NATURALIZIN⌐ ⌐

Essays on American Legal Realism and Naturalism
in Legal Philosophy

Naturalizing Jurisprudence

Essays on American Legal Realism and Naturalism in Legal Philosophy

BRIAN LEITER

The University of Texas at Austin

OXFORD

UNIVERSITY PRESS

OXFORD

UNIVERSITY PRESS

Great Clarendon Street, Oxford OX2 6DP

Oxford University Press is a department of the University of Oxford.
It furthers the University's objective of excellence in research, scholarship,
and education by publishing worldwide in

Oxford New York

Auckland Cape Town Dar es Salaam Hong Kong Karachi
Kuala Lumpur Madrid Melbourne Mexico City Nairobi
New Delhi Shanghai Taipei Toronto

With offices in

Argentina Austria Brazil Chile Czech Republic France Greece
Guatemala Hungary Italy Japan Poland Portugal Singapore
South Korea Switzerland Thailand Turkey Ukraine Vietnam

Oxford is a registered trade mark of Oxford University Press
in the UK and in certain other countries

Published in the United States
by Oxford University Press Inc., New York

British Library Cataloguing in Publication Data

Data available

Library of Congress Cataloging in Publication Data

Data available

Typeset by Newgen Imaging Systems (P) Ltd., Chennai, India
Printed in Great Britain
on acid-free paper by
Biddles Ltd., King's Lynn

ISBN 978–0–19–929901–0 (Hbk.)
ISBN 978–0–19–920649–0 (Pbk.)

1 3 5 7 9 10 8 6 4 2

for Maurice Leiter

Acknowledgements

I have benefited from conversations with many philosophers and legal scholars over the years. The footnotes to individual papers mention those who helped with particular projects, but here I should like to acknowledge more general intellectual debts. My philosophical outlook and development owes much to the many fine teachers and fellow students I spent time with in graduate school; I should mention especially John Doris, Allan Gibbard, Alex Miller, Thomas Pogge, Peter Railton, Crispin Wright, and José Zalabardo. Although not interested in jurisprudence, Maudemarie Clark and Ken Gemes have been important sources of philosophical ideas and stimulation for the last fifteen years. With respect to legal philosophy and its problems, I have learned a tremendous amount from the writings of and conversations with Jules Coleman, John Gardner, Leslie Green, Stephen Perry, Joseph Raz, and Scott Shapiro. My debt to Green is, by now, particularly substantial: he has taught me more about jurisprudence than anyone else, and he has also been an invaluable colleague. More recently, I have enjoyed the philosophical stimulation of two new colleagues, John Deigh and Larry Laudan.

The University of Texas School of Law has been an ideal professional home, and many colleagues—I should mention especially Hans Baade, Mitch Berman, Willy Forbath, Mark Gergen, Basil Markesinis, Scot Powe, Bill Powers, and Larry Sager—have done much to educate me about matters legal and jurisprudential. In the broader community of legal scholars, I have learned most from my oral and especially written exchanges with Ronald Allen and Richard Posner, as well as from my many conversations and correspondence with the late Milton Handler, from 1987 up until his death in 1998.

I particularly want to thank the many Deans and Associate Deans at Texas who offered unstinting support, and who provided me countless opportunities to try out many of the ideas and arguments in these essays with the many fine students who, over the past eleven years, have taken my courses and seminars, and helped me clarify and refine my thinking. Bill Powers, the former Dean and now President of the University, receives my special thanks for his commitment to our Law and Philosophy Program.

I am grateful to Jolyn Piercy, my wonderful administrative assistant, and Michael Sevel, one of our excellent JD/PhD students, for invaluable help in getting the manuscript ready for publication.

Sheila, Samuel, William, and Celia are, I am fairly sure, agnostic on whether jurisprudence should be naturalized, and for that, and so much else, I love them dearly. This collection is dedicated with warm gratitude to my father, Maurice Leiter, whose steadfast support—material, moral, and intellectual—of my academic pursuits across the decades has made this work possible.

B.L.

Austin, Texas
September 15, 2006

Sources

All essays have been reprinted with permission of the original publisher.

Essay 1: "Rethinking Legal Realism: Toward a Naturalized Jurisprudence," reprinted from *Texas Law Review*, vol. 76 (December 1997), pp. 267–315. Copyright 1997 by the Texas Law Review Association.

Essay 2: "Legal Realism and Legal Positivism Reconsidered," reprinted from *Ethics*, vol. 111 (January 2001), pp. 278–301. Published by the University of Chicago Press. This essay was also reprinted as "one of the ten best articles in philosophy" for 2001 in P. Grim et al. (eds.), *The Philosopher's Annual, Volume 24* (Stanford: CSLI Publications, 2003). Copyright 2001 by the University of Chicago.

Essay 3: "Is There an 'American' Jurisprudence?" reprinted from *Oxford Journal of Legal Studies*, vol. 17 (Summer 1997), pp. 367–87.

Essay 4: "Legal Realism, Hard Positivism, and the Limits of Conceptual Analysis," reprinted from J.L. Coleman (ed.), *Hart's Postscript* (Oxford University Press, 2001), pp. 355–70. This was itself a slightly revised version of "Realism, Hard Positivism, and Conceptual Analysis," which appeared in *Legal Theory*, vol. 4 (December 1998), pp. 533–47, published by Cambridge University Press.

Essay 5: "Why Quine is Not a Postmodernist," reprinted from *Southern Methodist University Law Review*, vol. 50 (July–August 1997), pp. 1739–54. This was part of a symposium on Dennis Patterson's book *Law and Truth*. Published by *Southern Methodist University Law Review* and the Southern Methodist University Dedman School of Law.

Essay 6: "Beyond the Hart/Dworkin Debate: The Methodology Problem in Jurisprudence," reprinted from *American Journal of Jurisprudence*, vol. 48 (2003), pp. 17–51. This was a symposium issue on "Law's Moral Foundations: Has It Any?"

Essay 7: "Moral Facts and Best Explanations," reprinted from *Social Philosophy & Policy*, vol. 18 (Summer 2001), pp. 79–101. It also appears in E.F. Paul et al. (eds.), *Moral Knowledge* (Cambridge University Press, 2001).

Essay 8: "Objectivity, Morality, and Adjudication," reprinted from Brian Leiter (ed.), *Objectivity, Morality, and Adjudication* (Cambridge University Press, 2001), pp. 66–98.

Essay 9: "Law and Objectivity," reprinted from Jules Coleman & Scott Shapiro (eds.), *The Oxford Handbook of Jurisprudence and Philosophy of Law* (Oxford University Press, 2002), pp. 969–89.

Contents

Introduction: From Legal Realism to Naturalized Jurisprudence

American Legal Realism was, quite justifiably, the major intellectual event in 20th century American legal practice and scholarship,[1] so it was somewhat disheartening to me, with my philosopher's hat on, to find that Realism was held in contempt, if noticed at all, by philosophers, even those with a substantial interest in law. The explanation for this state of affairs is, in retrospect, clear enough. On the one side, the Realists were not interested in philosophy, and tended to be intellectually reckless in some of their pronouncements. On the other side, the philosophers, who often knew little about law in practice (even those who were jurisprudents), were systematically misconstruing the kinds of questions Realists were asking.[2] Academic lawyers who tried to intervene[3] in some ways made matters worse in virtue of having a tin ear for philosophical questions and problems.[4] Other academic lawyers were content to offer useful intellectual histories of Realism, without regard for what was jurisprudentially significant.[5] What was needed was an explanation for why philosophers ought to care about the *actual* questions with which the Realists were concerned, and why the Realist questions were, in fact, questions within the purview of philosophical thinking about law.

Some time in the early 1990s, the relevant mediating consideration became clear to me: the legal philosophical tradition that had marginalized American Legal Realism was predicated on a conception of philosophy as beholden to the method of conceptual analysis via appeal to folk intuitions (as manifest, for example, in

---

[1] As I argue in Ch. 3, economic analysis of law (the most influential intellectual event in American law since the 1970s) is reasonably understood as a continuation of the Realist program.

[2] H.L.A. Hart presents a complicated case, since he was an experienced English lawyer. Here part of the explanation may have to do with the differences between the U.S. and English legal systems, and, in particular, the respective roles of the courts.

[3] I am thinking especially of Robert S. Summers, *Instrumentalism and American Legal Theory* (Ithaca: Cornell University Press, 1982).

[4] This is brought out usefully by Michael S. Moore (discussing Summers) in "The Need for a Theory of Legal Theories: Assessing Pragmatic Instrumentalism," reprinted in Moore's *Educating Oneself in Public: Critical Essays in Jurisprudence* (Oxford: Oxford University Press, 2000).

[5] Useful examples are William Twining, *Karl Llewellyn and the Realist Movement* (Norman: University Oklahoma Press, 1973) and G. Edward White, *Patterns of American Legal Thought* (Indianapolis: Bobbs-Merrill, 1978). Less satisfactory is the coverage of Realism in a more recent work of intellectual history, Neil Duxbury, *Patterns of American Jurisprudence* (Oxford: Oxford University Press, 1995), as I discuss in Ch. 3.

ordinary language), a method that was itself at risk of becoming an item of antiquarian interest in the context of the naturalistic revolution of late 20th century philosophy. Recognize the Realists as "prescient philosophical naturalists," and you now understand why most legal philosophers misunderstood them, and why they got so many things right.[6]

Legal philosophy, to be sure, made great strides fifty years ago when H.L.A. Hart, the giant of 20th century jurisprudence, brought its concerns and arguments into the mainstream of English-speaking philosophy, deploying, with enormous skill and insight, the then-dominant philosophical tools to fundamental questions about the nature of law and legal systems. Joseph Raz and some of his students subsequently refined and modified several of the basic Hartian theses, but by the turn of the century it was reasonably clear to most legal philosophers that the Hartian positivist tradition (as against its Kelsenian relative) had provided a powerful and compelling answer to some central jurisprudential questions about the "concept of law."[7] (An exception to this consensus has been Ronald Dworkin, but his influence within the core of legal philosophy has been limited, and his confusions about legal positivism widely recognized.[8]) Significant questions remain within the tradition of philosophical theorizing about law that Hart created,[9] but legal positivism stands as victorious as any research program in post-World War II philosophy.

In the small, hermetic—and rather incestuous—universe of Anglophone legal philosophy, the major developments in post-positivist philosophy passed almost entirely unnoted.[10] The ordinary language philosophy that influenced Hart had disappeared by the 1960s, as appropriate skepticism arose about why the linguistic practices of the masses—or even their upper-class brethren at Oxbridge—should be thought to contain nuggets of wisdom, let alone truths about the real world. Far more seriously, from the 1940s onward, the American philosopher Quine raised profound doubts about whether "philosophy" had some distinct method that actually contributed *anything* to understanding *what there is*, such that philosophy could stand apart from or "above" (as the spatial metaphor has it) the empirical sciences. Quine's attack on philosophy produced a double legacy,

---

[6] Chs. 1 and 2 try to make that case.

[7] As I argue in Ch. 6, John Finnis, the leading natural law theorist during this time, effectively concedes victory to Hartian positivism with respect to the theoretical questions that Hart was trying to answer.

[8] For an overview, see Brian Leiter, "The End of Empire: Dworkin and Jurisprudence in the 21st Century," *Rutgers Law Journal* 36 (2006): 165–81.

[9] There is a splendid, synoptic overview of these issues in Leslie Green, "General Jurisprudence: A 25th Anniversary Essay," *Oxford Journal of Legal Studies* 25 (2005): 565–80.

[10] The main exception, of course, was the interest in the 1980s and 1990s in how the "new" or "causal" theory of reference of Saul Kripke and Hilary Putnam might supply the requisite semantics for a natural law or Dworkinian theory of law. See, e.g., Michael S. Moore, "A Natural Law Theory of Interpretation," *Southern California Law Review* 58 (1985): 277–398; N. Stavropoulos, *Objectivity in Law* (Oxford: Oxford University Press, 1996); D. Brink, "Legal Interpretation, Objectivity, and Morality," in *Objectivity in Law and Morals*, ed. B. Leiter (Cambridge: Cambridge University Press, 2001).

one intended, the other not.[11] On the one hand, there was a "naturalistic turn" in English-speaking philosophy from the 1960s onward, that is, a recognition that to illuminate philosophical questions about knowledge, mind, and moral motivation (among many other topics), it would be necessary for philosophy to proceed in tandem with the sciences, acting as the abstract, reflective, and synthetic branch of empirical science. On the other—and this was the unexpected legacy—Quine's assault on the foundations of logical positivism (which viewed metaphysical questions as nonsensical) inadvertently opened the door to a new wave of metaphysical theorizing, especially about *modal* concepts like "necessity" and "possibility," which could then be deployed in understanding a range of questions about the nature of causation, free will, meaning, reference, and so on. Quine shared with the positivists what is called (pejoratively) "scientism", yet, ironically, his and others'[12] critique of logical positivism led, unexpectedly, to a new generation of armchair metaphysics.

"Scientism," as noted, is the epithet often applied to those, like Quine, who continue to take the Enlightenment seriously, which means taking seriously the epistemological and metaphysical consequences of the practical and, then, theoretical triumph of the sciences as our most reliable guide to what we can know and what there is. As Quine famously put it, "science is self-conscious common sense,"[13] which is to say that the epistemic standards of the sciences are merely formal extensions of the standards of evidence and justification that all of us employ all the time: we are all *practical* naturalists, and the only question is whether we are prepared to follow out the import of the epistemic norms that make human life possible. The opponents of naturalism—from the postmodernists, whom philosophers usually ignore, to the nostalgic religionists, to their unexpected allies, like Ronald Dworkin[14]—are largely in the position of those who would "have their cake and eat it too": they profess commitment, in theory or practice, to the naturalistic epistemology and metaphysics that is the legacy of the scientific revolution, but they would like to relax its demands when it comes to their preferred domains of "reality" like God or morality.

In one sense, all the essays in this volume are written with the aim of understanding where we can locate law and morality within a naturalistic picture of the world. This is not, it bears emphasizing, naturalism as Quine often presented it, which in its austere physicalism and behaviorism simply betrayed the *methodological* commitment at the core of naturalism (even Quine's own!), namely, to

[11] This is a capsule version of the account given in B. Leiter, "American Philosophy Today," in *The Oxford Companion to Philosophy*, 2nd ed., ed. T. Honderich (Oxford: Oxford University Press, 2005), pp. 27–8. See also my "Introduction," to *The Future for Philosophy*, ed. B. Leiter (Oxford: Clarendon Press, 2004).

[12] The critiques of positivist philosophy of science and epistemology by Paul Feyerabend, Norwood Russell Hanson, Thomas Kuhn, and Wilfrid Sellars were also decisive in dismantling the positivist edifice.

[13] W.V.O. Quine, *Word and Object* (Cambridge, Mass.: MIT Press, 1960), p. 3.

[14] See the discussion in Ch. 8.

defer to whatever ontology and epistemology falls out of successful scientific practice.[15] This is, as I have called it, a "relaxed" naturalism—it is "skeptical about
intuition-driven methods of philosophy and conceptual analysis; think[s] that the
facts matter for philosophy; take[s] philosophy to be continuous with empirical
science; and take[s] a far more Quinean (i.e., pragmatic) view of both ontology
and what counts as science than Quine (the arch-behaviorist-and-physicalist!)
himself"—since it allows for an ontology populated with whatever it is that[16] figures in successful predictive and explanatory practices, whether it be unreduced
mental states or norms. The proliferation of successful special sciences over the
last fifty years simply lends no naturalistic support to Quine's ontological and
evidential strictures, which are artifacts of the now-defunct research programs of
the middle of the 20th century.

Because it is a relaxed naturalism, however, it is also not simply a throw-back to
the Scandinavian Realism of Alf Ross and others, philosophers who also asked the
question where we could locate law and legal norms in a naturalistic picture of the
world. But for Ross and his allies, naturalism was understood through the lens of
logical positivism, and so the ontology, the epistemology, and the semantics of the
Scandinavians were largely circumscribed by physicalist and behaviorist views
that, like Quine's own, now seem poorly motivated. Hart demolished the
Scandinavian research program in jurisprudence a half-century ago,[17] and there is
no reason to think Hart was fundamentally mistaken. Norms and the "internal
point of view" are ineliminable features of the causal structure of the social world,
but, for naturalists, causality is still the benchmark of reality, and so no responsible
naturalized jurisprudence can eliminate the normative aspects of law and legal
systems. Naturalists can demand, to be sure, that any account of those features of
law which depends on "folk intuitions" as data points in theory-construction ought
to answer to empirically sound methods for ascertaining that data. As I note in the
Postscript to Part II, this kind of "experimental philosophy"[18] is likely to set much
of the agenda for naturalistic legal philosophy at the dawn of the 21st century.

---

[15] Even Quine famously observes that "telepathy and clairvoyance are scientific options, however
moribund. It would take some extraordinary evidence to enliven them, but, if that were to happen,
then empiricism itself—the crowning norm . . . of naturalized epistemology—would go by the
board." *Pursuit of Truth*, Rev. ed. (Cambridge, Mass.: Harvard University Press, 1992), pp. 20–1. In
other words, if telepathy actually *worked*, then our epistemology (and probably our ontology) would
have to be adjusted accordingly, and physicalism and behaviorism would likely go by the boards. But
that, of course, is exactly what a genuinely methodological naturalist should say.

[16] See my "Against Convergent Moral Realism: The Respective Roles of Philosophical Argument
and Empirical Evidence," in *Moral Psychology, Vol. 2: Intuition and Diversity*, ed. W. Sinnott-
Armstrong (Cambridge, Mass.: MIT Press, 2008).

[17] See H.L.A. Hart, *The Concept of Law*, 2nd ed. (Oxford: Clarendon Press, 1994), pp. 137–9; see
also Hart's 1959 essay on "Scandinavian Realism," reprinted in his *Essays in Jurisprudence and
Philosophy* (Oxford: Clarendon Press, 1983). In unpublished work, Brian Berry claims that Ross was
not insensitive to these kinds of worries. I bracket that issue here.

[18] The already "classic" study in the genre is Jonathan Weinberg, Shaun Nichols, and Stephen
Stich, "Normativity and Epistemic Intuitions," *Philosophical Topics* 29 (2001): 429–60.

The essays collected here reflect one philosopher's and legal scholar's attempt to make sense of what seems to be so compelling about American Legal Realism and, in the process, figure out where that jurisprudence fits into a naturalistic philosophy. The essays in Part I ("American Legal Realism and Its Critics") undertake the philosophical reconstruction and rehabilitation of American Legal Realism.[19] Chapter 1 ("Rethinking Legal Realism: Toward a Naturalized Jurisprudence") sets out the basic contours of my revisionary treatment of Realism, arguing that we can reconstruct the Realists as arguing for their "empirical" approach to the theory of adjudication as motivated by considerations analogous to those Quine invoked for naturalizing epistemology. In Chapter 2 ("Legal Realism and Legal Positivism Reconsidered"), I take up H.L.A. Hart's famous critique of Realism in Chapter VII of *The Concept of Law*, arguing that Hart both misconstrued the Realist position and failed to respond substantively to the genuine points of disagreement between his and the Realist views of indeterminacy and adjudication. In Chapter 3 ("Is There an 'American' Jurisprudence?"), the focus shifts from the philosophical response to Realism to that within academic law (something touched on briefly in Ch. 1). I use Neil Duxbury's interesting, if sometimes quite misleading, book *Patterns of American Jurisprudence*[20] to explore the nature of what is often called legal formalism (which the Realists rejected), the Critical Legal Studies misunderstanding of Realism, the relationship between economic analysis of law and Realism, and the nature of jurisprudential inquiry itself. Part I concludes with a new "Postscript" in which I take up some objections to my interpretation of Realism or the import of the naturalized jurisprudence I attribute to the Realists, objections lodged by Mark Greenberg,[21] Michael S. Moore,[22] and Alan Schwartz.[23]

The essays in Part II ("Ways of Naturalizing Jurisprudence") gradually move beyond American Legal Realism to address the broader question: what would it mean to bring legal philosophy within the "naturalistic turn" in modern philosophy? In Part I, naturalizing jurisprudence meant arguing for the importance of an empirical approach to *adjudication*. Chapter 4, "Legal Realism, Hard Positivism, and the Limits of Conceptual Analysis," notes that the Realist arguments for the indeterminacy of legal reasoning depend on a "Hard Positivist" (or Razian) conception of legal validity (according to which the criteria of validity in any legal system must themselves be source-based). I survey the traditional "conceptual"

---

[19] This book is almost entirely silent on Scandinavian Legal Realism, except to note (in Ch. 2) that Hart appears to have conflated it with its American cousin. I will say more about the profound differences between American and Scandinavian Realism in my forthcoming online *Stanford Encyclopedia of Philosophy* essay on the topic.   [20] (Oxford: Oxford University Press, 1995).

[21] Mark Greenberg, "Unnatural Proposal: Indeterminacy as a Motivation for the Naturalization of Legal Philosophy" (unpublished manuscript, presented at Columbia's Center for Law and Philosophy conference on "Naturalism and Other Realisms in Legal Philosophy" in April 2001).

[22] Michael S. Moore, "Introduction" to his *Educating Oneself in Public*, (n. 4 above) pp. 32–7.

[23] Schwartz, "Karl Llewellyn and the Origins of Contract Theory," in *The Jurisprudential Foundations of Corporate and Commercial Law*, ed. J. Kraus & S. Walt (Cambridge: Cambridge University Press, 2000).

arguments for and against the Razian theory of law, generally defending the Razian position. I conclude, however, by raising doubts about this whole way of proceeding in jurisprudence, suggesting, with a nod to Quine, that perhaps even questions about the nature of law itself might be settled by the results of the empirical sciences. Chapter 5 ("Why Quine is Not a Postmodernist") gives an overview of the Quinean attack on conceptual analysis for the novice, and argues against those[24] who have tried to misappropriate the Quinean naturalist assault on the traditional philosophical edifice as really constituting a precursor to post-modernism. Chapter 6 ("Beyond the Hart/Dworkin Debate: The Methodology Problem in Jurisprudence") returns, in a more systematic way, to the suggestion at the end of Chapter 4. I show how the denouement of the so-called Hart/Dworkin debate has been discussion of the methodology of legal philosophy itself. On one side, are defenders (in the spirit of Hart) of descriptive conceptual analysis, on the other, those who argue that we can not say *what law is* without saying *what it ought to be*. I consider and critique versions of the latter position offered by Ronald Dworkin, Stephen Perry, Julie Dickson, and John Finnis, before arguing that the real question is what role *conceptual analysis* should be playing at all. In the new Postscript to Part II, I take up some criticisms of naturalized jurisprudence in the more ambitious form considered in this section, as well as addressing replies to my criticisms of other legal philosophers concerned with methodology. I focus, in particular, on arguments by Jules Coleman,[25] Julie Dickson,[26] Ian Farrell,[27] John Finnis,[28] and Liam Murphy.[29] I also acknowledge a notable change of opinion in the Postscript. As I have delved deeper into the empirical science of law and legal institutions, the conclusion has become inescapable that its epistemic *bona fides* are in serious doubt. That means, I suggest, that the future for "naturalizing jurisprudence" will lie either with the program outlined in Part I or, in a different direction, namely, that suggested by the experimental philosophers, in which case it is likely, though not certain, to be an exercise in sophisticated conceptual ethnography.

The essays in Part III ("Naturalism, Morality, and Objectivity") are less directly concerned with the theory of law and adjudication, and more with the so-called

---

[24] Most notably in jurisprudence, Dennis Patterson in his *Law and Truth* (Oxford: Oxford University Press, 1996).

[25] Jules L. Coleman, *The Practice of Principle* (Oxford: Oxford University Press, 2001), pp. 210–14; Jules L. Coleman, "Methodology," in *The Oxford Handbook of Jurisprudence and Legal Philosophy*, ed. J. Coleman & S. Shapiro (Oxford: Oxford University Press, 2002), pp. 343–51.

[26] Julie Dickson, "Methodology in Jurisprudence: A Critical Survey," *Legal Theory* 10 (2004): 117–56.

[27] Ian Farrell, "H.L.A. Hart and the Methodology of Jurisprudence," *Texas Law Review* 84 (2006): 983–1011.

[28] John Finnis, "Law and What I Truly Should Decide," *American Journal of Jurisprudence* 48 (2003): 107–129.

[29] Liam Murphy, "Concepts of Law," *Australian Journal of Legal Philosophy* 30 (2005): 1–19.

"location problem,"[30] that is, how we understand the place of two kinds of norms, moral and legal, in a world whose essential nature is demarcated by its causal powers. Chapter 7 ("Moral Facts and Best Explanations") takes on the views of philosophers (like David Brink, Geoffrey Sayre-McCord, and Nicholas Sturgeon) who accept the premises of the location problem, but think morality earns its place in a world so conceived. I argue, against them, that there is no reason to think moral facts are part of the best causal explanation of experience. Chapter 8 ("Objectivity, Morality, and Adjudication") considers the views of two philosophers, Ronald Dworkin and John McDowell, who repudiate the premise of the location problem, namely, that causal efficacy is always the mark of the real. From the standpoint of legal philosophy, Dworkin's response is particularly significant, since his theory of law and adjudication makes a party's legal rights turn on the answer to moral questions: if those answers are not "objective," then Dworkin's theory is a license for extraordinary judicial discretion. I show that Dworkin has no good arguments against taking the location problem seriously, and that his and McDowell's alternative account of the objectivity of morality is both empty and entails counter-intuitive conclusions. Chapter 9 ("Law and Objectivity") surveys the whole landscape of issues about the objectivity of law (and, relatedly, morality), concluding with a rejoinder to Gerald Postema's interesting attempt to vindicate something like Dworkin's position.[31] I have not prepared a new Postscript for Part III, since the secondary literature has been both small and often sympathetic, and the most important critical response, Postema's, is dealt with in Chapter 9.

This collection is a genuine *selection* of essays on the topics indicated, and not an indiscriminate re-printing of everything I have written related to these issues over the past fifteen years or so.[32] I hope I have chosen wisely and effectively, and that these nine papers form a moderately coherent whole. I have made some quite minor revisions or cuts to some of the essays—the cuts with an eye to minimizing

[30] I believe the label is due to Frank Jackson, *From Ethics to Metaphysics: A Defence of Conceptual Analysis* (Oxford: Oxford University Press, 1998), pp. 1–5. My formulation of the "location problem" is not quite the same as Jackson's.

[31] See Gerald J. Postema, "Objectivity Fit for Law," in *Objectivity in Law and Morals* (n. 10 above), esp. pp. 133–7.

[32] There are no papers, for example, related to my efforts to understand the contribution of naturalistic approaches to epistemology to normative questions, especially about the law of evidence. See, e.g., Brian Leiter, "Naturalism and Naturalized Jurisprudence," in *Analyzing Law: New Essays in Legal Theory*, ed. B. Bix (Oxford: Clarendon Press, 1988), pp. 100–03; Brian Leiter, "The Epistemology of Admissibility: Why Even Good Philosophy of Science Would Not Make for Good Philosophy of Evidence," *Brigham Young University Law Review* 1997: 803–19; Ronald J. Allen & Brian Leiter, "Naturalized Epistemology and the Law of Evidence," *Virginia Law Review* 86 (2001): 1491–550; Brian Leiter, "Prospects and Problems for the Social Epistemology of Evidence Law," *Philosophical Topics* 29 (2001): 219–32. So, too, some early papers on legal indeterminacy and objectivity are not included: e.g., "Determinacy, Objectivity, and Authority," *University of Pennsylvania Law Review* 142 (1993): 549–637 (with Jules Coleman); "The Middle Way," *Legal Theory* 1 (1995): 21–31; "Legal Indeterminacy" *Legal Theory* 1 (1995): 481–92. Portions of the analyses in these papers do figure in Chs. 1, 8, and 9 in particular.

redundancies (though, alas, there remain some). But I have largely reprinted these essays intact,[33] in light of the fact that the previously published versions have already been the subject of discussion and comment, and part of the point of a volume like this is to make these ideas and arguments more easily available to other interested students and scholars who may want to follow the debates. I hope bringing them together, even with their existing deficiencies, will nonetheless serve to focus philosophical interest in American Legal Realism and scholarly discussion of the prospects for naturalized jurisprudence along its many dimensions.

---

[33] The most notable exception is Ch. 8, where I have rewritten a bit of the argument against the claim that the naturalistic conception of objectivity is irrelevant in order to bring out its *reductio* structure more clearly.

A Note on Legal Indeterminacy

Many of the chapters (especially in Parts I and II) will make reference to the idea of the indeterminacy of law or of legal reasoning. I want to set out here, for easy reference, the conceptual terrain that is presupposed or only articulated briefly in later portions of the book.[1]

To say that the law is indeterminate is to say that the class of legal reasons (hereafter "the Class") is indeterminate. Roughly speaking, the Class includes those reasons a court may properly give in justifying its decision. More precisely, the Class in some legal system consists of four components: (1) the legitimate *sources* of law (e.g., statutes, court decisions, morality, a constitution, etc.); (2) the legitimate methods of interpreting sources of law (e.g., intentionalism, originalism, purposive interpretation, structural interpretation, "strict" and "loose" readings of precedent); (3) the legitimate ways of characterizing the facts of a case in terms of their *legal* significance; and (4) the legitimate ways of reasoning with legal rules and legally described facts (e.g., deductive reasoning, reasoning by analogy). Indeterminacy may arise from any one of these four components. Perhaps, for example, there are too few sources of law, or perhaps too many conflicting ones. Jerome Frank emphasized indeterminacy with respect to (3), while other Legal Realists emphasized indeterminacy with respect to (2).

Let us say that the law on some point is *rationally indeterminate* if the Class (on some conception) is insufficient to *justify* only one outcome in that case.[2] Let us say that the law on some point *is causally indeterminate* if the Class does not causally explain the judge's decision. More precisely, Causal Indeterminacy is the thesis that the Class together with relevant Background Conditions is not causally sufficient to determine only one outcome. The relevant Background Conditions include two assumptions: (1) judges are rational, honest, competent, and error-free; and (2) the law exercises its causal influence through reasons. It is true, of

---

[1] This discussion draws on my earlier treatment in "Legal Indeterminacy," *Legal Theory* 1 (1995): 481–92.

[2] This formulation of the claim of rational indeterminacy has the virtue of being neutral as between indeterminacy and underdeterminacy. The law is indeterminate insofar as any outcome can be justified on the basis of the Class; the law is underdeterminate insofar as more than one, but not simply any, outcome can be justified on the basis of the Class. For those who are worried about the legitimacy of adjudication, however, this distinction does not matter: all that is needed is the claim of rational indeterminacy as formulated in the text. Lawrence Solum, for one, makes far too much out of this distinction and thus effectively misses the point of most indeterminacy arguments. See Solum, "On the Indeterminacy Crisis: Critiquing Critical Dogma," *University of Chicago Law Review* 54 (1987): 462–503.

course, that if judges are not rational, honest, or competent, or if they make mistakes, then the Class will be Causally Indeterminate, but this is plainly a less interesting point about the law. The thesis at issue here is that, even when the Background Conditions obtain, the law may still be Causally Indeterminate—typically because it is Rationally Indeterminate (when legal reasons do not justify only one outcome, then other psychological and sociological factors (e.g., the personality or the political ideology of the judge) must come into play to causally determine the decision).

The law can be Rationally Determinate and Causally Indeterminate, insofar as reasons are not causally effective—a thesis, in fact, embraced by some Legal Realists (notably, the arch-behaviorist Underhill Moore[3]). The converse, however, does not seem possible, assuming the Background Conditions obtain. Indeed, Causal Indeterminacy (or "Indeterminacy of Causes") follows necessarily from the truth of Rational Indeterminacy (or "Indeterminacy of Reasons") if we grant the following plausible thesis about causation in virtue of reasons:

(X) If reasons cannot rationally justify an event, then they cannot be causally sufficient for that event[4]

Thus, (X) supposes that for reasons to be Causally Determinate they must, at a minimum, be Rationally Determinate: if reasons A and B cannot constitute good reasons for uniquely deciding C, then it is hard to see how A and B could be causally sufficient for the unique decision C. If reasons are to be the sufficient cause of a decision, then they must, so thesis (X) supposes, determine C qua reasons. If, however, the law is Rationally Indeterminate, then the Class cannot determine (qua reasons) only one outcome, so granted (X) (and the Background Conditions), the truth of Causal Indeterminacy follows. The law can be Rationally Indeterminate in virtue of (1) deficiencies of the Class that are specific or peculiar to law ("Specific Indeterminacy of Reasons"); or (2) deficiencies of the Class in virtue of general deficiencies in all rational or semantic content ("General Indeterminacy of Reasons"). Karl Llewellyn's famous claim that the law is indeterminate in virtue of the existence of conflicting, but equally proper, canons of statutory construction is an example of an argument for the Specific Indeterminacy of Reasons.[5] The claim associated with the skeptical reading of Wittgenstein[6] and

---

[3] See the discussion of Moore in Ch. 1.

[4] Note that thesis (X) is compatible with the Humean thesis that our fundamental beliefs—e.g., in causation—do not admit of rational vindication. For even on the Humean picture, we must appeal to an additional factor (human nature, human sentiment, habit) to explain the fact that we believe in causation despite the absence of complete rational justification.

[5] See Karl Llewellyn, "Remarks on the Theory of Appellate Decision and the Rules and Canons About How Statutes are to be Construed," *Vanderbilt Law Review* 3 (1950): 395–406.

[6] See Saul Kripke, *Wittgenstein on Rules and Private Language* (Cambridge, Mass.: Harvard University Press, 1982). On the deficiencies of the skeptical reading, see Crispin Wright, "Kripke's Account of the Argument Against Private Language," *Journal of Philosophy* 81 (1984): 759–78.

with Derridean deconstruction[7] that there are no objective facts about meaning is an example of an argument for the General Indeterminacy of Reasons: in view of a general feature of semantic content (its lack of objective determinacy) the law, as but one domain dependent on semantic content, will also lack determinacy.[8] Hart's view that indeterminacy in law results from the indeterminacy (or "open texture") of language itself is a more plausible version of the thesis of the General Indeterminacy of Reasons.

Two more preliminary distinctions: the law suffers from Global Rational Indeterminacy if the Class is insufficient to justify only one outcome in any case. It suffers from Local Rational Indeterminacy if the Class is insufficient to justify only one outcome in some particular class of cases.

The plausibility of the thesis of the Rational Indeterminacy of law turns entirely on the plausibility of its conception of the Class and its constituents. Someone might have too cramped a view, for example, about the sources of law, in virtue of which the law appears to be Rationally Indeterminate. The "Positivist" believes that the law suffers from a type of Local Indeterminacy of Reasons—i.e., it is indeterminate in the "hard" cases. Ronald Dworkin can be understood as replying that this only appears to be so because the Positivist has too restricted a conception of the sources of law: if we expand the sources to include certain unpedigreed moral principles, we find that even putatively hard cases are Rationally Determinate. Conversely, someone might have a dim view of the determinacy of analogical reasoning—as a part of the Class—in virtue of which the law appears to be Rationally Indeterminate; indeed, such a view is espoused by writers in Critical Legal Studies who attack reasoning by analogy as a "method" of legal reasoning.[9] Against these writers, Cass Sunstein has argued for an optimistic view of the determinacy of analogical reasoning.[10]

Surprisingly, much of the legal academic literature on indeterminacy has been occupied not with the merits of the underlying conception of the Class, but rather with three general arguments that are supposed to constitute blanket refutations of the claim of indeterminacy (more precisely, of Rational Indeterminacy), independent of any particular account of the Class. The three most common arguments have been the arguments from easy cases, predictability, and the selection hypothesis. Each points to a (largely) uncontested legal phenomenon that is supposed to show that the law is not in fact Rationally Indeterminate. The three arguments are

[7] See, e.g., Clare Dalton, "An Essay in the Deconstruction of Contract Doctrine," *Yale Law Journal* 94 (1985): 997–1114; Gary Peller, "The Metaphysics of American Law," *California Law Review* 73 (1984): 1151–290 (see esp. 1160–70).

[8] For general criticism of these kinds of arguments, see Jules L. Coleman and Brian Leiter, "Determinacy, Objectivity, and Authority," *University of Pennsylvania Law Review* 142 (1993): 549–637, and esp. 571–2.

[9] See, e.g., Mark Tushnet, "Following the Rules Laid Down: A Critique of Interpretivism and Neutral Principles," *Harvard Law Review* 96 (1983): 781–827, esp. at 818–19; Roberto Unger, *The Critical Legal Studies Movement* (Cambridge, Mass.: Harvard University Press, 1986), pp. 8–11.

[10] Cass Sunstein, "On Analogical Reasoning," *Harvard Law Review* 106 (1993): 741–91.

themselves closely related: easy cases are also cases in which the outcome is clearly predictable, and the prevalence of easy cases has been obscured only because hard cases are typically "selected" for litigation through the stage of appellate review. Although these arguments are widely invoked as refutations of the indeterminacy thesis,[11] I have argued against them elsewhere,[12] showing that the argument from easy cases depends on the misleading conflation of global and local indeterminacy, and that the arguments from predictability and the selection hypothesis are, in turn, completely parasitical on the argument from easy cases and thus carry no independent weight. Those worried about indeterminacy—pro or con—would do better to concentrate on the real issue, namely, the underlying conception of the Class upon which every indeterminacy thesis is predicated. I return to that issue especially in Chapter 2.

[11] See, e.g., Ken Kress, "Legal Indeterminacy," *California Law Review* 77 (1989): 283–337; Solum "On the Indeterminacy Crisis" (n. 2 above); Frederick Schauer, "Easy Cases," *Southern California Law Review* 58 (1985): 399–440.
[12] See Leiter, "Legal Indeterminacy" (n. 1 above).

PART I

AMERICAN LEGAL REALISM
AND ITS CRITICS

1

Rethinking Legal Realism: Toward a Naturalized Jurisprudence*

I. Introduction

Considering the enormous influence Legal Realism has exercised upon American law and legal education over the last sixty years, and considering too, as the cliché has it, that "we are all realists now," it remains surprising how inadequate—indeed inaccurate—most descriptions of Realism turn out to be.

Ronald Dworkin, for example, claims that according to Realism, "judges actually decide cases according to their own political or moral tastes, and then choose an appropriate legal rule as a rationalization."[1] Dworkin is echoed by Judge Jon Newman of the Second Circuit who asserts that Realists believe that "the judge simply selects the result that best comports with personal values and then enlists, sometimes brutally, whatever doctrines arguably support the result."[2] John Hart Ely says the Realists " 'discovered' that judges were human and therefore were likely in a variety of legal contexts consciously or unconsciously to slip their personal values into their legal reasoning."[3] Steven Burton remarks that it is often "claimed, in legal realist fashion, that judges decide whatever they want to decide when the law is unclear (and it is often or always unclear)."[4] Fred Schauer

* For valuable comments on earlier drafts of this essay or related material on Realism, I am grateful to Steven Burton, Robert Clinton, Jules Coleman, Kent Greenawalt, Ken Kress, Douglas Laycock, Alan Schwartz, Scott Shapiro, Charlie Silver, Jay Westbrook, and the participants in a faculty workshop at the University of Iowa College of Law. For useful discussions about various aspects of Realism, I also thank Hans Baade and Charles Alan Wright. I am indebted to the discussants of a related paper on Realism at the Oxford-USC Legal Theory Institute at Oxford University in July 1995; I can recall particular helpful comments or questions on that occasion from Joseph Raz, Richard Warner, John Finnis, Jonathan Dancy, Jonathan Wolff, Marshall Cohen, Grant Lamond, Marty Levine, David Slawson, and Michael Stocker. My colleagues in philosophy, Daniel Bonevac, Cory Juhl, and Robert C. Koons, helped me in thinking about naturalism. Sheila Sokolowski offered useful suggestions on a penultimate draft. I am grateful to Matt Heffner, Saul Laureles, and Stefan Sciaraffa for research assistance, and to Jonathan Pratter of UT's splendid Tarlton Law Library for research support. Finally, it is a pleasure to thank Fred Schauer for introducing me to Realism more than a decade ago.

  [1] *Taking Rights Seriously* (Cambridge, Mass.: Harvard University Press, 1977), 3.
  [2] "Between Legal Realism and Neutral Principles: The Legitimacy of Institutional Values," *California Law Review* 72 (1984), 202–03.
  [3] *Democracy and Distrust* (Cambridge, Mass.: Harvard University Press, 1980), 44.
  [4] *Judging in Good Faith* (Cambridge: Cambridge University Press, 1992), 43. See also id., p. 112.

describes Realists as holding "that legal decision-makers are largely unconstrained by forces external to their own decision-making preferences."[5] And in a recent popular work, a Connecticut trial judge, Robert Satter, says that "Realists... assert that a judge exercises unbridled discretion in making decisions; he works backwards from conclusion to principles and uses principles only to rationalize his conclusions. They consider the judge's values all-important."[6]

Glosses on Realism like these are surely familiar to every student of the literature. It may help, however, to recast them in a slightly more systematic form so that we know precisely what picture of Realism it is that exerts such a powerful grip on the legal imagination. According to what I shall call the "Received View," Legal Realism is fundamentally: (1) a *descriptive theory* about the nature of judicial decision, according to which, (2) judges exercise *unfettered discretion*, in order (3) to reach results based on their *personal* tastes and values, which (4) they then *rationalize* after-the-fact with appropriate legal rules and reasons.

Like much "conventional wisdom," the Received View of Realism has an element of truth: the core of Realism is, indeed, a certain sort of *descriptive* claim about how judges decide cases according to which judges rationalize, after-the-fact, decisions reached on other grounds. But it is, or so I shall argue, quite misleading to think of Realism as committed to the claim that judges exercise "unfettered" discretion[7] or that they make choices based on "personal" values and tastes. That Realism has been saddled with these claims—what I shall call the claims of "Judicial Volition" and "Judicial Idiosyncrasy"—has contributed in no small measure to the frequent reduction of Realism to a whipping boy for legal common sense.[8]

As a preliminary matter, however, any talk about the core of "Realism"—or even of "Realism" *simpliciter*—invites the objection that there simply is no such thing: there is no doctrine of "Realism" as apart from the views of individual writers.[9] This sort of familiar skepticism is, I think, largely false. For *everyone* commonly thought to be a Realist—Karl Llewellyn, Jerome Frank, Underhill Moore, Felix Cohen, Leon Green, Herman Oliphant, Walter Wheeler Cook, and Max Radin, among others—endorses the following descriptive claim about adjudication: in deciding cases, judges respond primarily to the stimulus of the facts. The Received View can then be seen as simply one interpretation of certain aspects of what I shall call this "Core Claim" of Realism, to which I return below.

---

 [5] *Playing by the Rules* (Oxford: Oxford University Press, 1991), 191.

 [6] *Doing Justice: A Trial Judge at Work* (New York: Simon & Schuster, 1990), 64.

 [7] In Schauer's sense of being "unconstrained by forces external to their own decision-making preferences." *Playing by the Rules* (n. 5 above), 191.

 [8] See, e.g., Richard Posner, *Overcoming Law* (Cambridge, Mass.: Harvard University Press, 1995), 2–3, 20, 393.

 [9] For one recent version of this skeptical view, see Neil Duxbury, *Patterns of American Jurisprudence* (Oxford: Clarendon Press, 1995), 65. On the difficulties with Duxbury's conception of "jurisprudence" and of Legal Realism in particular, see Ch. 3.

Indeed, I will suggest something further: that the misleading presentation of the Received View as the essence of Realism really represents what we may call the "Frankification" of Realism, i.e., the now dominant tendency to treat Jerome Frank's particular interpretation of the Core Claim as identical to Realism.[10] Even among Realists, of course, Frank's view represented a particular sort of extreme—as Frank himself recognized.[11] Notwithstanding this, the Frankification of Realism has been the distinguishing feature of the long-term reception of Realism, as evidenced by the many quotations with which I began.[12] But Frank is not Llewellyn or Moore or Oliphant, and while Frank shares in the Core Claim, none of these other writers share in the Frankified Received View. In Part II of this paper, I will set out the Core Claim of Realism and explore (as well as defend) its differences with the Received View.

In Part III, I turn to broader questions of jurisprudence, in order to locate Realism's place within it. Although Realism had an undeniably powerful impact upon American legal education and upon how lawyers and judges think about what they do,[13] it has had almost no impact upon the mainstream of Anglo-American jurisprudence—the tradition running from Bentham and Austin in the 19th century, to Dworkin and Raz in the present. The cause of this neglect is clear: Hart's devastating critique of the Realists in Chapter VII of *The Concept of Law* rendered Realism a philosophical joke in the English-speaking world. The Realists, on Hart's reading, gave us a "Predictive Theory" of law, according to which by the concept "law," we just mean a prediction of what the court will do.[14] Hart easily demolished this Predictive Theory of Law. For example, according to the Predictive Theory, a judge who sets out to discover the "law" on some issue upon which she must render a decision is really just trying to discover what she

[10] Some writers are even explicit about this identification: cf., Anthony Kronman, *The Lost Lawyer* (Cambridge, Mass.: Harvard University Press, 1993), 186. For an unselfconscious "Frankification" of Realism, see Laura Kalman, *Legal Realism at Yale 1927–1960* (Chapel Hill: University of North Carolina Press, 1986), 3, 6. This is ironic given that Frank had nothing to do with Yale realism!

[11] See, e.g., Jerome Frank, "Are Judges Human?: Part One" *University of Pennsylvania Law Review* 80 (1931), 30 n. 31.

[12] These quotations may be usefully compared with the following apt summary of Frank's view:

[H]ow *do* judges decide cases? To Frank, they begin with the desired conclusion and search for premises to substantiate it. Oriented to achieving certain results, judges rationalize their decisions by finding facts and selecting rules that justify the desired conclusion. By manipulating those facts and rules, judges enjoy unfettered discretion. But what persuades judges to reach one conclusion rather than another? . . . Most important, according to Frank, are the "uniquely individual factors" that are the product of the judge's "entire life-history" . . . Frank reveled in unfettered judicial discretion . . .

Robert Jerome Glennon, *The Iconoclast as Reformer: Jerome Frank's Impact on American Law* (Ithaca: Cornell University Press, 1985), 45. Note, in particular, the prominent place given to the themes of Judicial Volition and Judicial Idiosyncrasy in this capsule summary of Frank's view. As I argue below, however, it is not clear that even Frank views judges as "unfettered."

[13] For a brief survey, see Leiter, "Legal Realism," in C.B. Gray (ed.), *The Philosophy of Law: An Encyclopedia* (New York: Garland, 1999).

[14] The abbreviated discussion in the text is borrowed from Leiter, "Legal Realism," in D.M. Patterson (ed.), *A Companion To Philosophy of Law and Legal Theory* (Oxford: Blackwell, 1996), 261–79.

will do, since the "law" is equivalent to a prediction of what she will do! These, and other manifestly silly implications of the Predictive Theory, convinced most Anglo-American legal philosophers that Realism was best forgotten.

Yet Hart misread the Realists as answering philosophical questions of conceptual analysis—the questions that Hart himself was concerned to answer (questions about what particular concepts—"knowledge," "morally right," "law"—mean). But the Realists were not "ordinary language" philosophers, and were not explicitly concerned with analyzing the "concept" of law as it figures in everyday usage.[15] Yet if we do not view the Realists on the model of philosophy-as-conceptual analysis, how can we understand them as engaged in recognizably jurisprudential inquiries? One possibility is to understand the Realists as forerunners of the deconstructionism and postmodernism that has recently swept the humanities— philosophy largely excepted. Such an approach, embraced by a number of writers associated more or less loosely with Critical Legal Studies ("C.L.S."),[16] is unattractive on two counts: first, it does not help us locate Realism within the questions and problems of jursiprudence;[17] and second, it seems to defeat the purpose of achieving a sympathetic philosophical understanding of the Realists to see them simply as forerunners of bad philosophy. Even more significant, though, is that the "postmodern" misreadings of Realism turn out to be fatally anachronistic. For the Realists, we must remember, came out of the intellectual culture of the 1920s and 1930s in the United States, a culture firmly in the grips of the world-view to which postmodernists are now reacting: a world-view in which natural science was considered the paradigm of all genuine knowledge; in which science was distinguished by its methods (e.g. observation, empirical testing); and in which the social sciences aimed to emulate the methods and successes of the natural sciences. Any plausible account of Realist jurisprudence can not lose sight of this intellectual background.

Yet there has been more to the C.L.S. reinvention of the Realists than the implausible reading of them as proto-postmodernists. In fact, two other themes have been quite prominent in the literature.[18] First, C.L.S. brought the economist Robert Hale, a marginal figure in the Realist movement,[19] to the center of its picture of Legal Realism. Yet whatever Hale's importance and interest in his

---

[15] For an extended discussion of these points, see Ch. 2.

[16] See especially, Gary Peller, "The Metaphysics of American Law," *California Law Review* 73 (1985), 1151–215.   [17] On these, see Ch. 3.

[18] See, e.g., Peller (n. 16 above); J. William Singer, "Legal Realism Now," *California Law Review* 76 (1988), 465; Morton Horwitz, *The Transformation of American Law 1870–1960* (New York: Oxford University Press, 1992); J.M. Balkin, "Some Realism About Pluralism: Legal Realist Approaches to the First Amendment," *Duke Law Journal* (1990), 375–430. Also illuminating in this regard are the introductory essays and editorial selections in William W. Fisher et al. (eds.), *American Legal Realism* (New York: Oxford University Press, 1993), a volume that views Realism through a C.L.S. lens.

[19] Milton Handler—himself an early Realist, professor at Columbia from 1927 to 1972, and a friend and colleague of both Hale and Llewellyn—has remarked regarding Hale that, "he carried very little influence with his colleagues . . . I'm amazed now to find him regarded as one of the great Legal Realists." Unpublished memo to Brian Leiter, p. 12 (April 27, 1995). Handler is identified as a

own right, he simply had nothing to contribute to the Realists' central jurisprudential concern with the theory of judicial decision-making.[20] Hale's crowning achievement, as C.L.S. presents it, is instead supposed to be a decisive argument against the public-private distinction.[21] In its contemporary form,[22] the argument typically runs as follows:

Since it is governmental decisions that create and structure the so-called "private" sphere (e.g. by creating and enforcing a regime of property rights), there should be no presumption of "non-interference" in this "private" realm (e.g. the marketplace) because it is, in essence, a public creature. There is, in short, no natural baseline against which government can not pass without becoming "interventionist" and non-neutral, because the baseline itself is an artifact of government regulation.

Unfortunately, this influential (and no doubt familiar) argument is based on a non-sequitur. From the fact that a "private" realm is a creature of government regulation it does not follow that government action in that realm is normatively indistinguishable from government action in the "public" realm: for the key issue is the normative justification for drawing the baseline itself, not simply the fact that one has been drawn by an exercise of public power. If the underlying normative reasons for drawing the baseline are sound (e.g. for demarcating a realm of "private" transactions), then *these reasons* provide an argument *against* intervention. That the "private" sphere is an artifact of government regulation is of no relevance.

Second, C.L.S. writers have frequently enlisted the Realists as authority for the C.L.S. claim that the law is indeterminate.[23] In so doing, they have introduced two important distortions of Realist jurisprudence. First, the Realists, unlike the C.L.S. writers, did not generally view the law as "globally" indeterminate,[24] that is, as indeterminate in *all* cases. To the contrary, Realists were mainly concerned to

---

Realist in Karl Llewellyn, "A Realistic Jurisprudence—The Next Step," *Columbia Law Review* 30 (1930), 454 and 454 n. 22, and in "Some Realism About Realism—Responding to Dean Pound," *Harvard Law Review* 44 (1931) 1237, 1240 n. 42, 1244 n. 55, 1245.

[20] I take it to be uncontroversial that the Realists were centrally concerned with what judges do. See, e.g., Edwin W. Patterson, *Jurisprudence: Men & Ideas of the Law* (Brooklyn: The Foundation Press, 1953), 541. ("The leading realists centered upon the judicial process".) The Realists, to be sure, also expressed interest in understanding the *effects* of legal rules in the real world, but this aspect of Realism does not, as I see it, bear on any recognizably jurisprudential questions. This concern of the Realists has been, in some ways, inherited by economic writers on law, especially institutional economists. For a useful overview, see Oliver E. Williamson, "Revisiting Legal Realism: The Law, Economics, and Organization Perspective," Working Paper No. 95-12, Program in Law & Economics, University of California, Berkeley, 1996.

[21] The argument is typically attributed to Hale and to the philosopher Morris Cohen—the latter being better known as a critic of Realism! For the relevant papers, see the excerpts reprinted in *American Legal Realism* (n.18 above).

[22] See, e.g., Cass Sunstein, "Lochner's Legacy," *Columbia Law Review* 87 (1987), 917–19. The C.L.S. reinvention of Realism has been so successful that even non-C.L.S. scholars have taken up these putatively "Realist" arguments.

[23] See the sources cited above, n. 18; see also the sources cited below, n. 28.

[24] For more on the terminology and conceptualization here, see my "Legal Indeterminacy," *Legal Theory* 1 (1995), 481–92.

point out the indeterminacy that exists in those cases that are actually litigated, especially those that make it to the stage of appellate review—a far smaller class of legal cases, and one where indeterminacy in law is far less surprising.[25] Second, the Realists based their argument for indeterminacy in law primarily on the existence of conflicting, but equally legitimate, *interpretive methods*: e.g., conflicting ways of reading statutes, or of construing precedents.[26] Because statutes or cases could be read in two ways, a statute or case could generate at least two different rules. Thus, even an honest application of the "methods" of legal reasoning and interpretation would fail to determine as a matter of law a unique decision. The C.L.S. writers, by contrast, have tended to locate the source of legal indeterminacy either (by loosely following Derrida and Wittgenstein) in general features of language itself[27] or (by loosely following Hegel via Lukacs via Unger) in conflicting moral and political principles that purportedly exist beneath the surface of the law, at some suitable level of abstraction.[28] The Realists made distinctively *lawyerly* arguments for legal indeterminacy, while C.L.S. writers have relied on more explicitly philosophical considerations—though considerations, it bears noting, that do not always do the work the C.L.S. writers think they do.[29]

If, then, we are indeed "all Realists now," this is a royal "we" that manifestly does not include legal philosophers. Within Anglo-American jurisprudence, Realism remains a joke, viewed simply as a movement that appealed to philosophically superficial lawyers, but which made no substantial contribution to philosophical thinking about law. Outside Anglo-American jurisprudence, meanwhile, legal theorists have selectively represented—or simply mispresented—Realism, and in ways that do not bode well for understanding the Realists as offering anything to a philosophical theory of law.

[25] See, e.g., Llewellyn, "Some Realism About Realism,"(n. 19 above) 1239 ("in any case doubtful enough to make litigation respectable the available authoritative premises . . . are at least two, and . . . the two are mutually contradictory as applied to the case at hand"); Max Radin, "In Defense of an Unsystematic Science of Law," *Yale Law Journal* 51 (1942), 1271 (judicial "decisions will consequently be called for chiefly in what may be called marginal cases, in which prognosis is difficult and uncertain. It is this fact that makes the entire body of legal judgments seem less stable than it really is").

[26] See Karl Llewellyn's seminal discussion of the "strict" and "loose" views of precedent in *The Bramble Bush: On Our Law and Its Study* (New York: Oceana Publications, Inc., 1951), 72–5, and of the conflicting "canons of statutory construction" in "Remarks on the Theory of Appellate Decision and the Rules and Canons About How Statutes Are to be Construed," *Vanderbilt Law Review* 3 (1950), 399–406.

[27] Though not, as Hart did, in the "open texture" of language. See H.L.A. Hart, *The Concept of Law* (Oxford: Clarendon Press, 1961), p. 124. Since this is Hart's focus in discussing the source of indeterminacy, this means that he never actually engages the arguments for indeterminacy most important to the Realists.

[28] For examples of these arguments for indeterminacy, see, e.g., Peller (n. 16 above); Clare Dalton, "An Essay in the Deconstruction of Contract Doctrine," *Yale Law Journal* 94 (1985), 997–1114; Mark Tushnet, "Following the Rules Laid Down: A Critique of Interpretivism and Neutral Principles," *Harvard Law Review* 96 (1983) 781–827; Roberto Unger, *The Critical Legal Studies Movement* (Cambridge, Mass.: Harvard University Press, 1986); Duncan Kennedy, "Form and Substance in Private Law Adjudication," *Harvard Law Review* 89 (1976), 1685–1778; Girardeau Spann, "Deconstructing the Legislative Veto," *Minnesota Law Review* 68 (1984) 473–544.

[29] For a representative critique, see Jules L. Coleman & Brian Leiter, "Determinacy, Objectivity and Authority," *University of Pennsylvania Law Review* 142 (1993), 549–637.

Thus our situation today: Realism is omnipresent in American law schools and legal culture, but almost entirely absent from serious legal philosophy. It is the aim of this essay to change that situation. I hope to show that the Realists laid the foundation for a jurisprudence distinguished by two novel philosophical commitments: *naturalism* and *pragmatism*. Naturalism is an unfamiliar term in the jurisprudential universe (though not, as I note, elsewhere in philosophy). Pragmatism, by contrast, is much talked about, but, I argue, poorly understood, especially as it applies to Realism. A *naturalized* jurisprudence predicated on a pragmatic outlook—in the precise sense with which I will be concerned—will turn out to be the real Realist legacy in legal philosophy.

A final methodological caveat bears noting. I regard what I am doing here as a *philosophical reconstruction* of Legal Realism. The Realists themselves were often badly confused about philosophical matters, which accounts, in part, for their sorry reputation among legal philosophers. Nonetheless, they had genuine insight into law and adjudication—more than most legal philosophers—and these insights reflect a philosophical sensibility of sorts. This essay tries to reconstruct and defend this sensibility. Such an account has been sorely missing from the literature on Realism.[30] While we now have a rich variety of *historical* materials on Realism,[31] there has been no *sympathetic* interpretation of Realism from a philosophical perspective. A philosophical interpretation of Realism will, of course, require us to sift through the mass of Realist writings, in order to produce a theory of law worthy of philosophical attention. This theory—what I call a "naturalized jurisprudence"—is one that remains, I hope to show, recognizably Realistic in spirit, if not in all its details.

II. The Real Legal Realism

A. The Core Claim

The Core Claim of Legal Realism consists of the following descriptive thesis about judicial decision-making: *judges respond primarily to the stimulus of facts.*[32] Put less formally—but also somewhat less accurately—the Core Claim of Realism is that

[30] Robert Summers tried, I think, to produce such an account in his *Instrumentalism and American Legal Theory* (Ithaca: Cornell University Press, 1982), but his book has had little impact on Anglo-American legal philosophy. Some of the reasons for this are persuasively set out in Michael S. Moore, "The Need for a Theory of Legal Theories: Assessing Pragmatic Instrumentalism," *Cornell Law Review* 69 (1984) 988–1013. In a nutshell: Summers never gives an adequate defense of the Realist turn to descriptive, empirical theory as a *jurisprudential* undertaking.

[31] See, e.g., William Twining, *Karl Llewellyn and the Realist Movement* (London: Weidenfeld and Nicolson, 1973); G. Edward White, *Patterns of American Legal Thought* (Indianapolis: Bobbs-Merrill, 1978); Kalman, *Legal Realism at Yale 1927–1960* (n. 10 above); Neil Duxbury, *Patterns of American Jurisprudence* (n. 9 above); John Henry Schlegel, *American Legal Realism and Empirical Social Science* (Chapel Hill: The University of North Carolina Press, 1995).

[32] Proper emphasis must be put on the word "primarily": no Realists (except perhaps Underhill Moore) claimed that rules never mattered to the course of decision.

judges reach decisions based on what they think would be fair on the facts of the case, rather than on the basis of the applicable rules of law.[33]

It is possible to find some version of the Core Claim in the writings of all the major Realists. Oliphant, for example, gives us an admirably succinct statement; he says that courts "respond to the stimulus of the facts in the concrete cases before them rather than to the stimulus of over-general and outworn abstractions in opinions and treatises."[34] Oliphant's claim was confirmed by Judge Hutcheson's admission that "the vital, motivating impulse for the decision is an intuitive sense of what is right or wrong for that cause."[35] Similarly, Jerome Frank cited "a great American judge," Chancellor Kent, who confessed that, "He first made himself 'master of the facts.' Then (he wrote) 'I saw where justice lay, and the moral sense dictated the court half the time; I then sat down to search the authorities . . . but I *almost always found principles suited to my view of the case*.' "[36] Precisely the same view of what judges really do when they decide cases is presupposed in Llewellyn's advice to lawyers that, while they must provide the court "a technical ladder" justifying the result, what the lawyer must really do is "on the facts . . . persuade the court your case is sound."[37] As Frank pointed out, the very same advice had been offered by a former president of the American Bar Association.[38]

---

[33] Obviously, an applicable rule of law makes certain facts relevant, and thus even a judge who is *following the legal rule* must take into account these facts. (Conversely, a judge must first look at the facts to see which legal rules are relevant.) But this is a plainly trivial sense of fact-responsive. The Realist idea is that judges are responding to the underlying facts of the case, facts that are not made relevant by any legal rule. An admirably succinct statement of the point comes from the eminent U.C.C. scholar James J. White, discussing what he correctly calls "the central tenet" of the Realists' Movement: namely that "judges' decisions are not merely from the rules they state in their opinions, but at least as much from unstated reasons—from the facts before them, from the expectation of the parties in the trade, and from the judges' own judgment about fairness." "The Influence of American Legal Realism on Article 2 of the Uniform Commercial Code," in Werner Krawietz et al. (eds.), *Prescriptive Formality and Normative Rationality in Modern Legal Systems* (Berlin: Duncker & Humblot, 1994), 401. In fact, I argue, below, that it was the dominant view among Realists that, at least in commercial disputes, what judges thought was fair on the facts tracked "the expectation of the parties in the trade."

[34] Herman Oliphant, "A Return to Stare Decisis," *American Bar Association Journal* 14 (1928), 75.

[35] Joseph Hutcheson, Jr., "The Judgment Intuitive: The Function of the 'Hunch' in Judicial Decision," *Cornell Law Quarterly* 14 (1929), 285.

[36] Frank, *Law and the Modern Mind* (New York: Brentano's, 1930), p. 104 note.

[37] Llewellyn, *The Bramble Bush* (n. 26 above), 76. This point is surely familiar to all litigators. When I wrote my first brief straight out of law school, the older litigator on the case put it to me (roughly) this way: "Cases are won or lost on the facts section of the brief. By the time the judge finishes the facts, you want him to think our client was screwed, and that fairness and justice dictate a decision for us. The law section of the brief just gives the judge a place to hang his hat." It is no small virtue of the Realists' Core Claim that it captures what every practicing lawyer knows.

[38] Frank, *Law and the Modern Mind* at 102–03 note. For a more recent statement of a similar point, see Judge Sam Sparks, "Tribute to the Honorable Homer Thornberry," *Texas Law Review* 74 (1996), 949–50 (describing the late Judge Thornberry of the U.S. Court of Appeals for the Fifth Circuit as having "a strong sense of what was 'right' and what was 'wrong.' When it appeared to the judge that the law presented a hurdle to what he thought was the fair and right thing to be done, he would struggle with this dilemma and argue with his law clerks or fellow judges until he was satisfied that his personal decision was both consistent with the law and the most fair determination under the circumstances").

Especially at the appellate level, Llewellyn maintained that one had to under-stand "how far the proposition which seems so abstract has roots in what seems to be the due thing on the facts before the court."[39] Later on, Llewellyn would speak of "the fact-pressures of the case"[40] and of "the sense of the situation as seen by the court"[41] as determining the outcome. Although the notion of "the situation-sense" was rendered cryptic by the later Llewellyn (who located it in a new cogni-tive "faculty" capable of detecting "immanent laws"[42]), it began life in Realist thought as a sensible, and naturalistically respectable,[43] phenomenon. Thus, Max Radin (in keeping with the Core Claim) suggested that the decision of a judge was determined by "a type situation that has somehow been early called up in his mind."[44] Type situations were simply "the standard transactions with their regu-latory incidents [which] are familiar ones to [the judge] because of his experience as a citizen and a lawyer."[45] We explain, in other words, the judge's "sense" of a particular situation by reference to the relevant psycho-social facts about the judge's professional and social history: by his having encountered such situations, say, in his prior practice as a corporate litigator and his having formed, accord-ingly, certain characteristic assumptions about what is right and fair in such circumstances, based in significant part on his familiarity with the local norms of conduct in that trade or practice. Judges are fact-responsive, and the facts, for Radin and Llewellyn, present themselves in ways that reflect what we might call the "sociological" profile of the judge.

The Realists, then, share a commitment to the view that in deciding cases, *judges respond primarily to the stimulus of the facts of the case*. Note, now, two points about this way of formulating the Core Claim.

First, the contrasting view here—usually dubbed "Formalism"—is committed to the descriptive claim that judges respond primarily (indeed, perhaps exclu-sively) to the rational demands of the applicable rules of law and modes of legal reasoning.[46] We can gloss the Formalist's descriptive claim as saying: judges are

---

[39] Llewellyn, *The Bramble Bush* (n. 26 above), 33.

[40] Llewellyn, "Some Realism About Realism," (n. 19 above) 1243. Cf. Karl Llewellyn, *The Common Law Tradition: Deciding Appeals* (Boston: Little, Brown and Company, 1960), 122.

[41] Id., p. 397.

[42] See id., p. 122 (quoting Levin Goldschmidt). For discussion, see Leiter, "Legal Realism" (n. 14 above). For a more sympathetic reading of the later Llewellyn, see Kronman, *The Lost Lawyer* (n. 10 above), 209–25.

[43] A naturalistically respectable faculty or property is one that has a place in the explanatory the-ories of successful natural and social sciences. I say more about naturalism, below.

[44] Max Radin, "The Theory of Judicial Decision: or How Judges Think," *American Bar Association Journal* 11 (1925), 362.

[45] Id., p. 358. A similar notion is developed at length by Underhill Moore in a series of papers in the late 1920s and early 1930s. See especially, Underhill Moore and Theodore S. Hope, Jr., "An Institutional Approach to the Law of Commercial Banking," *Yale Law Journal* 38 (1929) 703–19.

[46] As noted earlier (n. 33 above), the applicable legal rules also make certain facts relevant and thus require judges to respond to them; but this, of course, is a trivial sense of fact-responsiveness that no one denies.

(primarily) rule-responsive; while the Realist claims that judges are (primarily) fact-responsive.[47]

This gloss is potentially misleading in one respect. What the descriptive Formalist really claims is that judges are (primarily) responsive to *legal* reasons, while the Realist claims that judges are (primarily) responsive to *non-legal* reasons. This point is obvious enough in the case of the Formalist picture: statutes, precedents, and deductive inferences all give judges *legal reasons* for deciding one way rather than another.[48] But when a judge responds to the underlying facts of the case, what we are really saying is that the judge has *non-legal reasons* (e.g. "I think it wouldn't be fair to penalize the defendant here") for deciding the way she does.[49] The real dispute between the Formalist and the Realist then concerns whether the *reasons* that determine judicial decision are primarily legal reasons or non-legal reasons.[50] This means, of course, that this dispute presupposes a way of demarcating legal reasons from non-legal ones.[51] We shall have to revisit these issues below in discussing the naturalism of the Realists.

A second preliminary point, however, about my formulation of the Core Claim requires comment. My formulation invokes (intentionally, of course) the language of behaviorism, the dominant movement in psychology at the time the Realists were writing. According to the behaviorist, all human behavior can be explained in terms of the pairings of certain responses to certain stimuli; no reference to mental states (beliefs, desires, etc.) is required. The rhetoric of behaviorism—if not generally behaviorism itself—permeated the writings of the Realists: hence the sense of formulating the Core Claim in terms of fact-responsiveness. For the Realist-cum-behaviorist, the only question is: which stimuli trigger the judicial response? The Realists hold that it is primarily the underlying facts of the case, rather than the rules of law, that "trigger" the response.

---

[47] "Formalism" can also name a normative view, to the effect that judges *ought* to be primarily rule- and legal-reason-responsive. Theories of adjudication, of course, typically make both descriptive and normative claims. See Leiter, "Heidegger and the Theory of Adjudication," *Yale Law Journal* 106 (1996), 255–8.

[48] For a more precise characterization of the "Class of Legal Reasons," see Leiter, "Legal Indeterminacy" (n. 24 above).

[49] The only Realist who would deny this would have been Underhill Moore, who took behaviorism in psychology more seriously than other Realists. For the behaviorist, of course, the mind is a black box, not to be invoked in explaining behavior. Thus, reasons are only relevant as certain types of (aural, visual) stimuli, but are not relevant *in virtue of their rational content or meaning!* ("A proposition of law," says Moore, "is nothing more than a sensible object which may arouse a drive and cue a response." Underhill Moore & Charles Callahan, "Law and Learning Theory: A Study in Legal Control", *Yale Law Journal* 53 (1943), 3.) For the behaviorist, then, responsiveness to reasons really means nothing more than seeking out the lawful correlations between the stimuli that constitute the input (e.g. facts, laws, reasons, etc.) and the cognitive output (e.g. a judicial opinion). This, of course, was precisely Moore's program, under the heading of the institutional method. (For further discussion, see Leiter, "Legal Realism" (n. 14 above).) Since most of the Realists, happily, were not orthodox behaviorists, the notion of being responsive to reasons—legal or non-legal—is compatible with their work.

[50] I am grateful to Joseph Raz for clarification on this issue.

[51] On these points, see Leiter, "Legal Indeterminacy" (n. 24 above), and also Leiter, "Legal Realism" (n. 14 above).

Yet my formulation of the Core Claim is, importantly, still compatible with articulations of the same basic view by decidedly anti-behavioristic Realists, like Jerome Frank. Thus, when Frank quotes approvingly a former ABA President to the effect that "'the way to win a case is to make the judge want to decide in your favor and then, and then only, to cite precedents which will justify such a determination,'"[52] I take him to be supposing the truth of the Core Claim. In the same vein is Frank's observation that "the judge's innumerable unique traits, dispositions and habits...shap[e] his decisions" by determining "what he thinks fair or just with reference to a given set of facts."[53] Similarly, in formulating his own descriptive claim, Frank characterizes the opposing "conventional theory" as holding that, "*Rule* plus *Facts* = *Decision*", while his own view is that "the *Stimuli* affecting the judge" plus "the *Personality of the judge* = *Decision*."[54] It is, of course, Frank's injection of the "Personality of the judge" into the formula that puts the distinctive stamp on Frank's interpretation of the Core Claim: drop that and you have the Core Claim itself.

B. The Core Claim and the Received View

What interpretation of the Core Claim would not yield the Received View, one might wonder? Recall the two aspects of the Received View of Realism that are at issue here: first is the claim of "Judicial Volition," i.e. that judges exercise unfettered choice in picking a result; and second is the claim of "Judicial Idiosyncrasy," i.e. that judges make this choice in light of personal or idiosyncratic tastes and values. In its extreme, Frankified form, the theses of Judicial Volition and Judicial Idiosyncrasy lead to the conclusion that judicial decision is utterly unpredictable, as it is never possible to isolate the significant idiosyncratic facts about the individual judge that influence his essentially unconstrained choice of outcome.[55]

But it is precisely this upshot of the Received View that ought to raise a question about its adequacy. For surely one of the most familiar themes in the writings of the Realists is their interest in *predicting* judicial decisions (or *prophesying* them, as some Realists put it).[56] But if on the Received View of Realism, prediction of judicial decision is impossible (as Frank would have it), then the Received View could not possibly be an adequate account of the views of all those Realists who aimed to provide predictive theories of judicial decision.

---

[52] Frank, *Law and the Modern Mind* (n. 36 above), p. 102.   [53] Id., pp. 110–11.

[54] "Are Judges Human? Part Two," *University of Pennsylvania Law Review* 80 (1931), 242.

[55] A key theme, of course, of Frank, *Law and the Modern Mind* (n. 36 above). Of course, it is possible that we could formulate good predictive theories even in the absence of knowledge about the causes of decision. Knowledge of deterministic causation guarantees prediction, but plainly the reverse does not hold. Yet Frank seems to assume—with at least good epistemic reason—that absent a knowledge of what causes judges to decide as they do, we will not be able to predict how they will decide.

[56] See, e.g., O.W. Holmes, "The Path of the Law," *Harvard Law Review* 10 (1897), 461; Llewellyn, *The Bramble Bush* (n. 26 above), 4; Underhill Moore, "Rational Basis of Legal Institutions," *Columbia Law Review* 23 (1923), 609–17.

Notice, again, why the problem arises. Where decision is based on unfettered choice, then there is no way to predict decision: what gives us an anchor for prediction is precisely the presence of fetters.[57] If, for example, choice of decision is a rigid function of race or gender or class, then these fetters on decision—racial, gendered or class bias of some sort—form the basis for predicting decision.

But what "fetters" does the Frankified Received View offer? On the Received View, the foundation of judicial decision is the various idiosyncrasies of the individual judge, "the judge's innumerable unique traits, dispositions and habits... [which] shap[e] his decisions not only in his determination of what he thinks fair or just with reference to a given set of facts, but in the very process by which he becomes convinced what those facts are."[58] Here, then, the problem is epistemological: there are indeed determinants of decision (as, of course, Frank's vulgar armchair Freudianism would imply) but they are inaccessible to the observer, the would-be predictor of judicial decision. No lawyer or scholar could possibly track all the peculiarities of life history and psychological coloring that go into the process of decision to be able to predict what judges would do. When the "fetters" upon decision are *idiosyncratic*, the key to prediction will remain epistemologically opaque.[59]

We can now see the contours of the interpretation of the Core Claim that are needed to distinguish it from the Received View. First, choice of decision must, in fact, be sufficiently fettered so that prediction is possible. And second, these fetters upon choice must not consist in idiosyncratic facts about individual judges, but rather must be of sufficient generality or commonality to be both accessible and to admit the sorts of lawful[60] generalizations that make prediction possible. I shall call the former the Determinism Thesis and the second the Generality Thesis. Supplement the Core Claim with these two theses, and you get not the Frankified Received View, but a view which, I shall claim, is the dominant view among Realists.

C. Determinism and Generality

What facts about judges would constitute both *fetters* on decision and be sufficiently common among judges that they would form the basis for lawful (or at

---

[57] There are really two senses of "fetters" at issue here. The Received View claims that the Realists believe there are no fetters on judicial decisions in the sense of fetters *qua* legal reasons. All the Realists do, in fact, accept this part of the Received View, so understood. What they reject, however, is the claim that there are not fetters *qua* causal determinants of these decisions; thus, most Realists reject the image of judges as having unbounded volition in deciding cases—precisely the image that many writers infer from the Received View. (For clarification on these issues, I am indebted to Steven Burton.)   [58] Frank, *Law and the Modern Mind* (n. 36 above), 110–11.

[59] Notice that this means the emphasis on the theme of Judicial Volition is really mistaken even in the case of Frank: for Frank, judicial decisions are *determined*, so that, in reality, there is no room for judicial choice. It is just that both judges themselves, and we as observers of their behavior, will find it hard, if not impossible, to identify the determinants. For that, the hard work of Freudian psychoanalysis is required.   [60] "Lawful" in the scientific, not legal, sense.

least lawlike) predictive generalizations about patterns of decision? The Realists are, unfortunately, clearer about the patterns than about the fetters. Yet it is natural to construe them as offering something like an inference to the best explanation: given the actual existence of regular patterns of decision (which we Realists identify), the best explanation for the existence of such regularities must be that judges share certain features that channel their decisions into these patterns. We can make all this more concrete by considering some actual examples from the Realist literature.

The Realists tend to draw their best examples of the Core Claim from the realm of commercial law (rather, say, than constitutional law—a point of some significance, to which I return later). Typically, the Realists argue that what judges decide on the facts in such cases falls into one of two patterns: either (1) judges enforce the norms of the prevailing commercial culture; or (2) they try to reach the decision that is socio-economically best under the circumstances.

Oliphant gives this example: looking at a series of conflicting court decisions on the validity of contractual promises not to compete, Oliphant observes that in fact the decisions tracked the underlying facts of the cases:

All the cases holding the promises invalid are found to be cases of employees' promises not to compete with their employers after a term of employment. Contemporary guild [i.e. labor union] regulations not noticed in the opinions made their holding eminently sound. All the cases holding the promises valid were cases of promises by those selling a business and promising not to compete with the purchasers. Contemporary economic reality made these holdings eminently sound.[61]

Thus, in the former fact-scenarios, the courts enforced the prevailing norms (as expressed in guild regulations disfavoring such promises); in the latter cases, the courts came out differently because it was economically best under *those* factual circumstances to do so. Llewellyn provides a similar illustration.[62] A series of New York cases applied the rule that a buyer who rejects the seller's shipment by formally stating his objections thereby waives all other objections. Llewellyn notes that the rule seems to have been rather harshly applied in a series of cases where the buyers simply may not have known at the time of rejection of other defects or where the seller could not have cured anyway. A careful study of the facts of these cases revealed, however, that in each case where the rule seemed harshly applied, what had really happened was that the market had fallen, and the buyer was looking to escape the contract. The court in each case, being "sensitive to commerce or to decency,"[63] applies the unrelated rule about rejection to frustrate the buyer's attempt to escape the contract. Thus, the commercial norm—buyers ought to honor their commitments even under changed market conditions—is enforced by the courts through a *seemingly* harsh application of

61 Oliphant, "A Return to Stare Decisis" (n. 34 above) 159–60.
62 Llewellyn, *The Common Law Tradition* (n. 40 above), 122–4.   63 Id., p. 124.

an unrelated rule concerning rejection. It is these "background facts, those of mercantile practice, those of the situation-type"[64] that determine the course of decision.

Underhill Moore tried to systematize this approach in what he called "the institutional method."[65] Moore's idea was this: identify the normal behavior for any "institution" (e.g. commercial banking); then identify and demarcate deviations from this norm quantitatively, and try to identify the point at which deviation from the norm will *cause* a judicial decision that corrects the deviation from the norm (e.g. how far must a bank depart from normal check-cashing practice before a court will decide against the bank in a suit brought by the customer?). The goal is a predictive formula: deviation of degree X from "institutional behavior (i.e. behavior which frequently, repeatedly, usually occurs)"[66] will cause courts to act. Thus, says Moore: "the semblance of causal relation between future and past decisions is the result of the relation of both to a third variable, the relevant institutions in the locality of the court."[67] Put differently: what judges respond to is the extent to which the facts show a deviation from the prevailing norm in the commercial culture.

We may call this approach—to distinguish it from Frank's "Idiosyncrasy Wing" of Realism (in which he was joined by Judge Hutcheson and the Yale psychologist Edward Robinson)—the "Sociological Wing" of Realism (for reasons that will be made clear momentarily, if they are not apparent already). Notice, first, that the theory of the Sociological Wing—that judges enforce the norms of commercial culture or try to do what is socio-economically best on the facts of the case—should not be confused with the idea that judges decide based, for example, on how they feel about the particular parties or the lawyers. These "fireside equities"[68] may sometimes influence judges; but what more typically determines the course of decision is the "situation-type", i.e. the general pattern of behavior exemplified by the particular facts of the disputed transaction,[69] and what would constitute normal or socio-economically desirable behavior in the relevant commercial

---

[64] Id., p. 126.

[65] Moore and Hope, "An Institutional Approach to the Law of Commercial Banking" (n. 45 above).

[66] Id., p. 707.

[67] Underhill Moore and Gilbert Sussman, "Legal and Institutional Methods Applied to the Debiting of Direct Discounts—VI. The Decisions, the Institutions, and the Degree of Deviation," *Yale Law Journal* 40 (1931), 1219–72.   [68] Llewellyn, *The Common Law Tradition* (n. 40 above), 121.

[69] This becomes clear in the sort of instructional materials Realists prepared, which were organized *not* around doctrinal categories, but rather around factual scenarios, i.e. "situation-types". So, for example, Leon Green's torts casebook was originally organized not by the typical *doctrinal* categories (e.g. negligence, intentional torts, strict liability), but rather by the factual scenarios in which harms occur: e.g. "Surgical Operations" (Chapter 2), "Keeping of Animals" (Chapter 3), "Manufacturers, Dealers" (Chapter 5), "Builders, Contractors, Workmen" (Chapter 6), "Traffic and Transportation" (Chapter 9). Leon Green, *The Judicial Process in Tort Cases* (St. Paul: West Publishing Co., 1931), ix–x. There was for Green, the Realist, no law of torts *per se*, but rather a regime of tort rules for "surgical operations," another for "manufacturers," etc. For a similar approach to a different area of law, see Charles A. Wright, *Cases on Remedies* (St. Paul: West Publishing Co., 1955) (dividing the subject not by type of remedy, but by type of injury). A related view of law (notably contract law)

context. The point is decidedly not that judges usually decide because of idiosyncratic likes and dislikes with respect to the individuals before the court .[70]

But why would judges, with some degree of predictable uniformity, enforce the norms of commercial culture as applied to the underlying facts of the case? Here is where we must make an inference to the best explanation of the phenomenon: namely, there must be features of the "sociological" (as opposed to the idiosyncratic psychological) profile of the judges that explain the predictable uniformity in their decisions.[71] The Realists did little more than gesture, however, at a suitable psycho-social explanation. "Professional judicial office," Llewellyn suggested, was "the most important among all the lines of factor which make for reckonability" of decision;[72] "the *office* waits and then moves with the majestic power to shape the man."[73] Echoing, but modifying Frank, Llewellyn continued: "The place to begin is with the fact that the men of our appellate bench are human beings... And one of the more obvious and obstinate facts about human beings is that they operate in and respond to traditions... Tradition grips them, shapes them, limits them, guides them... To a man of sociology or psychology... this needs no argument... "[74] Radin suggested that "the standard transactions with their regulatory incidents are familiar ones to him [the judge] because of his experience as a citizen and a lawyer."[75] Felix Cohen, by contrast, simply lamented that "at present no publication [exists] showing the political, economic, and professional background and activities of our judges,"[76] presumably because such a publication would identify the relevant "social" determinants of decision.[77]

Thus, if the Sociological Wing of Realism—Llewellyn, Moore, Oliphant, Cohen, Radin, among others—is correct, then judicial decisions are causally determined (by the relevant psycho-social facts about judges), and at the same time judicial decisions fall into predictable patterns because these psycho-social facts about judges (e.g. their professionalization experiences, their backgrounds) are not idiosyncratic, but characteristic of significant portions of the judiciary. Rather than rendering judicial decision a mystery, the Realists' Core Claim, to the extent it is true, shows how and why lawyers can predict what courts do.

---

has been taken up more recently in transaction cost economics. See, e.g., Williamson, "Revisiting Legal Realism: The Law, Economics, and Organization Perspective" (n. 20 above), 13–16.

[70] Cf. Radin, "The Theory of Judicial Decision: or How Judges Think" (n. 44 above), 357.

[71] By dubbing the profile "sociological," I mean to be inclusive, rather than exclusive: the idea is that judges instantiate general characteristics, rather than idiosyncratic ones. What these general characteristics are may be illuminated by sociology, or social psychology, or anthropology.

[72] Llewellyn, *The Common Law Tradition* (n. 40 above), 45.   [73] Id., p. 46.

[74] Id., p. 53.

[75] Radin, "The Theory of Judicial Decision: or How Judges Think" (n. 44 above), 358.

[76] Felix Cohen, "Transcendental Nonsense and the Functional Approach," *Columbia Law Review* 35 (1935), 846.

[77] "A truly realistic theory of judicial decision," says Cohen, "must conceive every decision as something more than an expression of individual personality, as... even more importantly... a product of social determinants." Id., p. 843. This notion is taken up at length in the extensive political science literature on judicial decision-making.

Notice, too, that for the Sociological Wing it should also be possible to craft legal rules that really would "guide" decision, or at least accurately *describe* the course of decision actually realized by courts. This is precisely why Oliphant, for example, spoke of a "return" to *stare decisis*: the problem for Oliphant, as for most of the Realists in the Sociological Wing, was not that rules were pointless, but rather that the existing rules were pitched at a level of generality that bore no relation to the fact-specific ways in which courts actually decided cases.[78] Where it was impossible to formulate situation-specific rules, the Realists advocated using general norms, reflecting the norms that judges actually employ anyway. This formed a central part of Llewellyn's approach to drafting Article 2 of the Uniform Commercial Code—an undertaking that would seem impossible for the Realist-as-Rule-Skeptic of popular imagination. Since the Sociological Wing claimed that judges, in any event, enforced the norms of commercial culture, Article 2 tells them to do precisely this, by imposing the obligation of "good faith" in contractual dealings (Sec. 1-203). "Good faith" requires, besides honesty, "the observation of reasonable commercial standards of fair dealing in the trade" (Sec. 2-103). For a judge, then, to enforce the rule requiring "good faith" is just to enforce the norms of commercial culture—which is precisely what the Realists claim the judges are doing anyway!

III. Naturalism and Pragmatism in Legal Theory

A. Introduction

So far, we have seen that the dominant view among Legal Realists is not the Frankified Received View so common in the secondary literature, but rather the Core Claim as seen through the lens of the Determinism and Generality Theses. On this account, Realists advance (1) a *descriptive* theory about the nature of judicial decision, according to which (2) judicial decisions fall into (sociologically) determined patterns, in which (3) judges reach results based on a (generally shared) response to the underlying facts of the case, which (4) they then rationalize after-the-fact with appropriate legal rules and reasons. If this theory of judicial decision-making is different from Frank's psychologistic interpretation of the Core Claim, it is even more different from the inquiries constitutive of traditional jurisprudential theories. It is to these profound differences with the mainstream jurisprudential tradition that I want to turn in the remainder of this paper.

As a jurisprudential theory, Realism is marked by two distinctive philosophical commitments: what I shall call "Naturalism" and "Pragmatism." According to

---

[78] Charles Alan Wright, President of the American Law Institute and a self-identified Realist, points out to me that the Restatements have gradually moved in precisely this direction, reflecting the Realist insight.

Naturalism, a satisfactory theory of adjudication must be continuous with empirical inquiry in the natural and social sciences.[79] According to Pragmatism, a satisfactory theory of adjudication *for lawyers* must enable lawyers to predict what courts will do.[80] Naturalism and Pragmatism are linked in the following way: to predict reliably and effectively what courts will do one should know what *causes* courts to decide as they do; the *causes* of judicial decision, in turn, are only available to the sort of empirical inquiry modelled on the natural and social sciences that the Realists advocate.[81] A *naturalistic* theory of adjudication, then, is required to produce a *pragmatically valuable* theory for lawyers, i.e. one that will enable them to predict what courts will do.

In the following sections, I explicate the notions of naturalism and pragmatism and their relevance to legal theory—though I do so for differing reasons. In the case of naturalism, its import for jurisprudence has yet to be recognized; in the case of pragmatism, its import has been generally misunderstood or crudely understood. To construe the Realists as introducing naturalism and pragmatism into jurisprudence is, on my account, to understand them to be doing something quite precise.

B. Naturalism

Naturalism is a familiar development in recent philosophy: indeed, it would not be wrong to say that it is *the* distinctive development in philosophy over the last thirty years. The linguistic turn of the first half of the twentieth century (in which traditional philosophical problems were framed as problems about our use of language) has either given way to or been supplemented by the naturalistic turn, in which traditional philosophical problems are thought to be insoluble by the *a priori*, armchair methods of the philosopher, and to require, instead, embedding in (or replacement by) suitable empirical theories.[82] To name the major philosophical thinkers

---

[79] For some representative statements of the "naturalistic" position in philosophy, see Daniel Dennett, "Foreword," in Ruth Garrett Millikan, *Language, Thought and Other Biological Categories: New Foundations for Realism* (Cambridge, Mass.: MIT Press, 1984), ix, and Peter Railton, "Naturalism and Prescriptivity," in Ellen Frankel Paul et al. (eds.), *Foundations of Moral and Political Philosophy* (Oxford: Blackwell, 1990), 156–7. Railton calls this view "methodological" naturalism. Id.

[80] I will follow the Realists in analyzing these problems primarily from the standpoint of litigators rather than transactional lawyers.

[81] This assumes, of course, that the Realists are correct that the law is rationally indeterminate.

[82] In some measure, this may sound surprising to those who associate recent philosophy with "postmodernism," understood as a *philosophical* position to the effect that there is no objective truth, that objective knowledge of the world is impossible, that there are no "essences," that the era of "metanarratives" (in Lyotard's famous phrase) is past. Postmodernism in this *philosophical* sense, however, is distinguished by two characteristics: first, almost no philosophers believe it; second, it is supported by bad arguments. The two characteristics are obviously connected.

The bad arguments take two forms: what we may call the "Disappointed Absolutist" argument (to borrow Hart's apt term for a similar view in *The Concept of Law* (n. 27 above), 135) and the "Flesh & Blood" argument. The Disappointed Absolutist argument runs as follows: assuming some impossibly high standard for what will count as "justification" or "objectivity" or "semantic determinacy," it

of the last quarter century is to name philosophers with profoundly naturalistic commitments (of varying sorts): W.V.O. Quine, Jerry Fodor, David Armstrong, Jaegwon Kim, Stephen Stich, and Alvin Goldman, among others. It remains true, of course, that there are powerful philosophical voices aligned against naturalism,

turns out that no beliefs are justified, that no claims about the world are objective, and that no texts have determinate meanings. The problem with this argument, which leads almost all philosophers to dissent from it, is that it never queries whether the underlying standard of justification or objectivity or semantic determinacy is sensible or plausible or what we really mean when we talk about justification or objectivity or determinacy. (Some philosophers dissent for a slightly different reason: they think the high standard of justification or of objectivity *can* be met. The postmodernist literature never evinces even an awareness of these arguments.)

The Flesh & Blood argument runs this way: since, as knowers, we cannot escape our human situation—we cannot transcend, as it were, our flesh and blood (not to mention our race, our gender, our class, etc.)—we can never have objective knowledge of the world. To some extent, this argument piggy-backs on the Disappointed Absolutist argument. Yet it also introduces a new element, an explanation for why we cannot meet the high standards the latter argument presupposes: because we are always "situated." The mistake of this argument is to draw a false inference from the fact (is it an objective fact?) of our being "situated" to the conclusion that we cannot transcend our situation. There is certainly not a philosopher alive today who would deny that, as knowers, our beliefs about the world are shaped by our "situation": our particular cultural and historical moment, the particular traditions that inform our sensibility and judgment, the theoretical paradigms that determine how the world appears to us, the natural and bodily endowment that may make us who we are. Almost all of this is banal in the post-Kantian philosophical universe; and even in the pre-Kantian one, it has its adherents, like Hume (*contra*, e.g., Steven Winter's wildly mistaken claim that Hume was guilty of an "emphasis on Reason as a transcendent faculty..." "Bull Durham and the Uses of Theory", *Stanford Law Review* 42 (1990), 658). Even if we are situated—as no one denies—it may still be possible to have objective knowledge of a strongly objective world. This is precisely what post-Kuhnian and post-Quinean philosophers like Richard Boyd, Hartry Field, Philip Kitcher, and Peter Railton have been arguing for the last twenty years. Perhaps they are wrong. But if they are, it is not because they do not recognize the banal fact that we are "situated"; it is rather because their arguments for how we overcome the limits of our situation are wrong. But, once again, the postmodernist literature is blissfully unaware that there could even be such arguments.

The generally low intellectual level of "postmodern" scholarship has been the subject of much discussion recently, in the wake of the "Sokal Affair." Alan Sokal, a physicist, wrote a parody of postmodern scholarship, full of postmodern slogans and nonsensical science. The article was then accepted by and published in a trendy cultural studies journal, *Social Text*. For a brief overview, see Alan Sokal, "A Physicist Experiments with Cultural Studies," *Lingua Franca* 6 (May/June 1996), 62–4. The significance of this hoax is well put by two prominent philosophers: "The central issue raised by Alan Sokal's hoax... is the competence with which... [cultural] studies are conducted... For many years now, academics from a variety of disciplines have been grumbling... about the appallingly low standards of argument and evidence that appears to characterize work in this area... As philosophers... we have often been struck by the sloppy and naive quality of what passes for philosophical argument... and at the central role that such argument has been made to play." After giving an example from Sokal's piece, they observe, correctly, that, "Only the complete scientific, mathematical and philosophical incompetence of the editors of *Social Text* can explain how they were able to accept for publication such a tissue of transparent nonsense... [I]n accepting Sokal's parody, these [postmodern] scholars have made it clear that... they are unable to tell the difference between a statement that no sane person could credit and its opposite." Paul Boghossian & Thomas Nagel, "Letter to the Editor," *Lingua Franca* 6 (July/August 1996), 58–60. (As William Forbath points out to me, putatively "left" legal academics are overwhelmingly caught up in postmodernism. But as Sokal observes, "a scientific worldview, based on a commitment to logic and standards of evidence and to the incessant confrontation of theories with reality, is an essential component of any progressive politics." "Alan Sokal Replies", in id. 57.)

In any event, it is safe to say that outside of parts of academic culture in the humanities, social sciences, and law, postmodernism (in the *philosophical* sense described above) has been almost completely irrelevant. Recent years, in fact, have witnessed a proliferation of essentialist theories like that of Richard Rorty,[83] or recent Hilary Putnam,[84] or John McDowell.[85] It is beyond the scope of this paper to explain fully where these philosophers go wrong, though I shall make some responsive points in what follows.[86] Suffice it to say that theirs is a minority position in contemporary philosophy.[87]

What really bears noticing here is that while every area of philosophy—metaethics, philosophy of language, epistemology, etc.—has undergone a naturalistic turn over the last quarter-century, Anglo-American legal philosophy has remained untouched by these intellectual developments. Of course, this observation constitutes no argument; what I hope to show in the following pages is that the isolation of Anglo-American jurisprudence in this regard is a mistake, and that it is in the Realists themselves that we will find the first paradigm for a naturalized jurisprudence.

1. The Varieties of Naturalism

What is naturalism and how is it relevant to legal theory? This is a large question, which will receive only a partial answer here.[88] I propose to concentrate in what follows on that aspect of "naturalism" most relevant to an understanding of the Legal Realists.

---

about human beings and other naturalistic "metanarratives." Peter Kramer's best-seller is typical of the real *Zeitgeist*. "Our culture is caught in a frenzy of biological materialism," observes Kramer. "[The] impressive, close-up view of the power of biology over an unexpectedly broad spectrum of human behavior [provided by psychopharmacological drugs like Prozac] ... ha[s] done a good deal to move my assumptions about how people are constituted in the direction of the contemporary zeitgeist." Peter Kramer, *Listening to Prozac* (New York: Viking, 1993), xiii, xv. Postmodernists would do well to heed Nietzsche's methodological proclamation that "the basic text of *homo natura* must again be recognized": "To translate man back into nature ... to see to it that man henceforth stands before man as even today, hardened in the discipline of science ... Why did we choose this insane task? Or, putting it differently: why have knowledge at all?" *Beyond Good and Evil*, Section 230. (On Nietzsche's naturalism, see Leiter, *Nietzsche on Morality* (London: Routledge, 2002), Ch. 1.)

[83] *Philosophy and the Mirror of Nature* (Princeton, NJ: Princeton University Press, 1979).

[84] *Realism with a Human Face* (Cambridge, Mass.: Harvard University Press, 1990). See also Putnam's reply to me—in which the anti-naturalism is quite explicit—in "Replies," *Legal Theory* 1 (1995) 70–2.

[85] *Mind and World* (Cambridge, Mass.: Harvard University Press, 1994). McDowell views himself as a "naturalist," just not what he calls a "bald naturalist." Many philosophers, myself included, are inclined to think that McDowell's "naturalism" simply represents an unprincipled expansion of the category to encompass precisely those phenomena that seem to have a dubious status in a naturalistic conception of the world. See especially id. pp. 66–86.

[86] For a splendid critique of McDowell's cryptic brand of anti-naturalism, see Jerry Fodor, "Encounters with Trees," *London Review of Books* (April 20, 1995), 10–11 (reviewing Mcdowell, *Mind and World*). Of the many critiques of Rorty, one of the best and most-to-the-point remains Jaegwon Kim, "Rorty on the Possibility of Philosophy," *Journal of Philosophy* 77 (1980), 588–97.

[87] As Thomas Nagel (at NYU) has recently observed, the naturalistic approach "that sees philosophy as continuous with science, only more abstract and more general ... is now very common among analytic philosophers, including many of the best minds in the subject ... the Carnap-Quine [naturalistic] tradition has come to dominate the profession ...": Thomas Nagel, *Other Minds* (New York: Oxford University Press, 1995), 6.

[88] For a more substantial treatment, see Leiter, "Naturalism and Naturalized Jurisprudence," in *Analyzing Law: New Essays in Legal Theory*, ed. B. Bix (Oxford: Oxford University Press, 1998).

Naturalism in philosophy is always *first* a *methodological* view to the effect that philosophical theorizing should be continuous with empirical inquiry in the sciences.[89] The naturalist, following Quine, rejects the idea that there could be a "first philosophy", a philosophical solution to problems that proceeds *a priori*, that is, prior to any experience.[90] The philosophical naturalist demands continuity with the natural and social sciences in one or both of the following ways: what I will call "Results Continuity" and "Methods Continuity".

Results Continuity requires that the claims of philosophical theories be supported by the results of successful sciences. Epistemologists like Alvin Goldman look to the results of psychology and cognitive science to find out how the human cognitive apparatus really works; only with that information in hand, argues Goldman, can the epistemologist construct norms for how humans *ought* to form beliefs.[91] "Methods Continuity," by contrast, demands only that philosophical theories emulate the "methods" of inquiry and styles of explanation characteristic of successful sciences.[92] Historically, this has been the most important type of naturalism in philosophy, evidenced in writers from Hume to Nietzsche.[93] Hume and Nietzsche, for example, both construct "speculative" theories of human nature—modelled on the most influential scientific paradigms of the day (Newtonian mechanics, in the case of Hume; 19th-century physiology, in the case of Nietzsche)—in order to "solve" various philosophical problems.[94] Their speculative theories are "modelled" on the sciences most importantly in that they take over from science the idea that we can understand all phenomena in terms of deterministic causes.[95] Just as we understand events in

---

[89] The failure of philosophers to solve the so-called "demarcation problem"—i.e. the problem of what it is that demarcates genuine science from pseudo-science—does not, as far as I can see, doom this definition of naturalism; just as the "paradox of the heap" does not doom our ability to distinguish heaps from single grains—even if, in both cases, there are fuzzy borderline cases.

[90] It bears emphasizing here that most contemporary naturalists do *not* go as far as Quine in repudiating the idea of a "first philosophy" (or in embracing his austere physicalism; on the latter issue, see Christopher Hookway, *Quine: Language, Experience, and Reality* (Stanford: Stanford University Press, 1988), 124. While all would concur with Quine that philosophy can not be exclusively an *a priori* discipline, most naturalists still think there is significant work for conceptual analysis to do. A classic example is Alvin I. Goldman, *Epistemology and Cognition* (Cambridge, Mass.: Harvard University Press, 1986).   [91] See Goldman, id.

[92] Such a view does not suppose the methodological *unity* of the various sciences; so as not to be empty, it does require that the methods of the sciences not be so various as to encompass all possible methodological postures.

[93] On Hume, see the discussion in Barry Stroud, *Hume* (London: Routledge,1977) 1–16, 219–50; on Nietzsche, see Leiter, *Nietzsche on Morality* (London: Routledge, 2002), 6–10.

[94] The similarity between these two thinkers goes even deeper. Both can be read as arguing that given the failure of *rational* vindications of our beliefs—moral and otherwise—we must seek a *naturalistic* explanation for them. If there is an important difference between Hume and Nietzsche, it is that Nietzsche's speculative theories are generally more plausible than Hume's. See Leiter, *Nietzsche on Morality*, id.

[95] "[T]he key to understanding Hume's philosophy is to see him as putting forward a general theory of human nature in just the way that, say, Freud or Marx did . . . And the theories they advance are all, roughly, deterministic." Stroud, *Hume* (n. 93 above), 4. For Freud, the deterministic causes are various unconscious drives and desires; for Nietzsche, they include both drives and physiological causes.

the inanimate world by identifying the natural causes that determine them, so too we understand human beliefs, values, and actions by locating their causal determinants in various features of human nature.

Methodological Naturalists, then, construct philosophical theories that are continuous with the sciences either in virtue of their dependence upon the actual results of scientific method in different domains or in virtue of their employment and emulation of distinctively scientific ways of looking at and explaining things.[96] We must still distinguish, however, between two different branches of Methodological Naturalism: the Quinean and the Goldmanesque. The former I will call "Replacement Naturalism"; the latter "Normative Naturalism". Goldman's paradigm of Normative Naturalism has dominated philosophical research in the area,[97] though it is Quine's notion of Replacement Naturalism that bears most immediately on Legal Realism. Since both Replacement and Normative Naturalists share the *methodological* commitment distinctive of naturalism—to make philosophical theorizing continuous with and dependent upon scientific theorizing—the difference must be located elsewhere: not in methodology, but in goal. According to Replacement Naturalists, the goal of theorizing is description or explanation; according to Normative Naturalists, the goal is regulation of practice through the promulgation of norms or standards.[98] I plan to concentrate here

Other aspects of scientific "method" that have also been influential in philosophy include a commitment to seeking empirical confirmation of theoretical claims, and, concomitantly, a commitment to the experimental method.

[96] Many naturalists go beyond Methodological Naturalism, however, and embrace a *substantive* doctrine. "Substantive Naturalism" in philosophy is either the (ontological) view that the only things that exist are *natural* or *physical* things; or the (semantic) view that a suitable philosophical analysis of any concept must show it to be amenable to empirical inquiry. In the ontological sense, Substantive Naturalism is often taken to entail physicalism, the doctrine that only those properties picked out by the laws of the physical sciences are real. In the semantic sense, Substantive Naturalism is just the view that predicates like "morally good" can be analyzed in terms of characteristics (e.g. "maximizing human well-being") that admit of empirical inquiry (e.g. by psychology and physiology, assuming that well-being is a function of psychological and physical condition).

Many philosophers are drawn to some type of Substantive Naturalism in virtue of their Methodological Naturalism: being a philosophical naturalist in the methodological sense sometimes leads a philosopher to think that the best philosophical account of some concept or domain will be in terms that are substantively naturalistic. But it is important to notice that a commitment to Methodological Naturalism does *not* entail this conclusion: methodologically, it is an open question whether the best philosophical account of morality or mentality or law must be in substantively naturalistic terms.

Too often, it seems to me, philosophers conflate "naturalism" with *Substantive* Naturalism. See, e.g., Philip Pettit, "Naturalism," in Jonathan Dancy and Ernest Sosa (eds.), *A Companion to Epistemology* (Oxford: Blackwell, 1992), 296–7; Stephen J. Wagner & Richard Warner, "Introduction" in Stephen Wagner and Richard Warner (eds.), *Naturalism: A Critical Appraisal* (Notre Dame, Ind.: University of Notre Dame Press, 1993), 1–3. But from the standpoint of the Methodological Naturalist, this prejudges too many issues in precisely the *a priori* fashion that Methodological Naturalism was meant to rule out.

[97] See, e.g., the survey of recent literature in Philip Kitcher, "The Naturalists Return," *Philosophical Review* 101 (1992), 53.

[98] Notice that *this* goal is not peculiar to Normative Naturalism—it is equally the goal of traditional epistemology, from Descartes to the early Carnap. What distinguishes the Normative Naturalist from

on Replacement Naturalism; I will take up the relationship between Realism and Normative Naturalism elsewhere.[99]

The *locus classicus* of Replacement Naturalism is, of course, Quine's 1968 paper "Epistemology Naturalized."[100] The central enterprise of epistemology on Quine's view is to understand the relation between our theories of the world and the evidence (sensory input) on which they are based. Quine's target is one influential construal of this project: Cartesian foundationalism, particularly in the sophisticated form given to it in the twentieth century by Rudolf Carnap in *Der Logische Aufbau der Welt.*[101] The foundationalist wants an account of the theory-evidence relation that would vindicate the privileged epistemic status of at least some subset of our theories: our theories (in particular, our best theories of natural science) are to be "grounded" in indubitable evidence (i.e. immediate sense impressions).[102] As is quite familiar, foundationalism, for Quine, is a failure, rendered unrealizable by Quinean meaning holism on the one hand (theoretical terms get their meanings from their place in the whole theoretical framework, not in virtue of some point-by-point contact with sensory input), and the Duhem-Quine thesis about the underdetermination of theory by evidence on the other (there is always more than one theory consistent with the evidence, in part, because a theoretical hypothesis can always be preserved in the face of recalcitrant evidence by abandoning the auxiliary hypotheses that informed the test of the hypothesis).[103]

What becomes, then, of epistemology? Hilary Kornblith has summed up Quine's view as follows:

Once we see the sterility of the foundationalist program, we see that the only genuine questions there are to ask about the relation between theory and evidence and about the acquisition of belief are psychological questions.[104]

---

the traditional epistemologist is the methods employed to realize this goal. See Goldman, *Epistemology and Cognition* (n. 90 above), 6–9.

   [99] See "Naturalism and Naturalized Jurisprudence"(n. 88 above).

   [100] W.V.O. Quine, "Epistemology Naturalized," in *Ontological Relativity and Other Essays* (New York: Columbia University Press, 1969). See also, W.V.O. Quine, "Grades of Theoriticity," in Lawrence Foster and Joe Swanson (eds.), *Experience and Theory* (Amherst: University of Massachusetts Press, 1970). Further citations will only be to the former paper, not the latter.

   [101] (Berlin: Weltkreis, 1928); usually translated as *The Logical Structure of the World*, though the literal rendering of *Aufbau* as "building-up" conveys nicely the foundationalist flavor of the project.

   [102] For reasons of simplicity of presentation, I am blurring two issues here. The foundationalist program, at least in the early Carnap (who later repudiates it), has two parts: semantic and epistemic. The semantic program is to translate all sentences referring to physical objects into the language of sense-data (e.g. "I am being appeared to greenly now"). The epistemic program is to show that scientific theories about the physical world are uniquely justifed on the basis of sensory experience. Semantic holism dooms the first project. Hume on induction, and the Duhem-Quine thesis about underdetermination doom the second.

   [103] See the astute summary in Jaegwon Kim, "What is 'Naturalized Epistemology?'" *Philosophical Perspectives* 2 (1988), 385–6.

   [104] "Introduction: What Is Naturalistic Epistemology?" in Hilary Kornblith (ed.), *Naturalizing Epistemology*, Second Edition (Cambridge, Mass.: MIT Press, 1994), 4.

This view Kornblith aptly dubs Quine's "replacement thesis": "the view that epistemological questions may be replaced by psychological questions."[105] Here is how Quine puts it:

The stimulation of his sensory receptors is all the evidence anybody has had to go on, ultimately, in arriving at his picture of the world. Why not just see how this construction really proceeds? Why not settle for psychology? Such a surrender of the epistemological burden to psychology is a move that was disallowed in earlier time as circular reasoning. If the epistemologist's goal is validation of the grounds of empirical science, he defeats his purpose by using psychology or other empirical science in the validation. However, such scruples against circularity have little point once we have stopped dreaming of deducing science from observations.[106]

Several pages later, Quine continues that on his proposal,

Epistemology, or something like it, simply falls into place as a chapter of psychology and hence of natural science. It studies a natural phenomenon, viz., a physical subject. This human subject is accorded a certain experientally controlled input—certain patterns of irradiation in assorted frequencies, for instance—and in the fullness of time the subject delivers as output a description of the three-dimensional external world and its history. The relation between the meager input and the torrential output is a relation that we are prompted to study for somewhat the same reasons that always prompted epistemology; namely, in order to see how evidence relates to theory, and in what ways one's theory of nature transcends any available evidence.[107]

Thus Quine: the central concern of epistemology is the theory-evidence relationship; if the foundationalist story about this relationship is a failure, then that leaves only one story worth telling about this relationship: namely, the story told by "a purely descriptive, causal-nomological science of human cognition."[108] The science of human cognition *replaces* armchair epistemology: we naturalize epistemology by turning over its central question—the relationship between theory and evidence—to the relevant empirical science.

We can now generalize Quine's point as follows. Let us say that a Replacement Naturalist in any branch of philosophy holds that:

For any pair of relata that might stand in a *justificatory* relation—e.g. evidence and theory, reasons and belief, causal history and semantic or intentional content, legal reasons and judicial decision—if no normative account of the relation is possible, then the only theoretically fruitful account is the descriptive/explanatory account given by the relevant science of that domain.[109]

---

[105] Id., p. 3.   [106] Quine, "Epistemology Naturalized" (n. 100 above), 75–6.

[107] Id., pp. 82–3.   [108] Kim, "What is 'Naturalized Epistemology?'" (n. 103 above), 388.

[109] One might, of course, hold that the descriptive account just gives us all there is to justification: so, e.g., describing the causal history of a belief may be all there is to *justifying* that belief. See the discussion in Fodor, "Encounters with Trees." The possibility, however, has no bearing on the project here.

This generalizes Quine's point in one important respect: for Quine infers Replacement Naturalism only from the failure of *foundationalism*—which is simply one possible normative account of the evidence-theory relationship, but not the only one. Quine's arguments simply do not show that no other normative account of the evidence-theory relationship is possible. Quine has been extensively criticized on precisely this score.[110] The key to a successful defense of Replacement Naturalism, in my view, lies in the implicit notion of *fruitfulness* of theoretical investigation. The Quinean rejoinder must take the form of saying: "Once we give up on the foundational project of justification, nothing we have to say about justification will be of much theoretical interest; theorizing about justification will collapse, as it were, into a banal descriptive sociology of our justificatory practices."[111] Put more simply: if we cannot carry out the program of normative foundationalism, then we might as well do something useful and interesting, namely empirical theory.

Why is normative theory sterile without foundationalism? Let me give one brief example to illustrate the point. It is now a familiar result of cognitive psychology that human beings regularly make mistakes in logical reasoning.[112] So a mere descriptive theory of belief-formation, of the sort Quine appears to recommend,

[110] See, e.g., Barry Stroud, *The Significance of Philosophical Scepticism* (Oxford: Clarendon Press, 1984), 211–54; Stephen P. Stich, "Naturalizing Epistemology: Quine, Simon and the Prospects for Pragmatism," in Christopher Hookway and Donald Peterson (eds.), *Philosophy and Cognitive Science*, Royal Institute of Philosophy, Supplement no. 34 (Cambridge: Cambridge University Press, 1993), 3–5. See also, Kim, "What is 'Naturalized Epistemology?'" (n. 103 above), and Goldman, *Epistemology and Cognition* (n. 90 above), 2–3. For a rather different view, however, see Richard Foley, "Quine and Naturalized Epistemology," *Midwest Studies in Philosophy* 19 (1994), 243–60. Foley rejects the "standard interpretation of Quine's view" (id. at 246)—roughly, my interpretation in the text—calling attention instead to places where Quine affirms a *normative* role even for his naturalized epistemology. Id. at 248–50. While Foley correctly recognizes that for Quine these norms admit of no *a priori* justification (id. at 258), he seems to think this is trivial, since (1) the norms Quine favors are ones we could almost never give up anyway; and (2) Quine identifies them, according to Foley, from the "armchair" rather than empirically (id. at 253–9). Foley's provocative paper, in my view, underestimates how much of a break this really is from the tradition, and overestimates how much normative epistemology Quine really offers. But these issues would take me too far afield of my present concerns.

[111] This view of Quine is implicit in Rorty's provocative interpretation in Rorty, *Philosophy and the Mirror of Nature* (n. 83 above), 165–212. As Rorty says (regarding Wilfrid Sellars and Quine): "their holism is a product of their commitment to the thesis that justification is not a matter of a special relation between ideas (or words) and objects, but of conversation, of social practice . . . we understand knowledge when we understand the social justification of belief . . ." id. at 170. But this gets Quine wrong in an important respect, for it makes it sound like Quine has some *positive* view about justification, namely that it consists in "social practice." But Quine's point, as I read him, is that there is nothing to "understand [about] knowledge" at all, if "understanding knowledge" means understanding justification. If we could have told the foundationalist story about justification, that would have been interesting; but we cannot, thinks Quine, so justification just drops out of the picture as a topic for fruitful theoretical inquiry. Someone might do the descriptive sociology and map the "social justification of belief" as we find it; but that would not shed special light on *justification*. Quine's preferred alternative is to study the evidence-theory relationship as a matter of empirical psychology—again, not as a way of analyzing "justification," but as a way of understanding "knowledge"—i.e. the "theories" we construct on the basis of meager evidence—without understanding justification.

[112] For an overview of some relevant results, see Stephen Stich, "Could Man Be an Irrational Animal?," reprinted in *Naturalizing Epistemology* (n. 104 above).

would simply record these mistakes. But shouldn't epistemology tell us that beliefs *ought* not to be formed illogically? One can hardly imagine why Quine would disagree: one *ought* not to form beliefs illogically. But the question is whether this piece of banal advice adds up to a fruitful research program? Quine, I take it, thinks it does not. The descriptive project of Replacement Naturalism may record certain irrational cognitive processes in studying the evidence-theory relationship, but given the underdetermination of theory by evidence, even when we correct logical mistakes, we still will not have an account of which of our theoretical beliefs are warranted and which are not. The Quinean intuition is that we will learn more from the empirical inquiry than from systematizing our mundane normative intuitions about irrationality. Moreover, this latter project will collapse into the descriptive sociology of knowledge *unless* we have some foundational point outside our epistemic practices from which to assess the epistemic issues: otherwise we can do no more than report what it is we do. But it is precisely the viability of such an external standpoint that Quine denies.

2. Naturalism and Legal Theory

We saw that Quine's argument for Replacement Naturalism moved in two steps. Step one was *anti-foundationalism*: no unique theory is justified on the basis of the evidential input. Step two was *replacement*: since no foundational story can be told about the relation between input (evidence) and output (theory), why not replace the normative program with a purely descriptive inquiry, e.g. the psychological study of what input causes what output. We can find, I shall argue, analogues of both steps in the Realists' approach to the theory of adjudication.

Theory of adjudication is concerned *not* with the relationship between "evidence" and "scientific theory," but rather with the justificatory relationship between "legal reasons" (the input, as it were) and judicial decision (the output): theory of adjudication tries to tell judges how they *ought* to justify their decisions, i.e. it seeks to "ground" judicial decision-making in reasons that require unique outcomes.[113] The Realists are "anti-foundationalists" about judicial decisions in the sense that they deny that the legal reasons justify a unique decision: the legal reasons underdetermine the decision (at least in most cases actually litigated). More precisely, the Realists claim that the law is *rationally* indeterminate in the sense that the class of legal reasons—i.e. the class of legitimate reasons a judge may offer for a decision—does not provide a *justification* for a unique outcome.[114] Just as sensory input does not *justify* a unique scientific theory, so legal reasons, according to the Realists, do not *justify* a unique decision.

---

[113] I take it this last assumption about the ambitions of theory of adjudication is contested in Burton, *Judging in Good Faith* (n. 4 above), and in Kenneth Kress, "Legal Indeterminacy," *California Law Review* 77 (1989), 285–337. I take up the general worry below.

[114] That the Realists think the law is "indeterminate" is, of course, quite familiar. On some of the problems about how to formulate the Realist view about indeterminacy, see Leiter, "Legal Indeterminacy" (n. 24 above).

The Realists also take the second step that Quine takes: replacement. According to the Realist indeterminacy thesis, legal reasons underdetermine judicial decisions, meaning that the foundationalist enterprise of theory of adjudication is impossible. Why not replace, then, the "sterile" foundational program of justifying some one legal outcome on the basis of the applicable legal reasons, with a descriptive/explanatory account of what input (that is, what combination of facts and reasons) produces what output (i.e. what judicial decision)?[115] To give such a descriptive/explanatory account is just to vindicate the Core Claim of Realism. As Underhill Moore puts it at the beginning of one of his articles: "This study lies within the province of jurisprudence. It also lies within the field of behavioristic psychology. It places the province within the field."[116] Notice how closely this echoes Quine's idea that "Epistemology . . . simply falls into place as a chapter of psychology . . ."[117] Jurisprudence—or, more precisely, the theory of adjudication—is "naturalized" because it falls into place, for the Realist, as a chapter of psychology (or anthropology or sociology). Moreover, it does so for essentially Quinean reasons: because the foundational account of adjudication is a failure—a consequence of accepting the Realists' famous claim that the law is indeterminate.[118]

We must note immediately, however, four potential problems for this account. First, insofar as the Realists do *not* claim that the law is indeterminate in *all* cases, the analogy with Quine collapses. Second, insofar as theory of adjudication is not essentially a *foundationalist* program, the analogy with Quine collapses. Third, even if *legal* reasons underdetermine the decision, there still may be non-legal reasons (e.g. reasons of morality or policy) that do justify a unique decision—in which case, why think this must be described in strictly naturalistic or "causal" terms? Fourth, even if each of these problems is overcome, it still seems that not *all* of jurisprudence has been naturalized: for example, the Realist argument for the indeterminacy of law is parasitic upon a *conceptual* account of the criteria of legality (i.e. of the legitimate sources of law). I take up each of these issues in turn.

[115] Such a naturalized jurisprudence would be in tension with most of modern legal philosophy, which follows H.L.A. Hart in accepting a hermeneutic model for understanding the social world. According to this model, we do not look for lawful regularities in the external behavior of social actors; rather, to understand social actors we must adopt their "internal" point of view, and understand, for example, what their reasons mean to them. We can understand the Realists as contesting whether such an approach is really more explanatorily and predictively fruitful than their non-hermeneutic approach to the social world.

[116] Moore & Callahan, "Law and Learning Theory: A Study in Legal Control" (n. 49 above), 1.

[117] Quine, "Epistemology Naturalized" (n. 100 above), 82.

[118] If this account provides a philosophical pedigree for one strand in Realism, it does so, of course, at the cost of getting the chronology all wrong: Moore's remark, for example, predates Quine's by a quarter-century! Yet both Quine and the Realists were nurtured in a similar intellectual millieu—one dominated by "naturalism," and, more particularly, by behaviorism in psychology. In any event, the point of introducing Quine here is *only* to establish the *intellectual* credentials for the style of argumentation we find in the Realists. The Realists depart from Quine, needless to say, on many issues—as might many philosophers who nonetheless accept naturalism and the rejection of the analytic-synthetic distinction. See especially, Hookway, *Quine: Language, Experience, and Reality* (n. 90 above), 124.

(1) As noted earlier, the Realists, unlike the later writers of C.L.S., do not claim that the law is "globally" indeterminate: they do not claim that the class of legal reasons fails to justify a unique outcome in *all* cases; rather it fails to do so "locally," i.e. in a particular range of cases (e.g. the cases that reach the stage of appellate review). But to concede that there is some *other* range of cases where the law *is* determinate is just to concede that the "foundationalist" program can be carried out for those cases: that is, we can give an account of the unique decision justified by the applicable legal reasons. But the possibility of foundationalism eliminates the motive for replacement of the normative inquiry with a purely descriptive one. Thus, it appears the analogy with Quinean Replacement Naturalism breaks down.

The Realist may concede as much, and indeed, has no reason not to. For the Realist does not call for "naturalizing" theory of adjudication in that range of cases where legal reasons *are* satisfactory predictors of legal outcomes (i.e. precisely those cases where the foundationalist program can be carried out).[119] One may worry, again, about whether there is an *interesting* or *fruitful* normative story to be told (rather than a merely mundane one), but it suffices for the analogy with Quine that there remains some substantial domain of cases where the foundational program can not be carried out, so that the case for replacement remains intact.

(2) Perhaps, though, theory of adjudication—even for "hard" cases—is not a *foundationalist* theory: it may aspire to delimit the range of legal reasons that *ought* to be brought to bear in deciding some legal question, but it does not seek to delimit the reasons such that they justify a *unique* outcome. In that case, the fact that the reasons *under*determine the outcome does not threaten the genuine *normative* ambitions of theory of adjudication.

This objection is just a variation on one of the familiar objections to Quinean naturalism, namely, that it wrongly infers the futility of normative theorizing from the failure of only *one sort of normative program*, i.e. foundationalism.[120] The proper naturalistic rejoinder, as noted earlier, is to query whether non-foundational normative theorizing is a fruitful undertaking. This worry is particularly vivid in the case of theory of adjudication. If the objection under consideration is correct, then a *normative* theory that specifies what the anti-foundationalist concedes—namely, that there is more than one (though not simply any) judicial decision that can be justified on the basis of the class of legal reasons—must, in some measure, be a theory worth having. Arguably, such a theory might be adequate to deflect the challenge to the political *legitimacy* of adjudication based on the indeterminacy of law,[121] but does it provide the *normative* guidance to judges we want from a

---

[119] I defend a somewhat different view in Ch. 6; but see also the Postscript to Part II.

[120] Cf. Kim, "What is 'Naturalized Epistemology?' " (n. 103 above).

[121] See, e.g., Burton, *Judging in Good Faith* (n. 4 above), and Kress, "Legal Indeterminacy" (n. 113 above). I adopted a similar view in Coleman & Leiter, "Determinacy, Objectivity and Authority" (n. 29 above), but I now think that part of the argument is mistaken.

theory?[122] Does a theory that tells judges they would be justified (on the basis of the class of legal reasons) in deciding for the plaintiff on theory X *or* the defendant on theory Y (but not the plaintiff or defendant on theory Z!) really provide normative guidance for judges worth having? My lawyerly intuition is that normative guidance like this (which underdetermines the final outcome) is not of much value to judges *or to lawyers*. Indeed, if we take seriously the pragmatic ambition of the Realists—to enable lawyers to predict what courts will do—then formulating a non-foundational normative theory of adjudication will be inadequate, precisely because it provides the lawyer with insufficient tools for predicting the actual decision in the case at hand.[123]

(3) Yet even the Realists concede that judges decide for *reasons*, it is just that they do not decide for reasons *of law* (the latter being indeterminate). For example, in the context of commercial disputes, some of the Realists claim that what judges try to do is enforce the norms of commercial practice: the norms of commercial practice provide reasons for deciding one way rather than another.[124] Even granting the truth of anti-foundationalism regarding *legal* reasons, then, why think we should replace such theories with "naturalistic" ones, i.e. with descriptive accounts of what "inputs" cause what "outputs"? Moreover, if we *do* think such naturalistic explanations are called for in those cases that involve consideration of non-legal reasons, why confine naturalistic explanations *only* to those cases: why not, in other words, demand a naturalistic explanation of even "easy" cases, controlled by rationally determinate legal reasons? Put more simply, the challenge is this: why "naturalize" (in the sense of seeking deterministic causes) where reasons (legal or non-legal) will suffice to explain?

A Realist has at least four possible responses:[125]

First: conceding the relevance of (non-legal) reasons does not obviously defeat the naturalistic program. To give a *causal* explanation of decisions in terms of reasons does require taking the normative force of the reasons *qua* reasons seriously.[126] So to give a causal explanation of the decision (as the naturalist wants to do) we must attend, as it were, to the *rationality* of the reasons. But this is just a constraint on *naturalization* in the domain, not an objection to the naturalistic program.

The difficulty with resting content with this line of response is that it then suggests that we could just as well "naturalize" the decision of easy cases, where the

---

[122] Consider the analagous question that the Quinean might pose to the non-foundationalist epistemologist: do we provide useful *normative* guidance to scientists when we tell them that they are justified in accepting more than one (though not simply any) theory in light of the evidence?

[123] Writers like Burton who do not accept pragmatism (in my sense) as a constraint on theorizing will, presumably, be unmoved by this objection.

[124] As noted earlier, this descriptive claim informed Llewellyn's drafting work on Article 2 of the U.C.C. For a rich discussion, see White, *Patterns of American Legal Thought* (n. 31 above).

[125] The discussion that follows is indebted to fruitful debates on these issues with Jules Coleman, Joseph Raz, and Scott Shapiro.

[126] For the seminal discussion, see Donald Davidson, "Actions, Reasons, and Causes," reprinted in *Essays on Actions and Events* (Oxford, Clarendon Press, 1980), 3–19.

legal reasons are determinate. The rule says, "Anyone going faster than 55 m.p.h. shall pay a $50 fine." Newt was clocked going faster than 55 m.p.h. Therefore, the judge decides, Newt must pay the fine. No doubt we could tell a "naturalistic" story about this decision—e.g., about the psychological mechanisms that make deductive inferences possible and "intuitive" to creatures like us—but surely this seems like a pointless exercise. Where reasons *rationalize* a decision determinately, why think there is any *need* for a naturalistic explanation, even if one could be given? This suggests the need for a second, more promising, response.

Second: if we are going to invoke intuitions about whether *naturalistic* explanations (that do not invoke reasons as causes) are more or less *useful* (or *fruitful* or *"needed"*) than rationalizing explanations, then surely it is an open empirical question which sorts of explanations we should prefer. The enormous political science literature trying to correlate judicial decisions with the background of judges[127] is predicated on the assumption that the former, not the latter, explanations are more interesting and more illuminating. This literature seeks to "explain" judicial decisions *without* reference to reasons—not because such reasons could not be given (no doubt the Republican judges have "Republican" reasons for deciding as they do), but because it is thought that the "naturalistic" explanations here—cashed out in terms of correlations between decisions and psycho-social facts about the judges—are more useful, more fruitful, more informative than the explanations in terms of reasons. The Realist might concede, then, that we could understand judicial decisions in terms of responsiveness to non-legal reasons, but contend that naturalistic explanations that make no reference to reasons, but only to relevant psycho-social facts about judges, represent the more fruitful way to go.

But whether this is true, to repeat, is an open empirical question, and thus the Realist would do well to have additional responses.

Third: the most likely response for the Realist to make—and, indeed, the most plausible—is to claim that even the non-legal reasons (e.g. reasons of "policy" or of "morality") are rationally indeterminate: so just as the legal reasons underdetermine the decision, so too do the non-legal reasons. The fact that moral considerations are not "objective" makes it likely that moral reasons will be indeterminate.[128] We can also understand certain C.L.S. arguments as

---

[127] See, e.g., Jilda M. Aliotta, "Combining Judges' Attributes and Case Characteristics: An Alternative Approach to Explaining Supreme Court Decisionmaking," *Judicature* 71 (Feb.–Mar. 1988), 277–80; Sheldon Goldman, "Voting Behavior on the United States Court of Appeals Revisited," *American Political Science Review* 69 (1975), 491–506; Joel Grossman, "Social Backgrounds and Judicial Decisionmaking," *Harvard Law Review* 79 (1966), 1551–64; Stuart Nagel, "Political Party Affiliation and Judges' Decisions," *American Political Science Review* 55 (1961), 843–50; C. Neal Tate, "Personal Attribute Models of the Voting Behavior of U.S. Supreme Court Justices: Liberalism in Civil Liberties and Economics Decisions, 1946–1975," *American Political Science Review* 75 (1981), 355–67.

[128] On this issue, with particular reference to Ronald Dworkin's curious writings on the subject, see Ch. 8.

supporting the same point about the indeterminacy of moral and policy reasons.[129] If these considerations are correct, then any explanation of the decision in terms solely of reasons, legal or non-legal, will necessarily be incomplete. The Realist goal is to locate and articulate the real cause of the decision, which requires going beyond the domain of reasons.[130]

Fourth: even where reasons are rationally determinate, there is still work for a naturalistic story to do. For often it *is* interesting and informative—rather than trivial—to understand why it is persons respond to the reasons they respond to. Some law professors find considerations of efficiency compelling; others respond more to reasons arising out of empathetic engagement with the experiences of actual individuals. These differences, as is surely familiar, often track differences in character, personal style, temperament. Of course, if we assume that responsiveness to reasons is determined exclusively by considerations of rationality, then we will be confident that reason itself tells all the story there is to be told about why persons respond to the reasons they respond to (either they are rational or irrational). What is known as the "Strong Programme" in sociology of knowledge[131] denies this: what passes as "rationality" itself, as much as irrationality, requires explanation in terms of social and psychological forces. We need not go that far, however. It suffices to render naturalistic explanations illuminating if we assume that there are incommensurable rational systems, so that within any system, there are purely rational explanations for decisions, but the fact that an agent has adopted that rational system itself requires non-rational, naturalistic explanation. Philosophers, Nietzsche says,

...all pose as if they had discovered and reached their real opinions through the self-development of a cold, pure, divinely unconcerned dialectic...; while at bottom it is an assumption, a hunch, indeed a kind of "inspiration"—most often a desire of the heart that has been filtered and made abstract—that they defend with reasons they have sought after the fact.[132]

From this Nietzsche concludes we need a two-step naturalistic explanation of the views of a philosopher: we explain the philosophical views in terms of the "morality" at which he "aim[s]"; but we explain the "morality" at which he aims in terms of "the innermost drives of his nature."[133] Substitute talk of a judge's decision for the views of the philosopher, and we quickly recognize the Frank/Hutcheson

---

[129] For an illuminating overview, see Andrew Altman, "Legal Realism, Critical Legal Studies, and Dworkin," *Philosophy & Public Affairs* 15 (1986), 205–35.

[130] The assumption here is that reasons are insufficient to cause a decision when they do not rationally justify the decision, assuming the judges are rational. For more on this, see Leiter, "Legal Indeterminacy" (n. 24 above).

[131] See, e.g., Barry Barnes, *Scientific Knowledge and Sociological Theory* (London: Routledge, 1974); David Bloor, *Knowledge and Social Imagery* (London: Routledge, 1974); Barry Barnes and David Bloor, "Relativism, Rationalism and the Sociology of Knowledge," in Martin Hollis and Steven Lukes (eds.) *Rationality and Relativism* (Oxford: Basil Blackwell, 1982), 21–47.

[132] Nietzsche, *Beyond Good and Evil* (1886), Sec. 5.   [133] Id., p. Sec. 6.

"hunch" theory of judicial decision: we explain the decision in terms of the "hunch"; and we explain the "hunch" psychoanalytically (at least for Frank). But even the Sociological Wing of Realism could propose that responsiveness to reasons itself requires explanation, it is just that the relevant explanation is *sociological* in character, not psychological.

(4) Even if the Realist is successful in defending his case for the "naturalization" of theory of adjudication (on the Quinean model), this hardly shows that jurisprudence has been naturalized. Recall, for example, that to make the case for Replacement Naturalism we must make the case for anti-foundationalism which, in the legal case, is just the claim that the class of legal reasons does not justify a unique decision (i.e. the claim of the "rational" indeterminacy of law). But it is impossible to formulate an argument for rational indeterminacy of law without presupposing certain conceptual views about the criteria of legal validity.[134] When Holmes, for example, chalks up judicial decision not to law but to a half-conscious judgment of policy,[135] he is plainly presupposing that reasons of policy are *not* part of the "law" (i.e. the class of legitimate legal reasons). And in demonstrating the indeterminacy of *law* by concentrating on indeterminacy in the interpretation of *statutes and precedents*,[136] Realists like Llewellyn and Radin seem to be supposing that these exhaust the authoritative sources of law.[137] This means, of course, that the Realists are working with an implicit theory of the *concept* of law, a theory on which the argument for indeterminacy piggy-backs. (Indeed, in many respects they seem to hold to a fairly crude type of legal positivism as a conceptual theory.[138]) But this implicit conceptual theory is manifestly not a *naturalized* theory: the "concept" of law is not illuminated or fixed by empirical inquiry in the natural and social sciences. So it seems that there is still room for non-naturalized jurisprudence, after all.

And so there is! But I do not see that the Realist should argue otherwise. The Realists call for the "naturalization" of *theory of adjudication*; but in so arguing, they may require traditional philosophical help in crafting theories of the "concept" of law that analytic jurisprudents have typically provided. Jurisprudence *per se* is *not* naturalized; just that part of jurisprudence concerned with the theory

---

[134] On this issue, see my "Legal Indeterminacy" (n. 24 above) and Ch. 2.

[135] See Holmes, "The Path of the Law" (n. 56 above), 464.

[136] See, e.g., Llewellyn, *The Bramble Bush* (n. 26 above), 70–6; Max Radin, "Statutory Interpretation," *Harvard Law Review* 43 (1930), 863; Karl Llewellyn, "Remarks on the Theory of Appellate Decision and the Rules and Canons About How Statutes are to be Construed," *Vanderbilt Law Review* 3 (1950), 395–406. See the discussion in Leiter, "Legal Realism" (n. 14 above).

[137] Llewellyn even remarks on one occasion that judges take rules "in the main from authoritative sources (which in the case of the law are largely statutes and the decisions of the courts." Llewellyn, *The Bramble Bush* (n. 26 above), 13.

[138] See Ch. 2. I say "crude" positivism, because positivists have historically recognized customary practices as legitimate sources of law, while the Realists *often* seem to assume that law is exhausted by legislation and court decisions. Of course, even this assumption could be better defended within the contours of a positivistic theory than any of the typical "natural law" alternatives.

of adjudication. For Quine, of course, to naturalize philosophy is just to put philosophers out of business and turn the whole affair over to empirical inquirers.[139] But Quine's conception of naturalization is especially radical in this regard. Most "naturalistic" philosophers think that there remains some characteristically philosophical work to do (e.g., conceptual analysis[140]), even if philosophical questions ultimately require naturalistic answers.[141] The Realists *naturalize* theory of adjudication, but that still leaves conventionally philosophical work to be done in the broader field of jurisprudence.[142]

C. Pragmatism

1. What is Pragmatism?

Unlike naturalism, "pragmatism" is surely a familiar term to lawyers. Unfortunately, it has been so recklessly overused in recent years that it has been rendered, by now, either utterly banal or simply empty.[143] The banality is particularly evident in discussions of the "pragmatism" of the Realists. Thus, Joseph Singer writes that:

The legal realists wanted to replace formalism with a pragmatic attitude toward law generally. This attitude treats law as made, not found. Law therefore is, and must be, based on human experience, policy, and ethics, rather than formal logic. Legal principles are not inherent in some universal, timeless logical system; they are social constructs designed by people in specific historical and social contexts for specific purposes to achieve specific ends. Law and legal reasoning are part of the way we create our form of social life.[144]

---

139 Or it means that philosophers have to take up "armchair [empirical] learning theory," which Quine increasingly does. See Hookway, *Quine: Language, Experience, and Reality* (n. 90 above), 55.

140 Quine's famous attack on the analytic-synthetic distinction and the factuality of "meaning" has embarrassed a lot of philosophers out of saying openly that this is what they are doing (i.e. conceptual analysis or the analysis of meaning). But once one concedes the temporally and perhaps culturally relative character of the concepts to be analyzed—as most contemporary philosophers do (cf. Kim's response to Rorty, "Rorty on the Possibility of Philosophy" (n. 86 above))—then there is no reason to be worried about Quine's attack.

141 This is certainly true of Alvin Goldman's program which, as noted earlier, is the paradigm for most philosophical research in the area.

142 The essays in Part II raise doubts about this conclusion.

143 For relevant discussion, see, e.g., Steven D. Smith, "The Pursuit of Pragmatism," *Yale Law Journal* 100 (1990), 409–49; Steven Walt, "Some Problems of Pragmatic Jurisprudence," *Texas Law Review* 70 (1991), 317–64 (reviewing Richard Posner, *The Problems of Jurisprudence* (Cambridge, Mass.: Harvard University Press, 1990)). For other admissions of the "banality" of pragmatism, see Richard Rorty, "The Banality of Pragmatism and the Poetry of Justice," *Southern California Law Review* 63 (1990), 1811–13; Thomas Grey, "Holmes and Legal Pragmatism," *Stanford Law Review* 41 (1989), 814. For sturdier and more substantial accounts of pragmatism (with affinities to my own), see Richard Warner, "Why Pragmatism? The Puzzling Place of Pragmatism in Critical Theory," *University of Illinois Law Review* (1993), 539–45; Susan Haack, "Pragmatism," in *A Companion to Epistemology*, 351–56.

144 J. William Singer, "Legal Realism Now," *California Law Review* 76 (1988), 474. On Singer's penchant for the banal, see again Warner, "Why Pragmatism? The Puzzling Place of Pragmatism in Critical Theory," id., 539–40.

Although there is little to disagree with in this pleasantly innocuous "pragmatic" attitude, one ought to worry that this is because hardly anyone has ever disagreed with these sentiments.[145] If the Realists are pragmatists, it had better be in a sense more interesting than this.

But what is the more interesting sense of pragmatism? Contrary to the impression left by much recent "jurisprudential" writing,[146] to be a philosophical "pragmatist" is not simply to be a thinker who refuses to draw distinctions, engage in abstract argument, develop a coherent point of view, or construct theories.[147] "Pragmatism"[148] is, instead, characterized by a double commitment, pertaining,

[145] The usual suspects—Beale and Langdell—have been unfairly slurred as "legal Platonists." See the useful, corrective discussion in Anthony J. Sebok, "Misunderstanding Positivism," *Michigan Law Review* 93 (1995), 2078–90. Although I fully endorse Sebok's historical scholarship on this point, I reject his ultimate jurisprudential conclusions, which are deeply wrong-headed: e.g., that Realism is incompatible with Legal Positivism (id., p. 2094); that the Legal Process school is implicitly positivistic (id., p. 2110). Sebok's mistake is to conflate an historical fact—the reckless use of "formalism" and "positivism" as interchangeable labels—with the philosophical claim that positivism is committed to a particular theory of adjudication, namely formalism. (A claim specifically rejected by positivists: see H.L.A. Hart, "Analytic Jurisprudence in Mid-Twentieth Century: A Reply to Professor Bodenheimer," *University of Pennsylvania Law Review* 105 (1957), 955–6.) But positivism is primarily a conceptual theory about the nature of law, while formalism is a claim about how judges do—and ought to—decide cases. That the Realists rejected formalism as an adequate descriptive theory of adjudication has no bearing on whether or not they were positivists! See the discussion in Leiter, "Legal Realism" (n. 14 above). Additionally, I would have thought that Vincent Wellman had demonstrated decisively the close connections between Legal Process and Dworkin—not positivism. See Vincent A. Wellman, "Dworkin and the Legal Process Tradition: The Legacy of Hart & Sacks," *Arizona Law Review* 29 (1987), 413–74. *Qua* history, however, Sebok's discussion is highly illuminating. See my critique of Sebok in "Positivism, Formalism, Realism," *Columbia Law Review* 99 (1999), 1138–64.

[146] See, e.g., Margaret Jane Radin, "The Pragmatist and the Feminist," *Southern California Law Review* 63 (1990), 1699–1726; Margaret Jane Radin & Frank Michelman, "Pragmatist and Poststructuralist Critical Legal Practice," *University of Pennsylvania Law Review* 139 (1991), 1019–58; Pierre Schlag, "Missing Pieces: A Cognitive Approach to Law," *Texas Law Review* 67 (1989), 1195–250; Stanley Fish, "Almost Pragmatism: Richard Posner's Jurisprudence," *University of Chicago Law Review* 57 (1990), 1447–75.

[147] See, e.g., Margaret Jane Radin, "The Pragmatist and the Feminist", id., p. 1706 (pragmatists are not interested in definitions of concepts—like "pragmatism" or "feminism"—in terms of necessary or sufficient criteria), id., p. 1718 (pragmatists do not seek any "overarching universal conception or set of principles that could harmonize" conflicting notions), id., p. 1719 (pragmatists are neither "tough-minded," nor "tender-minded"—in William James' sense of those terms—but rather accept and embrace both), id., p. 1720 ("pragmatic distinctions" are not "hard and fast"). Radin does assert that it is a "misunderstanding" of pragmatism "to suppose that it scorns every rationalistic notion as so much jabber and gesticulation, that it loves intellectual anarchy as such and prefers a sort of wolf-world absolutely unpent and wild and without a master or a collar to any philosophic classroom product, whatsoever" (id., p. 1715). This is, unfortunately, a "misunderstanding" that Radin's discussion decidedly invites. Richard Posner, whose account of pragmatism suffers from other defects (see the discussion in Walt, "Some Problems of Pragmatic Jurisprudence") does, at least, try to mute the anti-intellectual tone of much recent legal pragmatism. See, e.g., Posner, *The Problems of Jurisprudence* (n. 143 above), 19.

[148] The "definition" that follows is only *partly* stipulative. In characterizing "pragmatism," we have two benchmarks to go by. One is the set of views embraced by self-identified "pragmatist" philosophers like Charles Peirce, William James, and John Dewey—who unfortunately disagreed about more than they agreed on (though they have more in common with each other, than any do with Richard Rorty). A second is the meaning of the word "pragmatist," and its cognates, in ordinary

on the one hand, to the enterprise of theorizing itself, and, on the other, to epistemology. The pragmatic view of theory-construction is essentially the view expressed most famously by Marx in the "Theses on Feuerbach": "Man must prove the truth, that is, the reality and power, the this-sidedness of his thinking in practice. The dispute over the reality or non-reality of thinking which is isolated from practice is a purely *scholastic* question" (Thesis II, emphasis added).[149] Theorizing, in other words, should make a difference to practice (or experience). Notice that this is centrally a *normative* maxim, concerning what sort of theorizing is *worth doing*. It is not a substantive metaphysical or semantic doctrine to the effect that, e.g., theoretical claims that make no difference to practice or experience are meaningless and without cognitive content. "The advice," contained in the pragmatic maxim, says Mark Johnston, "comes not from the right account of the concepts of meaning and truth, but from common sense as it applies to cognitive labor."[150] Pragmatism, as Johnston puts it, involves an "anti-speculative norm" to the effect that "it is idle to aim at inaccessible truth."[151]

The pragmatic commitment in epistemology is more philosophically substantial: namely, anti-foundationalism. Anti-foundationalism is a claim about the *justification* of belief, to the effect that all justification is inferential: all justification, in other words, is of the form, "we are justified in believing X, because we can infer it from our belief Y." Since all of our beliefs are justified only insofar as they are inferrable from other beliefs, it follows that our beliefs do not, ultimately, rest on a "foundation" of beliefs that are justified *simpliciter*, i.e. self-justified in some sense, without depending on any other belief. How, then, do we get started in epistemic matters? What beliefs should we start with and what norms of justification should we embrace? The distinctive pragmatic view is that at least some beliefs and norms must be accepted solely on the *a posteriori* criterion of *utility for particular human purposes*. Rather than think *all* acceptable beliefs must satisfy certain *epistemic* demands—e.g., "corresponding to reality," or "being warranted under ideal epistemic conditions," or "figuring in our best scientific account of the world," or

language. The two, happily, overlap in some measure. But as with any concept that has enjoyed wide and varied usage, the ultimate criterion for a definition of the concept must be its contribution to fruitful theory-construction (itself a pragmatic criterion!). For some pertinent discussion, see again, Warner, "Why Pragmatism? The Puzzling Place of Pragmatism in Critical Theory" (n. 143 above), and Haack, "Pragmatism" (n. 143 above).

149 This, in a nutshell, is also the central point of Mark Johnston's important recent paper, "Objectivity Refigured: Pragmatism Without Verificationism," in John Haldane and Crispin Wright (eds.), *Reality, Representation and Projection* (New York: Oxford University Press, 1993). Johnston argues powerfully against the tendency of modern so-called "pragmatists" (e.g. Hilary Putnam, Nelson Goodman, Richard Rorty) to construe "pragmatism" as a substantive view about the truth-predicate. (Some difficulties with Johnston's argument, however, are discussed in Alexander Miller, "Objectivity Disfigured: Mark Johnston's Missing Explanation Argument," *Philosophy and Phenomenological Research* 55 (1995), 857–68.

150 Johnston, id., p. 97. See also, id., p. 112: "Although the Pragmatism of John Dewey and William James is characteristically anti-metaphysical, it nowhere needs to claim that metaphysical statements, because neither verifiable nor falsifiable, are devoid of truth value. It is enough that an interest in such unconstrained claims is just idle."   151 Id., p. 117.

"being inferrable from some set of foundational beliefs"—the pragmatist holds that some beliefs have to be accepted simply because they "work" relative to various human ends.

So understood, of course, pragmatism clearly has nothing against distinctions, definitions, coherence, abstract argument, or theoretical edifices: it is, at best, an open question whether or not these tools of the intellect are or are not useful for human purposes. Indeed, in certain domains—e.g., scientific inquiry—it is clearly a closed question: such intellectual tools are plainly useful for human purposes (aeronautical engineering does not work without definitions and theories, and without such engineering the planes neither go up nor come down where we humans want them to). But even in ethical and social matters, it is hardly obvious that the intellectual's tools are a pragmatic vice. To the contrary, to eschew a self-consciously theoretical perspective, to forego a "totalizing" critique (in favor, say, of "confront[ing] each dilemma separately and choos[ing] the alternative that will hinder empowerment the least and further it the most"[152]) may really be a *political*, not *philosophical*, move—an implicit endorsement of "incrementalism" against radicalism. It may, after all, require an abstract theory[153] to reveal the pernicious character of incrementalism, so that it is nothing more than the self-serving palliative prattle of those invested in the status quo to renounce "theory" in favor of dealing with "concrete problems" in particular contexts.[154] Ultimately, it is an ironic commentary on the irrelevance of so much of the current academic Left, which talks about taking seriously "the perspective of the oppressed,"[155] that it should fail to notice that the perspective of the oppressed is decidedly *not* pragmatic, that the oppressed do not eschew "transcendence . . . and atemporal universality,"[156] but rather embrace and affirm absolute and universal human rights against their oppressors—who typically understand the meaning of pragmatism in political practice all too well.[157]

[152] Margaret Jane Radin, "The Pragmatist and the Feminist" (n. 146 above), 1704.

[153] Such a theory could come in two forms. First, one could have a theoretical view of social and historical causation that has *no* consequences for practice, because it reveals human actions to be impotent. A materialist view of history like Braudel's, in which the causal determinants of human affairs are geography, climate, and demography, arguably gives us such a picture. (Marx's materialism is often suspected of entailing a similar conclusion, though Marx did not embrace this view.) Alternatively, one could have a theoretical view of social and historical causation such that *incremental* changes (of the sort Radin recommends) in the service of some good (e.g. human liberation through the abolition of race, gender and class discrimination), turn out to make the realization of that good less likely. Such a view is also associated with various writers in the Marxist tradition. Radin's "pragmatism" would, on this latter view of historical and social evolution, actually preclude achievement of her moral and political agenda.

[154] For a really quite stunning example of precisely this tendency towards incrementalism among self-proclaimed "pragmatists," see Putnam, "Replies" (n. 84 above), 73.

[155] Margaret Jane Radin, "The Pragmatist and the Feminist" (n. 146 above), 1723.

[156] Id., p. 1707.

[157] This point is well made by Martha Nussbaum in "Valuing Values: A Case for Reasoned Commitment," *Yale Journal of Law & the Humanities* 6 (1994), 214 (replying to Pierre Schlag and Steven Winter). Of course, it is tempting to argue, à la Nietzsche, that it is simply *prudent* (or pragmatic) of the oppressed to employ the vocabulary of universal human rights. But even so, this would

I find a certain type of pragmatism attractive (indeed, unavoidable), but it is both more modest and more radical than the apology for fuzziness that masquerades as pragmatism in the law journals. This pragmatism is a relative of the type one finds in philosophers like Carnap and Quine,[158] and that has entered the philosophical lexicon in the metaphor of "Neurath's boat."[159] The radicalism of this pragmatism resides in its recognition that the only possible criteria for the acceptance of *epistemic norms*—norms about what to believe—are pragmatic: we must simply accept the epistemic norms that work for us (that help us predict sensory experience, that allow us to manipulate and control the environment successfully, that enable us to "cope"). Pragmatic criteria are, at the limit, the only possible criteria for the acceptance of epistemic norms precisely because we cannot defend our choice of any particular epistemic norm on *epistemic* grounds *ad infinitum*. At some point, we must reach an epistemic norm for which the best we can say is: it works.

But which norms actually work for us? Take an example: "Don't believe in a hypothesis that figures in a non-consilient explanation of experience" is a norm for belief—call it the "consilience" norm. A non-consilient explanation is one that posits an explanandum (the thing that does the explaining) that seems too narrowly tailored to the explanans (the event to be explained).[160] Here is how this consilience norm works in our lives. Suppose while sitting at home, all the lights in the house suddenly go out at the very same moment. What fact about the world explains this? Explanatory hypothesis #1:

Conspiring leprauchuans have simultaneously thrown all the light switches in the house.

---

still show that, on *pragmatic* grounds, there is no reason to bracket abstract, transcendent, universal theories. This point is helpfully discussed in Eric Blumenson, "Mapping the Limits of Skepticism in Law and Morals," *Texas Law Review* 74 (1996), 523–76.

[158] See especially, Rudolf Carnap, "Empiricism, Semantics and Ontology," in Leonard Linsky (ed.), *Semantics and the Philosophy of Language* (Urbana: University of Illinois Press, 1952), 208–28; W.V.O. Quine, "Two Dogmas of Empiricism," in *From a Logical Point of View* (Cambridge, Mass.: Harvard University Press, 1953), 20–46. Quine would, of course, reject Carnap's view that there is a timeless, immutable line between the "external" questions (which receive pragmatic answers) and the "internal" questions (which do not).

[159] Otto Neurath, "Protokollsätze," *Erkenntnis* 3 (1932) 204–14. Neurath analogizes our epistemological situation to sailors who are trying to rebuild their ship while at sea. Since they cannot rebuild the whole ship at once—they cannot step outside the ship, as it were, and rebuild it from scratch—they must choose to stand firm on certain planks in the ship while reconstructing others. They will, of course, choose to stand firm on the planks that work the best—a pragmatic choice—while rebuilding those that are less dependable or useful or necessary. Of course, at a later date, the sailors may choose to rebuild the planks they had stood on previously, and in so doing they will again stand on some other planks that serve their practical needs. Our epistemic situation, for Neurath, is the same: we necessarily stand firm on certain planks of our theoretical conception of the world—hypotheses, epistemic norms, and the like—while evaluating other claims about the world. The planks we choose to rest our epistemic edifice upon are just those that have worked the best for us in the past; but nothing precludes the possibility that at some point in the future, we will rebuild those planks as well, while relying upon a new set of hypotheses, epistemic norms, etc.

[160] On consilience, see Paul Thagard, "The Best Explanation: Criteria for Theory Choice," *Journal of Philosophy* 75 (1978), 79–85.

By contrast, explanatory hypothesis #2 proposes that:

There has been a general power failure, i.e. electrical current has stopped entering the house.

Both explanatory hypotheses suppose an ontology: mischievous leprauchuans on the one hand; electricity, wires, and currents on the other. But the appeal to leprauchuans is non-consilient: it seems a gratuitous ontological posit, precisely because supposing that leprauchuans exist does not help explain anything else. Their existence does not explain our observations—we have not seen any—nor does it help explain the restoration of power (we neither need to "exterminate" the leprauchuans in order to retain power, nor do we even need to turn on all the light switches they are hypothesized to have flipped). By contrast, assuming the existence of electrical currents proves a very fruitful ontological posit: it not only cues us to the appropriate steps to take to restore power in the house, but it helps explain a range of ordinary phenomena (like why the television goes off when unplugged from the socket). Since the consilience norm favors the electricity ontology over the leprachuan ontology, and since the former works better than the latter, it appears that a good reason to accept the consilience norm is because of its practical cash-value.

Indeed, the consilience norm—and its other relatives in a scientific epistemology—have worked very well for we humans: they helped depopulate our ontology of leprauchuans and gods and ethers, and they are foundational norms in scientific practice, a practice that sends the planes into the sky, keeps the food from spoiling in the refrigerator, and alleviates human suffering through modern medicine. From a philosophical standpoint, what bears special notice is that the epistemic norms of common sense and the epistemic norms of science are simply on a continuum. As Quine remarks, "The scientist is indistinguishable from the common man in his sense of evidence, except that the scientist is more careful."[161] The pragmatic necessity of successfully predicting the course of experience is central to ordinary life *and* to the scientific enterprise; but this means, in turn, that the pragmatic rationale for our most basic epistemic norms can be found in universal features of the human situation: the need to explain our experience with an eye to figuring out what will happen next. Science succeeds at this better than any other practice, and this is why Quine, unlike the anti-foundationalist postmodernists, continues to agree with the positivists that science is the paradigm of genuine knowledge.[162]

---

[161] W.V.O. Quine, "The Scope and Language of Science," in *The Ways of Paradox and Other Essays* (Cambridge, Mass.: Harvard University Press, 1976), 233. For more on these issues, see Peter Hylton, "Quine's Naturalism", *Midwest Studies in Philosophy* 19 (1994), 261–82, a paper whose interpretation of Quine's "naturalism" I do not fully endorse, but from which I have learned much.

[162] On this point, see especially Hookway, *Quine: Language, Experience, and Reality* (n. 90 above), 2–3. It is for this reason in particular that lumping Quine with the postmodernists, as Dennis Patterson does, seems a mistake. See Dennis Patterson, "Postmodernism/Feminism/Law," *Cornell Law Review* 77 (1992), 270–9; Dennis Patterson, *Law & Truth* (New York: Oxford University Press, 1996), 158–61. For more on this issue, see Ch. 3 in this volume.

Yet the modesty of this type of pragmatism should also now be apparent: for once we accept a framework of epistemic norms, then the criteria for belief acceptance need *not* be pragmatic, except to the extent that the epistemic norms we accept—on *pragmatic* grounds—themselves embody pragmatic criteria. But it is completely consistent for the pragmatic philosopher, in the sense being discussed here, to distinguish sharply between, say, facts and values,[163] precisely because he has accepted, on pragmatic grounds, epistemic norms that invite this distinction.[164] This is why, for example, the great pragmatist philosopher Quine is a thoroughly tough-minded philosopher in the Jamesian sense, and not Radin's wishy-washy pragmatist who accepts both the "tough-minded" and "tender-minded" philosophical virtues.[165] For Quine, the (tough-minded) epistemic norms characteristic of the world-view he calls "naturalism" have simply worked the best.[166] By pragmatic criteria, that is reason enough to repudiate "tender-mindedness"—at least, until experience forces us to think otherwise.

2. Pragmatism and Legal Theory

Although the Realists do not have worked-out epistemological views, the pragmatism we find in their writings is *analogous* to the pragmatic view in epistemology and, at the same time, reflects the basic pragmatic commitment to make theorizing relevant to practice. The analogy, simply put, is this: just as philosophical pragmatists hold that it is a criterion of acceptability for particular epistemic norms that they work for us humans—e.g. by helping us predict sensory experience—so too it is a criterion of acceptability for a theory of adjudication for the Realists that it *work for lawyers*. Work for lawyers, for the Realists, means that it enables them to predict what courts will do.

---

[163] *Contra*, e.g., Richard Thompson Ford, "Facts and Values in Pragmatism and Personhood," *Stanford Law Review* 48 (1995), 225 ("A characteristic feature of pragmatism is the blurring of the distinction between facts and values").

[164] See, e.g., Allan Gibbard, *Wise Choices, Apt Feelings: A Theory of Normative Judgment* (Cambridge, Mass.: Harvard University Press, 1990), 106. This point also helps vitiate Putnam's complaint that I am a "scientific imperialist." Putnam, "Replies," (n. 84 above) 70. "Scientific imperialism" implies that there is an unjustified and unjustifiable reaching out by the epistemic norms of science (e.g. only believe in facts that figure in the best explanation of experience) to foreign domains where they do not belong (e.g. the domain of value). But from the Quinean perspective, this gets it all backwards: the epistemic norms of science *work*—they have proved a fruitful way of coping with reality—so the burden is on the philosopher who would abandon such norms to give us a reason why (other than the blatantly question-begging reason that his favored properties can thereby secure a place in his ontology).

[165] James' "tough-minded" philosopher is an empiricist and materialist, among other things; James' "tender-minded" philosopher is sympathetic to rationalism, idealism, and religion. See Margaret Jane Radin's summary, "The Pragmatist and the Feminist" (n. 146 above), 1713.

[166] That Quine's criteria for naturalism are pragmatic becomes clearest when he says that if telepathy turned out to really work, then we would have to revise our naturalistic view of the world accordingly. But, he adds, "It is idle to bulwark definitions against implausible contingencies." See W.V.O. Quine, *Pursuit of Truth* (Cambridge, Mass.: Harvard University Press, 1990), 20–1.

It is only in this quite specific sense that I want to understand the Realists as pragmatists. For the Realists, it is a constraint on theory-construction in jurisprudence that such theories have practical cash-value, i.e. by making it possible to predict what courts will do. Notice, moreover, that there is nothing banal about this pragmatism. Indeed, in conjunction with the Realists' Core Claim, it entails a startling conclusion: that the dominant approach to theory of adjudication in the Anglo-American world is based on a mistake. Under the influence of Dworkin's writings, analytic theory of adjudication is predicated on the assumption that what the theory must account for is the reasons judges give in their opinions for their decisions. Indeed, it has been one of Dworkin's consistent charges against Hart's positivism that it does not describe adequately how judges decide hard cases. But if the Realist Core Claim is correct, then the construction of a theory that is descriptively adequate in Dworkin's sense is an idle exercise: judges decide for other reasons—their response to the facts—and not because of the legal reasons that fill their opinions. What but a fetish for pedantry would compel one to construct a theory around the latter (impotent) reasons, rather than the former (effective) reasons? The Realists' pragmatism, coupled with the truth of the Core Claim (if it is true!), would entail discarding most jurisprudential work on the theory of adjudication. This conclusion is indeed hinted at, though not drawn, in one of the seminal critiques of Dworkin's program, by John Mackie.[167] Mackie observes that,

[T]here is a distinction—and there may be a divergence—between what judges say they are doing, what they think they are doing, and the most accurate objective description of what they actually are doing. They may say and even believe that they are discovering and applying an already existing law, they may be following procedures which assume this as their aim, and yet they may in fact be making new law. Such a divergence is not even improbable, because even where new law is being made, it will seem fairer if this fact is concealed and the decision is believed to enforce only presently existing rights . . . [168]

Mackie, like a good Realist, would urge against Dworkin a descriptive claim about what it is judges are *really* doing: Mackie would, in other words, contest with Dworkin the data that the theory is supposed to capture. For Dworkin, it is "what judges say they are doing, what they think they are doing,"[169] while for Mackie and the Realists it is "what they are actually doing" that requires theoretical explication. For the Realist, this choice of data is easy to explain: a theory about anything else will not be *useful* for lawyers. Moreover, such a theory is necessarily a *naturalistic* theory, for the reasons set out above.

---

[167] John Mackie, "The Third Theory of Law," reprinted in Marshall Cohen (ed.), *Ronald Dworkin and Contemporary Jurisprudence* (Totowa, NJ: Rowman & Allanheld, 1983), 161–70.

[168] Id., p. 163.

[169] For evidence that this is Dworkin's view see especially Dworkin, *Taking Rights Seriously* (n. 1 above), 22, 112.

D. Do the Realists Deliver a Naturalized Jurisprudence?

It is well and good to talk about making jurisprudential theories continuous with empirical inquiry in the natural and social sciences, but do the Realists really help us in this regard? Many readers may sympathize with Richard Posner's recent observation that, "The empirical projects of the legal realists, which not only failed but in failing gave empirical research rather a bad name, illustrate the futility of empirical investigation severed from a theoretical framework."[170] It is, of course, slightly ironic to hear an advocate of *economics* attack any group of theorists for having a failed empirical research program.[171] And Posner is also plainly wrong that the failing of Realism was *lack* of a theoretical framework:[172] the problem, more often, was rather adherence to a bad theoretical framework— Watsonian behaviorism. But surely Posner is right to speak as he does of the "empirical studies that went nowhere"[173] that Realism bequeathed us.[174] In that case, why think of Realism as the fountainhead of a naturalized jurisprudence?

---

[170] Posner, *The Problems of Jurisprudence* (n. 143 above), 19. Posner continues: "Modern economics can furnish the indispensable theoretical framework for empirical research that the law so badly needs." Id.

[171] "[E]conomic theory [is] one of the more dismal empirical failures in the history of science." John Dupré, Book Review, *Philosophical Review* 104 (1995), 151 (reviewing Philip Kitcher, *The Advancement of Science* (New York: Oxford University Press, 1993).) Let us recall, for example, that even the predictions generated from the Coase Theorem have been empirically falsified. See Robert Ellickson, *Order Without Law: How Neighbors Settle Disputes* (Cambridge, Mass.: Harvard University Press, 1991). Despite all the "empiricist" rhetoric by proponents of economics, actual empirical researchers in various areas of law have found economic analysis distinctly indifferent to reality. The work of those we might call the "Texas Empiricists" is particularly instructive in this regard. See, e.g., Elizabeth Warren & Jay Lawrence Westbrook, "Searching for Reorganization Realities," *Washington University Law Quarterly* 72 (1994), 1257–89; Ronald J. Mann, "Explaining the Pattern of Secured Credit," *Harvard Law Review* 110 (1997) 625–83; Julius Getman and Thomas Kohler, "The Common Law, Labor Law, and Reality: A Response to Professor Epstein," *Yale Law Journal* 92 (1983), 1415–34; Julius Getman and Ray Marshall, "Industrial Relations in Transition: The Paper Industry Example," *Yale Law Journal* 102 (1993), 1803–95; Thomas O. McGarity, "The Expanded Debate Over the Future of the Regulatory State," *University of Chicago Law Review* 63 (1996), 1463–1532. For a balanced discussion of the failings of economics *qua* science, and an interesting (if contestable) philosophical account of why that should be so, see Alexander Rosenberg, *Economics: Mathematical Politics or Science of Diminishing Returns?* (Chicago: University of Chicago Press, 1992). For a more substantial discussion of the problems with economics understood as an empirical science, see Leiter, "Holmes, Economics, and Classical Realism," in Steven Burton (ed.), *The Path of the Law and Its Influence: The Legacy of Oliver Wendall Holmes, Jr.* (Cambridge: Cambridge University Press, 2000), 285–325.

[172] The same misguided complaint has been made by others besides Posner. See, e.g., Williamson, "Revisiting Legal Realism: The Law, Economics, and Organization Perspective" (n. 20 above), 1 ("That [Legal Realism] foundered while [law & economics] flourished is explained in large measure by the absence of an intellectual framework for Legal Realism and the use by law and economics of the powerful framework of neoclassical economics").

[173] Posner, *The Problems of Jurisprudence* (n. 143 above), 393–4.

[174] The most notorious—but also, I should add, the least well-conceived—is the infamous "parking study" reported in Moore & Callahan, "Law and Learning Theory: A Study in Legal Control" (n. 49 above). For a similar complaint about Hume's naturalism, and a reply, see Stroud, *Hume* (n. 93 above), 223–4.

The answer depends partly on what we expect from the philosophical proponents of a naturalized jurisprudence. The Realists, as seen through the lens of
philosophical naturalism, give us arguments *against* much of traditional theory of
adjudication, and in favor of empirical studies. They may not give us paradigms
of *good* empirical studies; but perhaps we should not look to them for that. The
Realists give us the philosophical motivation and cues for how we should proceed,
even if they do not carry off the project themselves.

Yet even this may concede too much. For contrary to Frank's skepticism about
predicting what judges will do, it appears that lawyers frequently are able to predict what courts will do: how else would they stay in business, after all? But if the
Realists are correct that judges decide in accordance with the Core Claim, yet have
failed to deliver (as Posner charges) a successful scientific theory of judicial decision, then how do lawyers predict what courts will do? To anyone who has litigated, the answer seems plain enough: lawyers work with some degree of informal
psychological, political and cultural knowledge about judges and courts that constitutes what we might call a "folk" social scientific theory of adjudication. The
success of this folk theory—which is, after all, largely coextensive with the talents
of lawyers (i.e. their ability to advise clients what to do, when to go to trial, when
to settle, etc.)—constitutes the core of a naturalized jurisprudence.

We should not be misled here by the fact that in certain domains "naturalization" is thought to require supplanting folk theories—that is, theories that rely
on our common sense categories of belief and desire to explain behavior.[175]
Philosophers of many persuasions have argued that the basic "folk" categories are
compatible with a naturalistic program.[176] In any event, such an objection would
be unavailable to someone like Posner who advocates economic explanations,
since such explanations are, of course, just one type of systematizing of folk-
psychological explanations (though predicated on a particularly simple-minded
folk psychology).[177]

---

[175] See, e.g., Paul M. Churchland, "Eliminative Materialism and the Propositional Attitudes,"
Journal of Philosophy 78 (1981), 67–90; Stephen P. Stich, *From Folk Psychology to Cognitive Science:
The Case Against Belief* (Cambridge, Mass.: MIT Press, 1983).

[176] See, e.g., Jerry A. Fodor, *The Language of Thought* (Cambridge, Mass.: Harvard University
Press, 1979); Terence Horgan and James P. Woodward, "Folk Psychology Is Here To Stay,"
Philosophical Review 94 (1985), 197–226; Jaegwon Kim, "Multiple Realization and the Metaphysics
of Reduction," in *Supervenience and Mind* (New York: Cambridge University Press, 1993), 309–35.
Note that for Kim "the scientific possibility of, say, human psychology is a contingent fact (assuming
it is a fact); it depends on the fortunate fact that individual humans do not show huge physiological-
biological differences that are psychologically relevant." Id., p. 329.

[177] See Alexander Rosenberg, "If Economics Isn't Science, What Is It?", reprinted in Daniel
Hausman (ed.), *The Philosophy of Economics: An Anthology*, 2nd edition (Cambridge: Cambridge
University Press, 1994), 381–2. Rosenberg's *philosophical* explanation for the failure of economics
qua science depends on the Davidsonian argument that psychology cannot promulgate genuine
causal explanations because causal laws must be *strict*. The Davidsonian premise, contrary to
Rosenberg, however, has been widely contested. See, e.g., Tyler Burge, "Philosophy of Language and
Mind: 1950–1990," *Philosophical Review* 101 (1992), 35 ("I do not think it a *priori* true, or even
clearly a heuristic principle of science or reason, that causal relations must be backed by any particular

Recall, too, what is required for a "naturalized" jurisprudence: we seek *methodological* continuity with the natural and social sciences. Folk theories plainly satisfy this demand: they are predicated on *empirical* observation of judicial decisions; they seek *causal* explanations for these decisions (i.e. they understand "reasons as causes"); and they look for regular, law-like (ideally: lawful) patterns of decision. Indeed, it is common in the extensive political science literature on judicial behavior to (correctly) identify Realism with precisely such a naturalistic research program.[178] That lawyers possess workable, if informal, folk theories of judicial decision serves to vindicate and instantiate Realism's naturalistic program.

Of course, the folk theories of adjudication that lawyers employ all the time seem to lack the systematicity characteristic of genuine *scientific* theories: in particular, they fail to generate *laws* of judicial behavior.[179] The political science literature—which dispenses with folk psychology in favor of seeking "lawful" correlations between (crudely) the demographic profiles of judges and their decisions—has not been much more successful.

But if the political science literature on judicial decision-making has not met with great success,[180] perhaps it is because it abandons too readily Frank's insight that "the personality of the judge is the pivotal factor in law administration."[181] To concede this would, of course, pull us away from the Generality Thesis embraced by the mainstream of Realism—a thesis, moreover, that does seem apt for the sorts of commercial law disputes on which the Realists focussed. But perhaps in areas like constitutional law—where the issues engage the personality of the judge in special ways—we need to reconsider the merits of Frank's approach. Of course, Frank conjoined his insight into the importance of personality with excessive skepticism about our capacity to attain epistemic access to the features of personality that are causally determinative. Certainly on an orthodox conception of

kind of law"). Cf. Brian Leiter & Alexander Miller, "Closet Dualism and Mental Causation," *Canadian Journal of Philosophy* 28 (1998), 161–81.

[178] See, e.g., Tracey E. George and Lee Epstein, "On the Nature of Supreme Court Decisionmaking," *American Political Science Review* 86 (1992), 324–5; Orley Ashenfelter, Theodore Eisenberg, and Stewart Schwab, "Politics and the Judiciary: The Influence of Judicial Background on Case Outcomes," *Journal of Legal Studies* 24 (1995), 257 ("Since the rise of legal realism, it has been axiomatic that the background and worldview of judges influence cases"). George and Epstein, however, wrongly think that the Realists utterly discounted the relevance of legal rules and reasons—no doubt because they suppose a Frankified version of Realism. See George and Epstein, id., p. 324.

[179] It is a contested topic among philosophers of science what constitutes a "law." A common idea is that "laws" state certain *necessary* truths about nature. This does not help too much, however, since the concept of "necessity" is equally hard to get a handle on. For a recent discussion, and critique, see Bas C. Van Fraassen, *Laws and Symmetry* (Oxford, Clarendon Press, 1989), 15–128.

[180] For one recent and pertinent discussion, see Ashenfelter et al., "Politics and the Judiciary: The Influence of Judicial Background on Case Outcomes" (n. 178 above). Although these authors "find surprisingly little evidence that the identity of the judge influences the case's outcome" (id. at 260), this may be because they characterize the judge's identity in gross sociological/demographic terms: "political party, sex, race, religion, law school, and age." Id. at 266. Perhaps what is really needed is a more fine-grained (though harder to get, of course) account of a judge's identity.

[181] Frank, *Law and the Modern Mind* (n. 36 above), 111.

psychoanalytic method, we as mere observers could not hope to get access to the deep facts about personality that determine the course of decision. But psycho-analytic explanations are, importantly, on a continuum with ordinary folk psycho-logical explanations,[182] and as with folk explanations, those of us living in the post-Freudian world have acquired a similar competence to observe and explain behavior in broadly Freudian terms. Perhaps, then, Frank's skepticism is unwar-ranted. Indeed, judicial opinions are a rich repository of material for the armchair "folk" psychoanalyst. Surely, for example, the astonishing rigidity of Justice Scalia's constitutional jurisprudence, especially his fear of "unconstrained" judgment;[183] or Justice Thomas's almost pathological incapacity for—or unwillingness to engage—empathetic feelings,[184] both cry out for psychoanalytic explanations. If the Sociological Wing of Realism describes the right program of research for understanding the area of commercial law, there may yet be reasons to think that the Idiosyncrasy Wing—minus Frank's skepticism—points the right way to a nat-uralized account of decision-making in other domains. I hope to show elsewhere that this approach is, indeed, fruitful.

IV. Conclusion

The reception of Realism, like the reception of any prominent and controversial movement, has been marked by misunderstandings: Realism was slurred as proto-fascism in the 1940s,[185] Realism suffered "Frankification" in the 1950s and 1960s,[186] and during the 1970s and 1980s, Realism was "CLSified." As we start a new century, I hope we may see Realism reborn yet again, this time as a *natural-ized* approach to jurisprudence. The Realists, we must remember, were very much a product of their intellectual milieu, which was decidedly not postmodern. The 1920s and 1930s marked the heyday of "positivism," in philosophy and the social sciences: natural science was viewed as the paradigm of all genuine know-ledge, and any discipline—from philosophy to sociology—which wanted to attain

---

[182] For a concise articulation of this point, see Thomas Nagel, "Freud's Permanent Revolution," in *Other Minds*, 26–44. For a stout defense of Freud's "science" of the mind, see David Sachs, "In Fairness to Freud", reprinted in Jerome Neu (ed.), *The Cambridge Companion to Freud* (Cambridge: Cambridge University Press, 1992), 309–38.

[183] See *Employment Division v. Smith*, 494 U.S. 872 (1990).

[184] See especially his dissent in *Hudson v. McMillian*, 503 U.S. 1, 18 (1992).

[185] See, e.g., Francis E. Lucey, "Natural Law and American Legal Realism: Their Respective Contributions to Theory of Law in A Democratic Society," *Georgetown Law Journal* 30 (1942), 494–531; Ben W. Palmer, "Hobbes, Holmes, and Hitler," *American Bar Association Journal* 31 (1945), 569–73.

[186] See, e.g., Grant Gilmore, "Legal Realism: Its Causes and Cure," *Yale Law Journal* 70 (1961), 1038 ("A judge's holding in a case is an *ad hoc* response to a unique state of facts, rationalized, after the event, with a dissimulation more or less conscious, and fitted willy-nilly into the Procrustean bed of approved doctrine. The motivations of the judicial response are buried, obscure, unconscious and—even to the judge—unknowable").

epistemic respectability had to emulate its methods, i.e. had to be "naturalized". (Even the Deweyan pragmatism of that era was heavily colored by Dewey's naturalism.[187]) While philosophical "positivism" may have been on the defensive in the 1950s and 1960s, its basic ideals—especially regarding natural science as the paradigm of objective knowledge—have been successfully defended and revived more recently.[188] The Realists came of intellectual age in a positivistic and naturalistic culture, and their approach to jurisprudential questions bears the mark of that origin. With the benefit of philosophical advances of the last thirty years, we are finally in a position to recognize what most jurisprudents have missed: that the Realists were not bad legal philosophers, but rather prescient ones, philosophical naturalists before their time.

[187] See, e.g., John Dewey, Sidney Hook, and Ernest Nagel, "Are Naturalists Materialists?", reprinted in John Ryder (ed.), *American Philosophic Naturalism in the Twentieth Century* (Amherst, NY: Prometheus Books, 1994), 102–120, and John Dewey, "Antinaturalism in Extremis," in Yervant Krikorian (ed.), *Naturalism and the Human Spirit* (New York: Columbia University Press, 1944), 1–16. One would not know about Dewey's naturalism, though, to look at how he figures in much recent legal pragmatism.

[188] Only the apparently widespread ignorance of recent developments in philosophy of science since Kuhn and Feyerabend in the 1960s leaves large portions of the academy with a contrary impression. For relevant discussion, see Larry Laudan, *Science and Relativism* (Chicago: University of Chicago Press, 1990) and Philip Kitcher, *The Advancement of Science* (Oxford: Oxford University Press, 1993). It bears noting that Quine, perhaps the most important philosophical critic of positivism, nonetheless "remained faithful to the underlying spirit of positivism." Hookway, *Quine: Language, Experience, and Reality* (n. 90 above), 2.

2

Legal Realism and Legal Positivism Reconsidered*

This paper challenges two widespread views about the relationship between the jurisprudential theories known as "Legal Realism" and "Legal Positivism." The first is that the two doctrines are essentially incompatible or opposed at the philosophical or conceptual level.[1] The second is that Legal Realism is a jurisprudential joke, a tissue of philosophical confusions[2]—confusions that the twentieth century's leading Positivist, H.L.A. Hart, exposed more than thirty years ago in the famous Chapter VII ("Formalism and Rule-Skepticism") of *The Concept of Law* ("CL").[3] The two views are connected in the following way: Hart, on this picture,

* I am grateful to workshop audiences at the law schools at Northwestern, Yale and the Universities of California (Berkeley), Chicago and Virginia for useful discussion of earlier drafts, as well as to Douglas Laycock, Scott Shapiro, and Charles Silver for helpful comments. I also thank the editors and anonymous referees for *Ethics* for their helpful suggestions on the penultimate version.

[1] Ronald Dworkin notes that, "Students are taught that the second rival to positivism [after Natural Law Theory] is the school of legal realism." *Law's Empire* (Cambridge, Mass: Harvard University Press, 1986), p. 36. Dworkin goes on to develop an account in which (under different names) Realism, Positivism, and Dworkin's own theory are set in opposition. See also, Theodore Benditt, *Law as Rule and Principle* (Stanford: Stanford University Press, 1978), p. 61 ("legal realism contrasts with positivism"); Harold J. Berman, "Toward an Integrative Jurisprudence: Politics, Morality, History," *California Law Review* 76 (1988): 779–801, 781 (Realism is "at the opposite pole of positivist jurisprudence"); Edgar Bodenheimer, "Analytical Positivism, Legal Realism, and the Future of Legal Method," *Virginia Law Review* 44 (1958): 365–78, 365 (Positivism and Realism "are customarily regarded as representing sharply antithetical viewpoints with respect to the nature of law"); Alan Mabe, "An Appraisal of Dworkin's Systematic Legal Theory," *Florida State Law Review* 15 (1987): 587–606, 588 (Hart's "positivism [is] a direct response to some of the more extreme claims of realism"); Jeffrie G. Murphy & Jules L. Coleman, *Philosophy of Law: An Introduction to Jurisprudence*, rev. ed. (Boulder: Westview, 1990), p. 33 (introducing Realism as being one of the movements that "maintain[s] that the entire outlook and perspective of legal positivism...seriously distorts the nature of law and legal systems"); Anthony Sebok, "Misunderstanding Positivism," *Michigan Law Review* 93 (1995): 2054–132, 2094 ("Legal realism and legal positivism were, in fact, deeply antagonistic theories.")

[2] See, e.g., Michael S. Moore, "The Need for a Theory of Legal Theories," *Cornell Law Review* 69 (1984): 988–1013, 1013 ("I believe that [the Realists]) lacked the necessary detail and philosophical sophistication to qualify the amalgam of their views as a distinct theory of adjudication."); Leslie Green, "The Concept of Law Revisited," *Michigan Law Review* 94 (1996): 1687–717, esp. 1694 (against the Realists, "Hart's arguments are decisive"). Cf. Benditt, *Law as Rule and Principle*, pp. 46–7.

[3] H.L.A. Hart, *The Concept of Law* (Oxford: Clarendon Press, 1961) [cited hereafter as CL in the body of the text].

sealed the tomb of Realism as a serious legal theory, and in so doing gave credence to the idea that Realism and Positivism were opposed doctrines.

I propose to contest both these views through a careful re-examination of Hart's influential critique.[4] Against the first claim, I shall argue that whereas Positivism is essentially a *theory of law*—a theory, in part, about what is distinctive of any society's *legal* norms (as opposed to, e.g., its moral, aesthetic, and social norms)—Realism is essentially a *descriptive theory of adjudication*, a theory about what it is judges really do when they decide cases. In defending their descriptive theory of adjudication, however, it turns out that the Realists must *presuppose* a theory of law, one that is, in fact, a kind of Positivism.[5] Only by (wrongly) construing the Realist theory of adjudication as a conceptual theory of law could Hart make it seem that Positivism and Realism are opposed doctrines.

It is this same conflation of theoretical aims and methods that sustains the second widespread view: that Realism is—as Hart purportedly demonstrated—a philosophical mess. While Hart successfully refutes a doctrine we may call "Conceptual Rule-Skepticism"—essentially skepticism at the level of a theory of law—it is unclear that the vast majority of Realists embraced this type of skepticism. The real dispute between Realism and Positivism, in fact, exists at the *empirical* level, i.e. the level of whether or not legal rules *causally determine* judicial decisions.[6] Although Hart recognizes both kinds of rule-skepticism (though without using these labels), it will turn out (surprisingly) that he never offers an argument against Empirical Rule-Skepticism at all.

Thus, at the *philosophical* or *conceptual* level, Realism and Positivism are quite compatible, and, in fact, the former actually needs the latter. At the *empirical* level, it will turn out that, while there is a genuine disagreement between the two theories, neither Hart nor any other legal philosopher has actually provided a real argument against the Realist view. It is time, I conclude, to reconsider the place of Legal Realism in the pantheon of jurisprudence.

We must begin, however, by saying something about the views and authors named by the labels "Realism" and "Positivism."

---

[4] Some earlier writers have noted limitations of Hart's critique, though, as the many sources cited in n. 1 indicate, these admonitions have gone largely unheeded. Murphy & Coleman, for example, comment on the unfairness of some of Hart's criticisms in passing in *Philosophy of Law* (n. 2 above), p. 35. The most systematic previous critique of Hart's reading of Legal Realism can be found in Andrew Altman, "Legal Realism, Critical Legal Studies, and Dworkin," *Philosophy & Public Affairs* 15 (1986): 205–35, esp. at pp. 207–12. While I endorse several of Altman's criticisms of Hart (as discussed below), his defense is hampered by a misunderstanding of Realism, largely borne of his distorting pairing of Realism with Critical Legal Studies ("C.L.S."). For discussion, see especially nn. 13, 55, and 63, below; for a general discussion of the C.L.S. misreading of Realism, see Ch. 3.

[5] This theme, which is central to the present paper, is unnoted by Altman in "Legal Realism, Critical Legal Studies, and Dworkin," (id.) in part because he is more interested in the legal indeterminacy debate as it plays out between Dworkin and the C.L.S. writers.

[6] There is, in fact, a jurisprudential disagreement between Realism and Hart over the sources of legal indeterminacy, but this dispute is conceptually severable from the dispute over Empirical Rule-Skepticism, as I will argue below.

I. Legal Realism

It is a commonplace—so oft-repeated that it now has the status of dogma—that Legal Realism cannot be "defined," that the movement is too disparate in its concerns to be characterized coherently.[7] If one actually reads the Realists, however—as opposed to reading *about them*—the opposite turns out to be the case. For those writers who are, by any account, major figures in Legal Realism[8]—e.g. Karl Llewellyn, Jerome Frank, Max Radin, Underhill Moore, Hessel Yntema, Felix Cohen, Herman Oliphant, Leon Green, Joseph Hutcheson— *all* shared an interest in understanding judicial decision-making[9] and, in particular, shared certain substantive views about how adjudication *really* works. This has long been clear to lawyers whose work is actually informed by Realism. As one leading First Amendment scholar writes: "The sine qua non of legal realism was the belief that doctrine obscured more than it explained about why a court decided as it did. *Thereafter*, legal realists split into a variety of approaches to the law."[10]

More precisely, the Realists all embraced the following *descriptive* thesis about adjudication:[11] in deciding cases, judges react primarily to the underlying facts of the case, rather than to applicable legal rules and reasons (the latter figuring primarily as ways of providing post-hoc rationales for decisions reached on other grounds).[12] Where the Realists differed was over *how* judges respond to the facts

---

[7] For one recent version of this skepticism, see Neil Duxbury, *Patterns of American Jurisprudence* (Oxford: Clarendon Press, 1995), p. 65.

[8] Getting a clear picture of Realism has been complicated in recent years by the "reinvention" of Realism by the Critical Legal Studies ("C.L.S.") writers. The C.L.S. writers typically treat as central to Realism the critique of the public-private distinction found in Realist contemporaries like the economist Robert Hale and the philosopher Morris Cohen. But Hale was, in fact, viewed as a marginal figure by his Realist contemporaries (and, indeed, had nothing to say about their central concern: adjudication), while Cohen was actually best known as a *critic* of Realism. For examples of the C.L.S. reinvention of Realism, see Gary Peller, "The Metaphysics of American Law," *California Law Review* 73 (1985): 1151–290; J. William Singer, "Legal Realism Now," *California Law Review* 76 (1988): 465–544; and Morton Horwitz, *The Transformation of American Law: 1870–1960* (Oxford: Oxford University Press, 1992). The introductory essays and editorial selections in *American Legal Realism*, ed. W.W. Fisher et al. (New York: Oxford University Press, 1993) also reflect an essentially C.L.S. vision of Realism.

[9] A point that was equally as commonplace among an earlier generation of commentators. See, e.g., Edwin W. Patterson, *Jurisprudence: Men and Ideas of the Law* (Brooklyn: Foundation Press, 1953), p. 541: "The leading realists centered upon the judicial process."

[10] L.A. Powe, Jr., "Justice Douglas After Fifty Years: The First Amendment, McCarthyism and Rights," *Constitutional Commentary* 6 (1989): 267–87, 271 (emphasis added).

[11] For a detailed defense of this interpretation, see Ch. 1.

[12] See, e.g., Herman Oliphant, "A Return to Stare Decisis," *American Bar Association Journal* 14 (1928): 71–6, 107, 159–62, at p. 75: judges "respond primarily to the stimulus of the facts in the concrete case before them rather than to the stimulus of overgeneral and outward abstractions in opinions and treatises." For further documentation and discussion, see Ch. 1.

Altman, in his otherwise sympathetic discussion, misses the centrality to Realism of this positive claim about adjudication because he conflates Realism with C.L.S. He claims that "the master theme of legal realism" is "that of the breakdown of any sharp distinction between law (adjudication) and

of a case. A minority of Realists—like Frank and Hutcheson—thought that idiosyncrasies of the judge's personality determined the decision (though neither held,
as popular lore would have it, that "what the judge ate for breakfast" determined
the outcome). As a result, predicting how courts will decide cases is impossible for
these Realists.

The majority of Realists—sensibly recognizing that lawyers can and do predict
judicial outcomes all the time—took a different view. Judicial decisions, these
Realists argued, fall into discernible patterns (making prediction possible), though
the patterns are not those one would expect from the existing legal rules. Rather,
the decisions fall into patterns correlated with the underlying factual scenarioes
of the disputes at issue: it is the judicial response to the "situation type"—i.e. the
distinctive factual pattern—that determines the outcome of the case.

Herman Oliphant offers a useful illustration of the point.[13] Oliphant examined
a series of conflicting court decisions on the validity of contractual promises not to
compete, cases that were utterly inexplicable by reference to the then-existing
rules of contract law. Why, then, did the courts uphold some promises but not
others? Oliphant finds the solution in the underlying "situation types" of the
cases: in cases involving a promise by a seller of a business not to compete with the
buyer, the promises were upheld; in cases involving a promise by an employee not
to compete with his employer, the promises were generally not enforced. In each
case, prevailing, but informal, "commercial norms" favored these differing outcomes. But instead of saying explicitly that what they were doing was enforcing
the norms of the prevailing "commercial" culture, the courts instead invoked general rules of contract law, rules that did nothing to explain the actual decisions.[14]

---

politics." "Legal Realism, Critical Legal Studies, and Dworkin" (n. 4 above), p. 206 n. 4. While this is
the "master theme" of C.L.S., to be sure, it is not a theme in the writings of Llewellyn, Oliphant,
Frank, and Moore, among other prominent Realists. The mistake here is in thinking that Realists
viewed "politics" as determining judicial decisions where legal rules and legal reasons did not. In fact,
the Realists emphasized the role of psychological factors (unrelated to politics) or uncodified commercial norms, rather than political preferences. See the further discussion, below, in the text.

[13] "A Return to *Stare Decisis*" id. pp. 159–60.

[14] Interestingly, the *Restatement of Contracts 2d* (St. Paul, Minn.: American Law Institute
Publishers, 1981) has actually incorporated Oliphant's distinction, now restating the rules in a more
fact-specific way. (I am grateful to Mark Gergen for pointing this fact out to me.)

But Oliphant's point hardly belongs only to the past. A seminal study by the leading scholar of the
law of remedies recently demonstrated that in 1,400 cases involving the "irreparable injury rule"—
the rule that says courts will not prevent harm, when money damages will compensate—"Courts do
prevent harm when they can. Judicial opinions recite the rule constantly, but they do not apply
it . . . When courts reject plaintiff's choice of remedy, there is always some other reason, and that reason has nothing to do with the irreparable injury rule. We identify the real reasons for decision, and
use those reasons to explain old cases and decide new cases." Douglas Laycock, *The Death of the
Irreparable Injury Rule* (New York: Oxford University Press, 1991), p. vii. Like the Realists, Laycock
also attributes the existing pattern of decisions to "[a]n intuitive sense of justice that has led judges to
produce sensible results" id., p. ix. For a similar argument regarding the law of federal courts, see
Michael Wells, "Naked Politics, Federal Courts Law, and the Canon of Acceptable Arguments,"
Emory Law Journal 47 (1998): 89–162.

This Realist insight—that in private law especially, what courts really do is enforce the prevailing, uncodified norms as they would apply to the underlying factual situation—is reflected in the teaching materials that Realists prepared. For the Realists, there was, for example, no law of torts, *per se*, but rather numerous laws of torts specific to differing situation-types. Thus, the Realist casebook was not organized by doctrinal categories—e.g. negligence, intentional torts, etc.— but rather by "situation types": e.g. "surgical operations," "keeping of animals," "traffic and transportation," etc.[15] So, too, the law of remedies was not to be understood in terms of the general legal remedies available, but rather in terms of the *types* of injury-situations for which remedies might be sought.[16]

Realists like Oliphant—who were, to repeat, the vast majority[17]—thought that the task of legal theory was to identify and describe—*not* justify—the patterns of decision; the social sciences were the tool for carrying out this non-normative task. While the Realists looked to behaviorist psychology and sociology, it is easy to understand contemporary law-and-economics (at least in its descriptive or "positive" aspects) as pursuing the same task by relying on economic explanations for the patterns of decision.[18]

As a result of this Realist orientation, there is a sense in which we may think of the type of jurisprudence the Realists advocated as a *naturalized* jurisprudence, i.e. a jurisprudence that eschews armchair conceptual analysis in favor of continuity with *a posteriori* inquiry in the empirical sciences.[19] Just as a *naturalized* epistemology—in Quine's famous formulation—"simply falls into place as a chapter of psychology"[20] as "a purely descriptive, causal-nomological science of human cognition,"[21] so too a naturalized jurisprudence for the Realists is an essentially descriptive theory of the causal connections between underlying situation-types and actual judicial decisions. (Indeed, one major Realist, Underhill Moore, even anticipates the Quinean slogan: "This study lies within the province of jurisprudence. It also lies within the field of behavioristic psychology. It places the

---

[15] See Leon Green, *The Judicial Process in Tort Cases* (St. Paul: West Publishing, 1931).

[16] See Charles Alan Wright, *Cases on Remedies* (St. Paul: West Publishing, 1955).

[17] What I call the "Frankification" of Realism over the last sixty years—the tendency to treat Jerome Frank's extreme views as typical of Realism—has obscured the centrality of the Oliphant approach to most of the Realist literature. On this point, see generally Ch. 1.

[18] An ambition clearest in the early work of Richard Posner. See, e.g., *Economic Analysis of Law* (Boston: Little, Brown, 1973), p. 6. There is, to be sure, a *normative* dimension to the writings of many Realists: the point to emphasize is that in looking at judicial decison-making they did not aspire to produce a theoretical *justification* of the actual pattern of decisions. As to what judges do, most Realists embraced a kind of "normative quietism:" judges do what they do, and while making the pattern explicit *might* facilitate future decision-making, there is no value to a general normative theory of decision that departs too far from existing practice. For documentation and discussion, see Leiter, "Legal Realism" in D.M. Patterson (ed.), *A Companion To Philosophy of Law and Legal Theory* (Oxford: Blackwell, 1996), p. 277.   [19] For a detailed development of the analogy, see Ch. 1.

[20] W.V.O. Quine, "Epistemology Naturalized," in *Ontological Relativity and Other Essays* (New York: Columbia University Press, 1969), p. 82.

[21] Jaegwon Kim, "What is 'Naturalized Epistemology'?" *Philosophical Perspectives* 2 (1988): 381–405, 388.

province within the field."[22]) There are, of course, competing conceptions of what it means to *naturalize* some domain of philosophy, and I do not want to enter here the debates on their merits and demerits.[23] All I do want to suggest is that the *method* that the Realists bring to bear in legal theory might, fruitfully, be thought of as a *naturalistic* method, akin to Quine's proposal for naturalizing epistemology.[24]

Notice, in particular, that both Quine and the Realists can be seen as advocating naturalization for analogous reasons. On one familiar reading, Quine advocates naturalism as a response to the failure of the traditional foundationalist program in epistemology, from Descartes to Carnap. As one commentator puts it: "Once we see the sterility of the foundationalist program, we see that the only genuine questions there are to ask about the relation between theory and evidence and about the acquisition of belief are psychological questions."[25] That is, once we recognize our inability to tell a *normative* story about the relation between evidence and theory—a story about what theories are *justified* on the basis of the evidence—Quine would have us give up the normative project: "Why not just see how [the] construction [of theories on the basis of evidence] really proceeds?"[26]

So, too, the Realists can be read as advocating an empirical theory of adjudication precisely because they think the traditional jurisprudential project of trying to show decisions to be *justified* on the basis of legal rules and reasons is a failure. For the Realists, the law is *rationally indeterminate*:[27] i.e. the class of legitimate legal reasons that a court might appeal to in justifying a decision fails, in fact, to justify a *unique* outcome in many of the cases.[28] If the law were determinate, then we might expect—except in cases of ineptitude or corruption—that legal rules and reasons would be reliable predictors of judicial outcomes. But the law in many cases is indeterminate, and thus in those cases there is no "foundational" story to be told about the particular decision of a court: legal reasons would justify just as

---

[22] Underhill Moore & Charles Callahan, "Law and Learning Theory: A Study in Legal Control," *Yale Law Journal* 53 (1943): 1–136, 1.

[23] On the competing conceptions, see Brian Leiter, "Naturalism and Naturalized Jurisprudence," in *Analyzing Law: New Essays in Legal Theory*, ed. B. Bix (Oxford: Oxford University Press, 1998). I particularly do not want to enter here the debate about the place of "normativity" in Quine's conception of a naturalized epistemology. For contrasting views, see, e.g., Richard Foley, "Quine and Naturalized Epistemology," *Midwest Studies in Philosophy* 19 (1994): 243–60; Kim, "What is 'Naturalized' Epistemology" (n. 21 above); Quine, *Pursuit of Truth* (Cambridge, Mass.: Harvard University Press, 1990), pp. 19–21.

[24] If the Realists are, in fact, *naturalists*, it is only with respect to the theory of adjudication. There is nothing in Realism that would constitute a naturalization of the theory of law proper, e.g. a naturalized account of the *concept* of law. See the further discussion in the text at the end of this section.

[25] Hilary Kornblith, "Introduction: What is Naturalistic Epistemology," in *Naturalizing Epistemology*, 2nd edition, ed. H. Kornblith (Cambridge, Mass: MIT Press, 1994), p. 4.

[26] Quine, "Epistemology Naturalized (n. 20 above)," p. 75.

[27] On the differing claims of indeterminacy, see Leiter, "Legal Indeterminacy," *Legal Theory* 1 (1995): 481–92.

[28] Strictly speaking, the claim is that the class of legal reasons *underdetermines* the outcome: the class justifies more than one, though not simply *any* outcome. I follow conventional practice in the literature, and speak simply of "indeterminacy."

well a contrary result. But if legal rules and reasons cannot *rationalize* the decisions, then they surely cannot *explain* them either: we must, accordingly, look to other factors to explain why the court actually decided as it did. Thus, the Realists in effect say: "Why not see how the construction of decisions really proceeds?" The Realists, then, call for an essentially *naturalized* and hence *descriptive* theory of adjudication, a theory of what it is that causes courts to decide as they do.

I do not want to overstate, though, the force of the analogy; it is helpful in suggesting where Hart may have gone wrong in assimilating Realism to the paradigm of philosophy-cum-conceptual-analysis, but it is misleading if we take it as implying a Realist commitment to proto-Quinean doctrines across the boards. We can see this at two places. First, as I will argue below, the Realists end up presupposing a theory of the concept of legality in framing their arguments for law's indeterminacy; thus, while they may believe the only fruitful account of *adjudication* is descriptive and empirical, not normative and conceptual, they themselves need a concept of *law* that is not itself empirical or naturalized. The analogy with naturalized epistemology, in other words, must be localized to the theory of adjudication, and not the whole of jurisprudence.

Second, the crux of the Realist position (at least for the majority of Realists) is that non-legal reasons (e.g., judgments of fairness, or consideration of commercial norms) *explain* the decisions. They, of course, explain the decisions by *justifying* them, though not necessarily by justifying a unique outcome (i.e., the non-legal reasons might themselves rationalize other decisions as well). Now clearly the descriptive story about the non-legal reasons is not going to be part of a non-mentalistic naturalization of the theory of adjudication: a causal explanation of decisions in terms of reasons (even non-legal reasons) does require taking the normative force of the reasons *qua reasons* seriously. The behaviorism of Quine or Underhill Moore is not in the offing here, but surely this is to be preferred: behaviorism failed as a foundation for empirical social science, while social-scientific theories employing mentalistic categories have flourished. Moreover, if the non-legal reasons are themselves indeterminate—i.e., if they do not justify a *unique* outcome—then any causal explanation of the decision will have to go beyond reasons to identify the psyco-social facts (e.g., about personality, class, gender, socialization, etc.) that cause the decision. Such a "naturalization" of the theory of adjudication might be insufficiently austere in its ontology for Quinean scruples, but it is still a recognizable attempt to subsume what judges do within a (social) scientific framework.

II. Legal Positivism

Positivism, in contrast to Realism, is a *theory of law* or about the *nature of law*. Such a theory aims to explain certain familiar features of societies in which law exists, and it proposes to do so by analyzing the "concept" of law. Conceptual analysis, of course, is not a mere exercise in lexicography.[29] As Hart observed: "the suggestion that inquiries into the meanings of words merely throw light on words is false" (CL, p. v). Rather, Hart endorsed J.L. Austin's view that "a sharpened awareness of words . . . sharpen[s] our perception of phenomena" (quoted in CL, p. 14). Thus, although Hart employs the *method* of conceptual analysis, he calls his project one of "descriptive sociology" (CL, p. v). As Joseph Raz puts it: "we do not want to be slaves of words. Our aim is to understand society and its institutions."[30] Conceptual analysis is simply the primary tool that the Hartian Positivist employs to this end.

What features of the concept of law require explanation for the Positivist? Two are particularly important. First, *legal* norms are typically demarcated from other norms in society: one violates a *legal* norm by going faster than 65 m.p.h. on most highways, while one violates a norm of *etiquette* by talking with one's mouth full at the table. A theory of law tries to articulate the *criteria of legality*, i.e. the criteria a norm must satisfy in order to count as a *legal* norm as distinct from some other type. Second, *legal* norms play a distinctive role in the practical reasoning of citizens, i.e. reasoning about what one *ought* to do. If I say, for example, "Don't go faster than 65 m.p.h. on the highway" that may give you reasons for acting, depending, for instance, on whether you think I am a good driver, knowledgeable about the roads, sensitive to your schedule and the like. But when the legislature issues the same prescription—"Don't go faster than 65 m.p.h. on the highway"— that adds certain reasons for action that were not present when I articulated the same norm. Thus, a satisfactory theory of law ought to explain this special *normativity* of law as well.

By Positivism I shall mean that family of views about the nature of law distinguished by its commitment to two broad theses:[31]

Social Thesis: What counts as law in any particular society is fundamentally a matter of social fact.

Separability Thesis: What the law *is* and what the law *ought* to be are separate questions.

Positivists, of course, differ among themselves about the correct interpretation of these two theses. The most important recent debate concerns whether or not the

---

[29]　Though it seems more than a little misleading to say, as Leslie Green does, that Hart's "book is not an exercise in linguistic philosophy." "The Concept of Law Revisited" (n. 2 above), p. 1688 n. 1.

[30]　Joseph Raz, "Legal Positivism and the Sources of Law," in *The Authority of Law* (Oxford: Clarendon Press, 1979), p. 41.

[31]　See Brian Leiter, "Realism, Hard Positivism, and Conceptual Analysis," *Legal Theory* 4 (1998): 533–47. This characterization differs slightly from the one presented in Jules L. Coleman & Brian Leiter, "Legal Positivism," in *A Companion to Philosophy of Law and Legal Theory*, p. 241, which now seems to me unduly narrow. The labels in the text were coined in Jules L. Coleman, "Negative and Positive Positivism," reprinted in *Ronald Dworkin and Contemporary Jurisprudence*, ed. M. Cohen (London: Duckworth, 1983), p. 29, and Raz, "Legal Positivism and the Sources of Law" (n. 30 above), p. 37, though both authors use them in a more narrow sense than that presented in Leiter, id., and Coleman & Leiter, id.

Social Thesis should be interpreted as stating merely the *existence-conditions* for a Rule of Recognition (the rule that sets out a society's criteria of legality) or whether the Social Thesis also states a constraint on the *content* of the test for legal validity that any Rule of Recognition can set out. If the Social Thesis merely states the existence-conditions, then a Rule of Recognition is simply whatever Rule is constituted by the social facts about how officials actually decide disputes; as a result, such a Rule can incorporate tests of legal validity that make reference to moral and other substantive criteria of legality if these are the criteria officials actually employ to decide disputes. If, however, the Social Thesis also states a constraint on the content of the Rule of Recognition, then the criteria of legality a Rule of Recognition sets out must themselves *consist* in social facts, e.g. facts about pedigree or source. The former "Inclusive" or "Soft" Positivism has been defended by a number of writers—including, importantly, Hart himself in the recently published "Postscript" to the second edition of *The Concept of Law*.[32] It is rejected in favor of "Hard" Positivism by Joseph Raz[33] and, in effect, by Ronald Dworkin, who thinks that Soft Positivism is not a positivistic view at all.[34] Although I agree with Raz in favoring Hard over Soft Positivism, a discussion of that issue would require a separate paper. Suffice it to note that the kind of positivism presupposed by Legal Realism will turn out to be *Hard* Positivism.[35]

The centerpiece of Hartian Positivism is the idea that in any society in which *law* exists there must exist a certain complex social fact (per the Social Thesis) constituting a "Rule of Recognition" that determines the criteria any norm must satisfy to count as a *legal* norm. Such a Rule of Recognition is just a particular instance of a more general phenomenon that Hart calls a "social rule." A social rule exists in a society when we find patterns of convergent behavior in accord with the rule and we find that participants in the practice view the rule as a standard of conduct, to which they appeal both to justify their own conformity to the rule and to criticize those who deviate from the rule (CL, pp. 55–56, 90). With respect to a Rule of Recognition, we are interested in the patterns of convergent behavior evinced by relevant officials: e.g. how do judges decide questions about what the binding legal standards are? In the United States, for example, we find that arguments like, "This statute is invalid because it conflicts with the First Amendment" or "This will is enforceable having been duly enacted in accord with the applicable state statute" accurately state criteria of legality, while the argument, "This statute is void because it is inconsistent with the principles set out in Book IV of Plato's *Republic*" does not. What we learn, in other words, by examining official practice is that the Rule of Recognition for our legal system identifies

---

[32] Edited by P. Bulloch and J. Raz (Oxford: Clarendon Press, 1994). For further discussion of Inclusive or Soft Positivism, see Coleman & Leiter, "Legal Positivism" (id.) and W.J. Waluchow, *Inclusive Legal Positivism* (Oxford: Clarendon Press, 1994). Cf. Stephen R. Perry, "The Varieties of Legal Positivism," *Canadian Journal of Law & Jurisprudence* 9 (1996): 361–81.

[33] See especially, Joseph Raz, "Authority, Law and Morality," *The Monist* 68 (1985): 295–324.

[34] *Law's Empire* (n. 1 above), p. 127.   [35] See Ch. 4.

the federal Constitution and state statutes as valid sources of law (among many others), while it accords no such significance to Plato's *Republic*.[36] The Positivist answer, then, to the conceptual question, "What is law?" is in essence: "Whatever satisfies the criteria of a society's Rule of Recognition," where the Rule of Recognition is a social rule as described above.[37]

III. Varieties of Rule-Skepticism

Hart thinks the Legal Realists are rule-skeptics, but he thinks their rule-skepticism is untenable. As we noted at the beginning, it is this famous critique that is probably most responsible for the perception that Positivism and Realism are incompatible positions, and that Realism is best forgotten as a jurisprudential theory. With the basic doctrines of Realism and Positivism set out above, we are in a position to see where Hart went wrong.

What is rule-skepticism? Early on, Hart characterizes it as "the claim that talk of rules is a myth, cloaking the truth that law consists simply of the decisions of courts and the predictions of them" (CL, p. 133). Indeed, much of the discussion is devoted to attacking this version of rule-skepticism. But Hart identifies a second type of rule-skepticism: "Rule-scepticism has a serious claim on our attention, but only as a theory of the function of rules in judicial decision" (CL, p. 135). This second rule-skeptic claims, in particular, "that it is false, if not senseless, to regard judges as themselves subject to rules or 'bound' to decide cases as they do" (CL, p. 135). I propose to call the former doctrine "Conceptual Rule-Skepticism" and the latter "Empirical Rule-Skepticism."[38]

---

[36] Of course, a Rule of Recognition for a complex legal system like the American one must be corresondingly complex. For example: "A rule is a valid rule of law in the United States if it has been duly enacted by a federal or state legislature and it is not inconsistent with the federal constitution and if (for a state law) it is also not inconsistent with federal law or the state constitution; *or* if it figures in the holding of a court, and it has not been overruled by a higher court, or (in the case of non-constitutional issues) if it has not been overruled by a subsequent legislative enactment." Even this is far from complete. For example, in the modern administrative state, administrative agencies are also sources of binding legal norms.

[37] "What is law?" is, of course, ambiguous as between, "Given a legal system in some society, which norms in the society are legal norms?" and "For any society, how do we know whether law or a legal system exists in that society?" The text only gives Hart's answer to the former, not the latter, question. I am also not discussing here the Positivist account of the "normativity" of law, which bears less directly on the argument. For discussion, see Coleman & Leiter, "Legal Positivism" (n. 31 above).

[38] There is a third variety of rule-skepticism—related to what I am calling "Conceptual Rule-Skepticism"—that Hart also discusses, but which is less important to understanding Hart's quarrel with Realism. This type of rule-skepticism denies "that there are any rules at all." This skepticism, says Hart, "cannot consistently be combined" with "the assertion that there are decisions of courts" since "the existence of a court entails the existence of secondary rules conferring jurisdiction on a changing succession of individuals and so making their decisions authoritative" (H.L.A. Hart, *The Concept of Law* (n. 3 above), p. 133). Even Hart concedes, however, that rule-skepticism was probably "never intended as a denial" of *all* rules in this way (id., p. 134).

Conceptual Rule-Skepticism proffers a skeptical account of the concept of law.[39] The account is skeptical insofar as it involves denying what we may call, for ease of reference, "the Simple View." This is the view that certain prior offical acts (like legislative enactments and judicial decisions) constitute "law" (even if they do not exhaust it). (The view is simple to be sure, but not false!) A Conceptual Rule-Skeptic offers an account of the concept of law which denies the Simple View: according to this rule-skeptic, rules previously enacted by legislatures or articulated by courts are not law. This follows from the skeptic's own account of the concept of law, according to which, "The law is just a prediction of what a court will do" or "The law is just whatever a court says it is on the present occasion." Positivism, by contrast, is a non-skeptical account, since the Positivist notion of a Rule of Recognition is fully compatible with the insight captured in the Simple View.

Empirical Rule-Skepticism, by contrast, need make no claim about the *concept* of law;[40] rather it makes an empirical claim about the causal role of rules in judicial decision-making. According to this skeptic, rules of law do not make much (causal) difference to how courts decide cases. In Hart's version of this type of skepticism, the skeptic is said to believe this because of his view that legal rules are generally indeterminate (CL, p. 135). We will consider Hart's reconstruction of the argument in greater detail below.

In what follows, I will argue, first, that Hart has good arguments against Conceptual Rule-Skepticism, but this form of skepticism is not, in fact, at stake in Legal Realism; and second, that Hart never offers any argument against Empirical Rule-Skepticism. It will turn out, then, that against the only form of rule-skepticism that is at issue, Hart has given us no reason to reject Legal Realism.

IV. Conceptual Rule-Skepticism

Surely the most famous part of Hart's treatment of rule-skepticism is his refutation of Conceptual Rule-Skepticism: he memorably demonstrates that the skeptic's analysis of the concept of law is manifestly silly. Given our ultimate conclusion (that the Realists are *not* Conceptual Rule-Skeptics), it will suffice here to illustrate Hart's critique briefly by reference to two familiar phenomena: the phenomena of judicial mistake and of a judge trying to decide a case.

---

[39] I should note that my "Conceptual Rule-Skepticism" collapses different aspects of Hart's discussion, but in ways that are both fair to Hart and heuristically valuable for focussing the dispute between Hart and the Realists.

[40] Empirical Rule-Skepticism could be grounded in a philosophical argument about the indeterminacy of law. In fact, the Realists have such arguments, and they differ from Hart's, as discussed below. But Empirical Rule-Skepticism can also be rendered as a *pure* empirical question about whether or not legal rules play a (significant? determinative?) causal role in judicial decisions. I take up these issues below.

Any satisfactory analysis of the concept of law must account for the familiar fact that sometimes we want to say that a court has made a mistake as to the law. Sometimes we as observers or critics of courts say that; sometimes a higher court says that in overturning a lower court's decision. The Conceptual Rule-Skeptic, however, has no way of accounting for this aspect of the concept of law; indeed, for the Conceptual Rule-Skeptic to complain that a court was mistaken about the law is simply unintelligible! For according to the skeptic, by the concept "law" we just mean either "a prediction of what a court will hold" or "whatever a court holds." If that were right, then someone who said, "The lower court's holding was mistaken as to the law" would, in effect, be saying that, "The lower court's holding was mistaken as to the lower court's holding," which is nonsense. The skeptical account makes it impossible to articulate the simple idea that the law is one thing, and a particular court's decision another. The skeptic eliminates the needed conceptual space for even *questioning* whether a court misunderstood the law.

Here is a second illustration of the deficiencies of the skeptic's analysis of the concept of law. Suppose a judge must decide the question whether a franchisor can terminate a franchisee in Connecticut with less than sixty days' notice. The judge would presumably ask herself something like the following question: "What is the law governing the termination of franchisees in this state?" But according to the Conceptual Rule-Skeptic, to ask what the "law" is on termination and notice is just to ask, "How will the judge decide this case?" So a judge who asks herself what the law is turns out—on the skeptic's reading—to really be asking herself, "What do I think I will do?" But this is clearly *not* what the judge is asking, and so once again the skeptical account generates a silly interpretation. As Hart puts it: the "statement that a rule [of law] is valid is an internal statement recognizing that the rule satisfies the tests for identifying what is to count as law in [this] court, and constitutes not a prophecy of but part of the *reason* for [the] decision" (CL, p. 102; cf. p. 143).

Given that Conceptual Rule-Skepticism is manifestly ridiculous, one might wonder why Hart never considered the possibility that he had simply misread the Realists. In fairness to Hart, at least one Realist was, arguably, a Conceptual Rule-Skeptic: Felix Cohen.[41] But Cohen is nowhere cited by Hart; Hart's Realism is an amalgamation, largely, of Frank, Holmes, and Llewellyn. It is undeniably true that these writers, like most Realists, talk about the importance of "predicting" what courts will do. The question is whether, in so talking, they are fairly read as offering an analysis of the concept of law. Only Hart's grossly anachronistic reading suggests an affirmative answer.

The idea that philosophy involves "conceptual analysis" via the analysis of language is an artifact of Anglo-American analytic philosophy of the twentieth century; indeed, as practiced by Hart, it really reflects the influence of fashionable

---

[41] See esp. Felix Cohen, "Transcendental Nonsense and the Functional Approach," *Columbia Law Review* 35 (1935): 809–49. Altman also attributes the view, wrongly, to Holmes. "Legal Realism, Critical Legal Studies, and Dworkin" (n. 4 above), p. 212 n. 18. See the further discussion, below, in the text.

views in philosophy of language current at Oxford in the 1940s and 1950s. The Realists were not philosophers, let alone analytic philosophers, let alone students of G.E. Moore, Russell, and the early Wittgenstein, let alone colleagues of J.L. Austin. The idea that what demands understanding about law is the "concept" of law as manifest in ordinary language would have struck them as ludicrous. While the Realists had much to say about adjudication and how legal rules work in practice, they had nothing *explicit* to say about the *concept* of law.[42]

How, then, do we understand their talk about "predicting" what courts will do? In *Law and the Modern Mind*, Jerome Frank cautions the reader early on that he "is primarily concerned with 'law' as it affects the work of the practicing lawyer and the needs of the clients who retain him."[43] Holmes begins "The Path of the Law" by emphasizing that he is talking about the meaning of law to lawyers who will "appear before judges, or . . . advise people in such a way as to keep them out of court."[44] Against this background, infamous statements like Llewellyn's—"What these officials do about disputes is, to my mind, the law itself"[45]—make perfect sense. This is not a claim about the "concept" of law, but rather a claim about how it is *useful* to think about law for attorneys who must advise clients what to do. For your client, the franchisee in Connecticut, does not simply want to know what the rule on the books in Connecticut says; he wants to know what will happen when he takes the franchisor to court. So from the practical perspective of the franchisee, what one wants to know about the "law" is what, in fact, the courts will do when confronted with the franchisee's grievance. That is all the law that matters to the client, all the law that matters to the lawyer advising that client. And that is all, I take it, the Realists wanted to emphasize.

In fact, there is a deeper theoretical reason why the Realists could not have been Conceptual Rule-Skeptics. For the Realist arguments for the indeterminacy of

---

[42] That it struck them as a ludicrous enterprise is not to say that they were right to so regard it. Indeed, as we shall see shortly, the Realists presuppose an account of the concept of law in making their argument for legal indeterminacy.

[43] Jerome Frank, *Law and the Modern Mind* (New York: Brentano's, 1930), p. 47 note.

[44] O.W. Holmes, Jr., "The Path of the Law," *Harvard Law Review* 10 (1897): 457–78, 457. Michael S. Moore contests my reading of these and related passages in the "Introduction" to his recent collection of papers, *Educating Oneself in Public: Critical Essays in Jurisprudence* (New York: Oxford University Press, 2000), esp. at note 74 and accompanying text. Moore cannot, of course, deny the obvious: the Legal Realists were not philosophers, and showed no interest in questions of conceptual analysis. Instead, Moore lays emphasis on the fact that to appear before a judge—as Holmes recognizes laywers do—one "must offer up good justifying reasons for deciding in his client's favor," and that is not compatible with the predictive theory. Id., n. 74. But this is to miss the point: it is not compatible with the predictive theory *understood as a conceptual claim about the nature of law*, but it is perfectly compatible with the predictive theory understood as a piece of pragmatic advice: a lawyer who will appear before a judge must have some predictive view about what the judge is likely to do and what considerations he is likely to find compelling in order to *effectively* frame his justifying reasons and to effectively counsel his client about what to expect as the outcome of taking the matter to court. Moore gives no reason for assigning to the Realist claims about prediction philosophical baggage they plainly did not intend.

[45] Karl Llewellyn, *The Bramble Bush* (New York: Oceana, 1930), p. 3.

law—like *all* arguments for legal indeterminacy[46]—in fact presuppose a non-skeptical account of the concept of law. Indeed, they presuppose an account with distinct affinities to that developed by the Legal Positivists![47] The central claim of legal indeterminacy is the claim of *rational* indeterminacy: the claim that the "class of legal reasons" fails to justify a unique outcome in some or all cases. The "class of legal reasons" is the class of reasons that may properly justify a legal conclusion (and thus "compel" it insofar as legal actors are responsive to valid legal reasons). So, for example, appeal to a statutory provision or a valid precedent are parts of the class of legal reasons, while appeal to the authority of Plato's *Republic* is not: a judge is not obliged to decide one way rather than another because Plato says so. Any argument for indeterminacy, then, presupposes some view about the *boundaries* of the class of legal reasons. When Oliphant argues, for example, that the promise-not-to-compete cases are decided not by reference to law, but by reference to uncodified norms prevalent in the commercial culture in which the disputes arose, this only shows that the law is indeterminate on the assumption that the normative reasons the courts are actually relying upon are not themselves *legal* reasons. So, too, when Holmes chalks up judicial decisions not to legal reasoning but to "a concealed, half-conscious battle on the [background] question of legislative policy"[48] he is plainly presupposing that these policy concerns are not themselves *legal* reasons. The famous Realist arguments for indeterminacy which focus on the conflicting, but equally legitimate ways, lawyers have of interpreting statutes and precedents[49] only show that the law is indeterminate on the assumption either that statutes and precedents largely exhaust the authoritative sources of law or that any additional authoritative norms not derived from these sources conflict. It is the former assumption that seems to motivate the Realist arguments. Thus, Llewellyn says that judges take rules "in the main from authoritative sources (which in the case of law are largely statutes and the decisions of the courts)."[50]

What concept of law is being presupposed here in these arguments for legal indeterminacy, a concept in which statutes and precedent are part of the law, but uncodified norms and policy arguments are not? It is certainly not Ronald Dworkin's theory, let alone any more robust natural law alternative. Rather, the Realists are presupposing something like the Positivist idea of a Rule of Recognition whose criteria of legality are exclusively ones of pedigree: a rule (or canon of construction) is part of the law in virtue of having a source in a legislative enactment

---

[46] On this point, see Leiter, "Legal Indeterminacy" (n. 27 above).

[47] Recall, too, that it is the argument for indeterminacy that motivates the Realist call for *naturalization*, i.e. for developing a descriptive account of what causes courts to decide as they do. More precisely, the Realists had a *pragmatic* goal of constructing theories of adjudication that would be *useful* for lawyers. And such a theory has to be a *naturalized* theory because of the rational indeterminacy of law. See Ch. 1.   [48] "The Path of the Law," (n. 44 above) p. 467.

[49] The classic discussions are Llewellyn, *The Bramble Bush* (n. 45 above), pp. 72–5; Max Radin, "Statutory Interpretation," *Harvard Law Review* 43 (1930): 863–85; and Karl Llewellyn, "Remarks on the Theory of Appellate Decision and the Rules and Canons About How Statutes are to be Construed," *Vanderbilt Law Review* 3 (1950): 395–406.   [50] *The Bramble Bush* (n. 45 above), p. 13.

or a prior court decision.[51] The Realists, in short, cannot be Conceptual Rule-Skeptics, because their arguments for the indeterminacy of law presuppose a non-skeptical account of the criteria of legality, one that has the most obvious affinities with that developed by Hard or Exclusive Positivists.

V. Empirical Rule-Skepticism

We have seen that there are no grounds for repudiating Realism just because Conceptual Rule-Skepticism is an implausible view. In fact, most Realists were not Conceptual Rule-Skeptics and, what is more, their other theoretical commitments preclude commitment to Conceptual Rule-Skepticism. But the Realists are, to be sure, skeptics of some sort, and the most plausible candidate is what I have been calling Empirical Rule-Skepticism. Here is Hart's characterization of the view:

[I]t amounts to the contention that, so far as the courts are concerned, there is nothing to circumscribe the open texture [of language in which rules are framed]: so that it is false, if not senseless, to regard judges as themselves subject to rules or "bound" to decide cases as they do. They may act with sufficient predictable regularity and uniformity to enable others, over long periods, to live by courts' decisions as rules. Judges may even experience feelings of compulsion when they decide as they do, and these feelings may be predictable too; but beyond this there is nothing which can be characterized as a rule which they observe. (CL, p. 135)

Empirical Rule-Skepticism on this rendering, then, involves two claims: (1) legal rules are indeterminate; and, as a result, (2) legal rules do not determine or constrain decisions.

Notice that Hart's way of framing the skeptical argument makes it depend upon a philosophical claim about law, i.e. that it is indeterminate. But (2) could be true even if (1) were false (that would be *pure* Empirical Rule-Skepticism, we might say). Yet Hart is surely correct that most Realists[52] argue for both (1) and (2). But he is wrong about the Realist argument for (1), and thus underestimates the amount of indeterminacy in law.

---

[51] One difference is that most Positivists recognize customary practices as sources of valid law, whereas it is not clear what the Realists think about this. Let me emphasize too that the claim in the text is only an *interpretive* point about the Realists: *their actual arguments and claims presuppose* a Hard Positivist conception of legality. But perhaps a Realist theory of law would do better if constructed on non-Positivist grounds, say by allowing for content-based criteria of legality (criteria like "commercially fair" and the like)? In fact, I think it a virtue of Realism that it is (tacitly) committed to Hard Positivism, but the reasons for that pertain to the general reasons for thinking natural law and Soft Positivism are not viable options. That is a discussion that would take us far afield of the central topics, but for some pertinent discussion see Chs. 4 & 8.

[52] Underhill Moore may be the exception. See the discussion in Leiter, "Legal Realism" (n. 18 above), p. 268.

The central strategic move of Chapter VII of *The Concept of Law* is to concede to the skeptic, right up front, that legal rules are indeterminate, but to argue that this indeterminacy is a marginal phenomenon, one insufficient to underwrite far-reaching skepticism. The skeptic is portrayed, accordingly, as having unrealistically high expectations for the determinacy of rules, as being "a disappointed absolutist" (CL, p. 135). The strategy depends, however, on Hart's account of the source of indeterminacy, an account, as we shall see, quite different from the Realist one.

According to Hart, legal rules are indeterminate because "there is a limit, inherent in the nature of language, to the guidance which general language can provide" (CL, p. 123). Language is, in Hart's famous phrase, "open-textured":

> There will indeed be plain cases constantly recurring in similar contexts to which general expressions are clearly applicable ("If anything is a vehicle a motor-car is one") but there will also be cases where it is not clear whether they apply or not. ("Does 'vehicle' used here include bicycles, airplanes, roller skates?"). The latter are fact-situations, continually thrown up by nature or human invention, which possess only some of the features of the plain cases but others which they lack. (CL, p. 123)

Language is "open-textured" in that while words have "core" instances—aspects of the world that clearly fall within the extension of the word's meaning—they also have "penumbras," cases where it is unclear whether the extension includes the aspect of the world at issue. In cases in which the facts fall within the penumbra of the key words in the applicable legal rule, a court "must exercise a discretion, [since] there is no possibility of treating the question raised . . . as if there were one uniquely correct answer to be found, as distinct from an answer which is a reasonable compromise between many conflicting interests" (CL, p. 128).

While some recent writers have challenged the implicit semantics that informs this argument for the indeterminacy of language (*a fortiori* of law),[53] I think we can agree with Hart (and, I would venture, with common-sense) that legal rules must necessarily be indeterminate in some measure given the indeterminacy of language itself, and that this type of indeterminacy resides "at the margin of rules" (CL, p. 132). What bears noting here is that the Realist argument for indeterminacy did *not* rely on these points at all.

The Realists located the indeterminacy of law not in general features of language itself, but in the existence of equally legitimate, but conflicting, *canons of interpretation* that courts could employ to extract differing rules from the same statutory text or the same precedent.[54] Indeterminacy, in short, resides for the

[53] See David O. Brink, "Legal Theory, Legal Interpretation, and Judicial Review," *Philosophy & Public Affairs* 17 (1988): 105–48. For the more recent version of Brink's view, see his paper, "Legal Interpretation, Objectivity, and Morality," in Leiter (ed.), *Objectivity in Law and Morals* (New York: Cambridge University Press, 2001).

[54] Altman makes a similar point in "Legal Realism, Critical Legal Studies, and Dworkin," (n. 4 above) p. 209, though he does not put the emphasis, as the Realists do, on conflicting *canons* of interpretation as the source of indeterminacy. He also fails to note the difficulties facing the Realists' tacit notion of "legitimate" canons of interpretation that underlies the indeterminacy argument. I take up these problems, below, in the text.

Realists not in the rules themselves, but in the ways we have of characterizing what rules statutes and precedents contain. Llewellyn, for example, argues that any precedent can be read "strictly" or "loosely," and that either reading is "recognized, legitimate, honorable."[55] The strict interpretation characterizes the rule of the case as specific to the facts of the case; the loose interpretation abstracts (in varying degrees) from the specific facts in order to treat the case as standing for some general norm. But if "each precedent has not one value [that is, stands for not just one rule], but two, and . . . the two are wide apart, and . . . whichever value a later court assigns to it, such assignment will be respectable, traditionally sound, dogmatically correct,"[56] then precedent, as a source of law, cannot provide reasons for a unique outcome, because more than one rule can be extracted from the same precedent.

Llewellyn thinks the same is true of statutory interpretation, where one can find "'correct,' unchallengeable rules of 'how to read' which lead in happily variant directions."[57] By mining the cases, Llewellyn shows that courts have endorsed contradictory canons of construction, like "A statute cannot go beyond its text," but also "To effect its purpose a statute must be implemented beyond its text."[58] But if a statute can properly be construed in contradictory ways to stand for different rules, then reasoning from the statute will not justify a unique outcome in the case at hand.[59]

One difficulty with these Realist arguments is that they rely on a tacit conception of *legitimate* legal argument. The assumption is that if lawyers and courts employ some form of argument—a "strict" construal of precedent, a particular canon of statutory construction—then that form of argument is *legitimate* in any and all cases. Put in this strong form, the assumption cannot be right: not *every* strict construal of precedent will be legally proper in every case. Even Llewellyn must recognize this, as suggested by his famous—but clearly facetious—example of the strict reading that yields, "This rule holds only of redheaded Walpoles in pale magenta Buick cars."[60] But that would *never* be a legitimate construal of a precedent (barring some bizarre scenario in which all these facts turned out to be legally relevant), and Llewellyn surely knows as much. The claim cannot be, then, that *any* strict or loose construal of precedent is *always* valid. It must only be that lawyers and judges have this interpretive latitude often enough to inject a considerable degree of indeterminacy into law.

Note that, even if we agreed with Hart that the open-texture of language affects rules only "at the margins," the Realists have now given us an *additional* reason

---

[55] *The Bramble Bush*, (n. 45 above) p. 74.   [56] Id., p. 76.
[57] "Remarks on the Theory of Appellate Decision," (n. 49 above) p. 399.
[58] Id., p. 401; cf. *The Bramble Bush* (n. 45 above), p. 90. See generally, Radin, "Statutory Interpretation" (n. 49 above), esp. pp. 881–2.
[59] Some Realists also locate indeterminacy in the wide latitude judges have in how to characterize the facts of a given case in legally significant ways. For discussion of this source of indeterminacy, see Frank, *Law and the Modern Mind* (n. 43 above), pp, 108–10; Llewellyn, *The Bramble Bush* (n. 45 above), p. 80.   [60] *The Bramble Bush*, (n. 45 above) p. 72.

(beyond Hart's) to expect indeterminacy in law. If the Realists are right, then not only do legal rules suffer from the open-texture that Hart describes, but statutes and precedents will frequently admit "manipulation"—legally proper manipulation, of course—and thus be indeterminate in this additional respect as well. The *combination* of sources of interdeterminacy (the open-texture of language, and the conflicting canons of interpretation) seems sufficient to move indeterminacy from the margins to the center of cases actually litigated.

Hart, of course, is not entirely insensitive to the Realist arguments, though he treats them extremely cursorily. In response to Llewellyn's point, for example, that a court can interpret a precedent both "loosely" and "strictly" and thus extract two different rules from the same prior decision, Hart says simply this: "in the vast majority of decided cases there is very little doubt [as to the rule of the case]. The head-note is usually correct enough" (CL, p. 131). But every first-year litigation associate knows that this approach to precedent would be a recipe for disaster. To extract "holdings" without regard to the facts of the case—which is all a head-note typically provides—is mediocre lawyering.[61] Skillful lawyers know exactly what Llewellyn describes: that the "rule" of a prior case can be stated at differing degrees of specificity, and so made to do very different rhetorical work depending on the needs of the case at hand.

It bears noting that the Realist argument for Empirical Rule-Skepticism is actually conceptually severable from the claim that the law is indeterminate. For centrally, it is based on the *observation* that the decisions courts reach do not fall in to patterns that correlate with the rules they invoke; rather the decisions reflect judges's response to the underlying facts of the cases.[62] This was the point of Oliphant's example of the promise-not-to-compete cases discussed earlier; it is Llewellyn's point too in his discussion of the New York sales cases.[63] What causes judges to decide as they do, according to the Realist, is not legal rules,[64] but a sense

---

[61] See Altman, "Legal Realism, Critical Legal Studies, and Dworkin" (n. 4 above), p. 210 for the same point.

[62] This is the aspect of Realism ignored by Altman, but which is central to motivating the Realist theory of adjudication. Cf. n. 13 above.

[63] *The Common Law Tradition* (Boston: Little, Brown, 1960), pp. 122–4. A series of New York cases applied the rule that a buyer who rejects the seller's shipment by formally stating his objections thereby waives all other objections. Llewellyn observed that the rule seemed to have been harshly applied in some cases where the buyers simply may not have known at the time of rejection of other defects or where the seller could not have cured in any case. Upon looking at the underlying facts of the cases, however, Llewellyn discovered that in each case where the rule seems to have been harsly applied what had really happened was that the market had gone sour, and the buyer was looking to escape the contract. The court, being "sensitive to commerce or to decency" (id., p. 124) applied the unrelated rule about rejection to frustrate the buyer's attempted violation of a basic norm of commercial conduct: namely, parties should honor their commitments even under changed market conditions. It is, in short, the "background facts, those of mercantile practice, those of the situation-type" (id., p. 126) that determine the court's decision.

[64] Some legal rules, of course, structure the presentation of facts to the court, and thus "the facts of the case at hand" are unintelligible *without* legal rules. Conceding this point does not change the fact, however, that there still may be a disjunction (as the Realists claim) between the substantive rules of law that judges invoke in their decisions and the *real* bases for their decisions.

of what would be fair on the facts of the case at hand. *All* Realists agreed on this point. Judge Hutcheson revealed that "the vital, motivating impulse for the decision is an intuitive sense of what is right or wrong for that cause."[65] Frank invoked the example of "a great American judge," Chancellor Kent, who had confessed that, "He first made himself 'master of the facts.' Then (he wrote) 'I saw where justice lay, and the moral sense decided the court half the time; I then sat down to search the authorities . . . but I almost always found principles suited to my view of the case . . . .'"[66] Llewellyn noted that to understand what appellate courts are really doing, one must appreciate "how far the proposition which seems so abstract has roots in what seems to be the due thing on the facts [before the court]."[67] As a result, Llewellyn's advice for the lawyer was "on the facts . . . [to] persuade the court your case is sound," even if the lawyer must also provide a "technical ladder"[68] to the "sound" result. Frank pointed out that the very same advice had been given by a former President of the American Bar Association.[69] Indeed, I have met very few appellate litigators who have dissented from the Realist view.[70] In short, the core of the Realist defense of Empirical Rule-Skepticism is, in fact, *empirical*: they looked at what the courts really did, and found that legal rules were clearly not the determining factors in a large number of cases.[71]

At the same time, the Realists—unlike many of the later Critical Legal Studies writers—did not overstate the irrelevance of rules. For one thing, Realists were (generally) clear that their focus was indeterminacy at the stage of appellate review, where one ought to expect a higher degree of uncertainty in the law. Cases that have determinate legal answers are, after all, less likely to be litigated to the stage of appellate review. Most of the time, the Realists seemed to understand this point. Thus, Llewellyn explicitly qualified his indeterminacy claim by saying that, "[I]n any case doubtful enough to make litigation respectable the available authoritative premises . . . are at least two, and . . . the two are mutually contradictory as applied to the case at hand."[72] And Max Radin noted that judicial "decisions will consequently be called for chiefly in what may be called marginal cases, in which prognosis is difficult and uncertain. It is this fact that makes the entire body of

---

[65] Joseph C. Hutcheson, Jr., "The Judgment Intuitive: The Function of the 'Hunch' in Judicial Decision," *Cornell Law Quarterly* 14 (1929): 274–88, 285.

[66] *Law and the Modern Mind*, (n. 43 above) p. 104 note.

[67] *The Bramble Bush* (n. 67 above), p. 29.   [68] Id., p. 76.

[69] *Law and the Modern Mind* (n. 43 above), p. 102 note.

[70] Recently, I had occasion to ask a litigation partner at a local firm—a very capable attorney with no jurisprudential instincts or training whatsoever—whether he thought appellate courts decided cases on the law or based on what they thought were the right results given the underlying facts of the case. He thought it was obviously the latter, not the former. A systematic empirical study on this point would be interesting, but all my anecdotal evidence to date—combined with my own litigation experience—makes me confident that the Realists had it right.

[71] Of course, cases that reach the stage of appellate litigation are but a small fraction of the universe of legal cases. In this sense, "the law" can be broadly determinate, even if litigated cases are often not.

[72] Karl Llewellyn, "Some Realism about Realism—Responding to Dean Pound," *Harvard Law Review* 44 (1931): 1222–64, 1239.

legal judgments seem less stable than it really is."[73] Empirical Rule-Skepticism is surely more plausible when it is not advanced as a *global* claim about adjudication and the law.

Moreover, the Realists did not completely discount the role of rules in adjudication. Llewellyn is representative when he asks, "Do I suggest that . . . the 'accepted rules,' the rules the judges say that they apply, are without influence upon their actual behavior?" and answers, "I do not."[74] The Realist approach, says Llewellyn, "admits . . . *some* relation between *any* accepted rule and judicial behavior" but then demands that *what* that relation is requires empirical investigation, since it is not always the relation suggested by the "logic" (or content) of the rule.[75] As he puts the point elsewhere: Realists deny that "traditional . . . rule-formulations are *the* heavily operative factor in producing court decisions."[76] But to deny only *this* claim is to admit that rules play *some* causal role in decisions.

Even with all these qualifications in hand, there still remains a genuine point of dispute between Hart and the Realists. While both acknowlege indeterminacy in law, and while both acknowledge, accordingly, that rules do not determine decisions in some range of cases, they clearly disagree over the *range* of cases about which these claims hold true. Theirs, in short, is a disagreement as to *degree*, but it is a real disagreement nonetheless. While Hart would locate indeterminacy, and thus the causal irrelevance, of rules "at the margin," Realist skepticism encompasses the "core" of appellate litigation.

So how does Hart, in the end, respond to the Realist contention that, at least in appellate adjudication, rules play a relatively minor role in causing the courts to decide as they do? Here is, I take it, the crux of Hart's rejoinder:

[I]t is surely evident that for the most part decisions . . . are reached either by genuine effort to conform to rules consciously taken as guiding standards of decision or, if intuitively reached, are justified by rules which the judge was antecedently disposed to observe and whose relevance to the case in hand would generally be acknowledged. (CL, p. 137)

What exactly is the argument here? As far as I can see, it consists in four words: "it is surely evident." But that is no argument at all. Hart simply denies what the Realist affirms, but gives no reason for the denial other than his armchair confidence in the correctness of his own view.

Of course, Hart *may* be correct.[77] But given the devastating impact Hart's chapter had upon Realism, it is surely more than ironic that on the crucial point of

---

[73] Max Radin, "In Defense of an Unsystematic Science of Law," *Yale Law Journal* 51 (1942): 1269–79, 1271.

[74] Karl Llewellyn, "A Realistic Jurisprudence—The Next Step," *Columbia Law Review* 30 (1930): 431–65, 444.   [75] Id.

[76] "Some Realism About Realism" (n. 72 above), p. 1237 (emphasis added).

[77] A large body of political science literature suggests, however, that Hart is not. See, e.g., Jeffrey A. Segal & Harold J. Spaeth, *The Supreme Court and the Attitudinal Model* (New York: Cambridge Universtiy Press, 1993). For a balanced overview of the pertinent literature, see Frank B. Cross, "Political Science and the New Legal Realism: A Case of Unfortunate Interdisciplinary Ignorance," *Northwestern University Law Review* 92 (1997): 251–326.

dispute with Realism—to what extent rules matter in appellate adjudication—
Hart never offers any argument at all.

VI. A Final Worry about Realism and Positivism

Even if Hart himself never gives us a genuine argument against Legal Realism,
there may still be reason to worry about the compatibility of Realism and Positivism arising from a different source: namely, that the Rule of Recognition is, for
Hart, a *social* rule.[78] The problem may be put this way: if the primary rules validated by a society's Rule of Recognition are indeterminate, then they do not really
guide judges in deciding cases. In that event, however, the Rule of Recognition is a
mere "paper" Rule of Recognition: it sets out the criteria judges *say* they are using,
but it does not reflect the *real* criteria, since the primary rules it validates do not
determine decisions. But a Rule of Recognition for Hart is a *social* rule, i.e. one
constituted by the actual practice of officials in deciding disputes, and thus cannot
be a "paper" rule in this way. Thus, it seems, Positivism and Realism are incompatible after all.

Or are they? Recall, to start, that the Realist view is not that *all* primary rules
are indeterminate. Because the Realists focus on appellate litigation, and because
such litigation constitutes only a small portion of the universe of legal cases and
questions, the Realists can allow that *most* primary rules (as validated under the
Rule of Recognition) are, indeed, determinate as applied to most situations. Thus,
primary rules do *guide* most decisions (and thus the Rule of Recognition that
validates them is a *social* rule), even if in appellate cases the primary rules do not
determine the outcomes.

Yet even this latter point still concedes too much. For there are different ways in
which the primary rules may prove to be indeterminate. The class of legal reasons
is *in*determinate if it justifies *any* outcome on a given question. The class of legal
reasons is *under*determinate if it justifies more than one but not simply any outcome on a given question. Any plausible thesis about the indeterminacy of law
is, strictly speaking, a thesis about the *under*determinacy of law.[79] Now the class
of legal reasons in a particular legal system is constituted, at least in part, by that
system's Rule of Recognition which validates the primary rules that figure in
legal reasoning. If the class of legal reasons is underdeterminate, that means that
it still constrains the decisions of officials even when the primary rules are not
determinate: for the rules simply fail to justify a *unique* outcome, but they still
do determine the range of *possible* outcomes. Thus, even on the Realist picture,
the primary rules validated under the Rule of Recognition *guide* decision in some
measure for appellate judges (as for other officials of the system), insofar as these

---

[78] I am indebted to Scott Shapiro for suggesting this argument.
[79] See Leiter, "Legal Indeterminacy" (n. 27 above), pp. 481–2 and n. 1.

primary rules constrain the range of possible decisions. So the Realist indeterminacy thesis is still compatible with the Positivist idea of a Rule of Recognition as a social rule.

VII. Conclusion

Even H.L.A. Hart acknowledged that the Realists "opened men's eyes to what actually goes on when courts decide cases."[80] This is quite familiar to lawyers, though largely lost on most legal philosophers. For what legal philosophers took from Hart was the demonstration that the Realists were just confused jurisprudents, defenders of an untenable Conceptual Rule-Skepticism. We have seen, however, that while Hart was right about Conceptual Rule-Skepticism, he was wrong in attributing it to Realism: he misread the Realists, anachronistically, as forerunners of his own brand of philosophy-cum-conceptual analysis. With that misreading cast aside, the relationship between Realism and Positivism takes on a very different appearance. The relationship, seen clearly, has three main features.

First, both Realists and Positivists think that the law is indeterminate, though they differ on the source of this indeterminacy *and* on its scope. Second, Realist arguments for indeterminacy seem to presuppose an essentially Positivistic account of the criteria of legality, one in which proper pedigree is the hallmark of a genuinely *legal* norm. Third, Realists and Positivists *do* disagree over how often legal rules matter in judicial decision-making. In some measure, this disagreement tracks the one about the *scope* of indeterminacy, and thus remains a philosophical dispute. But at bottom it is an *empirical* disagreement, not a conceptual one: the rules on the books either do, or do not, play a causal role in the decisions courts reach most (all, some, half) of the time. On this point of genuine disagreement, Hart, at least, never gives us any real argument against the Realist position at all. Perhaps, then, it is time for legal philosophers to stop treating Realism as a discredited historical antique, and start looking at the movement with the sympathetic eye it deserves.

---

[80] H.L.A. Hart, "Positivism and the Separation of Law and Morals," *Harvard Law Review* 71 (1958): 593–629, 606.

3

Is There an "American" Jurisprudence?

I. Jurisprudence

Defining intellectual movements by nationality or geography is probably as common as it is misleading. Consider, for example, the oft-noted contrast between "Anglo-American" analytic philosophy and so-called "Continental" philosophy. Although most students understand right away that these labels are really proxies for differences in philosophical style and concerns, it is still curious that the tradition of Hegel and Heidegger should be named after a "Continent" that was also the birthplace of foundational figures in the "opposed" analytic tradition (for example, Wittgenstein and Carnap). These geographic labels have become increasingly misleading in recent years—as prominent "Anglo-Americans" like John McDowell now regularly invoke Hegel and Gadamer in a prose style that often rivals theirs for opacity;[1] as Parisians like Jacques Bouveresse and Dan Sperber make contributions to the analytic tradition in philosophy of language and mind;[2] and as the most illuminating commentatory on "Continental" figures is done, almost without exception, by analytically-trained Anglo-American philosophers.[3] There remain, to be sure, some profound differences between the philosophical orientation and method of the traditions of Hegel, Marx, Nietzsche, and Heidegger versus that of Wittgenstein, Carnap, Quine, and Kripke,[4] but it is not a difference that is much illuminated by reference to geography or nationality.

   * Thanks to Sheila Sokolowski for useful advice on an earlier draft, and my colleagues Douglas Laycock, Sanford Levinson, Bill Powers, and David Rabban for helpful comments on the penultimate draft.

   [1] Cf. John McDowell, *Mind and World* (Cambridge, Mass.: Harvard University Press, 1994).

   [2] See, e.g., Dan Sperber & Deirdre Wilson, *Relevance: Communication and Cognition* (Oxford: Blackwell, 1986); Jacques Bouveresse, *Wittgenstein Reads Freud: The Myth of the Unconscious*, trans. C. Cosman (Princeton: Princeton University Press, 1995).

   [3] See, e.g., G.A. Cohen, *Karl Marx's Theory of History: A Defence* (Princeton: Princeton University Press, 1978); Michael Forster, *Hegel and Skepticism* (Cambridge, Mass.: Harvard University Press, 1989); Maudemarie Clark, *Nietzsche on Truth and Philosophy* (Cambridge: Cambridge University Press, 1990); Hubert Dreyfus, *Being-in-the-World: A Commentary on Heidegger's "Being and Time," Division I* (Cambridge, Mass.: MIT Press, 1991).

   [4] For some relevant discussion, see Leiter, "Nietzsche and the Morality Critics," *Ethics* 107 (1997): 250–85.

It is a curious feature of Neil Duxbury's book *Patterns of American Jurisprudence*[5] that it should display so little anxiety about whether its subject-matter—that is, "American jurisprudence"—is genuine; whether, in short, the label "American jurisprudence" makes much sense. Consider, for example, that of various major American figures currently active in "jurisprudence"—writers like Jules Coleman (Yale), David Lyons (Boston University), Gerald Postema (University of North Carolina), and Frederick Schauer (Harvard), to name just a few who are likely to be familiar to readers—not a single one is mentioned anywhere in the text of this 500-page study. This omission is both remarkable and revealing. Since it plainly does not suffice to be either an American or an influential contributor to legal philosophy to figure in the history of American jurisprudence by Duxbury's lights, what constitute, one wonders, the criteria of inclusion and exclusion?

One thing that all the aforementioned American jurisprudents have in common is that they have contributed, in various ways, to theorizing about the nature of law and of legal authority, and they have done so by the standards of argument characteristic of analytic philosophy. They are, roughly speaking, figures in "analytic" jurisprudence, that tradition whose seminal twentieth-century work is H.L.A. Hart's *The Concept of Law*[6]. Duxbury's fixation with the "geographical approach" to the history of ideas, however, leads him to refer even to Hart's monumental work—a work that has enjoyed a worldwide influence—as an example of "British jurisprudence" (67)! Positivism may loom particularly large on the English jurisprudential landscape, to be sure, but it seems silly to cabin it off as the phenomenon of a particular island in the north-east Atlantic. Hart's work, after all, is much indebted to the positivism of a German (Hans Kelsen), while much of the important recent work in Legal Positivism has been done by one Israeli (Joseph Raz) and several Americans (e.g. Coleman, Lyons, Postema, and Schauer, among others).[7] It bears noting, too, that the leading contemporary proponents of the opposed "natural law" theory are British (John Finnis) or teaching in Britain (Ronald Dworkin).

Perhaps, then, being dead is what distinguishes the members of the Duxburyean pantheon of "American jurisprudents"? In fact, however, the book is replete with references to living American law professors like Richard Delgado, Joseph William Singer, and Frances Olsen (U.C.L.A.)—representatives, respectively, of "Critical Race Theory," "Critical Legal Studies" ("C.L.S."), and "Feminist Jurisprudence." Indeed, each of the six chapters of this book is devoted to one of the "schools" or "movements" that constitute "American jurisprudence" in Duxbury's view: "Formalism," especially as defended by Christopher Columbus Langdell and Joseph Beale at Harvard and various turn-of-the-century judges (Chapter 1); "Legal Realism" in the writings of Karl Llewellyn, Jerome Frank, and others at Yale

---

[5] Neil Duxbury, *Patterns of American Jurisprudence* (Oxford: Clarendon Press, 1995). All citations will be included, by page number, in the body of the text.   [6] (Oxford: Clarendon Press, 1961).
[7] For an overview, see Wil Waluchow, *Inclusive Legal Positivism* (Oxford: Clarendon Press, 1994) and Jules L. Coleman & Brian Leiter, "Legal Positivism," in D.M. Patterson (ed.), *A Companion to Philosophy of Law and Legal Theory* (Oxford: Blackwell, 1996).

and Columbia in the 1920s and 1930s (Chapter 2); the "policy science" of Myres McDougal and Harold Lasswell at Yale during and after World War II (Chapter 3); the "Legal Process" school associated most prominently with Henry Hart and Albert Sacks at Harvard in the 1950s (Chapter 4); the law and economics movement originating at the University of Chicago in the 1960s and 1970s (Chapter 5); and Critical Legal Studies, Critical Race Theory, and Feminist Jurisprudence, "movements" of the 1970s, 80s and 90s (Chapter 6).[8] The American Ronald Dworkin—the most widely cited living legal philosopher in the English-speaking world—appears primarily (and only briefly) as a way of rounding out the discussion of Legal Process (pp. 293–7).

As a teacher of a course that goes under the heading "jurisprudence" at a leading American law school, I accord some brief attention to "formalism" and C.L.S., and somewhat more substantial attention to Legal Realism; no time is devoted at all, however, to the writers and themes that figure in Duxbury's Chapters 3, 4, and 5, or to the Critical Race Theory or Feminist Legal Theory of Chapter 6. There is, to be sure, something of at least moderate interest in all these movements. It is impossible, for example, to think seriously about private law doctrine in the United States without an understanding of economic analysis. One has a rather thin understanding of constitutional theory of the 1950s and 1960s without an appreciation of Legal Process. One can hardly participate in modern international law scholarship without a background in "policy science." And feminists have forever changed the terms in which social and political theorists must think about the inequitable ways in which benefits and burdens are distributed in human societies. But none of this, as I see it, has much direct bearing on jurisprudence, that is, on philosophical thinking about law. None of these theorists shed much light on core jurisprudential questions like: what is law? what is the relationship between legal norms and other norms in society? how do judges decide cases and how ought they to decide them? are legal norms authoritative (do they give rise to special obligations or reasons for action)? what are the legitimate sources of law? and the like. Indeed, from a jurisprudential standpoint, what almost all of Duxbury's writers and movements have in common is a lack of philosophical depth or sophistication in matters of legal theory. It would be rather a shame—and grossly unfair—if the distinguishing feature of "American jurisprudence" were to turn out to be philosophical ineptitude!

There has been, unfortunately, rather too little writing on the question of the distinctive subject-matter and concerns of jurisprudence.[9] But Duxbury simply

---

[8] These movements have had several institutional affiliations. Stanford, Georgetown, and Wisconsin have concentrations of both Critical Legal Studies ("C.L.S.") and Critical Race Theory writers; Harvard was the early "hotbed" of C.L.S.; Columbia has several prominent Critical Race Theorists. Interestingly, a number of the leading American law schools—Yale, Chicago, Michigan, N.Y.U., Texas, Virginia—have been untouched by C.L.S., and largely untouched by Critical Race Theory.

[9] A notable exception is Michael S. Moore, "The Need for a Theory of Legal Theories: Assessing Pragmatic Instrumentalism," *Cornell Law Review* 69 (1984): 988–1013.

brushes the issue aside by noting that the word is used in different ways and that "there can be no universal consensus concerning what makes an idea 'jurisprudential' " (1). But "universal consensus" is nowhere else taken as a necessary condition for analyzing or demarcating a concept, so why burden "jurisprudence" alone with meeting that impossible standard? While our account of the field of "jurisprudence" should do some justice to common understandings—"jurisprudence," after all, ought not to turn out to be coextensive with physics—in the end the more important question is whether, from the standpoint of inquiry and research, it is (or has proved to be) intellectually fruitful to conceive of the field as having certain boundaries.

In this regard, I find jurisprudence—as the study of philosophical problems about law—most helpfully thought of on the model of philosophy of science.[10] The philosopher of science, typically at least, does not critique scientific theories or engage in scientific work itself.[11] What he typically does do, however, is examine two broad types of issues: *epistemological* and *ontological*. First, he tries to describe and assess (in epistemic terms) the "methods" scientists employ to discover truths about the world. Thus, for example, philosophers of science frequently ask questions like: What is involved in "confirming" a theory? What constitutes giving an "explanation" of a phenomenon? Secondly, the philosopher of science tries to determine the *ontological* commitments scientific theories actually do have, or ought to have. Are scientific theories, for example, literally true, or should we conceive of the unobservable entities they posit as merely "useful fictions"?

If we take jurisprudence to stand in an analogous relationship to law, then we might say that the jurisprudent does not critique substantive legal doctrines or engage in legal work itself (e.g. arguing or deciding cases), but rather: (i) studies, elucidates and perhaps critiques or revises the *methods* used by lawyers and judges to "discover" legal conclusions (e.g. the "methods" of legal reasoning, of legal interpretation, etc.); and (ii) examines the *ontological* commitments actually manifest in the law or that ought to be part of our conception of law (e.g. what is the status of a claim like "Leiter is liable for his negligence in this case" or, more generally, what is it to say that law "exists" on some point?).[12] To take these questions as central to jurisprudence is to take the rich tradition of theories of adjudication and of law associated with names like Austin, Kelsen, Hart, Raz, and Dworkin as central to jurisprudence. This understanding of jurisprudence does, happily,

---

[10] The idea for the analogy was first suggested to me by my colleague William C. Powers, Jr.

[11] One exception is certain work in the philosophy of physics which is hard to distinguish from the work of theoretical physicists themselves. The work of the philosopher David Malament at the University of California at Irvine is a good example in this regard.

[12] It is important to note that views on both sets of questions are implicit in almost all our discussions about the law. To criticize a court's reasoning, for example, is to presuppose a view about judicial *method*; to accuse a judge (as so often happens in the United States) of imposing her "personal values" rather than applying the law presupposes a view about what the law is, about what law "exists" on point.

make a place for the Legal Realists and some of their heirs, writers who can be understood, for example, as launching skeptical attacks upon the claim of "method" in lawyering and judging. At the same time, much of the literature of "policy science", of law and economics, of Legal Process, and of feminism or Critical Race Theory—whatever its intrinsic interest—turns out not to be jurisprudential at all. Such work is, more often, a contribution to political or constitutional theory, to legal pedagogy or to the actual development of substantive law. Such literature, however, typically sheds no special light on the *methods* of legal reasoning or the *ontological* commitments of lawyers and judges.

None of the genuinely jurisprudential questions are much discussed or illuminated in Duxbury's book. This is no surprise. The introductory chapter is titled, "Jurisprudence as Intellectual History" (1), and it tells us that, "Ideas have histories, and jurisprudence is a much more enlightening and engaging enterprise when it focuses on those histories" (7). But surely this cannot be right: jurisprudence cannot be intellectual history, for without actual jurisprudence—without actual philosophical theorizing about law—there would be no ideas for "jurisprudence as intellectual history" to study in the first place. More than a generation after Hart expressed the pedagogic hope that his book "may discourage the belief that a book on legal theory is primarily a book from which one learns what other books contain,"[13] it is disappointing to see precisely this misconception at the core of a major work with "jurisprudence" in its title.

Duxbury's book, in short, does not offer much to readers who want to think philosophically about law—that is, precisely those who, in my view, are interested in jurisprudence. The book would have been more aptly, if not more attractively, titled, "Patterns of American Non-Philosophical Thinking About Law." So understood, there can be little question that Duxbury has provided us with an extremely engaging and useful survey of what American academic lawyers—and some non-academic ones as well—have said about law and judicial decision-making from the 1870s to the early 1990s. The question remains, though, whether even this geographical demarcation for the subject-matter of the book is a fruitful one.

II. Patterns, Revolts, and the History of Ideas

Duxbury is not the first writer to traverse this territory; the intellectual history of Legal Realism, for example, has been effectively covered before,[14] and Duxbury

---

[13] H.L.A. Hart, *The Concept of Law* (n. 6 above), p. vi.
[14] See, e.g., W.E. Rumble, *American Legal Realism: Skepticism, Reform, and the Judicial Process* (Ithaca: Cornell University Press, 1968); William Twining, *Karl Llewellyn and the Realist Movement* (Norman: University of Oklahoma Press, 1973); G. Edward White, *Patterns of American Legal Thought* (Indianapolis: Bobbs-Merrill, 1978); Laura Kalman, *Legal Realism at Yale: 1927–1960* (Chapel Hill: University of North Carolina Press, 1986); John Henry Schlegel, *American Legal Realism and Empirical Social Science* (Chapel Hill: University of North Carolina Press, 1995).

makes appropriate use of the work of his predecessors. What he has given us, that his predecessors have not, is a far more comprehensive picture of the "patterns" of American legal thinking, one that goes well beyond the familiar story of the Realist reaction to turn-of-the-century legal formalism (about which more below). In this regard, he has a more explicit historiographical aim, that bears on the question of whether "American" is a fruitful theoretical category in the history of legal thinking. Duxbury wants to contest what he calls the "pendulum swing" vision of American legal thought, according to which the last hundred years is characterized by a back-and-forth between "formalistic" views of law (e.g. Langdellianism, Legal Process) and "realistic" views (e.g. Legal Realism, Critical Legal Studies) (2). The virtue of the pendulum swing view, of course, is that it explains why all these writers ought to be considered together. In opposition to this, however, Duxbury claims that American legal thinking has been "character-ized not by the pendulum-swing view of history but by complex patterns of ideas" (2). Ideas, explains Duxbury, "tend to emerge and decline" (3); "rarely do we see them born or die" (3). These claims strike me as rather too mundane to warrant the prominent place Duxbury assigns them. Indeed, that Duxbury identifies no proponents of the "pendulum swing" version of American legal thought suggests that it may be a straw man.

This impression, unfortunately, is only reinforced by Duxbury's argument that there was never—as the title of a famous book by Morton White would have it— a "revolt" against formalism in American thought.[15] To the contrary, says Duxbury, "the movement away from formalist legal thinking was very slow and hesitant" (3), rather than leading "almost immediately to the birth of a new jurisprudence" (64). But this seems a rather thin argument, attributing, as it does, a silly view of timing to the historian of "revolts." Even political "revolts," like the Russian Revolution of 1917—the "revolt against Tsardom" we might say—have long, slow-moving prehistories, even if actual armed conflict occurs over a rather short period of time. This is even more the case in the realm of ideas, as everyone must certainly recognize: unlike political revolutions, there is rarely a moment in the history of ideas when the king's head is lopped off and we know the revolution has occurred. Duxbury, himself, concedes that there was a "movement away from for-malist legal thinking"; he contests only the proper description of the timing. Yet, again, it is not clear who holds the implausible, opposing view. Duxbury's is still a pendulum view of American legal thinking, it is just his is a slower moving pendu-lum. Happily, though, the pendulum view, as made more nuanced by Duxbury, provides precisely the rationale for this kind of book. For there can be no denying that the basic patterns of ideas—realistic and formalist—have indeed been influ-ential in American legal education and practice.

---

[15] Morton White, *Social Thought in America: The Revolt Against Formalism* (Oxford: Oxford University Press, 1976).

III. From Formalism to Realism

At the heart of any story about "American jurisprudence" are two movements dating from the late 19th-century and the first three decades of the 20th-century. The first is the "legal formalism" that both permeated decisions of the U.S. Supreme Court circa 1900 and that had as its leading academic proponent Christopher Columbus Langdell, first Dean of the Harvard Law School in the late 19th century. The second is the "Legal Realist" reaction to formalism that reached its peak in the 1920s and early 1930s, centered largely in a group of legal academics at Columbia and Yale, but taking its inspiration from late 19th-century writings of Oliver Wendell Holmes, Jr., among others.

Formalism, according to Duxbury's somewhat overbroad definition,[16] is "the endeavour to treat particular fields of knowledge as if governed by interrelated, fundamental and logically demonstrable principles of science" (10). In law, this basic formalistic impulse appears, says Duxbury, in two forms: in "Langdellian legal science" in the law schools, and in "the entrenched faith in *laissez-faire*" in the courts (11). According to the former, it was possible through study of prior judicial opinions to ascertain the fundamental principles of law in any domain; once those were firmly established, all the other rules could be deduced accordingly. The crux of Langdell's formalism is well-described by Anthony Kronman:

> To understand a given branch of legal doctrine in a scientific fashion, one must begin . . . by first identifying the elementary principles on which the field of law is based (for example, in the case of contract law, the principle that the minds of the parties must meet for a contract to be formed and that each must give or promise to give something of value to the other in return). These elementary principles are to be discovered by surveying the case law in that area. Once they have been identified, it is then the task of scholars to work out, in an analytically rigorous manner, the subordinate principles entailed by them. When these subordinate principles have all been stated in propositional form and the relations of entailment among them clarified, they will . . . together constitute a well-ordered system of rules that offers the best possible description of a particular branch of law—the best answer to the question of what the law in that area *is* . . . [I]ndividual cases that cannot be fit within this system must be rejected as mistakes.[17]

By contrast, formalism in the courts appeared in the guise of a "fundamental belief in individualism as a moral and economic ideal" (26), requiring, in particular, the preservation of economic exchange—whether of goods or labor—free of state regulation. This judicial formalism finds its most notorious expression in the U.S. Supreme Court's 1905 decision in *Lochner v. New York*[18] in which the Court

---

[16] See the discussion of Duxbury's mistaken description of the Realists as tacit formalists, below.

[17] Anthony Kronman, *The Lost Lawyer* (Cambridge, Mass.: Harvard University Press, 1993), p. 171; cf. Duxbury, (n. 5 above), pp. 15–23 for a somewhat less tidy account to the same effect.

[18] 198 U.S. 45 (1905).

invalidated a New York law regulating the working conditions of bakers on the grounds that it violated the "liberty of contract" protected by the Fourteenth Amendment to the U.S. Constitution (30–1). The decision, like many of that period, was indifferent to the rampant inequality in bargaining power between employers and employees.

One difficulty with this account of formalism is that Duxbury never quite explains how the two strands hang together. In particular, it is not clear how the commitment to *laissez-faire* in the courts embodies the "formalistic" impulse to make law scientific. One suspects that in calling this formalism, Duxbury is animated more by a desire to show Realism to be "one of the intellectual bedrocks of modern critical legal studies" (25). For he later (105–111; cf. 471) follows the C.L.S. writers[19] in treating the critique of free-market economics by the economist Robert Hale and the philosopher Morris Cohen as key elements of the "Realist" reaction to formalism. The difficulty is that Hale is, at best, a marginal figure in Realism,[20] having nothing to say about the central Realist project of developing a theory of adjudication, while Cohen was a well-known *critic* of Realism! One of the central features of the C.L.S. reinvention of Realism, which Duxbury unhappily recasts now as historical fact, was to treat these two figures, and their attack on *laissez-faire*, as central to (rather than simply contemporaneous with) Realism.[21]

Duxbury's two strands of formalism—academic and judicial—are really one: the formalism of Langdell, so aptly described by Kronman in the passage quoted above. Applied to courts, it simply becomes the view that judicial decisions should conform to the tidy deductive pattern of discovering an applicable rule or principle of law (as fixed by the Langedellian method), subsuming the facts under that rule, and inferring the outcome. Like Langdell's academic science of law, judicial formalism was distinguished by an absolute indifference to social and economic considerations: law and legal decision-making are to be understood as taking place within a hermetic logical universe of clear-cut legal rules and deductive inferences. Thus, in its formalistic opinion in *United States v. E.C. Knight Co.*,[22]

[19] See, e.g., Joseph William Singer, "Legal Realism Now," *California Law Review* 76 (1988): 465–544; Morton Horwitz, *The Transformation of American Law 1870–1960* (Oxford: Oxford University Press, 1992). See also, the selections and introductory materials in W.W. Fisher et al. (eds.), *American Legal Realism* (New York: Oxford University Press, 1993), a volume which views Realism through a C.L.S. lens.

[20] Milton Handler—an early Realist, Columbia law professor from 1927 to 1972, and friend of both Hale and Karl Llewellyn—has remarked that Hale "carried very little influence with his colleagues . . . I'm amazed now to find him regarded as one of the great Legal Realists" (unpublished memo, April 27, 1995, p. 12). Although Handler is better known as the leading antitrust scholar and litigator in the United States during the 1950s and 1960s, his early contributions to Realism are discussed in two famous papers by Llewellyn: "A Realistic Jurisprudence—The Next Step," *Columbia Law Review* 30 (1930), p. 454 and n. 22, and in "Some Realism About Realism—Responding to Dean Pound," *Harvard Law Review* 44 (1931), pp. 1237, 1240 and n. 42, 1244 and n. 55, and 1245.

[21] Towards the end of the book, Duxbury even starts referring to "the basic realist-cum-critical legal insight that law is political" (502). As I discuss below, however, it is hardly clear that the Realist view is well-described by the phrase "law is political," even if C.L.S. is.   [22] 156 U.S. 1 (1895).

the U.S. Supreme Court held that the regulation of a sugar manufacturer (responsible for 90% of sugar production in the United States!) was not within the power of Congress to regulate "interstate commerce," since, *by definition*, "interstate commerce" could not include *manufacturing*, which takes place wholly within a state. That, in reality, decisions by E.C. Knight Co. would affect the sugar market nationwide was of no concern to a formalistically-minded court applying "plain meanings" and clear-cut rules. Although it is true, then, that the formalist American courts of the turn-of-the-century were pro-*laissez-faire*, this is merely a contingent, not necessary, truth about their formalism: courts in communist societies could be just as formalistic. Formalism is a *style* of decision-making, not a substantive political program.

Whereas Duxbury does attempt to define "formalism," he takes a rather less satisfactory approach to Realism. It "was more a mood than a movement" he says, adding a few lines later it is "more appropriate to describe it as an intellectual tendency" (69). The heart of this "mood" was opposition to formalism along both the dimensions detailed in the prior chapter. Even so, says, Duxbury, we must in the end "recognize the formalist elements in realist thought" itself (130)! All of this strikes me as unduly vague and even misleading, for reasons I shall explain momentarily. Whatever the faults in his account of Realism, however, Duxbury has performed a very useful service to intellectual history by locating themes from the "Realist" literature—broadly construed—in their wider intellectual context: in empirically-minded political science (95–7), in institutional economics (97–111), in behaviorist psychology (126–7), in Progressive political thought (114–19), in the type of materialist history associated with Charles Beard (113–14), and in Veblenesque sociology (99 ff.). Although others have noted some of these influences on Realism, Duxbury is the first to bring them all together and to paint a complete picture of the whole landscape of ideas in which Realism took root.

The difficulty with Duxbury's approach is that "negative" definitions of Realism fail to do justice to a considerable amount of agreement among Realists about what courts *are* doing. Indeed, Duxbury himself correctly notes later on that the Realists shared the "assumption . . . that judges—stimulated, primarily, by the facts before them rather than by the rules to which those facts might be fitted—work backwards, 'from a desirable conclusion to one or another of a stock of logical premises'" (123) (quoting Max Radin). But this descriptive thesis about what judges are really doing when they decide cases surely constitutes a positive (as opposed to merely negative) thesis about adjudication: what I have called elsewhere "the Core Claim" of Realism.[23] The Realists then divide over the question of what it is that determines how judges respond to the facts: whether it is idiosyncratic facts about each judge's personality (as Jerome Frank believed) or whether it is far more common "sociological" facts about judges (e.g. their background, their professional socialization experiences, and the like) (as Karl Llewellyn, Felix

---

[23] See Ch. 1.

Cohen, Underhill Moore, and the majority of the Realists held). Over time, our image of Legal Realism has suffered "Frankification," resulting in what Duxbury rightly calls "the popular burlesque" of Realism according to which judicial decisions are determined by "the moods and whims of the particular judge" (67–8). Unfortunately, Duxbury never clearly demarcates the Frankified burlesque of Realism from the mainstream of Legal Realism, which was far more influential.

Had Duxbury organized his discussion around this positive doctrine—the "Core Claim" shared by all the key Realists—he would have been able to tell a more principled story about the Realist interest in social science. Instead, he ends up claiming that "little effort was made by any of the so-called realists to explain, why, exactly, the integration of law with the broader social sciences should prove to be such an enlightened initiative" (130). This comment, however, betrays a fairly serious lack of understanding of what motivated the Realists.

Roughly, we may reconstruct the Realist line of thought this way. Starting from a pragmatic commitment to producing theories of law that would be useful to lawyers, the Realists recognize that a Langdellian legal science fails on that score: cases are not decided on the basis of purely "legal" rules and reasons, but rather on the basis of a court's "response" to the facts of the case. A lawyer who takes his cues from Langdell will not have a very good idea why courts do what they do; to figure out what courts are *really* up to, we must attend to the ways they respond to particular, recurring factual scenarios (to "situation-types"). These responses, happily, appear to fall into certain patterns (at least according to the "sociological" wing of Realism, noted above), sometimes reflecting the "norms" of the commercial culture in which a dispute had originally arisen,[24] sometimes reflecting shared fact-specific judgments about "fairness" or "socio-economic" utility in particular contexts.[25] A useful legal theory, then, ought to identify and describe these patterns, stating, as it were, the correlations between situation-types and judicial decisions. The social sciences then—conceived "positivistically" (that is, on the model of the natural sciences)—were the tool for performing this crucial task. By approaching law like a behaviorist psychologist, an anthropologist, or an empirical sociologist, the Realists hoped to discover the real patterns of judicial decision-making, thus providing information of practical value to lawyers.

Elements of this story do make scattered appearances in Duxbury's version of events (especially *circa* pp. 96 and 128), but the big picture never comes in to focus. This lack of a more refined jurisprudential picture of Realism also allows Duxbury to say much later that, "Legal realism...constituted a rather half-hearted, largely unsuccessful attack on legal formalism" (206). But this misses the

---

[24] This aspect of Realism is well discussed by the eminent American scholar of the Uniform Commercial Code, James J. White, in "The Influence of American Legal Realism on Article 2 of the Uniform Commercial Code," in W. Krawietz et al. (eds.), *Prescriptive Formality and Normative Rationality in Modern Legal Systems* (Berlin: Duncker & Humblot, 1994), esp. at p. 401.

[25] Thus, Realist texts characteristically rejected the idea that there was a uniform body of law; instead, there are many sub-bodies of law specific to particular factual contexts. See, e.g., Leon Green,

very profound impact the sociological wing of Llewellyn, Moore, and Herman Oliphant has had on American law, even if the Realists themselves never did much serious social-scientific work. My colleague Charles Alan Wright, the leading American authority on civil procedure and federal courts, describes himself as a Legal Realist, yet he is also now the first law professor to serve as President of the American Law Institute, which oversees the "Restatements of Law." The Restatements, as Duxbury notes (147–8), were an object of bitter attack by the early Realists, who viewed them as a mere exercise in Langdellian folly! Yet as Wright-the-Realist points out to me, the Restatements have internalized the important lesson of Oliphant and other Realists: that there is no "law of contracts" *per se*, but rather many laws of contracts for the many concrete but recurring contexts in which contractual disputes arise. Increasingly, then, the Restatements "restate" the law not in terms of broad, generally applicable rules, but rather in terms of fact- and context-specific legal rules.[26] In other words, the Restatements now try to accomplish precisely what the Realists thought one needed positivistic social science to accomplish: a statement of the fact-specific patterns of decision followed by the courts. That Duxbury—an English lawyer, unduly influenced it seems by the C.L.S. version of Realism—should have neglected this particular legacy of Realism is not surprising.

Yet Duxbury does recognize that the Realists shared the Langdellian ideal of certainty in law—though he puts the point misleadingly. The Realists, he says (quoting Grant Gilmore), were "Langdellians *malgré eux*," adding that we must "recognize the formalist elements in realist thought" (130). Duxbury explains that for the Realists,

... judicial decisions "could and should become more predictable" [citation omitted] ... [P]redictivist-inspired realism treats as notionally desirable the facilitation of a formally certain, "prediction-friendly" system of law ... And it is thus that realism ... appears to

---

The Judicial Process in Tort Cases (St. Paul: West Publishing, 1931) (organizing the law of torts not by doctrinal categories—e.g. negligence, intentional torts, etc.—but by situation-types, like "surgical operations," "keeping of animals," and "traffic and transportation"); Charles Alan Wright, *Cases on Remedies* (St. Paul: West Publishing, 1955) (organized not by type of legal remedy, but by type of injury).

This type of Realist approach to legal doctrine continues to be influential in the United States. For example, the leading American authority on the law of remedies, Douglas Laycock, begins his seminal attack on the irreparable injury rule (the rule that says courts will not prevent harm, when money damages will compensate for the harm) by noting that a survey of 1,400 cases shows that, "Courts do prevent harm when they can. Judicial opinions recite the rule constantly, but they do not apply it ... When courts reject plaintiff's choice of remedy, there is always some other reason, and that reason has nothing to do with the irreparable injury rule. We can identify the real reasons for decision, and use those reasons to explain old cases and decide new cases." *The Death of the Irreparable Injury Rule* (New York: Oxford University Press, 1991), p. vii. Laycock goes on to note that, "An intuitive sense of justice has led judges to produce sensible results, but there has been no similar pressure to produce sensible explanations." id., p. ix. Laycock's project, in other words, is to make "doctrine reflect ... reality," i.e. the reality of how the courts really decide these cases, id., p. 281. Cf. Herman Oliphant, "A Return to Stare Decisis," *American Bar Association Journal* 14 (1928): 71–6, 107, 159–62.

26 Indeed, Oliphant's own interesting example (in "A Return to Stare Decisis," id.) about conflicting court decisions regarding contractual promises not to compete has now been incorporated into

attempt to discredit one formalist conception of law only to replace it with another...
The assumption that it may be possible to predict future legal decisions with considerable,
if not quite total, accuracy is hardly less formalist...than the basic Langdellian belief that
legal doctrine is reducible to a handful of common law principles which may be applied
uncontroversially to future legal disputes. (131)

The difficulty with this confused analysis is that, to the extent it is true, it is trivial
and familiar, and to the extent it is not familiar, it is false. Let me explain.

It is well known that the Realists, like Langdell, wanted to develop a science of
law; their dispute with Langdell was over what that meant.[27] This should not be
surprising to anyone: roughly the mid-19th century to the mid-20th century
marked the heyday of philosophical "Positivism," by which I mean the view that
natural science is the paradigm of all genuine knowledge. For any discipline to
constitute "knowledge," on the Positivist view, it must emulate natural science.
Langdell was inspired by this model (as Duxbury correctly notes at p. 15), as were
the Legal Realists. The 1920s, let us remember, was manifestly *not* the age of postmodernism and deconstruction![28] That the Realists should not have shared the
impulse to be "scientific" would have been the real surprise.

But only by equating "formalism" with the scientific impulse does Duxbury's
accusation of formalism make any sense. Yet this is an equation that obscures
more than it reveals. What has always distinguished "formalism" in law is *not*
simply the thought (common to the Realists and Langdell) that adjudicative outcomes might have causal determinants and thus be predictable, but rather that
they are predictable in virtue of the law being *rationally* determinate: that is, in
virtue of the class of legitimate legal reasons justifying a unique decision in each
case.[29] It is the latter that distinguishes Langdell's science of law, and legal formalism proper, from Legal Realism. For the formalist, decisions can be predicted
because the law is rationally determinate: if you know the relevant legal rules and
you know the distinctive methods of legal reasoning, you know what courts will
do. For the Realists, this is pure mythology: the prior cases and statutes can be
legitimately manipulated in different ways, so that there is rarely a determinate
answer as a matter of law, at least not in those cases that reach the stage of review
by higher courts. For the Realists, cases are predictable, to the extent they are, not
because the legal reasons are determinate, but because a social-scientific inquiry
can identify those non-legal factors that really determine the course of decision.
To say, as Duxbury does, that the "more general realist view" is "that there is an

the Restatement of Contracts. See especially §188 and "Comment" in *Restatement of Contracts 2d*
(St. Paul: American Law Institute Publishers, 1981). (I am grateful to Mark Gergen for bringing this
to my attention.)

[27] For one recent example of someone who makes this point, see Kronman, (n. 17 above).

[28] *Contra*, e.g., the quite anachronistic reading of Realism in Gary Peller, "The Metaphysics of
American Law," *California Law Review* 73 (1985): 1151–290.

[29] For the important distinction between "rational" and "causal" indeterminacy, see Leiter, "Legal
Indeterminacy," *Legal Theory* 1 (1995): 481–92.

implicit rationality about the legal process which allows for the possibility of pre-dicting future decisions with a fair degree of accuracy" (133–4) is a non-sequitur: that outcomes be determinate does not require that they be *rationally* determin-ate. (Think of Freud's psychic determinism.) To collapse Realism into formalism because of the Realist interest in predicting outcomes is to obliterate one of the crucial theoretical distinctions between Legal Realism and Langdell's formalistic jurisprudence.

IV. After Realism

I have concentrated on Duxbury's problematic discussion of Realism because it is in Legal Realism that the most important jurisprudential issues are broached. But almost two-thirds of Duxbury's book is devoted to surveying the movements in American law schools that followed Realism.

As Duxbury astutely notes (157–8), Realism tended to focus disproportion-ately on private law; two of the initial post-Realist developments, by contrast, took as their focus the many important areas of law not concerned primarily with relations in the marketplace. In the 1940s and after, Harold Lasswell and Myres McDougal at Yale focused on international law in launching their "policy science," "which purported to accord far more significance to the matter of policy formation than so-called legal realists had ever done" (164). In particular, Lasswell and McDougal wanted to go beyond the Realists in using social science not simply for *describing* what courts do, but as "an invaluable source of normative guidance" (172). "The purpose of the social sciences," for policy science, "is to demonstrate that liberal-democratic values are essentially correct values" (175).

How exactly "policy science" discharges this latter task is a bit unclear. Indeed, in retrospect, policy "science" looks rather silly, a "science" in name only. Although it had its biggest impact on international law scholarship—where it soon devolved, in the hands of McDougal and many of his followers (not, most notably, the radical international lawyer Richard Falk), into lame apologetics for American impe-rialism—its attempt to make policy-formation scientific through systematic thinking about values has borne no fruit. The significance of policy science, according to Duxbury, is that it "marks the first American attempt to conceive of . . . lawyering . . . as an overtly political endeavour" (164).

By contrast, the Legal Process "school" of the 1950s has proved more enduring—in part because, as Duxbury notes, it was less a "school" than a certain long-standing attitude towards lawyering, "an attitude premised in every instance on the belief that those who respect and exercise the faculty of reason will be rewarded with the discovery of a priori criteria which give sense and legitimacy to their legal activities" (208). This "faith in reason" (205) reworks, in more sophisti-cated garb, the formalistic ideal of a rationally determinate legal order, but one in which it is not simply "deductive logic" that does the work but rather the "reason which is embodied in the fabric of the law itself" and which is expressed in such themes as "principle, purpose, integrity and prudence" (205).

In perhaps the book's most valuable chapter, Duxbury traces the key themes of what he calls "process jurisprudence"—reasoned, principled decision-making as the crux of the judicial function; the distinct roles of judiciary and legislature; judicial restraint and the limits of discretion—through the work of John Dickinson in the 1930s, Lon Fuller in the 1940s, Henry Hart and Albert Sacks in the 1950s (whose classic text, *The Legal Process*,[30] gave the movement its name), constitutional theorists like Herbert Wechsler and Alexander Bickel in the late 1950s and 1960s, and Ronald Dworkin's theory of adjudication of the 1960s and 1970s.[31] Although part of his purpose in recounting this lengthy history is to show that "process jurisprudence did not emerge in response to legal realism" (298), Duxbury himself concedes the obvious fact that, "the process perspective was at its most vital during the years following the Second World War" (298). In other words, even if there were "process"-type themes before the 1950s, it was only when the Realists had been discredited as giving comfort to totalitarianism by undermining faith in the "rule of law" that "process jurisprudence" came to dominate American legal thinking.

Duxbury argues, somewhat more plausibly, that "process" thinking was not unique to the law schools, that from the political science of Robert Dahl to the political philosophy of John Rawls, there was a shared "attitude concerning the importance of rationality within a democracy" (297). But I think Duxbury overstates his case when he says that "faith in reason lies at the heart of the American jurisprudential culture" as "the effort to preserve the image of adjudication as an apolitical activity" (298). To the contrary, this is but one pole of American "jurisprudential" culture; the other is precisely the realistic perspective, from Legal Realism to C.L.S., which does not share this romanticized "faith in reason". Although "process jurisprudence"—at least until Dworkin—is notably unclear or sometimes just superficial on all the key philosophical questions—the nature of practical reason, the distinction between good and bad reasoning, the goals of a legal or political system, the legitimate sources of law—Duxbury is surely right that the "faith in reason," the faith that we may understand judicial decisions as determined within the space of legal reasons, is a recurring one in American legal thought. But what we might call "skepticism about reason"—the no-nonsense realistic appraisal of what courts are really doing—has equal claim to being the

---

[30] Widely circulated in mimeographed form since the late 1950s, the materials were finally published forty years later: Henry Hart & Albert Sacks, *The Legal Process*, ed. W. Eskridge & P. Frickey (Mineola: Foundation Press, 1994).

[31] Somewhat less plausibly, Duxbury tries to trace "process" thinking back to Langdell, John Chipman Gray, and Benjamin Cardozo. Here, however, his own critical comments about Herbert Hovenkamp's attempts to identify a "first" law and economics movement at the turn of the century seem especially apt: "while, in the early part of the century, certain themes were identified which would come to feature prominently in the development of [process jurisprudence], these themes were merely sketched or suggested rather than explored" (322).

opposing pole of "American jurisprudential culture." Despite his claims at the beginning of the book, then, Duxbury's own work supports a variation on the "pendulum swing" view of American legal thought.

This brings us, however, to the vexed question of where to locate law and economics, the subject of Duxbury's Chapter 5.[32] Duxbury usefully canvasses different arguments construing economic analysis as a continuation of both the "formalistic" (including process) and "realistic" strands in American legal thinking (301–09, 312–13), concluding that to understand its influence in American law schools, "we must appreciate the degree to which law and economics is profoundly distinct from, rather than how it bears superficial affinities to, realist thought" (309). Yet the three points Duxbury calls attention to in this regard do not really make the case: he mentions that there was work in law and economics prior to Realism (310); that unlike the Realists, economic analysts of law were not interested in the social sciences *per se*, but only in economics (310); and that economic analysis, unlike Realism, was not concerned "with the processes of reasoning" by which judges decide cases (311).

On the first point, Duxbury himself again concedes the obvious: that turn-of-the-century economic work in law is a distant relative of the economic analysis of Richard Posner and company (310; cf. 405–06). The second point presupposes that central to Realism is an indiscriminate interest in all the social sciences, a view, as we have already seen, that is superficial. The Realists were interested in social science because they found conventional legal argument and analysis did not illuminate the real patterns of judicial decision. In this respect, Realism has much in common with those strands of economic analysis which see economics as describing the real, underlying logic of the common law (cf. 410–14). Finally, it is unclear in what sense, exactly, the Realists were interested in "the processes of judicial reasoning": given that they thought such processes indeterminate, they, like the economists, are driven to look for explanations of judicial decisions elsewhere.

Indeed, Duxbury articulates the main reason to view economic analysis as the "realistic" swing of the pendulum: for unlike the Legal Process writers, and very much like the Legal Realists, economists in law "make no pretence that there exist principles which provide objectively correct solutions to adjudicative controversies" (312). Economic analysis, like Realism, seems predicated on a thoroughgoing skepticism about the adequacy of existing legal categories, and the need for an alternative explanation of the actual course of decisions. Duxbury quotes Richard Posner saying that, "the positive role [of economics]—that of explaining

---

[32] I should note that Duxbury does an admirably clear-headed job reviewing the main themes of law and economics, from the logic of its assault on governmental regulation (namely "that the absence of regulation facilitates free market pricing, that free market pricing engenders competition, and that competition engenders allocative efficiency"(376–77)), to a pithy account of Ronald Coase's views ("Market forces...internalize costs irrespective of rules imposing liability" (387)), to the core assumption about human beings as rational utility-maximizers that animates neo-classical economics (cf. 378). I particularly liked Duxbury's characterization of the widespread view of Richard Posner's application of economics to non-market arenas of life as "Swift without the satire" (416).

the rules and outcomes in the legal system as they are—is . . . even more important" than generating normative proposals (410). But surely this is precisely the
Realists' view too, even if they did not think economics would provide the best
explanation. Elaborating on Posner's view, Duxbury writes: "Owing to the fact
that judicial opinions are frequently suffused with rhetoric, it is invariably very
difficult to figure out what types of concerns lead judges to reach the decisions
that they do" (410). Yet the resonance with Realist views here is striking; thus
Llewellyn writes:

[I]f I am right, finding out what the judges *say* is but the beginning of your task. You will
have to take what they say and compare it with what they *do*. You will have to see whether
what they say matches with what they do. You will have to be distrustful of whether they
themselves know (any better than other men) the ways of their own doing, and of whether
they describe it accurately, even if they know it.[33]

The task Llewellyn identifies is, of course, precisely the task the Posnerian lawyer-
economist would discharge, as Duxbury himself makes clear.

What makes Duxbury's resistance to understanding economic analysis as the
"Realist" swing of the pendulum in American legal thought so peculiar—despite
the obvious affinity in program (if not in details) between the two movements—is
that without such a way of understanding law and economics he is forced, finally,
to say that, "Economic analysis of law has generally evolved independently of
modern American jurisprudential concerns" (416)! But if that is the case, then
what is this lengthy and useful overview of economic analysis of law even doing in
a book on "Patterns of American Jurisprudence"? The answer—the one Duxbury
resists—is that while lawyer-economists may not have been taking their intellectual cues from Realism, the basic descriptive and explanatory project is strikingly
similar to the one the Realists advocated.

In a final chapter, Duxbury takes us from the 1970s to the 1990s in American
law schools, looking primarily at C.L.S., as well as more recent offshoots, like
Feminist Legal Theory, Critical Race Theory, pragmatism, deconstruction, and
postmodernism. He takes as a focal point the question: "how did [C.L.S.] touch a
nerve in the American law schools?" (423)—referring to the substantial controversy that C.L.S. generated during the 1980s. Duxbury's answer is that C.L.S. threat-
ened the "quest for consensus" that had "dominated" American "jurisprudence"
since World War II: "At the heart of both process jurisprudence and law and economics rests not only a faith in consensus but also a belief that the liberty of the
individual is something which legal theory ought to affirm and promote" (424).

C.L.S., according to Duxbury, shattered this "consensus," though it did not try
to put a new, positive program in its place. He writes:

Critical legal studies has been written off for failing to supply answers to the problems
which realism merely posed: adjudication is still a political affair; economic freedom still

---

[33] Karl Llewellyn, *The Bramble Bush* (New York: Oceana, 1930), p. 5.

conceals coercion. Yet if there is a fundamental lesson which critical legal studies teaches, it is that there are no right answers to the problems which realism posed. The basic conclusion of critical legal studies is that lawyers must constantly be reminded of these problems... (427–8; cf. 470)

If this were right, this would indeed render C.L.S. a rather boring footnote to American Legal Realism. But it is almost surely wrong, and Duxbury's own subsequent discussion undermines this picture. Several respects in which C.L.S. goes beyond Realism immediately come to mind:

(1) The Realists argued that the "law" was indeterminate largely by appealing to familiar methods of legal and judicial reasoning, and showing how these methods often conflicted, leading, e.g., to a "strict" and a "loose" interpretation of a precedent, or to opposed ways of reading the same statutory provision.[34] C.L.S. writers, by contrast, take a rather different, and more philosophically ambitious tact. They locate the source of "indeterminacy" in law in one of two sources: either in general features of language itself (drawing here—not always accurately—on the semantic skepticism associated with Wittgenstein and Derrida[35]); or in the existence of "contradictory" moral and political principles that they claim underlie the substantive law, understood at a suitable level of abstraction.[36] Duxbury himself recognizes this strand of C.L.S., which he aptly describes as claiming,

... that liberal consciousness is somehow a false or corrupted consciousness, that there exists within liberal thought—liberal legal thought included—a tension so fundamental, so irresolvable, that it must ultimately implode and make way for radical social transformation. (455)

(2) This strategy of argument signals the rather curious intellectual pedigree of C.L.S., a pedigree that Duxbury does not appear to recognize.[37] For what C.L.S.

[34] For discussion, see Ch. 1. Remarkably, in the book's worst howler, Duxbury asserts that the Realists "neglected to consider in detail the question of why there is uncertainty in law" (460)! This leads him to think that C.L.S. was the first "to figure out from where it is that legal indeterminacy springs" (460).

[35] For a critical discussion of this aspect of C.L.S., see Jules L. Coleman & Brian Leiter, "Determinacy, Objectivity, and Authority," *University of Pennsylvania Law Review* 142 (1993): 568–72.

[36] The most famous example of this strategy of C.L.S. argument is Duncan Kennedy, "Form and Substance in Private Law Adjudication," *Harvard Law Review* 89 (1976): 1685–778. Another, somewhat more sweeping example of this argumentative strategy can be found in Mark Kelman, *A Guide to Critical Legal Studies* (Cambridge, Mass.: Harvard University Press, 1987). Kelman's arguments, however, strike me as philosophically unsound.

[37] Duxbury *does* note the influence of Hegel on the C.L.S. idea that there is a "fundamental contradiction" in society between our need for other people and our fear of being dominated by them (460–1). See Duncan Kennedy, "The Structure of Blackstone's Commentaries," *Buffalo Law Review* 28 (1979): 205–382. This theme is vaguely evocative of Hegel's notion that the self can only be constituted through the recognition of other persons. (More precisely, Hegel's view is that there is a contradiction between wanting to be a "self-consciousness" and wanting to be "independent": to be self-conscious is just to be dependent on the recognition of other self-consciousnesses. Cf. G.W.F. Hegel, *Phenomenology of Spirit*, trans. A.V. Miller (Oxford: Oxford University Press, 1977), pp. 104–19.) But Duxbury does not note that Hegel would have rejected Kennedy's view that the "contradiction" is insurmountable (cf. 461): in this respect, Kennedy remains a philosophical liberal

has done in American legal thought is to revive a certain strategy of left-wing critique that dates back to the Left Young Hegelians of the 1830s in Germany. Seizing upon the Hegelian notion that *ideas* are the engine of historical change, the Left Hegelians sought to effect change by demonstrating that the prevailing conservative ideas were inherently contradictory and thus unstable. To resolve these contradictions, it would be necessary to change our ideas, and thus change the world.

This strand of Hegelianism was a dead issue by the 1850s—in part because of Schopenhauer's devastating anti-Hegelian polemics, in part because of Marx's criticisms (about which more below), and in part because of the more general "materialistic" and "positivistic" turn in German intellectual life associated with Feuerbach and the so-called "German Materialists."[38] It was not revived until 1922 when Georg Lukács re-introduced Left Hegelian themes into the Marxist tradition of social critique in *History and Class Consciousness*, especially in the central chapter on "The Antinomies of Bourgeois Thought." C.L.S., however, acquires the style of argument less from Lukács—though he is a favorite figure in the footnotes of C.L.S. articles—than from Harvard Law School professor and C.L.S. "founding father" Roberto Unger, whose 1975 book *Knowledge and Politics* is quite obviously a replay of the central arguments and themes of *History and Class Consciousness*.

What is slightly ironic in this intellectual genealogy—one that most C.L.S. writers seem only vaguely aware of—is that C.L.S. should have revived precisely the tradition in left-wing thought that Marx had so viciously lampooned 150 years earlier![39] Indeed, with certain obvious emendations, we find Marx and Engels articulating a critique one often hears, with some cause, of C.L.S.:

Since [the C.L.S. writers] consider conceptions, thoughts, ideas, in fact all the products of consciousness ... as the real chains of men ... it is evident that [the C.L.S. writers] have to fight only against these illusions of the consciousness. Since, according to their fantasy, the relationships of men, all their doings, their chains and their limitations are products of their consciousness, [the C.L.S. writers] logically put to men the moral postulate of exchanging their present consciousness for human, critical or egoistic consciousness, and thus of removing their limitations. This demand to change consciousness amounts to a demand to interpret reality in another way, i.e., to recognize it by means of another interpretation ... They forget, however, that to these phrases [constituting the old interpretation] they are only

who views the "conflict" between individual and society as a perennial feature of the human situation. For Hegel, by contrast, the "contradiction" is dissolved in the recognition that to be autonomous is necessarily to be involved with other persons: others are not a threat to autonomy, but a precondition of it. All of this depends, of course, on Hegel's particular conceptions of "autonomy" and "freedom"; but the point that bears noting is that Kennedy, like the other C.L.S. writers, never really leaves the philosophical camp of the "liberals" on this issue.

[38] See, e.g., Frederick Gregory, *Scientific Materialism in 19th Century Germany* (Dordrecht: D. Reidel, 1977).

[39] See especially, the attack on Left Hegelians like Bruno Bauer in Karl Marx & Friedrich Engels, *The German Ideology: Part I*, reprinted in Robert Tucker (ed.), *The Marx-Engels Reader*, 2nd edition (New York: Norton, 1978).

opposing other phrases, and that they are in no way combating the real existing world when they are merely combating the phrases of this world.[40]

Showing the right-wing professors that their ideas are incoherent and demanding that they change their ideas is politically irrelevant for Marx: it is, of course, "contradictions" in the material circumstances of life that are the real engine of historical change.[41] What C.L.S. has done is to revive precisely this discredited strand of critical theory—the critique of ideas or "consciousness"—in the legal domain.[42] It is not obvious that these critiques are any more plausible or relevant now than they were in 1840.

(3) There is, however, another much more interesting strand of C.L.S., that bears on the criticism, lodged by Duxbury and many others, that C.L.S. simply has no positive program.[43] This strand of C.L.S. concentrates less on the (putatively) contradictory moral and political principles that (putatively) lie beneath the surface of the law, and describes instead the gap between the "ideals" professed by the law and the actual reality of life in capitalist America.[44] These critiques are often astute and powerful, and are typically accompanied by quite specific proposals for reform to bridge the gap between the "ideals" and the reality. Some of these proposals are quite radical (given the generally conservative cast of the American political landscape), but they are positive proposals nonetheless. The C.L.S. writers, it bears emphasizing, are not New Deal liberals like the Legal Realists. More than anything else, what accounts for the controversy they engendered is that for the first time in American law schools there was a significant group of legal scholars who did not support the capitalist system—either in its *laissez-faire* form or its corporate welfare-state form. Although a lot of superficial and amateurish work was done under the banner of C.L.S., that hardly distinguishes it from many other trendy movements that legal academia absorbed more peacefully (e.g. "policy science," postmodernism, pragmatism, Critical Race Theory, "feminist jurisprudence" and the like). It was the anti-capitalist politics of much of C.L.S. that set it apart.

---

[40] Id., p. 149.

[41] For the classic modern exposition of this view, see Cohen, *Karl Marx's Theory of History* (n. 3 above). And for pertinent critical discussion of Cohen's interpretation, see Peter Railton, "Explanatory Asymmetry in Historical Materialism," *Ethics* 97 (1986): 233–8.

[42] Besides Kennedy and Kelman, (n. 36 above), see also Peter Gabel, "Intention and Structure in Contractual Conditions: Outline of a Method for Critical Legal Theory," *Minnesota Law Review* 61 (1977): 601–43; Clare Dalton, "An Essay in the Deconstruction of Contract Doctrine," *Yale Law Journal* 94 (1985): 997–1114. Cf. Duxbury's discussion of the work of Mark Tushnet and others, pp. 443–9.

[43] The two strands are effectively discussed and contrasted in David Trubek's useful paper, "Where the Action Is: Critical Legal Studies and Empiricism," *Stanford Law Review* 36 (1984): 575–622.

[44] See especially the essays by Richard Abel (discussing torts), Karl Klare (discussing labor law), and the late Alan Freeman (discussing antidiscrimination law) in David Kaiyrs (ed.), *The Politics of Law: A Progressive Critique*, Rev. edition (New York: Pantheon, 1990). Cf. the quotes and discussion in Duxbury, p. 443.

Duxbury touches on many of these themes, though, as with Realism, they never quite come in to focus in the right way. The overview of C.L.S., like the overview of economic analysis, is a useful one, though it is occasionally derailed by Duxbury's penchant for gossip and "soap opera," as in his recounting of the politics of appointments at Harvard Law School in the 1980s (494–498) (who really cares, one wonders?).

V. Concluding Observations

If there is a more serious worry about Duxbury's lively survey of what American law professors have been saying these past one hundred years, it is that many of the "ideas" whose history Duxbury charts and whose content he summarizes may not really merit the sort of extended treatment he gives them. Duxbury himself has correctly observed elsewhere that, "American legal theorists [i.e. Duxbury's 'jurisprudents' as opposed to legal philosophers] are nothing if not slaves to fashion."[45] In this context, he mentions law and economics, C.L.S., pragmatism, feminism, post-modernism, Critical Race Theory, and civic republicanism as examples of "fashionable" ideas that have swept American legal scholarship.[46] Yet many of these "fashions"—some barely a decade old, and some already fading from the intellectual scene in American law schools—are the subject of large portions of Duxbury's book! Do we really need a "history" of what Andy Warhol would have called their "fifteen minutes of fame"? Does every fashionable idea that law professors lift from some other discipline, apply to law, and then pronounce as "theory" really warrant dialectical investigation and description—as opposed, say, to simply explanation?

Duxbury, unfortunately, seems oblivious to these concerns. The book is replete with pleasant paraphrase of "arguments" and "theories" that cry out for critical comment, but receive either none or merely tepid comments:[47] Felix Cohen's preposterous legal "functionalism" (a poor imitation of the now defunct "operationalist" program in philosophy of science) (132); the "predictivism" of Holmes and other Realists which treated "law" as simply a prediction of what courts would do (a view demolished decisively by H.L.A. Hart in Chapter VII of *The Concept of Law*) (125–8);[48] Lon Fuller's confused criticisms of Legal Positivism and his

---

[45] Neil Duxbury, "History as Hyperbole," *Oxford Journal of Legal Studies* 15 (1995): 487. Cf. Duxbury (n. 5 above), p. 468 for similar remarks.

[46] Duxbury "History as Hyperbole," id., n. 12.

[47] This problem is certainly not peculiar to Duxbury. A similarly uncritical recent study is Gary Minda, *Postmodern Legal Movements: Law and Jurisprudence at Century's End* (New York: New York University Press, 1995).

[48] Hart, as I have argued elsewhere, misconstrued the Realist interest in predicting what courts would do as a conceptual claim about law. See Ch. 2. Duxbury, however, leaves the reader with the impression that it *was* a conceptual claim, without even discussing the fact that such a view would be silly, as Hart demonstrated.

opposed claims about the "internal morality of law" (224–7) (suitably dismissed by Dworkin in remarks Duxbury quotes much later at 295); the familiar pretension of economists—from Milton Friedman to Richard Posner—to be practicing an "empirical science," pretensions presented by Duxbury as simply controversial, instead of fantastic (371–9, 409–14);[49] and the C.L.S. critique of "legal liberalism," which even Duxbury finally admits has "been castigated as caricaturing the liberal jurisprudential project" (489).

There is no justification, at this stage in the history of "jurisprudence," for simply summarizing so many half-baked ideas, without subjecting them to more rigorous critical comment; there can be no progress in philosophy or "legal thought" without shared recognition of the deficiencies of earlier views. Indeed, the fact that many of the theories considered in this book seem so poorly supported by reasons suggests the need for a very different sort of "history of ideas" than Duxbury provides. For Duxbury's is essentially an "idealistic" history, one that pursues the logic of ideas largely in isolation from the social and economic world. But the failure of the "logic" of many of these ideas to amount to much suggests that we need to look elsewhere for a real explanation of why these ideas have captured the attention of academic lawyers (and others).

An opposed "materialist" history of post-World War II American legal thought might, for example, examine the use of "policy science" at a time when ruling elites were intent on maximizing American opportunities for world domination and exploitation after the war had destroyed both the European colonial empires and the European economies.[50] How did the rhetoric of promoting—as "policy science" would have it—"democratic values" play into the actual U.S. policy of subjugating third-world peoples and appropriating their natural resources?[51]

Such a history might ask too about the connections between the rise of the pseudo-science of economics in law and the redistribution of wealth from the poor

[49] For pertinent discussion, see Alexander Rosenberg, *Economics: Mathematical Politics or Science of Diminishing Returns?* (Chicago: University of Chicago Press, 1992). For a brief overview of the central issues, see Alexander Rosenberg, "If Economics Isn't Science, What Is It?" reprinted in D. Hausman (ed.), *The Philosophy of Economics: An Anthology*, 2nd edition (Cambridge: Cambridge University Press, 1994). Note that the question is not whether economists produce predictions—all of us, applying common sense psychology, make testable predictions about behavior all the time—but whether economics yields predictions of scientific quality, in terms of their precision and reliability. It is well known to everyone but economists, it seems, that economics does not: hence the omnipresent boundary conditions in economic predictions (i.e. the "*ceteris paribus*" clauses) and the failure to make any real progress in the last one hundred years in specifying the causally relevant parameters of the boundary conditions.

[50] On the U.S. position after World War II, see Eric Hobsbawm, *The Age of Extremes* (New York: Vintage Books, 1994), Chs. 5 & 8. See also, Gabriel Kolko, *The Politics of War: The World and U.S. Foreign Policy 1943–1945* (New York: Random House, 1969).

[51] On American foreign policy and conduct during the post-War era through the 1970s, see Noam Chomsky, *American Power and the New Mandarins* (New York: Pantheon, 1969); Noam Chomsky & Edward Herman, *The Political Economy of Human Rights*, 2 volumes (Boston: South End Press, 1979); Gabriel & Joyce Kolko, *The Limits of Power: The World and United States Foreign Policy, 1945–1954* (New York: Harper & Row, 1972); Gabriel Kolko, *Confronting the Third World: United States Foreign Policy, 1945–1980* (New York: Pantheon, 1988).

to the rich that has been a striking feature of American economic policy since 1980. And what is the relation, the materialist historian might wonder, between the rise of Critical Race Theory and Feminism—movements that abandon the central Left issues of economic justice and systemic overhaul—as the dominant forms of "leftish" legal scholarship in American law schools and "the decline of actual left-wing movements outside academia . . . [and] the development in the 1980s of an academic celebrity system that meshes in funny, glitzy ways with the worlds of art and entertainment, with careerism . . . "?[52]

No doubt such a materialist history would leave out much, though not obviously any more than is left out by Duxbury's meticulous recounting of so many ill-conceived theories. What these extreme materialist alternatives to Duxbury's history of legal thought help to emphasize is that where ideas have not much intellectual content in their own right, it may pay to go beyond the latest fad in the journals and monographs to ask about the social and material world in which these ideas took hold. That is not, to be sure, Duxbury's project, but perhaps it should have been. There *is* an American "jurisprudence" (in Duxbury's sense of that term)—one marked by the realistic and formalistic swings of the pendulum—but significant portions of it seem more deserving of materialistic explanation along the lines sketched above. But that is not to suggest that all "jurisprudential" ideas should be "explained away" in this fashion. Indeed, a hermetic history of ideas might do very well for real philosophical thinking about law—"jurisprudence" in my sense. For real jurisprudence, however, the demarcation "American" (or "British") would make no sense.

[52] Katha Pollitt, "Pomolotov Cocktail," *The Nation* (June 10, 1996), p. 9.

Postscript to Part I:
Interpreting Legal Realism

A number of interpretive questions about and challenges to my philosophical reconstruction of American Legal Realism have been raised over the last decade. I want to take this opportunity to respond to a few of these, which are meant to be representative rather than exhaustive.

The legal philosopher Michael S. Moore is not alone in raising questions about the interpretive adequacy of my reading of American Legal Realism,[1] though I should at least note in passing that most academic lawyers interested in the Realists have generally responded favorably to my way of reconstructing them.[2] Moore writes:

Leiter brings a theory to Legal Realism with a vengeance. Utilizing his considerable philosophical sophistication, Leiter would reconstruct the Realist programme in light of the contemporary philosophical movements known as naturalism and pragmatism. On Leiter's reconstruction, the Legal Realists had good naturalist and pragmatist grounds for turning jurisprudence into a social science of judicial behavior.[3]

Moore allows that my reconstruction would render Realism a legitimate jurisprudential competitor, but retorts:

My doubt about Leiter's project is historical: I do not think the Legal Realists had anything like Leiter's philosophically sophisticated reasons for replacing conceptual and normative jurisprudence with an explanation-giving social science. I think they were simply confused. True enough, some of their views can be fitted to the philosophically sophisticated views Leiter describes; yet as the sayings go, even a broken clock tells the correct time twice every twenty-four hours . . .[4]

---

[1] Donald R. Davis, Jr., for example, raises related questions in a very learned piece on "A Realist View of Hindu Law," *Ratio Juris* 19 (2006): 287–313, which nonetheless relies extensively on my interpretation. I focus on Moore as putting the challenge to my reading most systematically.

[2] For example, Herbert Hovenkamp, the leading American antitrust scholar and an accomplished legal historian, says that my account is "a particularly good analysis of legal realism's basic analytic approach, less cluttered by *au courant* ideology than many others." "Knowledge About Welfare: Legal Realism and the Separation of Law and Economics," *Minnesota Law Review* 84 (2000), p. 845 n. 162. Hovenkamp is no doubt thinking of the pernicious influence of the Critical Legal Studies reinvention of Realism, which I critique in Chs. 1 and 3. My late colleague, Charles Alan Wright, the pre-eminent American procedure scholar in the second half of the 20th century, did much to both influence and confirm my reading.

[3] Michael S. Moore, *Educating Oneself in Public: Critical Essays in Jurisprudence* (Oxford: Oxford University Press, 2000), pp. 32–3.　　　　　　　　　　　　　　　　　　　[4] Id., p. 33.

We, of course, need to be careful here about sliding from the *reasons* the Realists had for turning to a descriptive theory of adjudication, and my own *reconstruction* of a philosophical motivation for those reasons. Nothing turns on the biographical fact about what Karl Llewellyn or Jerome Frank thought about philosophical matters: what matters are the positions they took and the reasons offered for them, and then whether there is any philosophical motivation to be supplied for those kinds of reasons and for taking those kinds of positions. My interpretation is, after all, a *reconstruction*: it "puts back together" in philosophical terms the largely unphilosophical arguments and positions of the American Legal Realists. The philosophy is mine, the basic arguments and ideas theirs.

Moore, however, has some specific grievances with my reconstruction. He allows that the reconstruction meets familiar objections to Realist positions,[5] but has two main doubts about whether these are the views of the Realists.[6]

1. Moore objects that "the only *explicit* concept of law the Realists held was the predictive definition of Holmes,"[7] adding that,

> It is a curious historiographic method to attribute beliefs to individuals in a way that: (a) discounts what they explicitly said, in favour (b) of a concept [of law] allegedly implicit in their discussion of something else. Leiter attempts to diminish the curiosity of (a) by confining their "law is prediction" pronouncements to contexts of practical advice by lawyers to clients. Yet the very texts Leiter cites support no such confinement; they propounded the identification (of law with predicted judicial decision) as an eye-opening, refreshingly frank, general theory of law applicable to judges and laypersons alike.[8]

This passage might serve as a cautionary tale for intellectual historians about the dangers of anachronism. Contrary to Moore, Holmes—like every other Realist— *never* made any explicit claim about the "concept of law," because that topic (namely, the "concept") was not a topic either Holmes or any other legal scholar recognized as a real one. (It was not even a central topic in philosophy until the middle of the twentieth century!) There is law, there are questions about law, there are the decisions of courts: but the "concept of law" as an abstract object to be elicited from all these practices simply did not exist as a topic of intellectual inquiry for Holmes or any of the later Realists. The texts I relied upon in Chapters 1, 2, and 3 in offering an interpretation of the Realist "law as prediction" talk are entirely consistent with my plausible characterization of their import, namely, that they constitute (as Moore himself aptly puts it) "practical advice by lawyers to clients." Holmes like every other Realist made the now banal, and obviously correct, observation that when your client, who is paying money for your services,

---

[5] Id., p. 35.

[6] Moore's final complaint (id., p. 37) pertains, as far as I can see, to the whole enterprise of philosophical reconstruction of the views of authors who are not themselves philosophically motivated, and raises no questions specific to my reconstruction of the Realists.

[7] This is the view that by the concept of "law" we just mean a "prediction of what the courts will do." This is the view that I argue briefly in Ch. 1 and at greater length in Ch. 2 is wrongly ascribed to Realism.   [8] *Educating Oneself in Public* (n. 3 above), p. 35.

asks "what is the law?" what she really wants to know is "what will judges do if we go to court?" or "what will legal officials do if we pursue this matter?" The client does not want to know what the esteemed legal authorities have to say on the question, or what the "paper rule" says will happen: the client wants to know what will *really* happen (e.g., will she be able to reclaim her property or get monetary damages for her losses? Or will she be told to go home?).

Moore calls attention[9] to the fact that in the second sentence of "The Path of the Law"[10] Holmes refers to "appear[ing] before judges" as one of the things lawyers do, which shows, Moore claims, that Holmes was, indeed, confusing the *predictive* and *justificatory* roles of law. Simple interpretive charity, though, would suggest that the passing reference to judges be put into context; here is the full paragraph:

[In studying law] [w]e are studying what we shall want in order to appear before judges, or to advise people in such a way as to keep them out of court. The reason why it is a profession, why people will pay lawyers to argue for them or to advise them, is that in societies like ours the command of the public force is entrusted to the judges in certain cases, and the whole power of the state will be put forth, if necessary, to carry out their judgments and decrees. People want to know under what circumstances and how far they will run the risk of coming against what is so much stronger than themselves, and hence it becomes a business to find out when this danger is to be feared. The object of our study, then, is prediction, the prediction of the incidence of the public force through the instrumentality of the courts.[11]

Holmes distinguishes quite clearly (with the "or") between two roles lawyers undertake, but then the bulk of the discussion is clearly given over to the second role, that of advising clients. *With respect to this latter role*—with respect, that is, to helping people who "want to know under what circumstances and how far they will run the risk of coming against what is so much stronger than themselves"— Holmes suggests what we are studying is "the prediction of the incidence of the public force through the instrumentality of the courts." What Moore needs, but cannot adduce (without the anachronism), is evidence that Holmes or other Realists had any general view about the *concept* of law, let alone one that confused *justification* and *prediction*.

Indeed, if we go a bit further into "The Path of the Law," we find the following famous passage, which sits rather uneasily with Moore's unflattering reading of Holmes:

The training of lawyers is a training in logic. The processes of analogy, discrimination, and deduction are those in which they are most at home. The language of judicial decision is mainly the language of logic. And the logical method and form flatter that longing for certainty and for repose which is in every human mind. But certainty generally is illusion, and repose is not the destiny of man. Behind the logical form lies a judgment as to the relative worth and importance of competing legislative grounds, often an inarticulate

---

[9] Id., p. 35 n. 74.   [10] *Harvard Law Review* 10 (1897), p. 457   [11] Id.

and unconscious judgment, it is true, and yet the very root and nerve of the whole proceeding. You can give any conclusion a logical form. You always can imply a condition in
a contract. But why do you imply it? It is because of some belief as to the practice of the
community or of a class, or because of some opinion as to policy, or, in short, because of
some attitude of yours upon a matter not capable of exact quantitative measurement, and
therefore not capable of founding exact logical conclusions.[12]

Holmes, obviously, is using "logic" here quite loosely to mean "legal reasoning" of
the traditional kind (the processes of "analogy, discrimination, and deduction")
which both lawyers, and importantly courts, employ: "The language of judicial
decision is mainly the language of logic." All of *this language* is, of course, justificatory in character, not predictive, as Holmes, like everyone else, is aware. The difficulty, he thinks, is that "you can give any conclusion a logical form,"[13] which is to
say that he thinks the justifications do not really *explain* the decisions. So a lawyer
has to persuade the court to, e.g., "imply a condition in a contract," but for that
argument to be *causally effective* in getting the judge to act, the good lawyer will
have to appeal, directly or indirectly, to the normative considerations that will
elicit the desired "judgment as to the relative worth and importance of competing
legislative grounds," since it is these that are actually *effective* and explanatory.[14]
To be sure, Holmes suggests it would be better if judges talked openly about the
legislative considerations,[15] but that recommendation is necessarily predicated on
full awareness that they do not so argue at present.[16] In other words, Holmes

---

[12] Id., pp. 465–6.

[13] This is, admittedly, a careless formulation of the claim about the indeterminacy of legal reasoning, since it implies that legal reasoning does not constrain at all the outcomes, which is obviously
false, and inconsistent with other things Holmes and all the later Realists remark upon.

[14] Notice that Holmes, anticipating Llewellyn and the "Sociological Wing" of Realism more
generally, allows that "the practice of the community" might also be the relevant explanatory factor in
the judge's decision.

[15] Jerome Frank, sitting as a judge on the U.S. Court of Appeals for the Second Circuit, explicitly
embraced Holmes's advice in his concurrence in *Ricketts v. Pennsylvania R. Co.*, 153 F. 2nd, 757,
768–9 (1946), noting that, "As Mr. Justice Holmes often urged, when an important issue of social
policy arises, it should be candidly, not evasively, articulated." Accordingly, Judge Frank argued that
the question of the validity of a release of claims against an employer (the railroad) for injury on the
job should be determined *not* through an analysis of the validity of the contract containing the
release, but rather based on consideration of the most efficient way to allocate the costs of accidents,
which must be borne by someone.

[16] Moore confuses Holmes's recommendation that judges *ought* to talk openly about issues of
social policy with his earlier discussion in "The Path of the Law" of how the "bad man" understands
talk of *legal* duties, such as the duty to perform a contract. *Educating Oneself in Public* (n. 3 above),
p. 35 n. 74. In that prior discussion, Holmes is making an *epistemological* point, namely, that you can
know what the law is without knowing anything about what is morally right and wrong; the device of
the "bad man" is used to bring that out (even a "bad man," someone who either does not know what
is right and wrong, or does not care, can understand what the law is). In that specific context, Holmes
claims that one should treat a *legal duty to perform a contract* as equivalent to a prediction about what
a court will do if one fails to perform. But when he speaks later ("The Path of the Law," *Harvard Law
Review* 10 (1897) p. 467) about the judge's duty to weigh questions of policy, he is obviously not
speaking about a *legal* duty, but about what he thinks judges *ought* to be doing, quite apart from what
their official legal obligation might be.

recognizes judicial practices of *justification* for what they are, but thinks that, at present, their rhetoric of justification is not what Holmes thinks it *ought* to be, since the rhetoric does not really reflect the *actual* (normative *and* causal) grounds of their decisions.

2. Regarding my claim that the Realist thesis about the indeterminacy of law is best understood as the claim that the class of legal reasons underdetermines the outcome in cases that reach the stage of appellate review, Moore's response eschews any reference to the actual textual evidence I presented,[17] opting instead for an odd form of "how could so many people be so wrong?":

> Leiter would make the Realists such reasonable fellows you have to wonder what all the fuss was about. The conventional wisdom has always been that if there are hard cases, where the legal materials do not yield unique answers, so there are easy cases where they do....Unless the contemporaries of the Realists of the 1920s and 1930s were paranoid, Leiter's low-key interpretation of the Realists cannot be right. Mainstream views can hardly generate the apoplexy the Realists generated within the more traditional legal academy.[18]

There are two bits of anachronism that mar this complaint: one about the "conventional wisdom," and one about the reception of Realism. Today's "conventional wisdom" after H.L.A. Hart may be as Moore describes it, but what is the evidence that in the 1920s and 1930s academic lawyers thought it was uncontroversial that appellate cases were decided largely on the basis of non-legal consideration? Moore cites none, and for obvious reasons. Of course, as I argued in Chapter 2, the real dispute between Hart and the Realists concerns precisely the *scope* of indeterminacy, and even on this issue, the Realists out-flank the Hartian "conventional wisdom" in ways that are controversial among legal philosophers, though not, I think, among lawyers.

That latter point is implicated in the second bit of anachronism that characterizes Moore's objection. What "the fuss was about" had partly to do with the phenomenon I called (in Ch. 1) "the Frankification" of Realism, that is, the tendency, even then, to treat Jerome Frank's most radical pronouncements as the core of Realism; and partly to do with the fact that claiming that the law was largely indeterminate in the range of cases that reached the stage of appellate review was, already, a controversial thesis. But it is also easy to overstate the controversy by focusing on indignant Harvard law professors protecting their turf[19] and Catholic lawyers enacting one of the many iterations of the Church's resistance to modernity.[20] Among those who considered themselves, without controversy, to be Legal Realists, were the primary drafter of the Uniform Commercial Code,[21] the name partner of one of Washington, DC's leading law firms,[22] the leading tort reform

---

[17] See Ch. 1, esp. pp. 22–30.   [18] *Educating Oneself in Public* (n. 3 above), p. 36.

[19] See, e.g., Roscoe Pound, "The Call for a Realist Jurisprudence," *Harvard Law Review* 44 (1931): 697–711.

[20] Ben W. Palmer, "Hobbes, Holmes and Hitler," *American Bar Association Journal* 31 (1945): 569–73.   [21] Karl Llewellyn.

[22] Thurman Arnold, who founded the firm now known as Arnold & Porter.

scholar in America in the twentieth century,[23] the pre-eminent antitrust lawyer and scholar in America of the post-World War II decades,[24] and the leading American authority on court procedure.[25] Perhaps this quite distinguished and "mainstream" cast of adherents is explained by the fact that the Realists, when you actually read them, were, in fact, "reasonable fellows."[26]

Indeed, one theme in the work of the second, though less aggressive, critic I want to consider is precisely that Karl Llewellyn, in particular, was not the "rule skeptic" he was portrayed to be.[27] Alan Schwartz, in his illuminating study of the actual articles Llewellyn wrote on contracts and sales law in the 1920s and 1930s,[28] says that Llewellyn "believed that rules could seriously constrain a decisionmaker's discretion,"[29] singling out me as one of those purportedly denying this.[30] Schwartz's Llewellyn, then, is not just Moore's "reasonable fellow," he is more "reasonable," so it appears, than even I present him!

Schwartz's presentation trades, however, on ambiguities about the scope of the thesis about rule skepticism and about the meaning of "rule" in Llewellyn's discussions. The Realist interest in the indeterminacy of legal reasoning—this is especially true of Llewellyn—concerned indeterminacy at the level of appellate litigation; that is compatible, of course, with significant determinacy in legal reasoning at every other level of the legal system. Certainly if one thought that "rule skepticism" meant *global* skepticism about the efficacy of rules in constraining conduct, then one might reasonably note that Llewellyn is *not* that kind of rule skeptic. But that has never been at issue in my interpretation of Realism.

The second ambiguity on which Schwartz trades is even more significant. Llewellyn, like all Realists,[31] thought that judges were significantly constrained in their decisions by *non-legal* normative considerations (considerations we might

[23] Leon Green, who taught law at Yale, Texas, and Northwestern (where he was Dean), and who even was offered (but declined) the job of Solicitor General of the United States right after World War II.

[24] Milton Handler, who taught at Columbia Law School from the 1920s until the 1970s, and who was name partner of a leading New York City law firm.

[25] My late colleague Charles Alan Wright, former President of the American Law Institute and lead author of the most influential procedure treatise.

[26] Moore also claims that, "The Realists thought that if the psychology of judging were as they described it, then they would have shown the rational indeterminacy of legal materials." *Educating Oneself in Public* (n. 3 above), p. 37. Unfortunately, Moore cites no text in support of this claim about what "the Realists thought," and the attribution seems obviously inconsistent with the extensive non-psychological arguments the Realists actually gave in support of the claim that legal reasoning was indeterminate. See, e.g., Karl Llewellyn, *The Bramble Bush* (New York: Oceana, 1930), pp. 74–6; Karl Llewellyn, "Remarks on the Theory of Appellate Decision and the Rules and Canons about How Statutes are to be Construed," *Vanderbilt Law Review* 3 (1950): 395–406; Max Radin, "Statutory Interpretation," *Harvard Law Review* 43 (1930): 863–85.

[27] Alan Schwartz, "Karl Llewellyn and the Origins of Contract Theory," in *The Jurisprudential Foundations of Corporate and Commercial Law*, ed. J. Kraus & S. Walt (Cambridge: Cambridge University Press, 2000), pp. 40–1.

[28] Schwartz's presentation, which emphasizes Llewellyn's belief in the importance of efficiency in the rules of contract, complements my reading of Llewellyn in Ch. 1, since Llewellyn (as Schwartz puts it) "used commercial practice as the best evidence of the efficient transaction" (id., p. 16), a reasonable epistemic practice given that commercial actors are more likely than most actors to be interested in efficient outcomes from an economic point of view.   [29] Id., p. 41.

[30] Id., p. 53 n. 147.   [31] See Ch. 1, esp. pp. 26–30.

call "rules," and which the Realists themselves sometimes referred to as "the real rules," meaning to contrast them with the merely "paper rules"), but what he denied, even in the material Schwartz discusses, is that the primary constraints were effected by *legally valid* norms or rules (often called "doctrine" or "announced rules" by Llewellyn). Schwartz, unfortunately, runs these kinds of normative considerations together, so misses the fact that in Llewellyn's detailed writings on contracts and sales, like his more theoretical writings, he was, indeed, committed to the Core Claim that judges respond primarily to factual situation-types rather than legally valid norms or doctrines.

Schwartz quotes a series of striking statements[32] in which Llewellyn appears to affirm the role of rules and doctrine in constraining decision, statements which Schwartz takes to be inconsistent with "rule skepticism." So, for example, Schwartz quotes Llewellyn from the "Introduction" to his *Cases and Materials on the Law of Sales*[33] saying that "doctrine is 'a convenient and fairly accurate summation of past decisions and of apparent trends, one which makes possible the intelligent decision of a new case in the light of its bearing on doctrine and on life.'"[34] Yet this claim about doctrine being "convenient and fairly accurate" is preceded immediately by the characteristic Realist theme—which we saw in both Llewellyn and Oliphant[35]—about the shortcomings of doctrine, namely, that it suffers from "academic abstraction and remoteness from life" which "threatens to issue in sterility."[36] Llewellyn then turns immediately to one of his familiar discussions about the indeterminacy of legal reasoning by the courts, concluding with a fairly typical and quite clear formulation of what I have called the Core Claim of Realism:

> [I]f [a law teacher] wishes either to predict the course of court decisions, or to train a student to foresee or to influence decisions, he must take full account of the effect of facts upon the courts. He must recognize too, that some facts of common life reach the court in the raw and as they are; that others are seen by the court and can influence the court only after . . . distortion . . . by legal procedure . . . and the law of evidence. There is that . . . most important distortion produced by the existing legal concepts in terms of which lawyers select and present facts, and in terms of which courts perceive and weigh them. And yet . . . we know that raw facts repeatedly, and in defiance of our legal "safeguards," break through undistorted to the court's consciousness in some cases and influence decision.[37]

Llewellyn then reiterates his famous view about the "strict" and "loose" view of precedent, now speaking in terms of "doctrine," before drawing the key conclusion, nowhere noted by Schwartz:

> [W]e must become prepared at the same moment, and in regard to the same pending case, to anticipate *either* a triumph of the felt needs of the case, with a consequent reshaping of doctrine to fit the result; *or* the triumph of mechanical, deductive reasoning from formulae which crush to death some needed, budding, economic institution. This forked expectation goes to the essence of an understanding of the law.[38]

---

[32] "Karl Llewellyn and the Origins of Contract Theory" (n. 27 above), p. 24.
[33] (Chicago: Callaghan & Co., 1930).   [34] Id., pp. ix–xx.   [35] See Ch. 1.
[36] *Cases and Materials on the Law of Sales* (n. 33 above), p. ix.   [37] Id., p. x.
[38] Id., pp. x–xi.

All of this should make absolutely clear that Llewellyn was a "rule skeptic" in the only sense that ever mattered: he recognized that purportedly legally binding rules and doctrine did not, in fact, determine the decision of the courts in a significant range of cases, which is exactly why students of the law had to be educated about the influence on judges of "the felt needs of the case" and why they must "take full account of the effect of facts upon the courts." None of this is to deny that legally valid rules or doctrine play some role in decision; it is to deny what all Realists denied, namely, that you will really understand what the courts, especially the appellate courts are doing, if you think "verbal formulations" of doctrine are the end of the story. As Llewellyn elsewhere puts it: "Do I suggest that . . . the 'accepted rules,' the rules the judges say they apply, are without influence upon their actual behavior?" and answers, "I do not."[39] The Realist approach, continues Llewellyn, "admits . . . *some* relation between *any* accepted rule and judicial behavior" but then demands that *what* that relation is requires empirical investigation since it is *not* necessarily the relationship that would be suggested by the content of the doctrine.[40] The Realist, Llewellyn writes in 1931, denies that "traditional . . . rule-formulations are the heavily operative factor in producing court decisions."[41] But to deny only *this* claim is to admit that rules play *some* causal and justificatory role in decisions. Yet that is all Realist rule-skepticism ever claimed.

These points are, I think, clear even in the materials that Schwartz cites. So, for example, summing up his *real* point about "doctrine" in the casebook on sales, Llewellyn writes:

> The book is much occupied in this connection with the difference between doctrine as a causal factor in inducing a decision and doctrine as a mere *ex post facto* justification of a decision already taken . . . . Doctrine is therefore emphasized, as doctrine must be; but it is emphasized as the first step in a wider process of seeing what law means of bringing it to bear on facts . . . .[42]

Schwartz, alas, leaves readers with the impression that understanding doctrine was not merely a "first step in a wider process of seeing what law means."

In fact, Schwartz's misreading of Llewellyn's views is even more dramatic in the case of one of Llewellyn's 1938 contract law studies.[43] Schwartz quotes the following as representing Llewellyn's article:[44]

> A rule which states accurately the outcome of the cases, seen as *cases*, incorporates *pro tanto* such wisdom on the cases as prior courts have shown, and such similarity of reaction as

---

[39] Karl Llewellyn, "A Realistic Jurisprudence—the Next Step," *Columbia Law Review* 30 (1930), p. 444.   [40] Id. (emphasis added).

[41] Karl Llewellyn, "Some Realism about Realism—Responding to Dean Pound," *Harvard Law Review* 44 (1931), p. 1237.   [42] *Cases and Materials on Sales* (n. 33 above), p. xi.

[43] Karl Llewellyn, "The Rule of Law in Our Case-Law of Contract," *Yale Law Journal* 47 (1938): 1243–71.

[44] "Karl Llewellyn and the Origins of Contract Theory" (n. 27 above), p. 45 n. 48, quoting "The Rule of Law in Our Case-Law of Contract" id., p. 1257.

courts are likely to continue to show... [The rule] gives some guidance (to the judge) about wherein his more personal judgments on such matters may be wisely tempered. It further sets... the picture of how far he is or is not really free to move unimpeded, and shows where the penumbra of his honest freedom lies to make further use of the given multiple case-law techniques.

But what does Llewellyn actually mean by a "rule" here? The real meaning becomes apparent from the context Schwartz omits. In the introduction to the article in question, Llewellyn calls the reader's attention right away "to the degree of implicit fluidity of case-law rules": "The correct doctrinal *possibilities* of case-law are hydra-headed, in the most settled field. It is the *probabilities* which move within a much narrower range, and which give guidance to counselor and court. But the probabilities turn not on the fixity of doctrine, but on the relative predictability of courts' reactions to new cases," i.e., the facts or situation-types presented by new cases.[45]

So Llewellyn draws at the very start the contrast between doctrine and "the relative predictability of courts' reactions to new cases" which depends *not* only on doctrine. As he puts it a few pages later (but still preceding the portion Schwartz quotes): "There is often enough very considerable implicit and silent consistency in actual decision even when announced rules are at odds"[46]—the "announced rules" being the doctrine or "paper rules" that non-Realists would take to be fully descriptive and explanatory of the decision. The "ideal," says Llewellyn, would be a situation where the rule both "fits rather accurately the actual recorded outcome of a rather consistent body of cases examined *as cases*, on facts and result" *and* "is announced in those cases as the rule."[47] And *it is this ideal* that Llewellyn is describing in the passage Schwartz quotes. What Schwartz quotes, in other words, is *not* the claim that the doctrine or rules courts *actually* articulate are in fact constraining their decisions; it is, rather, a claim about a legal universe in which a Realist revolution had taken place, such that the rules actually announced by the courts were ones cast at the requisite level of fact-specificity such that they track the normative judgments courts make as they respond to situation-types. Indeed, the very next sentence after the last one Schwartz quotes begins: "If the rules announced in past cases or in the books are substantially at odds with the decisions,"[48] then attorneys cannot rely on the announced rule (precisely because it will not constrain, and so will not help predict future decisions) and judges should "ponder whether to follow the announced rules."[49] But that, of course, is to deny what Schwartz wants to imply: namely, that Llewellyn thought the rules courts announce are generally constraining decisions.

As Schwartz notes,[50] in my view the "Sociological Wing" Realists think that what explains the predictable patterns into which appellate decisions fall are

[45] "The Rule of Law in Our Case-Law of Contract", n. 43 above, p.1244.   [46] Id., p. 1252.
[47] Id., p. 1256.   [48] Id., p. 1257.
[49] Id.   [50] "Karl Llewellyn and the Origins of Contract Theory" (n. 27 above), pp. 45–6 n. 52.

the psycho-social facts about judges—their background and professionalization experiences—which lead them to respond to situation-types in stable ways. Curiously, in this context Schwartz effectively acknowledges the points made above, for he writes (in a footnote): "Llewellyn did not deny the relevance of 'psycho-social facts' in the articles reviewed here, but did believe that courts decide accord-ing to rules, so that knowing the actual rules (rather than the doctrinal rules) would permit moderately accurate predictions."[51] So here the distinction so central to Llewellyn's discussion—between "actual rules" and "doctrine"—is explicitly noted. It was, of course, never any part of the rule-skepticism of the Sociological Wing of Realism to deny that normative considerations constrain the decisions of courts; the point was that these normative considerations were gener-ally not the same as the "doctrinal" or "announced" rules. The *actual* rule (or the "ideal" rule) is not necessarily the announced one, though in an ideal Realist legal universe, it would be. What the Realist needs to explain—and what I was talking about in referring to "psycho-social facts"—is precisely the phenomenon that Llewellyn aptly described in the 1938 article, namely, the "very considerable implicit and silent consistency in actual decision even when announced rules are at odds."[52] Obviously, in this case no appeal to doctrine or "announced rule" will do the explanatory work.

Mark Greenberg has raised a very different kind of objection to my reading in a stimulating but, alas, unpublished manuscript:[53] he thinks I have misappropri-ated the analogy to Quine's argument for naturalized epistemology. Because Greenberg's paper is still unpublished, it would not be appropriate to quote exten-sively from it, but a brief comment on its central thesis may prove illuminating and will hopefully stimulate Greenberg to make his interesting paper, in some suitably revised form, public. Since Greenberg's exposition is eloquent and lucid, I want to quote at least some of his own words:

A proposal to replace an area of philosophy with natural science can be sound only if there is reason to conclude that the philosophical project is in some way confused or bankrupt. I clarify the respect in which Quine concluded that foundationalism in epistemology was a failed project. At bottom, the idea that philosophy could validate science from the outside, on the basis of armchair standards of justification more demanding than those internal to science, was a confusion, an overreaching on the part of philosophy. The conclusion was not an indictment of science, but of certain philosophical preconceptions . . . .

[T]here is no parallel philosophical confusion or overreaching in the legal case. The analogue [for Leiter] to the failure of foundationalism is supposed to be the thesis that the law is indeterminate. I argue, however, that the epistemological parallel to the legal

---

[51] Id.   [52] "The Rule of Law in our Case-Law of Contract" (n. 43 above), p. 1252.

[53] Mark Greenberg, "Unnatural Proposal: Indeterminacy as a Motivation for the Naturalization of Legal Philosophy," which was presented at a conference on "Naturalism and Other Realisms in Legal Philosophy" organized by Joseph Raz and sponsored by Columbia Law School's Center for Law and Philosophy in April 2001. Papers by Greenberg and David Brink at that conference took issue with my work on naturalized jurisprudence, and I much benefited from the ensuing discussion that took place with them and the other participants.

indeterminacy thesis would be the philosophical conclusion that scientific theories could not be justified, an anti-naturalistic conclusion that could not have warranted a replacement of philosophy by science. In effect, Quine took that anti-naturalistic conclusion to provide a *reductio ad absurdum* of the foundationalist project. The closest parallel in the legal case to Quine's position would thus be the rejection of the arguments that seem to support the indeterminacy thesis.

This is a cleverly framed objection—certainly the most intriguing one registered against my account over the last decade, which is why I accord it attention here— but I believe it gets both Quine, and my own use of Quine, wrong in subtle ways.

Let us start by recalling my account of the analogy from Chapter 1:[54]

The central enterprise of epistemology on Quine's view is to understand the relation between our theories of the world and the evidence (sensory input) on which they are based. Quine's target is one influential construal of this project: Cartesian foundationalism, particularly in the sophisticated form given to it in the twentieth century by Rudolf Carnap in *Der Logische Aufbau der Welt*. The foundationalist wants an account of the theory-evidence relation that would vindicate the privileged epistemic status of at least some subset of our theories: our theories (in particular, our best theories of natural science) are to be "grounded" in indubitable evidence (i.e. immediate sense impressions).[55] As is quite familiar, foundationalism, for Quine, is a failure, rendered unrealizable by Quinean meaning holism on the one hand (theoretical terms get their meanings from their place in the whole theoretical framework, not in virtue of some point-by-point contact with sensory input), and the Duhem-Quine thesis about the underdetermination of theory by evidence on the other (there is always more than one theory consistent with the evidence, in part, because a theoretical hypothesis can always be preserved in the face of recalcitrant evidence by abandoning the auxiliary hypotheses that informed the test of the hypothesis).

What becomes, then, of epistemology? Hilary Kornblith has summed up Quine's view as follows:

> Once we see the sterility of the foundationalist program, we see that the only genuine questions there are to ask about the relation between theory and evidence and about the acquisition of belief are psychological questions.[56]

This view Kornblith aptly dubs Quine's "replacement thesis": "the view that epistemological questions may be replaced by psychological questions."[57] Here is how Quine puts it:

> The stimulation of his sensory receptors is all the evidence anybody has had to go on, ultimately, in arriving at his picture of the world. Why not just see how this construction really proceeds? Why not settle for psychology? Such a surrender of the

---

[54] P. 36 in this volume.

[55] For reasons of simplicity of presentation, I am blurring two issues here. The foundationalist program, at least in the early Carnap (who later repudiates it), has two parts: semantic and epistemic. The semantic program is to translate all sentences referring to physical objects into the language of sense-data (e.g. "I am being appeared to greenly now"). The epistemic program is to show that scientific theories about the physical world are uniquely justified on the basis of sensory experience. Semantic holism dooms the first project. Hume on induction, and the Duhem-Quine thesis about underdetermination doom the second.

[56] Hilary Kornblith, "Introduction: What Is Naturalistic Epistemology?" in *Naturalizing Epistemology*, 2nd edition, ed. H. Kornblith (Cambridge, Mass.: MIT Press, 1994), p. 4.   [57] Id., p. 3.

epistemological burden to psychology is a move that was disallowed in earlier time as circular reasoning. If the epistemologist's goal is validation of the grounds of empirical science, he defeats his purpose by using psychology or other empirical science in the validation. However, such scruples against circularity have little point once we have stopped dreaming of deducing science from observations.[58]

Several pages later, Quine continues that on his proposal,

Epistemology, or something like it, simply falls into place as a chapter of psychology and hence of natural science. It studies a natural phenomenon, viz., a physical subject. This human subject is accorded a certain experientially controlled input—certain patterns of irradiation in assorted frequencies, for instance—and in the fullness of time the subject delivers as output a description of the three-dimensional external world and its history. The relation between the meager input and the torrential output is a relation that we are prompted to study for somewhat the same reasons that always prompted epistemology; namely, in order to see how evidence relates to theory, and in what ways one's theory of nature transcends any available evidence.[59]

Thus Quine: the central concern of epistemology is the theory-evidence relationship; if the foundationalist story about this relationship is a failure, then that leaves only one story worth telling about this relationship: namely, the story told by "a purely descriptive, causal-nomological science of human cognition."[60] The science of human cognition *replaces* armchair epistemology: we naturalize epistemology by turning over its central question—the relationship between theory and evidence—to the relevant empirical science.

This was offered as a rather uncontroversial gloss on Quine's argument; I essentially followed the familiar accounts by Jaegwon Kim and Hilary Kornblith, neither of whom note the presence of any *reductio* in Quine's argument, and for good reason: there is none. The argument against foundationalism is not, *contra* Greenberg, in the form of a *reductio*, but rather based on the failure of its semantic and epistemic premises.[61] The analogy I then proposed was, to put it crudely, as follows: epistemology stands to science, as (one part of) philosophy of law stands to adjudication. In particular, epistemological foundationalism stands to science as jurisprudential "foundationalism" stands to adjudication: both are attempts to provide *a kind of* foundation for the associated practice (science on the one hand, legal reasoning and adjudication on the other), and both fail (the former for the reasons Quine gives, the latter for the reasons the Realists give about the indeterminacy of legal reasoning). There is certainly neither an "indictment of science" (as Greenberg puts it), nor an indictment of law, and I did not claim otherwise. Science goes on as always, with or without foundationalism, and so too does legal reasoning and judicial decision-making. There is, however, an indictment of *the philosophical practice*: in both cases, the proposal is to naturalize the failed

---

[58] W.V.O. Quine, "Epistemology Naturalized," in his *Ontological Relativity and Other Essays* (New York: Columbia University Press, 1969), pp. 75–6.   [59] Id., pp. 82–3.
[60] Jaegwon Kim, "What is 'Naturalized Epistemology,'" in *Naturalizing Epistemology* (n. 58 above), p. 388.   [61] See esp. Ch. 5, pp. 144–5.

foundationalist enterprise and replace it with a suitable empirical inquiry into the relata (e.g., theory and evidence, or judicial decision and legal reasoning) which the philosophical theory had tried to reconstruct unsuccessfully.

What then is Greenberg's quarrel with this analogy? Greenberg says that Quine rejected the idea that "philosophy could validate science from the outside, on the basis of armchair standards of justification more demanding than those internal to science," and so suggests that the *proper* analogy to philosophy of law would be the conclusion that the thesis of the indeterminacy of law, itself, involves imposing "armchair standards of justification more demanding than those internal" to law. Those who recall the Realist arguments for the indeterminacy of law from Chapters 1 and 2[62] will remember, however, that there is an important sense in which those arguments do not exploit a standard of justification *external* to the law or legal reasoning; they exploit rather the very ways in which lawyers and judges actually handle precedents and statutory materials to show that more than one judgment can be warranted based on the legal materials in the kinds of cases that reach the stage of appellate review. The Realist arguments show—to put it in new terms that are apt here—that legal reasoning does not always live up to the foundationalist ideal it sets itself. This is an ideal legal reasoning sets itself precisely in the sense that later writers like Dworkin try to exploit, namely, that courts defend their judgments as *required* by the applicable legal reasons, not as a non-legal *choice* among two or more legally defensible outcomes. Greenberg takes the moral of the Quinean critique to be that philosophy had imposed "armchair standards of justification more demanding than those internal to science," but the standards of justification exploited by the Realists in arguing for the indeterminacy of law are *precisely those internal* to legal reasoning. And an upshot of their critique is that appellate decisions do, indeed, lack one kind of justification, the kind that would be supplied if the legal reasoning were rationally determinate. But—*and this is key*—this is not, for the Realists, an indictment of adjudication, since they do not (unlike Dworkinians like Greenberg) think such determinacy is necessary for adjudication to be a defensible and justified practice.

What Greenberg has done is run together two kinds of justificatory questions when it comes to adjudication. One question is whether the decision in appellate cases is *justified* in the sense of rationally determinate as a matter of law (a standard, in fact, *internal* to legal reasoning). The Realists deny this, and in so doing there is, I argued, a useful analogy to be drawn to Quine's attack on (internalist) foundationalism in epistemology. But the Realists, like Quine, do not think this undermines the associated practice—adjudication for the Realists, science for Quine. But a different *justificatory* question about adjudication would be whether courts are *morally or politically justified* in deciding appellate cases if the decision is not rationally determinate as a matter of law. If the Realists thought that adjudication were not morally justified in virtue of the indeterminacy of legal reasoning in

appellate cases, then it would be reasonable to level Greenberg's charge of imposing external standards of justification. Ironically, though, it is not the Realists, but
Dworkinians like Greenberg, who impose this requirement. Greenberg simply
confuses the Realist critique with the Dworkinian question about the moral justification of the exercise of coercive power by the courts when he claims that "the
epistemological parallel to the legal indeterminacy thesis would be the philosophical conclusion that scientific theories could not be justified." That would be true,
however, only if the indeterminacy thesis were offered by the Realists as showing
that adjudication were morally illegitimate; but the Realists, like Hart and almost
everyone else, do not accept Dworkin's strange assumption that rational determinacy of legal reasoning is a necessary condition for adjudication to be morally
legitimate.

Greenberg only seems to find a disanalogy by claiming that epistemological
foundationalism is an "armchair" or "external" standard of justification with respect
to science. Indeed, it seems superficially plausible to say, as Greenberg does, that
Quine repudiates the idea that "philosophy could validate science from the outside, on the basis of armchair standards of justification more demanding than
those internal to science," but there is an important ambiguity in the notion of
"justification" here that Greenberg's phrasing elides. The failed foundationalist
program would have *justified* science in the sense of vindicating its special epistemic standing *in epistemic terms*. The standards of justification "internal to science" do no more than set the standards of evidence and inference for accepting or
rejecting particular scientific hypotheses and theories—in this regard, they are just
like the legal reasons whose indeterminacy the Realists diagnose. The standards of
evidence and inference internal to science do *not* supply a justification for science
of a kind the foundationalist sought, and which Quine critiqued. So it is not that
Quine thinks the "internal" standards of scientific justification themselves provide
an epistemic validation of science as an alternative to the foundationalist program;
it is rather that Quine thinks we have no vantage point on the kind of question
about justification the foundationalist was asking, since that would suppose we
could step out of Neurath's boat and rebuild the "ship of science" from scratch. As
I write in Chapter 5:

One crucial upshot of Quine's naturalism is that "there is no Archimedean point of cosmic
exile from which to leverage our theory of the world."[63] All theory is *scientific* theory for
Quine; there is no theoretical standpoint from which we can ask, "But is our science
true?" . . .

As Quine himself puts it elsewhere:

In my naturalistic stance I see the question of truth as one to be settled within science, there
being no higher tribunal. This makes me a scientific realist. I keep to the correspondence

---

[63] Roger Gibson, "Willard van Orman Quine," in *A Companion to Metaphysics*, ed. J. Kim &
E. Sosa (Oxford: Blackwell, 1995), p. 427.

theory of truth, but only holophrastically: it resolves into Tarski's disquotational version of truth rather than a correspondence of words to objects.[64]

But why is there no "higher tribunal" than science? Quine is often evasive on this issue, though at bottom I think it is safe to say that his posture is a pragmatic one: science is the highest tribunal *because science works*, and "science is self-conscious common sense,"[65] that is, science is just the formal and careful version of our ordinary "common sense" tools for predicting the future course of experience. "Our cognitive position is always internal to a body of substantive theory,"[66] and that theory is a scientific one because that, Quine thinks, is the theory that has proven most successful for creatures like us. That means, of course, that Quine does not think science supplies the *epistemic* justification for itself that foundationalism failed to; it just means that Quine thinks we can get no purchase on the question about the epistemic foundations of science, since we owe all our epistemic standards to our most successful epistemic practice, science.[67]

Greenberg gives the impression that Quine's main complaint was about "over-reaching on the part of philosophy," without giving due emphasis to Quine's main objective, namely, *replacing* the sterile philosophical questions with meaningful empirical questions. Thinking that philosophy has "overreached" by imposing armchair standards of justification would not, by itself, constitute a naturalization of epistemology, but it is the *latter* that Quine explicitly commends. Epistemology is "naturalized" for Quine in the sense that an aspect of its central question—namely, the relation between sensory input and theoretical output—is to be turned over to the highest tribunal, i.e., it is to be treated as an empirical question for scientific study. It is that idea of what it means to naturalize a philosophical domain—to replace a failed foundationalist project with an empirical study of the relata—that I suggested makes some sense of what it is the Realists were doing in their approach to adjudication.

There are, as I note in Chapter 1, reasons to wonder whether epistemology is bankrupt just because foundationalism of the internalist variety is bankrupt, and reasons to doubt that non-foundationalist normative philosophical programs will necessarily be sterile ones. Greenberg shares some of these worries as well, and I hope to address some of those issues after his paper his published. But I believe the central analogy on which I rely stands, for the reasons detailed above.

---

[64] W.V.O. Quine, "Comment on Lauener," in *Perspectives on Quine*, ed. R. Barrett & R. Gibson (Oxford: Blackwell, 1990), p. 229.

[65] W.V.O. Quine, *Word and Object* (Cambridge, Mass.: MIT Press, 1960), p. 3.

[66] Christopher Hookway, *Quine* (Cambridge: Polity Press, 1990), p. 209. Cf. *Word and Object* id., p. 22 ("we can never do better than occupy the standpoint of some theory or other, the best we can muster at the time").

[67] This suggests an apparent disanalogy with the Realists, but one that does not matter: namely, that the Realists did argue for their "anti-foundationalism" on the basis of standards "internal" to law. That means that legal decisions are *not* justified, *in one sense*, i.e., they are not rationally determinate. But that is compatible with thinking adjudication is *justified* in a moral or political sense, as noted earlier, in the text.

No doubt other objections to my interpretation of American Legal Realism will be forthcoming, but I hope I have at least succeeded in deflecting some of the most important and interesting objections to my reading to date.[68]

[68] I should say something, albeit brief, about a recent, very long, ambitious, but, in the end, extra-ordinarily confused paper by Michael Steven Green on "Legal Realism as Theory of Law," *William and Mary Law Review* 46 (2005): 1915–2000. Green, surprisingly, thinks the Realist theory of law—the view discredited by Hart, but wrongly ascribed to the Realists (as I argue in Ch. 2)—deserves philosophical attention. He thinks this, however, for odd reasons. On the one hand, Green seems to think the Realists are natural law theorists who deny that apparent laws, like statutes, are *really* laws (law "in the relevant sense" he calls it) since they fail to provide decisive reasons for action. Id., p. 1920. But sometimes his Realists sound like Positivists: "The fact that something is valid law [for a Realist] does not give those to whom the law applies an objective reason for obedience." Id., p. 1925. Indeed, later he says (echoing the argument in my Ch. 2) that "the realists' theory of law was remark-ably similar to Hart's." Id., p. 1940. But this is just to say, as I do, that Realists are tacit Legal Positivists; it certainly would not warrant the curious claim that Realists deny that norms are legally valid because they "may not provide a rebellious judge with any reason to adjudicate as the [law] instructs." Id., p. 1920. One explanation for this odd vacillation is that Green seems to think that Hart thought a theory of law had to explain "why law provides reasons for actions" (id., p. 1940), as opposed to taking account of the social fact that actors within a legal system *take law* to provide rea-sons for action. Indeed, Green writes:

Hart and the realists disagree about whether the social facts standing behind the law are *normative*—that is, whether these facts create objective reasons for obedience to the law. Hart thought the law was normative. The realists disagreed, and it is this rejection of legal rules ... that is the foundation of their novel theory of law.

Id., pp. 1957–8. But Hart, as little as the Realists, thought the social conventions constituting law generated "objective reasons for obedience to law," so the misunderstanding of Hart is as curious as the misunderstanding of the Realists (though this way of misreading Hart has, to be sure, a distin-guished pedigree via Dworkin—see the discussion in Ch. 6, esp. pp. 157–8—and Green, alas, simply adopts many of Dworkin's misreadings wholesale [cf. pp. 1969 ff. in Green's paper]).

In any case, Green's curious construal of the Realist theory of law seems motivated *not* by the texts of the Realists (one is hard-pressed to find the Realists expressing much interest in questions of politi-cal obligation!), but by ascribing to the Realists the rather striking (and not very plausible) philosop-hical view that, "Because objective reasons for action could not be observed to play a role in human action (particularly adjudication), the realists denied that they exist." Id., p. 1958. Instead, says Green, "attitudes *about* objective reasons for action ... empirically explain conformity with the law." Id., p. 1960. Putting the interpretive question to one side (the textual evidence is, in my view, quite thin), it is hard to take this seriously as an argument. Green says he wants to show that the view he is ascribing to the Realists "is philosophically *plausible*" (id., p. 1962), even if not convincing. But he has not even made a threshold case for plausibility. To start, Green does not even gesture at a serious showing that the *best* explanation will be the one in terms of *attitudes*; that would require probing the explanations in some detail, and comparing them with alternatives. But Green thinks it is decisive that "the attitudes [about the reasons] are sufficient to explain conformity" with the law (id., p. 1960) and therefore, there is no reason to assume the existence of the reasons. But what is the best explana-tion of the attitudes? Might it not be that they are responsive to the objective reasons? Why not think, alternatively, that the best explanation for judicial decisions might include the following kind of *nor-mative* social fact: namely, that there exists a *valid* legal rule (valid by whatever that legal system's crite-ria of validity are, e.g., "duly enacted by the legislature"), where the import of its being valid is that it creates *legal reasons* for decision. When judges recognize this social fact, they decide accordingly. But the social fact they recognize is intrinsically normative: to recognize it at all is to recognize its reason-giving character.

There are other points of detail with which one might take issue—Green, for example, misreads Holmes (id., pp. 1936–8) in much the way Moore did, as discussed earlier in this Postscript—but the confusions and problems noted above are the central ones.

PART II

WAYS OF NATURALIZING JURISPRUDENCE

4

Legal Realism, Hard Positivism, and the Limits of Conceptual Analysis*

I. Introduction

The American Legal Realists, as I read them, are *tacit* legal positivists: they presuppose views about the criteria of legality that have affinities with positivist accounts of law in the sense that they employ primarily pedigree tests of legal validity.[1] Since Dworkin's well-known critique of Hart's positivism a generation ago, however, it has been hotly contested whether there is anything about positivism as a legal theory that requires that tests of legal validity be pedigree tests. So-called "Soft" or "Inclusive" versions of positivism are willing to relax the restrictions on the content of a Rule of Recognition to admit non-pedigree criteria of legal validity; "Hard" or "Exclusive" versons of positivism deny that such a move is compatible with the central commitments of positivism. Hard Positivism, of which Raz has been the leading proponent,[2] thus competes with various Soft Positivisms,[3] defended by, among others, Coleman, Lyons, Soper, Waluchow, and now, explicitly, Hart himself in the "Postscript."[4] If the Realists are positivists, as I claim, then

* I am grateful to the students in my Fall 1997 seminar at UT Austin on "Legal Positivism" for help in thinking about these issues and to Brian Bix, Jules Coleman, Neil MacCormick, Scott Shapiro, and Stephen A. Smith for useful comments on earlier drafts.

[1] For the arguments to this effect, see Brian Leiter, "Legal Realism," in Dennis Patterson (ed.), *A Companion to Philosophy of Law and Legal Theory* (Oxford: Blackwell, 1996), 268–9, and Ch. 2 in this volume.

[2] See, e.g., Joseph Raz, "Legal Positivism and the Sources of Law," in *The Authority of Law* (Oxford: Oxford University Press, 1979), 37–52 and Joseph Raz, "Authority, Law and Morality," *The Monist* 68 (1985), 295–324.

[3] Some writers call the view "Inclusive Positivism" or "Incorporationism." I follow Hart's terminology in the text, even though "soft" runs the risk of a pejorative connotation.

[4] Jules Coleman, "Negative and Positive Positivism," reprinted in Marshall Cohen (ed.), *Ronald Dworkin and Contemporary Jurisprudence*, (London: Duckworth, 1983), 28–48; Jules Coleman, "Incorporationism, Conventionality and the Practical Difference Thesis," *Legal Theory* 4 (1998), 381–425; David Lyons, "Principles, Positivism and Legal Theory," *Yale Law Journal* 87 (1977), 415–35; E. Philip Soper, "Legal Theory and the Obligation of a Judge: The Hart/Dworkin Dispute," *Michigan Law Review* 75 (1977), 473–519; W.J. Waluchow, *Inclusive Legal Positivism* (Oxford: Clarendon Press, 1994); H.L.A. Hart, "Postscript," in *The Concept of Law*, 2nd ed. (Oxford: Clarendon Press, 1994). Leslie Green argues, plausibly, that *The Concept of Law* by itself does not support attributing Soft Positivism to Hart. See Leslie Green, "The Concept of Law Revisited," *Michigan Law Review* 94 (1996), 1705–07.

it cannot be the case that Soft Positivism is a genuinely positivistic doctrine. But there is more at stake here than just labels. Realist arguments for the indeterminacy of law—arguments central to the whole Realist enterprise—depend crucially on their tacit Hard Positivism.[5] If, in fact, positivism has a more relaxed view of the criteria of legality than Hard Positivism supposes, then Realist arguments depend on unsound tacit premises about legal validity. What is at stake, then, is not whether Realists should be called (tacit) "Positivists" or merely (tacit) "Hard Positivists," but whether their underlying view of the criteria of legality is sound. It can only be so if the best arguments favor Hard Positivism.

II. Positivism

Let us try to say now, more precisely, what is at stake in the dispute between Hard and Soft Positivists. All positivists accept what we may call the "Separation Thesis" (what the law *is* and what the law *ought* to be are separate questions) and the "Social Thesis" (what counts as law in any society is fundamentally a matter of social fact).[6] They differ over the proper interpretation of these theses.

Soft Positivists interpret the Separation Thesis as involving only a modal, existential generalization of the following form: it is (conceptually) *possible* that there exists *at least one* rule of recognition, and thus one legal system, in which morality is not a criterion of legal validity.[7] Hard Positivists, by contrast, interpret the

---

[5] See Brian Leiter, "Legal Indeterminacy," *Legal Theory* 1 (1995), 481–92, and Leiter, "Legal Realism" (n. 1 above), pp. 268–69.

[6] This differs slightly from the characterization offered in Jules Coleman and Brian Leiter, "Legal Positivism," in Dennis Patterson (ed.), *A Companion to Philosophy of Law and Legal Theory* (n. 1 above) 241–60, a characterization which now seems to me too narrow to do justice to the full panoply of positivist doctrines.

[7] See Coleman, "Negative and Positive Positivism" (n. 4 above). Coleman arrives at this doctrine by characterizing the Separation Thesis with a modal operator, i.e., there is no "necessary" relationship between law and morality. (In fact, Hart's classic 1958 paper does not use the modal operator. See H.L.A. Hart, "Positivism and the Separation of Law and Morals," *Harvard Law Review* 71 (1958), 593–629). The resulting "Negative Positivism" (as Coleman calls it) would be a weak enough doctrine if it claimed only that there exists at least one system in which the Rule of Recognition does not make morality a criterion of legality. But Coleman makes the doctrine even weaker than that by introducing yet a *further* modal element. He says that for Negative Positivism there need only be "at least one *conceivable* rule of recognition . . . that does not specify truth as a moral principle among the truth conditions for any proposition of law" and that it is enough that "we can *imagine* a legal system in which being a principle of morality is not a condition of legality for any norm" (id., pp. 30, 31; emphases added). As Coleman has noted, even Dworkin need not deny Negative Positivism in this sense. Indeed, a natural law theorist could accept Coleman's modal interpretation of Negative Positivism as well, as long as the natural-law claim that morality is a criterion of legality is taken to state a contingent, not necessary, truth about the concept of law, i.e., a truth that holds in this world, but not in all possible worlds. Of course, natural lawyers typically want to make a stronger claim than this.

Coleman does note elsewhere that, "Some might take the separability thesis to mean that law and morality are distinct in that no moral principles can count as part of a community's law." "Authority and Reason," in Robert George (ed.), *The Autonomy of Law: Essays on Legal Positivism* (Oxford: Clarendon Press, 1996), 287, 315 n. 5. I think it a desideratum in a characterization of the separability

Separation Thesis as requiring a universal generalization of the form: for all rules of recognition, hence for all legal systems, it is not the case that morality is a criterion of legality; *unless* some content-neutral criterion makes it so.[8] Soft Positivists interpret the Social Thesis as saying only that a society's Rule of Recognition is constituted by the social facts about how officials actually decide disputes; thus, for example, if it is the "practice" or "convention" of officials to decide disputes by reference to morality, then morality, in that society, is a criterion of legality. Hard Positivists, by contrast, interpret the Social Thesis as a constraint on the *content* of the Rule of Recognition, not simply on its existence-conditions. Thus, for Hard Positivists the Social Thesis says *not only* that a Rule of Recognition is constituted by social facts (e.g., facts about the conventional practice among officials in resolving disputes) but also that the criteria of legal validity set out by any society's Rule of Recognition must *consist* in social facts (e.g., facts about pedigree or sources).

III. Conceptual Arguments

All important arguments for Hard Positivism to date have been *conceptual* arguments, i.e., they defend Hard Positivism on the grounds that it provides a better explanation for various features of the concept of law. But what exactly is the "concept" of law? The nature of conceptual analysis in legal theory is rarely discussed explicitly or at great length,[9] though it is widely acknowledged to be the dominant *modus operandi* of jurisprudents. We may start by asking: what is a "concept"? A cynic might say that a "concept" is just what philosophers used to call "meaning" back when their job was the analysis of meanings. But ever since Quine embarrassed philosophers into admitting they did not know what "meanings" were, they started analyzing "concepts" instead. The cynical view has, I think, a modicum of truth, but it is hardly the whole story.

To start, there is the obvious point that the philosophical interest in "concepts" (or "meanings") is not like the lexicographer's interest in "meaning": the philosophical aim is not to track and then regulate linguistic practice and usage. As Raz puts it: "we do not want to be slaves of words".[10] At the same time, we cannot ignore words, because words and concepts stand in a close (partly evidentiary, partly constitutive) relationship. Yet one important difference between words and concepts is that it is concepts, and not words, that are the objects of propositional

---

thesis that it allow for this possible reading, especially since Coleman's preferred "modal" interpretation renders the thesis trivial, as Coleman himself acknowledges.

[8] Even in this latter scenario, Hard Positivists may want to deny that morality is an actual *standard* that *constrains* judicial decision.

[9] One recent exception is Brian Bix, "Conceptual Questions and Jurisprudence," *Legal Theory* 1 (1995), 470–5. Judging from recent work circulating in manuscript, it now appears the subject is attracting more attention from legal philosophers.

[10] Raz, "Legal Positivism and the Sources of Law" (n. 2 above), p. 41.

attitudes. "You can't do that, it's against the law" and "You can't do that, the legislature has prohibited it" both express the same concept—namely that of illegality—though one speaks of "the law" and the other of the actions of a legislature. So when jurisprudents appeal to the concept of law they are appealing to the object of a diverse set of propositional attitudes held by those who engage in "law-talk": the law-talk has as its object the concept of law, and the various types of law-talk different people (lawyers, judges, legal scholars, ordinary citizens) engage in has both evidentiary and sometimes constitutive value as to the contours of the concept. The objects of propositional attitudes, though, are abstract objects, and this invariably presents epistemic difficulties: the objects are not there to be picked up, weighed, measured, and scrutinized. We may sometimes wonder whether the object of all propositional attitudes concerning law is really the same "thing." Such a worry can prove fatal to the project of conceptual analysis. One reason ethical non-cognitivists think there is no fruitful analysis of "good" in the offing is because they think the objects of propositional attitudes about goodness are, in fact, different. A similar worry could arise about law.

The concept "law" seems, of course, to have referential content—it represents some feature of the real world—and it must be this point that Raz is making when he says that the argument for Hard Positivism "is not an argument from the ordinary sense of 'law' or any other term. It relies on fundamental features of our understanding of a certain social institution, the primary examples of which are contemporary municipal legal systems...".[11] An "understanding" of a social institution is, I take it, just our "concept" of that institution—precisely what all our law-related propositional attitudes have as their common object, even though they are couched in differently worded sentences-in-the-head. But if the referent of the concept is the ultimate object of inquiry, are we still "slaves" to words, at least at an evidential level? Not necessarily. Hart, it will be recalled, accepted J.L. Austin's (perhaps mistaken) rationale for "looking at words," namely that we "are using a sharpened awareness of words to sharpen our perception of phenomena".[12] But if we are skeptical about the Hart/Austin view, then the rationale for "looking at words" is less clear. Analyzing law-talk *may* be instrumental to the goal of understanding the real world. There is no particular reason, though, to think it is the only or even the best instrument. Yet it is the one legal philosophers, at least, continue to claim, distinctively, as their own.

Legal philosophers, then, who defend Hard Positivism typically appeal to specific features of the *concept* of law—the concept manifest in all kinds of law-talk, the concept that is the *real* object of all the many propositional attitudes people have when they engage in law-talk—for which Hard Positivism alone provides the best explanation. To date, the major conceptual arguments for Hard Positivism have been *functional* arguments, i.e., arguments that appeal to some aspect of our

---

[11] Id., p. 50.
[12] H.L.A. Hart, *The Concept of Law* (Oxford: Clarendon Press, 1961), p. 14, quoting Austin.

concept of the *function* of law. We may distinguish two main types of Functional Arguments: arguments from Public Guidance and from Authority.[13] Sections IV and V examine these arguments in detail, considering and, in some cases, responding to certain now familiar objections. In the end, I argue that only the argument from Authority succeeds, at least as a conceptual argument. Section VI concludes, however, by revisiting some of the worries about this whole style of argument. Satisfactory resolution of these debates, I suggest, requires that jurisprudence move beyond mere conceptual analysis.

IV. Public Guidance

Dworkin ascribes to Positivism (and Raz, among others, accepts) the claim that the function of law is to "provide a settled public and dependable set of standards for private and official conduct, standards whose force cannot be called into question by some individual official's conception of policy or morality."[14] Against Soft Positivism, then, it is argued that if morality can be a criterion of legality, then law cannot discharge this function, since the inherently controversial nature of moral claims and arguments will leave the law unsettled and the boundary between settled law and an "individual official's conception of . . . morality" vague.

Put this way, however, the argument claims too much: a claim about function may, indeed, be part of our concept of law, but it cannot plausibly be part of the *concept* that law functions *well* or *successfully*.[15] For this latter claim would then render a *conceptual impossibility* what seems, manifestly, to be an actuality: namely, that some legal systems function poorly. Thus, a successful functional argument against Soft Positivism must take the form of a pure *impossibility* argument: it must show that it is *impossible* for law to fulfill its function *at all* given the Soft Positivist theory of law. We can try to do this by recasting the argument in explicitly *epistemic* terms.[16]

---

[13] Yet a third genre, which appeals to our concept of what it means to be guided by a rule, has recently been developed by Scott Shapiro. See Scott J. Shapiro, "The Difference That Rules Make," in Brian Bix (ed.), *Analyzing Law: New Essays in Legal Theory* (Oxford: Clarendon Press, 1998), 33–62, and "On Hart's Way Out," *Legal Theory* 4 (1998), 469–507. I do not discuss these interesting new arguments here.

[14] Ronald Dworkin, *Taking Rights Seriously* (Cambridge, Mass.: Harvard University Press, 1977), 347. Raz accepts this as a commitment of Positivism in "Authority, Law and Morality" (n. 2 above), p. 320. Raz does not, however, invoke this as an argument *for* Hard Positivism; only Dworkin does that. Hart, in the "Postscript", seems to acquiesce in this move, as discussed in n. 16, below.

[15] I am indebted to Scott Shapiro for clarification on this issue.

[16] Dworkin's argument for Hard Positivism based on the "ideal of protected expectations" is really a variation on the *epistemic* version of the Public Guidance argument. See Dworkin, *Law's Empire* (Cambridge, Mass.: Belknap Press, 1986), 117 ff. According to Dworkin, the Positivist theory of law must answer the fundamental question of political philosophy: how can the exercise of coercive power be justified? It can only be justified, for Dworkin's Positivist, if the law "give[s] fair warning by making the occasions of coercion depend on plain facts available [i.e. epistemically accessible] to all rather than on fresh judgments of political morality, which different judges might make differently."

On the epistemic version of the argument, the claim is that it is a distinctive feature of the Rule of Recognition (hence of law) that it fulfill an *epistemic* function, i.e., empowering (at least) officials to recognize what the law is, if not with absolute certainty all the time, then at least with some reasonably high degree of certainty most of the time.[17] The conceptual claim, then, is that we do not have a legal system when officials cannot recognize law with a high degree of certainty most of the time. The argument is that Soft Positivism is not compatible, in principle, with this possibility, i.e., with the Rule of Recognition discharging this essential epistemic function.

According to Soft Positivism, the only constraint on a Rule of Recognition is that its existence-conditions are constituted by social facts, e.g., facts about how officials actually decide disputes. This means Soft Positivism is compatible, in principle, with what we may call the "Extreme Scenario," that is, the scenario in which it is the practice or convention of officials to decide all disputes by reference to Natural Law.[18] Such a Rule of Recognition could not discharge its epistemic function, unless (a) there are moral truths, and (b) we can have reliable knowledge of these truths most of the time. There is little reason to think that Soft Positivism could carry the heavy metaphysical and epistemological burden demanded by the prospect of the Extreme Scenario which Soft Positivism itself licenses. Since Soft Positivism is compatible, in principle, with the Extreme Scenario, Soft Positivism is incompatible, in principle, with the Rule of Recognition fulfilling its epistemic function.

Id., p. 117. As an argument for Hard Positivism, this is vulnerable to the objection that it builds too much into the concept of law, insofar as it assumes (as Hart puts it) "that the point or purpose of law and legal practice is to justify coercion." "Postscript" (n. 4 above), p. 248. Even if we do not go as far as Hart in claiming that "positivism . . . makes no claim to identify the point or purpose of law and legal practices as such," we can agree with Hart's (not obviously consistent) claim that it is "quite vain to seek any more specific purpose which law as such serves beyond providing guides to human conduct and standards of criticism of such conduct." Id., p. 249. In other words, Dworkin's more particularized version of the Public Guidance argument attributes to our *concept* of the function of law more than might uncontroversially be found there. For further discussion, however, of the problem with appeals to our "concept" of law, see the final section of this paper.

[17] Thus, I reject Coleman's view that the *semantic* sense of the Rule of Recognition is primary. Coleman, "Negative and Positive Positivism" (n. 4 above), pp. 30–31. Treating the semantic interpretation as primary seems contrary both to what Hart actually says (e.g. "Postscript" (n. 4 above), p. 251) and to the label he chose: it is, after all, a rule of "*recognition,*" and recognition is an epistemic capacity.

In recent work, Coleman has recast his earlier distinction between *semantic* and *epistemic* versions of the Rule of Recognition in terms of the difference between the Rule of Recognition fulfilling a "validation" function and an "identification" function. While the Rule always fulfills a validation (or semantic) function, it does not, says Coleman, fulfill an identification (or epistemic) function for ordinary citizens. See Coleman, "Authority and Reason" (n. 7 above) 307 ff., and "Incorporationism, Conventionality and the Practical Difference Authority" (n. 4 above), 416 ff. While this distinction seems, initially, to have some force against Raz's authority argument (see the discussion in the text, below), it has no force against the argument from epistemic function considered in the text, since the Rule of Recognition must still serve an epistemic function for officials if no one else.

[18] This would still be a weaker doctrine than traditional Natural Law Theory, since Natural Law is a criterion of legality in the Extreme Scenario only because of a contingent fact, i.e., this is how officials actually decide disputes.

Notice that it does not help the Soft Positivist to respond, as Waluchow does, that even a Rule of Recognition that satisfies Raz's Sources Thesis can still involve uncertainty.[19] This, of course, is true. But the only relevant question is one of degree, since Positivists do not maintain that the Rule of Recognition must eliminate all uncertainty.[20] Hard Positivism does require that there be truths about social facts and that we can have reliable knowledge of these truths. When comparing the ability of Hard and Soft Positivism to explain how a Rule of Recognition can fulfill its epistemic function, the crucial issue is whether we have reason to think that uncertainy will be compounded by the need to carry the metaphysical and epistemological burdens for both social facts *and* moral facts. But how could it not? How could ontological promiscuity and the resulting epistemological complexity such promiscuity entails *not* increase the burdens, hence increase uncertainty?

Of course, it remains possible that even though Soft Positivism necessarily *increases* uncertainty, it does not (in principle) increase it beyond the threshold that renders the fulfillment of the Rule of Recognition's epistemic function *impossible*. I do not see any way to rule out conclusively this latter possibility. In that event, the argument from Public Guidance can only make us skeptical about Soft Positivism, but cannot show it to be incompatible with law's function so conceived.

Interestingly, Hart acknowledges a related difficulty posed by permitting morality to be a criterion of legality, and it is worth looking at what he (as a defender of Soft Positivism) says about it. Hart writes:

[A] moral test can be a test for pre-existing law only if there are objective moral facts in virtue of which moral judgments are true... [I]f there are no such facts, a judge, told to apply a moral test, can only treat this as a call for the exercise by him of a law-making discretion in accordance with his best understanding of morality and its requirements and subject to whatever constraints on this are imposed by the legal system.... [I]f the question of the objective standing of moral judgments is left open by legal theory, as I claim it should be, then soft positivism cannot be simply characterized as the theory that moral principles or values may be among the criteria of legal validity, since if it is an open question whether moral principles and values have objective standing, it must also be an open question whether "soft positivist" provisions purporting to include conformity with them among the tests for existing law can have that effect or instead, can only constitute directions to courts to *make* law in accordance with morality.[21]

Law, in short, fails to provide public guidance if moral criteria of legality are tantamount to a license for judicial discretion, which is what they will be in the absence of an objectivist metaethic.

Note that nothing of importance in this passage turns on Hart's particular conception of what is required for the objectivity of morals, i.e., "objective moral facts

---

[19] Waluchow, *Inclusive Legal Positivism* (n. 4 above), 122.
[20] See, e.g., Hart's "Postscript" (n. 4 above), 251.   [21] "Postscript" (n. 4 above), pp. 253–4.

in virtue of which moral judgments are true." What is important is Hart's concession that Soft Positivism requires the objectivity of morality *in some sense*. Yet Hart adopts a rather casual posture towards this metaethical issue because he thinks that "the judge's duty will be the same" regardless of our metaethical stance: "It will not matter for any practical purpose whether in so deciding cases the judge is *making* law in accordance with morality (subject to whatever constraints are imposed by law) or alternatively is guided by his moral judgment as to what already *existing* law is revealed by a moral test for law".[22] This response seems unsatisfactory on a couple of scores.

First, it is not clear why *making a practical difference* is a relevant consideration in this context. We are seeking a sound theoretical understanding of the social phenomenon of law. It suffices to defeat a candidate theory if it generates an intractable theoretical dilemma, like being unable to account for how law could possibly fulfill its "public guidance" function or how the Rule of Recognition could possibly fulfill its epistemic function. Second, the issue at stake may, in any case, make a *practical* difference, in two different ways. Insofar as we view any incorporation of moral criteria of legal validity into a Rule of Recognition as tantamount to a licence for the exercise of judicial discretion, then judges who are adverse to exercising discretion at the first-order level of deciding a case on the merits[23] may "avoid the substance of the [moral] test and appeal instead to more familiar considerations like framers' intention, community consensus, or plain meaning."[24] Moreover, if an objectivist metaethic is correct, then it seems that would *necessarily* make a practical difference to how judges *ought* to decide cases that involve appeal to moral criteria of legality.

If these two points are correct, and if Hart were also correct in his meta-jurisprudential claim that "legal theory should avoid commitment to controversial philosophical theories of the general status of moral judgments",[25] then it would follow that Soft Positivism is untenable. For Soft Positivism requires taking a stand on controversial metaethical questions, and thus would violate the meta-jurisprudential scruples Hart endorses. But it seems unfair to rest an argument against Soft Positivism solely on Hart's particular, and perhaps idiosyncratic, meta-jurisprudential scruples.

---

[22] Id., p. 254.

[23] As distinct from the meta-level of deciding which rule of interpretation to employ.

[24] W.J. Waluchow, "Hart's 'Postscript'", *APA Newsletters* 96 (Fall 1996), 54.

[25] "Postscript" (n. 4 above), pp. 243–54. Curiously, Hart does not avail himself of what would seem to be the easiest line of response, which would allow him to avoid metaethics and simply rely on the tacit semantics that informs his argument about the "open texture" of language. For presumably moral predicates can have core and penumbral instances just like other predicates (e.g., "vehicle"): the core of a moral predicate is just the extension to which most competent speakers of the language would readily assent. Now while the core meaning of moral predicates would generally be smaller, and the penumbral instances larger, it would still be the case that where the facts of the case fall within the core of the moral predicate, Soft Positivism would not simply license discretion *and for exactly the same reason it does not license discretion in the case of a rule like "No vehicles in the park."*

V. Authority

The most important functional argument in favor of Hard Positivism is Raz's argument from authority. According to this argument, it is essential to law's function that it be able to issue in *authoritative* directives—even if it fails to do so in actuality. Raz claims that only his Sources Thesis is compatible with the possibility of law possessing authority. According to Raz, a legal system can only claim authority if it is possible to identify its directives without reference to the underlying ("dependent") reasons for that directive. This is a "prerequisite" for authority because what distinguishes a (practical) authority in the first place is that its directives pre-empt consideration of the underlying reasons (including, e.g., moral reasons) for what we ought to do, and in so doing actually makes it more likely that we will do what we really ought to do. But Soft Positivism makes the identification of law depend on the very reasons that authoritative directives are supposed to pre-empt, and thus makes it impossible for law to fulfill its function of providing authoritative guidance.

Soft Positivists have ventured three kinds of rejoinders to Raz's argument from authority. First, Soft Positivists might contest whether identifying laws by reference to moral considerations necessarily requires taking into account the dependent reasons on which those laws are based. "The set of all moral reasons," Waluchow notes, may "not [be] identical with the set of dependent reasons under dispute . . .".[26] Even if this were right, it would not prove enough. For it suffices to defeat Soft Positivism as a theory compatible with the law's authority if there exists *any* case in which the dependent reasons are the same as the moral reasons which are required to identify what the law is; that there remain some cases where these reasons "may" be different is irrelevant.[27] Moreover, if moral reasons are always overriding in practical reasoning—a view accepted, in fact, by most moral theorists[28]—then moral reasons will *always* be among the dependent reasons for any authoritative directive. Therefore, if identifying that directive requires recourse to moral reasons, the preconditions for authority will fail to obtain.

Second, Coleman has argued that Soft Positivism is compatible with the law's claim to authority because the Rule of Recognition is not the rule by which

[26] Waluchow, *Inclusive Legal Positivism* (n. 4 above), 139. For a similar objection, see Coleman, "Incorporationism, Conventionality and the Practical Difference Thesis" (n. 4 above), pp. 414–5.

[27] Waluchow has responded to this objection by claiming that "the preconditions of the authority of *some* directives does not require the authority of *all* directives." W.J. Waluchow, "Authority and the Practical Difference Thesis," *Legal Theory* 6 (2000), 71. But this misses the point that the authority argument is a *possibility* argument, i.e., an argument showing that the authority of law is *impossible* if one allows content-based criteria of legality. Thus, while it is surely true that *in actuality* some directives may prove to be authoritative and some not, what matters for the possibility argument is that it is even *possible* that some might fail to be authoritative, which is precisely the upshot of the Soft Positivist view of legality.

[28] Philippa Foot and Bernard Williams come to mind as exceptions. See the discussion in Brian Leiter, "Nietzsche and the Morality Critics," *Ethics* 107 (1997), 258–60.

ordinary people (those subject to the law's authority) *identify* what the law is.[29] Recasting his earlier, well-known distinction between the "semantic" and "epistemic" senses of the Rule of Recognition in terms of "validation" versus "identification" functions, Coleman argues as follows:

For there to be law there must be a validation rule—one that is as broad as incorporationism [i.e., Soft Positivism] allows. For law to be authoritative, however, there must be an identification rule—one that may not be so broad. There is a problem for incorporationism only if those two rules must be identical. They need not be, however, and often they are not. The Sources Thesis . . . imposes a constraint [only] on whatever rule ordinary citizens employ to identify the law that binds them. Since most ordinary citizens are able to determine the law that binds them, whereas few, if any, are able to formulate or state the prevailing rule of recognition, it is unlikely that the rule of identification [i.e. the *epistemic* guise of the rule of recognition] is the [*semantic*] rule of recognition.[30]

Coleman's argument calls attention to an important point: the *in-principle* authority of law is only impugned if the rule used to *identify* the law requires recourse to dependent reasons. The difficulty is that the Rule of Recognition must still perform an epistemic function for *officials*, and so Soft Positivism would still undermine the Rule's authority vis-à-vis them. Since Coleman has abandoned the claim about ordinary people in more recent work,[31] and since nothing turns on it, I refer the interested reader to an earlier version of this paper for a detailed (but now moot) refutation of that claim.[32]

Finally, some Soft Positivists have wanted to deny that *authority* involves *exclusionary* reasons, i.e., excluding from consideration the dependent reasons on which the authority bases his directive. "There is no reason," says Waluchow, "to think that authority is an all or nothing exclusionary matter."[33] Waluchow endorses Perry's view that an authoritative directive provides only "a second-order reason [which is] a reason for treating a first-order reason as having a greater or lesser weight than it would ordinarily receive, so that an exclusionary reason is simply the special case where one or more first-order reasons are treated as having zero weight."[34]

If authoritative directives are *not* exclusionary reasons, then the fact that one might need to consider dependent reasons in order to identify law—a consequence of Soft Positivism—would not be fatal to law's claimed authority. The crucial question then is whether it is central to the concept of authority that an

[29] "Authority and Reason" (n. 7 above), 307–308; "Incorporationism, Conventionality and the Practical Difference Thesis" (n. 4 above), 416 ff.

[30] "Authority and Reason" (n. 7 above), p. 308.

[31] Coleman now denies that the issue is "about the ways in which, as an empirical matter, ordinary folk come to learn the law of their community." "Incorporationism, Conventionality, and the Practical Difference Thesis" (n. 4 above), 420.

[32] "Realism, Hard Positivism, and Conceptual Analysis," *Legal Theory* 4 (1998) 542–43.

[33] Waluchow, *Inclusive Legal Positivism* (n. 4 above), 136.

[34] Stephen R. Perry, "Judicial Obligation, Precedent, and the Common Law," *Oxford Journal of Legal Studies* 7 (1987), 223.

authoritative directive *exclude* from consideration all dependent reasons. Let us take the example of precedent, on which both Perry and Waluchow rely. If a court overrules a precedent, surely the natural thing to say is that the overruling court did not treat the precedent as authoritative. It is natural to say this precisely for Razian reasons: the overruling court went back and struck the balance among the dependent reasons differently than did the overruled court. That is, it did not treat the prior court's decision as constituting an exclusionary reason for deciding the instant case a particular way, and in failing to do so, it did not treat the precedent as authoritative.

But on the Perry/Waluchow view, an overruled precedent may still be spoken of as authoritative insofar as the overruling court was required to "weigh [it] . . . more heavily than normal, i.e. more heavily than in other contexts in which authority is not present and reasons compete equally on their respective merits alone."[35] Yet this way of looking at the matter entails the bizarre conclusion that an overruled precedent may be described as "authoritative," when that is precisely what it seems not to be in virtue of having been overruled! Should we really say that an overruled precedent is "authoritative" just because the overruling court says, "We accord this precedent considerable weight in our decision, but in the end we decide the same issue the opposite way?"[36] The crucial idea behind the Razian analysis of the concept is precisely that what distinguishes authority is not simply that its pronouncements get taken "seriously" (whatever that means[37]) but that they are taken so seriously that they exclude further consideration of the reasons pertaining to the matter at hand. That the Razian analysis coincides with our intuitive way of thinking about the status of overruled precedents suggests that it captures something essential about the concept of authority.

VI. The Limits of Conceptual Analysis

We have seen that the leading arguments for Hard Positivism all depend upon claims about the concept of law, in particular, about our concept of the function

---

[35] Waluchow, *Inclusive Legal Positivism* (n. 4 above), 137.

[36] Waluchow does not share my intuitions about how the rhetorical question should be answered. See "Authority and the Practical Difference Thesis" (n. 27 above), 69–70. Waluchow thinks it equally "natural . . . to say that [the later court] deemed the precedent's authority to be *outweighed* by *especially strong reasons*." Id., p. 70. Saying a precedent's authority is "outweighed" is just a roundabout way of saying—to my ear at least—that it is not authoritative. But given my doubts about this mode of philosophical argumentation (see Section VI, below), I will not belabor the point here.

[37] Part of the difficulty here attaches to the critically ambiguous notion of "weight" on which Perry relies. How much weight must we assign to a particular directive before it constitutes an authoritative directive? If the Supreme Court were to treat *Roe v. Wade* 410 U.S.113 (1973) as a serious constraint on deciding whether a woman has a constitutional right to choose an abortion, but in the end, decides that a woman has no such right, does it make any sense in this context to speak of *Roe* as "authoritative" because the court "weighed" it seriously before ignoring it?

of law. Stephen Perry has argued in a number of papers[38] that such arguments are incompatible with what he calls "methodological positivism," which "maintain[s] that legal theory is a purely descriptive, non-normative enterprise that sets out, in the manner of ordinary science, to tell us what one particular corner of the world we inhabit is like."[39] His argument, in a nutshell, runs as follows: (1) we always require a background conceptual framework that demarcates the data that our theory aims to describe and explain; we do not, for example, think an adequate theory of adjudication must account for decision-making by judges who accept bribes, or that an adequate theory of American politics must account for the technology of voting booths, or that an adequate theory of history must account for the evolution of human language, even though this too transpires in real historical time; (2) part of the background conceptual framework essential for jurisprudence is a view about the *function* of law, a view which allows us to see which features of law the jurisprudential theory must capture; but (3) we cannot specify the function of law without engaging in normative argument, i.e., argument about what the function of law *ought* to be. Thus, we cannot do jurisprudence and be methodological positivists (as Hart, Waluchow, and others claim to be).

(1) is, or should be, an uncontroversial thesis in the general philosophy of science (including social science). (2) should be an equally uncontroversial observation about jurisprudence as one type of social-scientific inquiry. (3) is the important claim for our purposes since it supposes that conceptual analysis—appeal to the *concept* of law (or to a *concept* of law's function)—cannot suffice in jurisprudence. For conceptual analysis *would* be a method consistent with methodological positivism, yet Perry's point is precisely that we cannot remain methodological positivists and still have access to the crucial notion of law's "function" (or "purpose" or "point"). Why does Perry think this?

At bottom, Perry must think that our concept of the "function" of law does not hang together sufficiently well to admit of analysis: there are too many incompatible understandings of the concept, for the jurisprudent simply to fall back upon appeal to "our" concept. Perry thinks, for example, that both the Dworkinian idea that "the fundamental function of the common law is not the guidance of conduct but rather principled adjudication, i.e., the settlement of disputes in accordance with applicable moral principles"[40] or the Holmesian idea that the central concept is that of "sanctions" which "create . . . [prudential] reasons for action which are truly central to an accurate understanding of law"[41] have equal claims to being

---

[38] See especially, Stephen R. Perry, "Interpretation and Methodology in Legal Theory," in A. Marmor (ed.), *Law and Interpretation: Essays in Legal Philosophy* (Oxford: Clarendon Press, 1995), 97–135 and Stephen R. Perry, "The Varieties of Legal Positivism," *Canadian Journal of Law & Jurisprudence* 9 (1996), 361–81.

[39] "The Varieties of Legal Positivism" id., p. 361. For a related line of argument against (what Perry calls) "methodological positivism," see John Finnis, *Natural Law and Natural Rights* (Oxford: Clarendon Press, 1980), 3–22, esp. 3 and 16.   [40] "The Varities of Legal Positivism", id., p. 377.

[41] "Interpretation and Methodology in Legal Theory" (n. 38 above), 113.

"concepts of law" along with the Positivist idea of law as providing public guidance. (He also contests, of course, the Razian analysis of the concept of authority.) Conceptual analysis, by itself, gives us no reason to prefer one concept to the other; only a further, normative argument can do that—or so Perry argues.[42]

Now even the arguments for Hard Positivism reviewed above presupposed somewhat different concepts of the function of law (e.g., providing public guidance, or providing authoritative directives). That there should be different concepts of the function is not *per se* worrisome, as long as a single theory of law (e.g., Hard Positivism) provides the best account of all the genuine features that have a claim to being part of the concept. What is worrisome, however, is if the differing conceptual claims are in tension such that no one theory can account for the viable concepts. That is the position we find ourselves in if Perry's analysis of the situation is correct.

Is it correct? We might still fall back on the claim that certain intuitions about the concept of law really are more fundamental than others, e.g., that there is no "more specific purpose which law as such serves beyond providing guides to human conduct and standards of criticism of such conduct;"[43] or that authority *really does* demand exclusionary reasons. Can the Dworkinian or Holmesian conceptions plausibly claim to capture as fundamental a feature of law as the one Hart identifies? Can the Perry/Waluchow view of authority claim to be as plausible and intuitive as Raz's?

Philosophy becomes unsatisfying, though, when it turns into intuition-mongering and armchair sociology about what is really fundamental to "our" concepts.[44] One way to avoid the hopeless morass of warring conceptual intuitions is to take Perry's route, and abandon methodological positivism as a constraint on jurisprudence.[45] There is, however, another option consistent with methodological positivism, but which requires heeding a more general lesson of modern philosophy of language. Although Quine's seminal attack on the analytic-synthetic

---

[42] For some doubts about Perry's argument, see Coleman, "Incorporationism, Conventionality and the Practical Difference Authority" (n. 4 above), esp. at p. 392 n. 23. Even Coleman claims, however, that "*our* concept" of law has "certain essential features," he just denies that we need recourse to law's function to say what these features are (and thus denies (2), above, in the text). Id., pp. 393–43. We can identify these "essential features," says Coleman, by recognizing "law's institutionality," i.e. "the complex thought that part of the distinguishing feature of law's authority is the idea that legal rules are the result of institutional action of various kinds." Id., p. 395. Pitched at this level of abstraction, however, it is unclear how this is responsive to Perry's worry: what concept of law *exactly* flows from the "institutionality" of law?   [43] Hart, "Postscript" (n. 4 above), p. 249.

[44] Is it not this feature that makes most normative ethics so tiresome and pointless? Note that I can agree with Coleman that, "It does not follow from the existence of controversial cases that there is disagreement at the core, or that the core is empty." Id., p. 389. The worry, however, is precisely that the intuitions conflict *at the core*.

[45] Another possibility is to contest Perry's slide from the claim that the concept of law does not hang together sufficiently well to admit of analysis to the claim that we need *moral and political norms* in order to individuate the subject-matter of jurisprudence. But perhaps *epistemic* norms will suffice, e.g., simplicity, consilience, minimum mutilation of existing theoretical claims, and the like. Perry needs to motivate the turn to moral and political philosophy as the only normative solution.

distinction occasionally gets a polite nod from contemporary philosophers, it is less often that theorists take seriously its upshot: namely, that the claims of conceptual analysis are *always* vulnerable to the demands of *a posteriori* theory construction. It is, in many ways, a strange state of affairs that philosophers continue blithely with conceptual analysis, considering the disastrously bad record of pseudo-truths delivered by this method. As Gilbert Harman has recently written:

When problems were raised about particular conceptual claims, they were problems about the examples that had been offered as seemingly clear cases of a priori truth—the principles of Euclidean geometry, the law of excluded middle, "cats are animals," "unmarried adult male humans are bachelors," "women are female," and "red is a color." Physics leads to the rejection of Euclidean geometry and at least considers rejecting the law of the excluded middle. We can imagine discovering that cats are not animals but are radio controlled robots from Mars. Speakers do not consider the Pope a bachelor. People will not apply the term "bachelor" to a man who lives with the same woman over a long enough period of time even if they are not married. Society pages in newspapers will identify as eligible "bachelors" men who are in the process of being divorced but are still married. The Olympic Committee may have rejected certain women as insufficiently female on the basis of their chromosomes. Just as a certain flavor is really detected by smell rather than taste, we can imagine that the color red might be detected aurally rather than by sight.[46]

But if these "classics" of conceptual analysis all failed for *a posteriori* reasons, why in the world think conceptual analysis in jurisprudence will fare any better? If a proposed conceptual analysis is to be preferred to others, it must be because it earns its place by facilitating successful *a posteriori* theories of law and legal institutions. Such is, I take it, the final ambition of general jurisprudence, as Hart conceives it. And from this perspective, what is objectionable, say, about the Dworkinian take on the "concept of law" is that it is excessively parochial, frustrating the ambitions of general jurisprudence. In other words, what would ultimately vindicate the conceptual arguments for Hard Positivism is not simply the assertion that they best account for the "real" concept of law, but that the concept of law they best explicate is the one that figures in the most fruitful *a posteriori* research programs, i.e., the ones that give us the best going account of how the world works. That would require jurisprudence to get up from the armchair and find out what anthropologists, sociologists, psychologists, and others can tell us about the social practices in and around law. The Realists, in fact, undertook such inquiries, and they did so, as noted at the beginning, employing a (tacit) Hard Positivist view of legality. That is surely defeasible evidence in favor of Hard Positivism—though perhaps too easily defeasible given the mixed success of the Realist research program.[47] But more recent research programs in the spirit of

---

[46] Gilbert Harman, "Doubts About Conceptual Analysis," in M. Michael & J. O'Leary-Hawthorne (eds.), *Philosophy in Mind* (Dordrecht: Kluwer Academic Publishers, 1994), 43, 45. Harman's citations to supporting secondary literature are omitted.   [47] See Ch. 1, p. 56.

Realism have often fared better.[48] These programs, which try to understand the operation of courts in terms of the economic and social demographics that explain their behavior, typically assume that law-based explanations of behavior are confined to explanations in terms of pedigreed norms. At the same time, these social scientific approaches give us a picture of courts which fits them into a broader naturalistic conception of the world in which deterministic causes rule, and in which volitional agency plays little or no explanatory role. Thus, what commends these accounts is that they effect an explanatory unification of legal phenomena with the other phenomena constituting the natural world which science has already mastered. And since these research programs rely (implicitly) on the Hard Positivist "concept" of law, Hard Positivism would be vindicated by its implicit role in our best *a posteriori* theories of law and its place in the causal order of nature.

[48] See, e.g., Frank B. Cross, "Political Science and the New Legal Realism: A Case of Unfortunate Interdisciplinary Ignorance", *Northwestern University Law Review* 92 (1997), 251–325, for a useful survey of the literature.

5

Why Quine is not a Postmodernist*

I. Introduction

Dennis Patterson's wide-ranging book *Law and Truth*[1] has the great virtue of
locating questions of legal theory within their broader (and rightful) philosophical context: that is, as special instances of more general problems in metaphysics
and the philosophy of language. It also sets out a position in jurisprudence that
has some undeniable attractions. Although I have a number of disagreements with
Patterson's treatment of the substantive philosophical issues at stake, there can
be no doubt that he has performed a useful service in forcing legal philosophers
to think seriously about the distinctively *philosophical* problems that define the
discipline of jurisprudence.

I want to organize my discussion around one topic in particular: namely,
Patterson's identification of the great American philosopher Willard van Orman
Quine (b. 1908) as a pivotal figure in the transition from "modernity" to "post-
modernity" (158–9). This characterization, I will argue, involves an important
misunderstanding of Quine's thought. Both the "postmodernism" of its most
famous advocates (e.g. Derrida, Lyotard) and Patterson's "sanitized" postmodernism have only a superficial affinity with the philosophy of Quine. This should
not be surprising to those who, correctly, recognize Quine as a key figure in the
"naturalistic" turn in philosophy over the last thirty years.[2] Philosophers who have
taken the naturalistic turn reject the idea of philosophy as a purely *a priori* discipline, whose methods and results are antecedent to—indeed stand above and

* My thanks to Mark Gergen, William Powers, Jr., Sheila Sokolowski, and Ben Zipursky for helpful comments on earlier drafts. I am especially grateful to Douglas Laycock for impressing upon me
the force of Patterson's position, and thus helping me to clarify my critique. I am very pleased to contribute this paper to the symposium on *Law and Truth*, as but a small token of my gratitude to Dennis
Patterson for his unflagging encouragement and support over the last five years.

   [1] (Oxford: Oxford University Press, 1996). All further citations will be included, by page number,
in the body of the text.

   [2] He is not, I hasten to add, the only figure. Indeed, the Quinean program for "naturalizing" philosophy seems too radical to most philosophers. Far more influential is the paradigm for "naturalizing" philosophy developed in Alvin Goldman's work since the late 1960s, culminating in Alvin I.
Goldman, *Epistemology and Cognition* (Cambridge, Mass.: Harvard University Press, 1986). For an
overview of some of the major issues (with attention to Goldman's influence), see Philip Kitcher,
"The Naturalists Return", *Philosophical Review* 101 (1992), 53–114 .

adjudicate among—the claims of science; philosophy for the naturalist is rather a discipline whose methods and answers must be continuous with (perhaps supplanted by) scientific inquiry. Like the logical positivists, then, Quine remains committed to the primacy of science (especially physical science) in constructing our best theory of the world. He does so for different reasons than the positivists, to be sure, but in the end it is crucial to recognize (as one commentator has aptly put it) that Quine "remained faithful to the underlying spirit of positivism."[3] This central aspect of Quine's thought is lost in Patterson's assimilation of Quine to "postmodernism," with its emphasis on the idea that "no practice or discourse enjoys a privileged position vis-à-vis others" (182). Quine, as we shall see, plainly repudiates such a posture of "tolerance". I, of course, have a particular interest in correcting this misunderstanding because of the central role Quine plays in my arguments for "Naturalized Jurisprudence," a jurisprudence with few affinities to the "postmodern" jurisprudence Patterson defends.[4]

I proceed as follows. In Part II I set out briefly my understanding of Patterson's core jurisprudential position, as defended in Chapters 7 & 8 of *Law and Truth*. This sets the stage for his particular interpretation of Quine, which is the subject-matter of Part III. I demonstrate the inadequacies of this understanding of Quine, and offer an alternative interpretation of the structure of Quine's thought.

II. Legitimacy in Adjudication, Truth in Law

Patterson draws on the work of the well-known constitutional theorist Philip Bobbitt in introducing his conception of "truth" in law.[5] Bobbitt's work is widely recognized for its rich and subtle portrait of the different "modalities" of constitutional argument, a portrait that must resonate immediately with anyone who has spent time studying the twists and turns of constitutional argument in the courts, the law journals, or lawyers' briefs. But Bobbitt's ambition is to do more than provide the definitive descriptive sociology of how constitutional lawyers argue. According to Patterson, Bobbitt's work also shows that the debate about the legitimacy of judicial review "is a pseudodebate, driven by a mistaken picture of the nature of truth in constitutional law" (129). While conventional theorists have thought that constitutional argument must be "legitimated" (129), Bobbitt shows that, "To be legitimate, a constitutional argument must not veer from use of the modalities" (128).

---

[3] Christopher Hookway, *Quine: Language, Experience, and Reality* (Stanford: Stanford University Press, 1988), 2.   [4] See Ch. 1.

[5] See Philip Bobbitt, *Constitutional Fate: Theory of the Constitution* (New York: Oxford University Press, 1982) and Philip Bobbitt, *Constitutional Interpretation* (Oxford: Blackwell Publishing, 1991). I shall not be concerned with the adequacy of Bobbitt's view itself, but only with the adequacy of the view Patterson finds in Bobbitt. For a penetrating critique of Bobbitt's position (one with ramifications for Patterson's view as well), see J.M. Balkin and Sanford Levinson, "Constitutional Grammar", *Texas Law Review* 72 (1994), 1771–803. For Bobbitt's response, see "Reflections Inspired by My Critics", *Texas Law Review* 72 (1994), esp. 1910–26.

This whole line of thought seems to trade on an ambiguity in the meaning of the word "legitimate." Legitimacy in the *philosophical* sense has to do with whether a particular practice is *justified*. Legitimacy in the *sociological* sense has to do with whether a particular practice is "accepted" or "viewed as legitimate" by participants in the practice. The question about the legitimacy of judicial review is the question of how the exercise of coercive political power by courts can be *justified* in a democratic society.[6] From an answer to this familiar question of political philosophy, we may derive morals about which forms of constitutional interpretation are proper in a society such as ours, which are consistent, in other words, with the exercise of coercive power by courts.

By contrast, the sense of legitimacy at stake in claims like, "To be legitimate, a constitutional argument must not veer from use of the modalities" (128) seems to be purely sociological: in effect, Patterson is saying that Bobbitt's descriptive sociology of the modalities of argument actually used by constitutional lawyers is such a good descriptive sociology, that a constitutional argument that fits one of those modalities will be recognized and accepted immediately by good constitutional lawyers.[7] But a practice of argument can be quite legitimate in the sociological sense—i.e. parties to the practice can all feel, "Yes, this is a proper way to argue"— and still be utterly illegitimate in the philosophical sense, in the sense that exercising political power on the basis of such arguments cannot be adequately justified or defended in a democratic society. Bobbitt probably has the right theory of sociological legitimacy of constitutional arguments, but this has no bearing on the question of whether judicial review is legitimate in the philosophical sense, i.e. justified. What we would need is an *argument* to the effect that philosophical questions of justification just collapse into sociological questions about what participants in a practice are willing to "accept as legitimate." But I do not see such an argument in Patterson, and without such an argument, the Bobbitt point is (contrary to Patterson) simply a non-sequitur on the question about the legitimacy of judicial review.

Yet the more important idea Patterson wants to extract from Bobbitt's work is that "truth in law is a matter of the forms [or modalities] of legal argument" (150), i.e., a proposition of law is true if it is supported by one or more of the modalities of legal argument. Truth in law, then, is "internal" (in some sense that remains vague) to the practice of legal argument.

Patterson's point here, as I understand it, relies on an attractive intuition, one widely shared, I suspect, by lawyers. The intuition might be put this way: when

---

[6] I am puzzled by Patterson's assertion that the conventional debate about judicial review is "driven by a mistaken picture of the nature of truth in constitutional law" (129) or that it "treats propositions of constitutional law as if they were propositions about the world (empirical propositions)" (133). I do not see that the traditional debate about judicial review presupposes either of these claims.

[7] Cf. this passage from Bobbitt which Patterson quotes at 146: "Judicial review that is wicked, but follows the forms of argument, is legitimately done; and review that is benign in its design and ameliorative in its result but which proceeds arbitrarily or according to forms unrecognized within our legal culture, is illegitimate." Quoting Philip Bobbitt, *Constitutional Interpretation* (n. 5 above), 28.

Dworkin gives a belabored argument of moral philosophy for the constitutionality of affirmative action[8] or Posner gives a complex efficiency argument for the law of negligence,[9] whatever it is they are doing it does not look much like law. Their arguments in short, whatever their intellectual merit and ingenuity, do not sound much like *lawyers'* arguments, the sorts of arguments lawyers could stand up and make in court without being laughed out of the courtroom or cited for contempt.

We can also put the point more broadly. There has been an unsurprising tendency among the professional class of legal academics to want to develop "theories" of the law: tort law is *really* about efficiency or about corrective justice; constitutional law is *really* about enforcing the rights individuals have as a matter of moral argument; and the like. These "theories" may be the stuff of academic debates and tenure decisions, but they have not much to do with legal argument, with what lawyers and judges really do. In their quest to "reduce" legal categories and legal arguments to economic or philosophical ones, they actually miss the distinctive "internal" logic and integrity of the actual practice of legal argument as we find it in countless oral arguments and lawyers' briefs every day throughout the country.

This is, I hope, a sympathetic re-statement of the intuition that animates Patterson's position (and perhaps also Bobbitt's). As attractive as this intuition may initially appear, it also seems to me inadequate as an objection to the theories of scholars like Dworkin and Posner. The objection strikes me as false insofar as it denies that someone like Dworkin *describes* the practice of legal argument, since that is precisely what Dworkin does—though at a deeper level than the superficial level of how theoretically unreflective judges and lawyers argue.[10] As Dworkin says in *Law's Empire*: though real judges are less methodical than Hercules, Dworkin's ideal judge, "Hercules [nonetheless] shows us the hidden structure of their judgments and so lays these open to study and criticism."[11]

But if the objection is, instead, that this putative description of legal argument at a "deeper" level does *not* really succeed in describing the practice of argument by lawyers and judges, then the objection is question-begging: for that is precisely what Dworkin argues it does. What we would need, and what I do not find in Patterson, is an argument against Dworkin's descriptive claim, against the claim

[8] See, e.g., Ronald Dworkin, "Reverse Discrimination", in *Taking Rights Seriously* (Cambridge, Mass.: Harvard University Press, 1977), 223–9.

[9] See generally, Richard Posner, *Economic Analysis of Law*, 3rd ed. (Boston: Little, Brown, 1986).

[10] As two commentators have aptly observed: "Dworkin's account of legal principles is, of course, abstract and theoretical. But its force as an account comes from how well it tracks the standard methodologies of legal scholars, advocates, and judges... [This "reconstructive" methodology that Dworkin describes] is the dominant methodology in both the practice of law and in legal scholarship." Larry Alexander and Ken Kress, "Against Legal Principles", in Andrei Marmor (ed.), *Law and Interpretation: Essays in Legal Philosophy* (Oxford: Clarendon Press, 1995), 288.

[11] Ronald Dworkin, *Law's Empire* (Cambridge, Mass.: Belknap Press, 1986), 265. That this is also Posner's view is made explicit in Richard Posner, *The Problems of Jurisprudence* (Cambridge, Mass.: Harvard University Press, 1990), 373.

that his theory of adjudication describes "the hidden structure" of legal arguments. To assert that Dworkin (or Posner or anyone else) makes propositions of law "true" by reference to something "outside" of the law constitutes not an argument but the conclusion of an argument that still needs to be made.

How does the foregoing connect with "postmodernism"? Patterson's view is that theories like Dworkin's and Posner's are still in the grips of a "modernist" conception of language as essentially *representational*, as "picturing" facts about the world. On this view, a particular proposition like, "Leiter is liable for his intentional infliction of emotional distress," is true just in case the "facts" are as the sentence pictures them. Sentences are "true," we might say, insofar as they correspond to the facts about the world.

The "postmodern" alternative—which is attributed, variously, to Wittgenstein, Quine, Rorty, and Putnam—involves:

…a shift from a concept of language as representation to language as practice (meaning as use). It is a move from [language as] picturing to [language as] competence, with competence being a manifested ability with and facility in language. (169)

But how do we know that a particular use of language—e.g., saying "It is true that Patterson is liable for his negligence"—is a competent use of language? Patterson quotes Putnam saying that the measure of such competence is whether "a sufficiently well-placed speaker who used the words in that way would be fully warranted in counting the statement as true of that situation" (168). This answer, however, seems to be in tension with another one of Patterson's central themes: namely that "the realism/antirealism debate is phony" (166).

Let me say a few quick words about the debate to which Patterson alludes. The "realist" holds that the meaning of a sentence is given by its "truth-conditions" (i.e. the facts that would have to obtain in the world for the sentence to be true), and that these truth-conditions can, in principle, transcend our best capacities to verify them. The anti-realist denies that "truth" (or "truth-conditions") can transcend our epistemic capacities: "truth" for the anti-realist is "epistemically" constrained. In that sense, "truth" for the anti-realist is often said to be a matter of "warranted assertibility": what is "true" is what we (given our epistemic capacities) would be warranted in asserting.

We can put this all more informally: the realist holds that the "truth" is whatever it is, regardless of whether we human beings now know it or could ever come to know it; the anti-realist holds that "truth" cannot outrun our capacity for verifying or knowing it. The anti-realist view suggests a type of "relativism or crass conventionalism" (169), in the sense that "truth" is relativized to our epistemic capacities or to our existing (or potential) conventions for establishing what the "truth" is.

Now we can articulate the tension between Patterson's claim to have transcended the realism/anti-realism debate and his invocation of Putnam's view that a "competent" use of language is one in which "a sufficiently well-placed speaker who used the words in that way would be fully warranted in counting the statement as true of that situation." The problem is that Putnam's account of "competence" ties correct and incorrect usage to to what we "would be fully warranted in counting . . . as true," i.e. it relativizes "competence" to epistemic capacities, and thus sounds like a classic anti-realist position![12] So "postmodernism" on Patterson's account turns out to be indistinguishable from anti-realism—a result that would not be surprising to some.[13]

Patterson, however, follows Rorty (166–8) in arguing that by rejecting "representationalism"—the view that language and truth are matters of accurate representation rather than of social practice and approval—the realism/relativism debate has been rendered unintelligible.[14] The idea, roughly, is this: once we dispense with the idea of language as representing the way things are, then we no longer have to worry about whether our ways of talking about the world correspond to the (realist) truth (i.e. the way things really are, regardless of what we think) or whether they merely reflect some "relative" truth (i.e. the way we happen to be warranted in taking them to be). So by rejecting the view that language is representational we are supposed to eliminate any worries about the objectivity or relativity of truth.

This argument, however, seems to miss the force of the charge of relativism. For if the core of relativism is that conflicting views can be equally "valid" (where valid means "true" *or* "warranted" *or* "competent"), then precisely by rejecting representationalism (and a substantive notion of "truth") *and* by relativizing warrant to existing social or linguistic practice, Patterson (and Rorty) embrace relativism in precisely the sense anyone has ever cared about. Conflicting views can be "equally valid" on this view as long as they are sanctioned by (conflicting) linguistic or argumentative practices.

So Patterson's "postmodernism" devolves into a type of familiar relativism or anti-realism—a view that is certainly Putnam's view circa the early 1980s and is probably also Rorty's view; I very much doubt it is the position of Wittgenstein,[15] but my main concern is to make clear why this view could not be Quine's.

Before doing so, however, I want to say something about the connection of Patterson's "postmodernism" to better-known versions in the work of various

---

[12] Cf. the worries expressed about the potential relativism in Putnam's view in Brian Leiter, "The Middle Way", *Legal Theory* 1 (1995), 26 n. 32.

[13] See, e.g., Michael S. Moore, "The Interpretive Turn in Modern Theory: A Turn for the Worse?", *Stanford Law Review* 41 (1989), 871–957.

[14] See, e.g., Richard Rorty, "Introduction: Antirepresentationalism, Ethnocentrism and Liberalism", in *Objectivity, Relativism, and Truth* (Cambridge: Cambridge University Press, 1991), 1–20.

[15] This type of interpretation of Wittgenstein was developed in Crispin Wright, *Wittgenstein on the Foundations of Mathematics* (Cambridge, Mass.: Harvard University Press, 1980), and was, in turn, aptly criticized in John McDowell, "Wittgenstein on Following a Rule", *Synthese* 58 (1984), 325–63. Wright himself later rejected his earlier "anti-realist" interpretation of Wittgenstein. See Wright, "Wittgenstein's Rule-Following Considerations and the Central Project of Theoretical Linguistics", in Alexander George (ed.), *Reflections on Chomsky* (Oxford: Blackwell, 1989), 233–64.

"French" theorists. In Lyotard's influential work,[16] for example, postmodernism is associated with the demise of "metanarratives," with the notion that we could ever formulate a comprehensive theory of the world, social and natural, that would give us a "truer" picture of reality. The "postmodern" stance is marked by a spirit of epistemic tolerance: there are many viable ways of understanding the world, many different, equally valid "perspectives," no one of which can claim an epistemic privilege over all the others. This "tolerant" spirit is surely familiar from the work of Derrida, Lyotard, Rorty, Fish, Putnam, Feyerabend, and Goodman, among others.[17] How is it implicated in Patterson's version of postmodernism?

Patterson's account avoids, happily, the sophomoric obscurantism of Derridean ramblings in favor of locating the ground of the "postmodern" perspective in substantive philosophical theses. The core notion is, once again, the idea that language is *not* essentially representational, but is rather a certain sort of "social practice," in which the standards of correct and incorrect usage are the product of the practice itself (rather than "the way the world really is" or the like). But once we give up the idea of language as "representational" (so the argument goes) then we also give up the possibility of defending any one region of discourse—say, science—as better "representing" reality than all the others. The anti-representationalist position in semantics—the view that language is not a medium for representing the world, but rather a "practice" by which we cope with the world[18]—underwrites the postmodern spirit of epistemic tolerance by showing that all "meaning arises from human practices and that no practice or discourse enjoys a privileged position vis-à-vis others" (182), since the notion of "privilege" would only have been intelligible if the "representational" view of language had proved correct.

III. Patterson's Quine versus Quine the Naturalist

It is impossible to understand Quine's contributions to philosophy without an appreciation of the philosophical background of Logical Positivism, to which Quine is reacting. Although Patterson correctly alludes to this point in passing (158), his failure to pay it sufficient attention in the subsequent discussion has deleterious consequences. The basic story has been richly described elsewhere;[19] let me just recap the main points here.

---

[16] Jean-Francois Lyotard, *The Postmodern Condition: A Report on Knowledge* (Minneapolis: University of Minnesota Press, 1984).

[17] It is also often attributed, wrongly, to Nietzsche. See Leiter, "Perspectivism in Nietzsche's *Genealogy of Morals*", in Richard Schacht (ed.), *Nietzsche, Genealogy, Morality: Essays on Nietzsche's "On the Genealogy of Morals"* (Berkeley: University of California Press, 1994), 334–57. Much of the discussion there bears on the issues at stake here.

[18] How exactly it does this without "representing" the world is a matter on which Patterson and other anti-representationalists are not ideally clear.

[19] See especially, George Romanos, *Quine and Analytic Philosophy* (Cambridge, Mass.: MIT Press, 1983).

For the Positivists, truths were of two kinds: truths of meaning, and empirical truths. The latter were the domain of scientic inquiry, while the former consti-tuted the special domain of philosophy. Philosophy had as its task to analyze the meanings of the central concepts necessary for empirical inquiry in science, as part of the more general Positivist project of giving a "rational reconstruction" of science, that is, of vindicating the epistemically special status of science.

Quine's classic early papers—especially "Two Dogmas of Empiricism" (which Patterson discusses), but also "Carnap and Logical Truth" and "Truth by Con-vention" (which Patterson does not mention)—attack the idea that there is a real distinction between statements that are "true in virtue of meaning" versus those that are "true in virtue of empirical fact": in effect, he argues that all statements are answerable to experience (to fact), that none are "true in virtue of meaning" alone. Those we tend to call "analytic" are simply those that we are least willing to give up at that particular point in the history of inquiry: whatever the empirical facts are, we are going to adjust other parts of our theory of the world to accomodate those facts, before we think about rejecting the "analytic" statements.[20]

The collapse of the analytic/synthetic distinction—the distinction between "true in virtue of meaning" versus "true in virtue of fact"—has ramifications for philosophy. For on the Positivist picture, the "analytic" side of the divide was the business of philosophy, while the "synthetic" side was the business of empirical science. But if Quine is right, then there is just nothing there on the "philosophy" side of the divide: there are no "truths in virtue of meaning" for philosophers to analyze and explicate. The only truths are empirical truths, and thus all questions are scientific questions. Philosophy, then, gets "naturalized," i.e. it gets subsumed into science. This is the conclusion Quine explicitly draws in his later work, beginning especially with the classic 1968 paper "Epistemology Naturalized."[21]

There is, of course, another related line of argument running through Quine's work (most clearly in "Epistemology Naturalized"), which is directed at the specif-ically epistemological problems that animated Logical Positivism. The "founda-tionalist" program in epistemology, from Descartes to Carnap, aimed to provide scientific knowledge with an indubitable basis. Taking, once again, Carnap as the key philosophical figure, Quine argues against Carnap's foundationalist program in the *Aufbau* along two fronts: semantic and epistemic. Carnap's semantic program was to translate all sentences referring to physical objects into sentences referring

[20] In 1962, Hilary Putnam argued, persuasively I think, that: (a) contrary to Quine, there really are some (trivial) analytic statements (e.g. that a "bachelor" is "an unmarried man" is "true in virtue of meaning"); but (b) this concession costs Quine nothing in terms of the more substantial philosoph-ical point against Positivism: namely, that in science there are no statements which are genuinely ana-lytic, so that the proposed Positivist reconstruction of scientific practice cannot get off the ground. The history of science, Putnam points out, is full of examples of purportedly "analytic" statements that are, at a later date, treated as revisable empirical statements. See Hilary Putnam, "The Analytic and the Synthetic", reprinted in Hilary Putnam, *Mind, Language and Reality: Philosophical Papers*, vol. 2 (Cambridge: Cambridge University Press, 1975), 33–69.

[21] In W.V.O. Quine, *Ontological Relativity and Other Essays* (New York: Columbia University Press, 1969), 69–90.

only to sense-data; the semantic program cannot be carried out because of meaning holism, the Quinenan doctrine that theoretical terms get their meanings from their place in the whole theoretical framework, not in virtue of some point-by-point contact with sensory input. Carnap's explicitly epistemic program is to show that scientific theories are uniquely justified on the basis of sensory experience. The so-called "Duhem-Quine" thesis about the undetermination of theory by evidence dooms this project. There will always be more than one theory supported by the evidence because for any piece of recalcitrant data, we always have two options: abandoning the theoretical hypothesis being tested, or preserving the hypothesis, but abandoning the auxiliary hypotheses that informed the test of the theoretical hypothesis.[22] With the failure of epistemological foundationalism, Quine thinks we must "repudiate the Cartesian dream of a foundation for scientific certainty firmer than scientific method itself."[23] Epistemology gets "naturalized" in the sense that its central question—the relation between sensory input and theoretical output—is to be answered by science (especially empirical psychology). Philosophy, for Quine, has nothing to contribute by way of *justifying* science, as the failure of the foundationalist program makes plain. This does not mean we can no longer talk about epistemic *norms*; it just means that these norms will themselves be the deliverances of science.[24]

One should not be misled here (as it appears Patterson may have been) by the apparent isomorphism between Quine's view that philosophy has nothing to contribute by way of *justifying* science and Patterson's view that, e.g. philosophy or economics, has nothing to contribute by way of *justifying* law. First, the justificatory problem at issue for Quine and for Patterson is different. Quine is concerned with the question whether philosophy can give a rational defense of science as an epistemically superior mode of knowledge: a "justification" here amounts to showing that science has an epistemically privileged foundation as compared to astrology or religion or metaphysics. In law, by contrast, the question of justification is simply whether the exercise of coercive power by courts is defensible in a democratic society (given certain normative principles that are central to a democratic society).

[22] Here is what I hope is a useful example of the point. Recall the Biblical story of King Solomon, in which Solomon must decide which of two women is the real mother of a particular child. Suppose Solomon hypothesizes that woman A is the *real* mother of the child, while woman B is not. Solomon tests the hypothesis by proposing that the women each get half of the child. If his hypothesis is correct, then he predicts that A will decline to "split" the child, and will let woman B keep the whole child. But notice that this prediction depends on an *auxiliary hypothesis* that the Biblical story never mentions: namely, that a *real* mother's concern for the well-being of her child is always stronger than her jealousy that another should have *her* child. Suppose, now, that, contrary to the prediction, A is eager to split the child, rather than let B just have the child. Logically, this is compatible with the hypothesis that A is the real mother, *if we reject the auxiliary hypothesis*. If we remain committed, however, to the auxiliary hypothesis, then experience falsifies the original hypothesis. But notice that *experience itself appears to do no work in determining which hypothesis we discard*. (I owe the idea for this charming example to Gila Sher.)

[23] W.V.O. Quine, *Pursuit of Truth* (Cambridge, Mass.: Harvard University Press, 1990), 19.

[24] Id.

Notice, now, that the different content of the justificatory problem in each domain is mirrored in the *grounds* or *reasons* for then claiming that philosophy has no justificatory role to play. For Quine, philosophy cannot justify science because: (a) the foundationalist program in epistemology is doomed to failure (because of meaning holism and the Duhem-Quine underdetermination thesis); and (b) the collapse of the analytic-synthetic distinction, in any event, puts all questions—including justificatory questions—within the domain of science; there is no distinctive domain in which philosophy can do its work.

But where are the analogues of these arguments in Patterson's case against the possibility of justifying judicial review? As far as I can see, there are none proferred, nor are there any in the offing. In asking for a justification of judicial review in a democratic society we are not trying to solve any analogue of the foundational problem in epistemology: we are simply asking the familiar and intelligible question of whether, given the norms of a democratic society (which may not, themselves, have any "foundation"), it is permissible for courts to exercise coercive power, and if so, when. I do not see how meaning holism or the Quine-Duhem thesis make any difference in this context. Similarly, the collapse of the analytic-synthetic distinction puts all questions into the domain of science *because science is already the domain in which synthetic questions—questions of fact—are answered.* I have no idea how this Quinean consideration would support Patterson's view that "justification" in law is "internal" to law. It seems to me that the more obvious point to make is that Quine's attack on the analytic-synthetic distinction—indeed Quine's whole philosophical posture which assigns primacy to science—is simply irrelevant to the question of whether judicial review is justified. I cannot imagine this conclusion on my part will be surprising to lawyers or to political philosophers.

One crucial upshot of Quine's naturalism is that "there is no Archimedean point of cosmic exile from which to leverage our theory of the world."[25] All theory is *scientific* theory for Quine; there is no theoretical standpoint from which we can ask, "But is our science true?" This looks superficially like Patterson's claim that "there is no Archimedean point of cosmic exile [or simply from outside law] from which to leverage the practice of judicial review." But the affinity, as I have just argued, is merely superficial. Quine's arguments for the claim that there is no standpoint outside science from which to ask questions like, "What do we know?" and "What is real?" simply have no bearing on Patterson's modest (but, as far as I can see, unsupported) claim that there is no standpoint outside law from which to answer the question, "Is the practice of judicial review justified?" For Quine, all theory is scientific theory because all questions are really questions of empirical fact—there are no non-empirical, purely analytic questions—and science is the practice that has had the most success handling questions of empirical fact. But it is perfectly easy to distinguish the question, "Is the Religious Freedom Restoration

---

[25] Roger Gibson, "Willard van Orman Quine", in Jaegwon Kim & Ernest Sosa (eds.), *A Companion to Metaphysics* (Oxford: Blackwell, 1995), 426–8. For an interesting, extended treatment of this theme, see Peter Hylton, "Quine's Naturalism", *Midwest Studies in Philosophy* 19 (1994), 261–82.

Act constitutional?"—a question "internal" to law, as it were—from the question, "Is it defensible in a democratic society for a court to decide this question?"

Because for Quine all theory is scientific theory, Quine explicitly repudiates the relativism that we have seen Patterson's "postmodern" position entails. Thus, in 1960 he writes:

Have we . . . so far lowered our sights as to settle for a relativistic doctrine of truth—rating the statements of each theory as true for that theory, and brooking no higher criticism? Not so. The saving consideration is that we continue to take seriously our own particular aggregate science, our own particular world-theory or loose total fabric of quasi-theories, whatever it may be. Unlike Descartes, we own and use our beliefs of the moment, even in the midst of philosophizing, until by what is vaguely called scientific method we change them here and there for the better. Within our own total evolving doctrine, we can judge truth as earnestly and absolutely as can be; subject to correction, but that goes without saying.[26]

Far from thinking that this view permits him to move beyond "realism" and "antirealism"—to leave this dispute behind as a vestige of the "modernist" conception of language—Quine draws the opposite conclusion:

In my naturalistic stance I see the question of truth as one to be settled within science, there being no higher tribunal. This makes me a scientific realist. I keep to the correspondence theory of truth, but only holophrastically: it resolves into Tarski's disquotational version of truth rather than a correspondence of words to objects.[27]

But why is there no "higher tribunal" than science? Here is where I think Quine's underlying pragmatism becomes important—though this is not the type of pragmatism Patterson finds in Quine, which he refers to as Quine's "pragmatism on questions of truth" (159).[28] But Quine explicitly repudiates such an approach to truth: "Any so-called pragmatic definition of truth is doomed to failure. . . ."[29] Pragmatism enters not at the level of a theory of truth for Quine—Quine retains the correspondence theory of truth, as we have just seen—but at the level of *justification*. The reason all inquiry proceeds from within science is that science works: it "delivers the goods" one might say. Science, for Quine, is simply on a continuum with common sense,[30] which like science aims to predict the future course of experience in order to facilitate our coping with the world. It is just that science,

---

[26] W.V.O. Quine, *Word and Object* (Cambridge, Mass.: MIT Press, 1960), 24–5.

[27] W.V.O. Quine, "Comment on Lauener", in Robert Barrett & Roger Gibson (eds.), *Perspectives on Quine* (Oxford: Blackwell, 1990), 229.

[28] Patterson cites Hookway, *Quine: Language, Experience, and Reality* (n. 3 above), 50–58 [sic] on this point, but Hookway does not attribute to Quine a pragmatic theory of truth, only an appreciation of the role of pragmatic considerations to questions of what we are justified in believing. Indeed, Hookway lays emphasis on the point that "references to pragmatism vanish from Quine's [later] work" (id., p. 50) and that Quine "describes himself as a realist" (id., p. 52).

[29] *Word and Object* (n. 26 above), 23.

[30] "The scientist is indistinguishable from the common man in his sense of evidence, except that the scientist is more careful." W.V.O. Quine, "The Scope and Language of Science", in *The Ways of Paradox and Other Essays* (Cambridge, Mass.: Harvard University Press, 1976), 233. See also *Word and Object* (n. 26 above), 3 ("science is self-conscious common sense").

unlike, say, folk psychology or economics, predicts the future course of experience with much greater precision and reliability. For creatures like us, it is a pragmatic necessity to figure out what will come next. This pragmatic need puts us all "within" science as it were. "Our cognitive position is always internal to a body of substantive theory,"[31] and that theory is scientific because that is the theory that works for creatures like us. This Quinean pragmatism, once again, has no implications for the question whether or not judicial review is justified or "legitimate" in a democratic society.

Patterson's misconstrual of the role of pragmatism in Quine's thought is connected to his more general misreading of Quine. He claims, for example, that Quine embraced "holism, the view that the truth of any one statement or proposition is a function not of its relationship to the world but of the degree to which it 'hangs together' with everything else we take to be true" (159).[32] But this gets Quine wrong, insofar as it makes Quine's holism sound like the coherence theory of truth: i.e. a proposition is "true" just in case it " 'hangs together' with everything else we take to be true." But truth, for Quine, *is* not a matter of coherence, but of correspondence "to the world" (it is just that, for Quine, there is nothing philosophically substantial to say about truth-qua-correspondence (beyond what Tarski gives us) and there is nothing more to the world than the world as depicted by science).

Putnam's talk about "truth" as attaching to what competent speakers would be "fully warranted" in asserting is similarly anathema to Quine, as is the notion that understanding or knowledge is a matter of "practice, warranted assertibility, and pragmatism" (161).[33] The primacy of science may, ultimately, be justified on pragmatic grounds, but that does not mean that our norms for what we ought to believe (our norms for knowledge) are pragmatic ones. For science gives us our

---

[31] Hookway, *Quine: Language, Experience, and Reality* (n. 3 above), 209. Cf. *Word and Object* (n. 26 above), 22 ("we can never do better than occupy the standpoint of some theory or other, the best we can muster at the time").

[32] Patterson proceeds (also at 159) to quote a long passage from "Two Dogmas" which does not, as far as I can see, support his interpretation. The passage is *not* proposing a theory of "truth"—e.g., a proposition is "true" if it "hangs together" with everything else—but simply describing our epistemic situation, one aptly captured in Quine's favored metaphor of "Neurath's boat."

Neurath analogizes our epistemological situation to sailors who are trying to rebuild their ship while at sea. Since they can not rebuild the whole ship at once—they cannot step outside the ship, as it were, and rebuild it from scratch—they must choose to stand firm on certain planks in the ship while reconstructing others. They will, of course, choose to stand firm on the planks that work the best—a pragmatic choice—while rebuilding those that are less dependable or useful or necessary. Of course, at a later date, the sailors may choose to rebuild the planks they stood on previously, and in so doing they will again stand on some other planks that best serve their practical needs at that point.

Our epistemic situation, for Neurath and for Quine, is the same: we necessarily stand firm on certain "planks" (hypotheses, epistemic norms, etc.) of our theoretical conception of the world while evaluating other claims about the world. The planks we choose to rest our epistemic edifice upon are just those that have worked the best for us in the past. For Quine, these are the "planks" constitutive of science. Of course, nothing precludes the possibility that at some point in the future, we will rebuild the scientific planks as well (while standing firm on other planks), but Quine does not, for good reason, see much evidence that pragmatic considerations will give us any reason to stand firm on other planks in our ship of knowledge.

[33] For a similar misinterpretation of Quine, see Richard Rorty, *Philosophy and the Mirror of Nature* (Princeton, NJ: Princeton University Press, 1979), 170, and the attendant criticism in Ch. 1.

norms for belief, and the norms of science are not "pragmatic": science does not say, "Believe what's useful," but rather, "Believe only those hypotheses that answer to the test of experience" and the like. From within science—the only vantage point we even have on the questions of what is real and what is not—truth is a matter of correspondence, knowledge is fixed by the epistemic standards of science (which are not, themselves, ones of "warranted assertibility" or "pragmatism"), and science is not simply one "practice" among many, one which fails to "enjoy . . . a privileged positions vis-à-vis others" (182). Science is *the* practice— the only game-in-town as it were—insofar as we are interested in knowledge. There is no spirit of "epistemic tolerance" in Quine. Science, for Quine, sorts the wheat from the chaff when it comes to different "perspectives" on reality, and the upshot is fairly austere: the chaff includes not only religion, metaphysics, poetry, and astrology, but also non-behavioral psychology and all the special sciences insofar as they are irreducible to physics.[34]

Of course—to repeat—science enjoys its special status on Quine's view in virtue of its delivering on the pragmatic desiderata of helping us cope with experience better than any other practice. Creatures like us have to be able to anticipate the future course of experience, we have to figure out what will come next. Only science "delivers the goods" on that crucial pragmatic requirement. But once science is so enshrined, there is simply no standpoint from which to get a purchase on the notion whether science describes the "real" world or whether science constitutes "genuine" knowledge: talk about what is "real" or what we "know" are just scientific questions. Quine's "scientism"—his privileging of scientific discourse— is lost in Patterson's assimilation of Quine to "postmodernism." And Patterson affects this assimilation because he neglects Quine's naturalism and because he misunderstands Quine's pragmatism. Patterson's Quine, then, is not the Quine who has so profoundly influenced late-20th-century philosophy.

But perhaps there is yet another way of understanding the isomorphism between Quine's position and Patterson's.[35] Just as Quine rejects "foundationalism" in epistemology—showing that science can have no, nor does it need any, foundation—so too Patterson wants to show—*contra* writers like Posner, Dworkin et al.—that law needs no foundation beyond the practice of legal argument itself. Patterson's anti-foundationalism in law is isomorphic, then, with Quine's anti-foundationalism in epistemology.

Once again, however, the similarity between the two positions is illusory, and for two reasons, the second more substantial than the first.

First: foundationalism in epistemology[36] aims to *justify* our system of knowledge by showing that it rests on a foundation of (a) beliefs that are justified

---

[34] Quine's austere physicalism is a feature of his own substantive view that may not be entailed by his naturalism and pragmatism. For discussion, see Hookway, *Quine: Language, Experience, and Reality* (n. 3 above). [35] Here I am indebted to Bill Powers.

[36] I refer to the classical foundationalist tradition, from Descartes to Carnap. Foundationalism has had new life breathed into it by externalist reliabilism in the work of philosophers like Goldman, David Armstrong, and Fred Dretske.

in virtue of their being inferrable from other justified beliefs; and ultimately (b) "foundational" beliefs, i.e. those beliefs that are "justified" (or "warranted") without their justification depending on their receiving inferential support from any other beliefs. So the foundationalist thinks (contrary to Quine) that our body of scientific knowledge can be justified, *in the sense of being defended or upheld as epistemically special.* "Epistemically special" here just means: supported, at bottom, by foundational beliefs that enjoy a non-inferential warrant.

Now I do not see that when various writers propose that tort law is "really" about efficiency (e.g. Posner) or about corrective justice (e.g. Jules Coleman[37]) that this is equivalent to claiming that the substantive body of tort doctrine can be justified, *in the sense of being defended or upheld as "normatively" special (whether the norms are moral or economic).* Writers like Posner and Coleman aim to "explain" tort law: either conceptually (by explaining the underlying logic of the seemingly disparate doctrines of tort law[38]) or empirically, by licensing predictions of what the courts will do in the future in this domain. But it is perfectly possible to "explain" (either conceptually or empirically) tort law in terms of, e.g., "efficiency" without thinking that this then provides a *justification* for the present structure of tort doctrine. It is the latter claim that we would need for the analogy with Quine to work.

Of course, someone might retort, writers like Posner plainly think that the fact that, e.g., tort law is "efficient" constitutes a justification for the present structure of tort doctrine. The question, in that case, is whether Quinean arguments against epistemological foundationalism give us reason to reject Posner's justificatory "foundationalism" about tort law. This brings us to the second fatal problem with the analogy: the structure of Posner's putative foundationalism is not, in fact, isomorphic with that of the epistemological foundationalism which Quine critiques.

The epistemological foundationalist wants to justify science by showing that it satisfies a particular *epistemic norm*: namely, that science can be "built up" from (a) foundational beliefs (i.e. those which enjoy a non-inferential epistemic warrant); and (b) beliefs inferrable from foundational beliefs. The thrust of Quine's anti-foundationalist argument is to show that such a procedure of "building up" is not possible: we cannot satisfy the justificatory demands of the foundationalist's epistemic norm. But notice, now, that it is the *content* of this epistemic norm itself that is *foundational*, and not simply the fact that we are seeking to "justify" science by reference to some norm.

It is on this latter point that the structure of the Posnerian position differs, thus rendering Quine irrelevant. The Posnerian wants to *justify* tort law by showing that it satisfies a particular norm of what we might call "political morality": namely, efficiency. But the *content* of this efficiency norm is not, itself, foundational in structure. A practice is "efficient," roughly, if it mimics the transactional

---

[37] Jules L. Coleman, *Risks and Wrongs* (Cambridge: Cambridge University Press, 1992).
[38] See Brian Leiter, "Tort Theory and the Objectivity of Corrective Justice," *Arizona Law Review* 37 (1995), 46–7.

outcomes of an ideal market (i.e. one in which there is perfect information, no transaction costs, etc.). To be "efficient," then, is not to be "built up" via a justificatory process grounded in foundational beliefs. But since Quine's anti-foundationalism is an argument against such a justificatory process of "building up"—and not simply an argument against the enterprise of justification, *per se*— then Quine's anti-foundationalism is irrelevant to whether or not tort law can (or needs to be) justified by reference to efficiency.

We can put the point a bit differently. Merely seeking a justification for a practice is not, in itself, "foundational" in the sense to which Quine objects. A foundational justification is one with a very particular structure: one that aims to show that a unique outcome can be justified ("built up") out of constituent elements that rest ultimately on some foundational beliefs (i.e. ones that enjoy a non-inferential warrant). But not all attempts to justify a practice involve seeking a "foundationalist" justification in the objectionable sense. Quine's own defense of science, for example, is decidedly not foundational, but pragmatic, as we have seen. So, too, Posner's attempt to justify tort law or Dworkin's to justify judicial review are not "foundationalist" in the sense to which Quine objects. The isomorphism between Quine's anti-foundationalism and Patterson's (putative) anti-foundationalism turns out to be spurious: it trades on an ambiguity in the word "foundational," in the fact that we can talk about justifying a doctrine or theory by giving it a "foundation" without meaning what the epistemological "foundationalist" means: namely, that it is a unique theory that is justified through a building-block process that rests on claims that enjoy a non-inferential warrant.

All of the foregoing, of course, leaves open the possibility that Patterson's approach to law may yet be defended on other grounds. In that sense, my conclusion is quite modest relative to the ambitious scope of Patterson's book. Simply put: I hope I have succeeded in showing that, contrary to Patterson, Quine the naturalist provides no help in defending a postmodern jurisprudence.

6

Beyond the Hart/Dworkin Debate: the Methodology Problem in Jurisprudence*

For three decades now, much of the Anglo-American legal philosophy curriculum has been organized around something called "the Hart/Dworkin debate," a debate whose starting point is Ronald Dworkin's 1967 critique[1] of the seminal work of Anglophone jurisprudence in the twentieth-century, H.L.A. Hart's 1961 book *The Concept of Law*.[2] Hart's final word on that debate is now available to us in the posthumously published 1994 "Postscript" to *The Concept of Law*, while Dworkin has not published anything substantially new about the debate since his book *Law's Empire* in 1986.[3]

* Thanks to Les Green for helpful comments on an earlier draft; to the audiences at the Legal Philosophy Colloquia at Oxford University in March 2002 and at Cambridge University in November 2002 for valuable comments on and discussion of earlier versions; to the audience and conferees at Notre Dame in April 2003; and to the students (Stephen Bero, Brian Berry, Ian Farrell, Michael Sevel, Sean Whyte) in my Advanced Topics in Jurisprudence course at Texas in the Spring of 2003 for their critical and illuminating engagement with these issues. I am especially grateful to John Finnis for affording me the opportunity to revise the essay taking into account the first version of his critical remarks at the Notre Dame conference—though I am sure I have failed to make as many changes as he would have deemed warranted.

[1] Ronald Dworkin, "The Model of Rules I," reprinted in *Taking Rights Seriously* (Cambridge, Mass.: Harvard University Press, 1977).

[2] Citations will be to the second edition, which includes Hart's Postscript, edited by Penelope Bulloch & Joseph Raz (Oxford: Clarendon Press, 1994).

[3] Ronald Dworkin, *Law's Empire* (Cambridge, Mass.: Harvard University Press, 1986). Most of Dworkin's efforts in the last two decades have been directed at issues in political philosophy (especially the theory of equality) and "applied" constitutional theory, apart from a brief, and rather badly confused, foray into the metaethical questions posed by his famous "right answer" thesis during the 1990s. See esp., Ronald Dworkin, "Objectivity and Truth: You'd Better Believe It," *Philosophy & Public Affairs* 25 (1996): 87–139. For detailed criticism, see Ch. 8.

There is currently an unpublished draft by Dworkin in circulation in which he purports to respond to Hart's "Postscript." This material is "not for quotation," so I will not discuss it here, except to note that it finds Hart guilty of the kind of "Archimedeanism" which Dworkin thinks has afflicted metaethical debate as well, one of the points he argued in "Objectivity and Truth." The failure of the arguments in this latter paper are, I venture, mirrored by the failures of this more recent reply to Hart.

Even more recently, Dworkin has published a bizarre polemic against legal positivism under the guise of a review of a recent book by Jules Coleman. See Ronald Dworkin, "Thirty Years On," *Harvard Law Review* 115 (2002): 1655–87. The polemic is marked by ten pages of relentless mischaracterizations of the views of Joseph Raz—to which I return below—as well as the astounding *ad hominem* accusation that what *really* motivates legal positivists is the desire to mark off "legal philosophy as an independent, self-contained subject and profession" which need not attend to "the academic study of substantive

The moment now seems opportune to step back and ask whether the Hart/ Dworkin debate deserves to play the same organizing role in the jurisprudential curriculum of the twenty-first century that it played at the close of the twentieth.[4] I am inclined to answer that question in the negative, though not, to be sure, because I can envision a jurisprudential future without Hart's masterful work at its center. Rather, it seems to me—and, I venture, many others by now—that on the particulars of the Hart/Dworkin debate, there has been a clear victor, so much so that even the heuristic value of the Dworkinian criticisms of Hart may now be in doubt.

The point is not, I hasten to add, that there remain no challenges to legal positivism, but rather that the significant issues that face legal positivists are now different, often in kind, from the ones Dworkin made famous. These, I shall argue, fall in to two broad categories: first, the correct account of the content of the rule of recognition and its relationship to the possibility of law's authority ("the Hart/Raz debate"); and second, the proper methodology of jurisprudence. I shall say relatively little about the Hart/Raz debate, since it is intramural, taking place against a background of some shared positivist assumptions. The methodology debate, by contrast—at least as it has been shaped by renewed appreciation[5] of John Finnis's seminal challenge in *Natural Law and Natural Rights*[6]—is, in my view, more significant: it promises to show that there is a relevant sense in which law and morality are not separable by challenging the methodological presuppositions of legal positivists. If the very enterprise of understanding the concept of law requires positive moral appraisal of law, then it turns out that questions about the moral foundations of law can not be treated as conceptually severable from questions about the nature of law. Legal positivism does, to be sure, score a partial victory, as Finnis himself concedes when he notes that positivism, in either Hart's or Raz's version, does give an adequate account of "what any competent lawyer . . . would say are (or are not) intra-systemically valid laws, imposing 'legal requirements.'"[7] What it fails to do, according to Finnis, is explain the "central cases" of law,[8] and that would be an inexcusable failing in any compelling theory of law.

and procedural fields of law" or "normative political philosophy." Id., p. 1679. Curiously, he makes this accusation in a review of a book by Jules Coleman, a third of which is devoted to examining the philosophical foundations of the substantive law of torts! More remarkably, he makes this accusation after excoriating Joseph Raz, most of whose work in the last two decades has concerned normative political and moral philosophy! (Hart, too, made important contributions to normative political philosophy.) *So what in the world is Dworkin thinking?* It is utterly mysterious.

    4 The question is not purely scholastic. My own doubts about the central place of Dworkin in the jurisprudential curriculum have arisen as a result of teaching his work, in opposition to Hart's, for a number of years now.
    5 See esp. Stephen R. Perry, "Hart's Methodological Positivism," in *Hart's Postscript: Essays on the Postscript to the* Concept of Law, ed. J. Coleman (Oxford: Oxford University Press, 2001), p. 313 n. 5 ("My thinking about methodology in legal theory has greatly benefited from Finnis's general discussion of this topic, and in particular from his illuminating critique of Hart"). See also, Julie Dickson, *Evaluation and Legal Theory* (Oxford: Hart Publishing, 2001), esp. Chs. 3 and 4.
    6 (Oxford: Clarendon Press, 1980), esp. Ch. 1.
    7 John Finnis, "On the Incoherence of Legal Positivism," *Notre Dame Law Review* 75 (2000), p. 1611.
    8 *Natural Law and Natural Rights* (n. 6 above), p. 11.

Methodology, then, implicates substance—that is, the correctness of any proposed substantive theory of law—and so, given the victory of Hart's positivism in the Hart/Dworkin dialectic, it makes good sense that legal philosophers have now given renewed attention to the methodological issues: for it is here that a new vulnerability of legal positivism has been identified.

In section I, I shall review the Hart/Dworkin and Hart/Raz debates; this review is elementary, and may be safely bypassed by anyone familiar with the shape of that dialectic. In section II, I turn to questions of methodology in jurisprudence. I shall argue for five propositions in this section: first, that Dworkin's constructive interpretivism presents no pertinent challenge to legal positivism, since it is thoroughly question-begging; second, that the pertinent methodological challenge to positivism comes from Finnis, and that Dworkin himself needs Finnis-style argument to motivate interpretivism; third, that positivists can respond to and (with some qualifications) defeat this methodological challenge; fourth, that positivists can also (with some qualifications) rebut Perry's more recent version of Finnis-style arguments; and fifth, that Dickson's attempt to stake out a position (what she calls "indirectly evaluative legal theory") intermediate between the methodological positivism or descriptivism of Hart and Finnis's position is a failure.

Finally, in section III, I turn to a larger debate about methodology that has come to the fore in epistemology, philosophy of mind, and ethics. Here I identify some possible weaknesses of the descriptivist rebuttal to Finnis from section II—the source of the "qualifications" previously noted—and argue for a different way of framing the methodology problem in jurisprudence.

I. The Hart/Dworkin Debate and the Hart/Raz Debate

The Hart/Dworkin debate begins with Dworkin's 1967 paper "The Model of Rules," which attributes to Hart four doctrines, all of which Dworkin rejects: that law consists of "rules" (understood as legal standards that differ from what Dworkin calls "principles"); that *legal* rules are identified via a "rule of recognition," that is, "by tests having to do not with their content but with their *pedigree*"; that where a rule does not control a case, judges have discretion; and that in those cases where judges have discretion, neither party has a pre-existing legal right to prevail.[9]

It is now well known, of course, that Dworkin misrepresented Hart's views on all but the last point.[10] Hart does think that when judges have discretion (in *Hart's* sense of discretion, not Dworkin's—more on that in a moment), no party has a

---

[9] "The Model of Rules I" (n. 1 above), p. 17.

[10] Dworkin's difficulty in representing his opponent's views fairly is one of the peculiar features of his corpus. In Hart's final rejoinder to Dworkin, in "The Postscript" (n. 2 above), I count roughly a dozen occasions where Hart has to complain that Dworkin has misstated Hart's views. (Dworkin fares no better with Raz; see the discussion n. 32 below.) Indeed, it is striking that Hart begins the "Postscript" by referring to a (never written) "second section" of the "Postscript," where he considers

legal right to prevail. But he did not intend the talk of "rules" in *The Concept of Law* to exclude the possibility that in some legal systems the standards that Dworkin calls "principles" can be legally binding;[11] he does not think there is anything about his account of a Rule of Recognition that prevents it from incorporating, as a matter of judicial convention, content-based tests of legal validity;[12] and while there is a sense in which Hart thinks that when "rules"—understood capaciously, as Hart intended, to include what Dworkin calls "principles"—do not control the outcome of a case, judges have discretion, the thrust of Hart's doctrine of discretion is not, in fact, captured by Dworkin's distinction between "strong" and "weak" discretion. This last point warrants further comment.

Dworkin distinguishes a doctrine he calls "strong" discretion—the kind of discretion a decision-maker has when he "is simply not bound by standards set by the authority in question"[13]—from the doctrine he calls "weak" discretion, which says only that "the standards an official must apply cannot be applied mechanically but demand the use of judgment."[14] Weak discretion is both trivial and inescapable, Dworkin thinks, once we recognize that the law can include what he calls "principles," that is legal standards which do not apply in an all-or-nothing fashion even when their factual predicate is satisfied,[15] but rather have to be weighed by the judge against other principles in reaching a decision. Therefore, the only *interesting* doctrine of discretion for a positivist to defend would be the strong version, but, Dworkin argues, once we admit that principles can be law, then it is never the case that judges are "not bound by [authoritative] standards": it is true they may have to exercise judgment in applying principles like "no man should profit from his own wrongdoing," but that is just to acknowledge that judges have weak discretion whenever principles are involved.

The distinction between strong and weak discretion is Dworkin's, not Hart's, and it seems to obscure rather than illuminate Hart's actual reasons for thinking judges have discretion. Hart need not maintain that in cases of discretion, judges are bound by *no* authoritative standards: there may, indeed, be binding standards that narrow the range of possible decisions. Yet even though authoritative standards delimit the range of possible decisions, "None the less there will be points where the existing law [whether "rules" or "principles"] fails to dictate any decision as the correct one," such that judges must exercise "law-making powers."[16] Introducing principles in to the canon of authoritative legal standards does not eliminate this possibility, since principles, as much as rules, can be indeterminate

---

critics other than Dworkin; about these other critics, Hart comments, "I have to admit that in more instances than I care to contemplate my critics have been right . . . " *The Concept of Law* (n. 2 above), p. 239. There is only one point (discussed below in the text) where Hart credits Dworkin with a similar insight.

  [11] *The Concept of Law* (n. 2 above), pp. 259–63.   [12] Id., p. 247.
  [13] "The Model of Rules I" (n. 1 above), p. 32.   [14] Id., p. 31.
  [15] As Hart puts it, "principles" are standards which are "non-conclusive" (*The Concept of Law* (n. 2 above), p. 261): even when legally valid, and thus binding on judges, they do not conclusively decide the matter at hand.   [16] *The Concept of Law* (n. 2 above), p. 273.

insofar as the facts of particular cases fall within the penumbra of the meaning of the operative words in the principle. The rule "No vehicles in the park" may be indeterminate as applied to motor scooters, but so too is the principle "No man may profit from his own wrongdoing" when applied to the heir whose reckless conduct leads to his benefactor's death. Reasoning by analogy, or appealing to the general purposes of particular laws, "certainly defers... [but] does not eliminate the moment for judicial law-making" in all cases, "since in any hard case different principles supporting competing analogies may present themselves and a judge will often have to choose between them, relying, like a conscientious legislator, on his sense of what is best and not on any already established order of priorities prescribed for him by law."[17]

If "The Model of Rules I" is notable mainly for leading Hart to clarify his views (in ways that, arguably, should have been clear from a fair reading of the 1961 book[18]), Dworkin's 1972 paper "The Model of Rules II"[19] caused Hart to change his "practice theory of rules" first articulated in the 1961 book. According to the strong version of that theory, promulgated in 1961, for any "duty" to exist in a community there must exist a "social rule", that is, a practice of convergent behavior among individuals in that community, where the individuals accept the rule describing that behavior from an "internal point of view," that is, they accept it as a standard justifying their own conformity with the pattern and as a basis for criticizing deviation from the pattern. The strong version of the theory, Dworkin shows, is too strong: the vegetarian who says we have a moral duty not to eat meat is not asserting that it is the general practice of individuals *not* to eat meat; so, too, the American abolitionist in 1825 who asserts that it is our duty not to hold other human beings as slaves is not asserting the existence of a pattern of convergent behavior, let alone one which is accepted from an internal point of view. Thus, the practice theory of rules, Hart now says, applies only when "general conformity of a group to [the rules] is part of the reasons which its individual members have for acceptance" of the rules.[20] Thus, Hart acknowledges that the practice theory is not "a sound explanation of morality, either individual or social."[21] But Hart maintains that the practice theory is "a faithful account of conventional social rules," including "the rule of recognition, which is in effect a form of judicial customary rule existing only if it is accepted and practiced in the law-identifying and law-applying operations of the courts."[22] To Dworkin's charge that such an account still does not explain how such a rule can create a *duty* or *reason for action*, Hart retorts that Dworkin confuses the claim "that the participants who appeal to rules as establishing duties or providing reasons for action must believe that there

---

[17] Id., p. 275.

[18] For a more balanced treatment than Dworkin's of what was clear, and what not, in the first edition of *The Concept of Law*, see the illuminating review essay by Leslie Green, "The Concept of Law Revisited," *Michigan Law Review* 94 (1996): 1687–717.

[19] Reprinted in *Taking Rights Seriously* (n. 1 above).

[20] *The Concept of Law* (n. 2 above), p. 255.   [21] Id., p. 256.   [22] Id.

are good moral grounds or justification for conforming to the rules" with the claim "that there must actually be such good grounds."[23]

Unfortunately, Hart, even in the Postscript, encourages this confusion. The practice theory of rules, consistent with the ambitions of descriptive jurisprudence, should be taken as stating only what is true of social practices that *are taken* by members of a community to impose duties, rather than as stating the *actual* grounds of duties that arise from social practices. But when Hart speaks of the "general conformity of a group to" rules as "part of the reasons which its individual members have for acceptance" of the rules, he invites precisely Dworkin's misunderstanding: he makes it sound like *the fact* of convergent behavior is, or needs to be, a *reason* for acting.[24] But all Hart needs for his "descriptive sociology" is the far weaker claim that the existence-conditions for some (not all) talk of "duties" is merely the fact of convergent behavior conjoined with acceptance of the rule describing that behavior from an internal point of view.

After his early critical papers on Hart's positivism, Dworkin turns to the elaboration of his own theory of adjudication and law, according to which the right answer to a legal question is the one that coheres with the "best" theory of the institutional history of the legal system (i.e., its statutes, precedents, constitution, etc.). The "best" theory, in turn, is one that both explains or fits some significant portion of that institutional history and provides the best moral justification of it. The theory was first set out in the 1975 paper "Hard Cases" (reprinted in *Taking Rights Seriously)* and then developed in the 1986 book *Law's Empire.*[25] Although the theory is usually presented by Dworkin as in competition with Hart's positivism, Dworkin, in fact, alters so many terms of the debate, that he is largely talking past Hart. As Hart puts it: "It is not obvious why there should be or indeed could be any significant conflict between enterprises so different as my own and Dworkin's conception of legal theory."[26] In particular, Dworkin simply assumes that, "A conception of law must explain how what it takes to be law provides a general justification for the exercise of coercive power by the state."[27] But this assumption is obviously not shared by Hart, nor is it even clear why any theorist should share it. As Hart writes,

My aim in this book was to provide a theory of what law is which is both general and descriptive. It is *general* in the sense that it is not tied to any particular legal system or legal culture, but seeks to given an explanatory and clarifying account of law as a complex social and political institutions with a rule-governed (and in that sense "normative") aspect. This

[23] Id., p. 257.

[24] Jules Coleman and I pursued that line of argument in our essay on "Legal Positivism," in *A Companion to Philosophy of Law and Legal Theory,* ed. D.M. Patterson (Oxford: Blackwell, 1996), pp. 247–9, but that now seems to me an error, for the reasons explained in the text.

[25] I am inclined to agree with Larry Alexander, in his discussion of *Law's Empire* (n. 3 above), that, "Most of what has changed from *Taking Rights Seriously* are the labels." Larry Alexander, "Striking Back at the Empire: A Brief Survey of Problems in Dworkin's Theory of Law," *Law and Philosophy* 6 (1987), p. 419.   [26] Id., p. 241.

[27] *Law's Empire* (n. 3 above), p. 190.

institution, in spite of many variations in different cultures and in different times, has taken the same general form and structure, though many misunderstandings and obscuring myths, calling for clarification, have clustered around it . . . My account is *descriptive* in that it is morally neutral and has no justificatory aims: it does not seek to justify or commend on moral or other grounds the forms and structures which appear in my general account of law, though a clear understanding of these is, I think, an important preliminary to any useful moral criticism of law.[28]

But Dworkin, by limiting his account of law only to those cases where the exercise of coercive power in accordance with law can be morally justified, has, plainly, changed the topic. Thus, Hart is surely right to say that his own enterprise is "radically different" from Dworkin's, since the latter puts the justification of coercive power at its core, and takes a particular legal culture, the Anglo-American, as its central concern. The only possible challenge Dworkin's theory could present to Hart's is if the former's *particular* jurisprudence of Anglo-American legal systems were deemed correct, but could not be accounted for within the framework of Hart's *general* jurisprudence. In particular, the question for Hart's positivism is whether it can make sense of the phenomenon of judges treating some principles as legally binding, not in virtue of their pedigree but simply in virtue of their content. Hart, famously, thinks his theory can.

In arguing that legal positivism can make room for the possibility of legally valid "principles" (in Dworkin's sense), Hart made two claims: (1) that some principles are, *contra* Dworkin, legally valid in virtue of their pedigree (e.g., principles of the common law like "no man shall profit from his own wrongdoing" are legally valid in virtue of having been adopted by a large number of courts for a long period of time); and (2) that there is nothing in the positivist notion of a Rule of Recognition that precludes content-based tests of legal validity—tests like, "this rule is legally valid in virtue of being a requirement of fairness"—which might account for those principles which are legally binding but lack a pedigree.

It is the second of Hart's two responses to Dworkin that is the entry point for what has become one of the most lively debates in core analytic jurisprudence in the past two decades, what I will call the Hart/Raz debate. This debate poses deep issues about the subsidiary components of the "concept of law" that concerned Hart: for example, what concept of authority is required by the concept of law,[29] and what it means to be guided by a rule.[30] To see what is at stake here, we need to return to Hart's notion of a Rule of Recognition, the secondary rule that sets out the criteria of legal validity in a legal system.

The Rule of Recognition, according to Hart, is a *social* rule, meaning that it is constituted by a customary practice of convergent behavior among judges, where the rule describing that pattern of behavior is accepted by those officials from an

---

[28] *The Concept of Law* (n. 2 above), pp. 239–40.
[29] See Joseph Raz, "Authority, Law, and Morality," *The Monist* 68 (1985): 295–327.
[30] See Scott J. Shapiro, "On Hart's Way Out," in *Hart's Postscript: Essays on the Postscript to the Concept of Law*, ed. J. Coleman (Oxford: Oxford University Press, 2001).

internal point of view. Thus, the Rule of Recognition of a particular society is constituted by the actual practice of officials in deciding disputes about the legal validity of particular rules: do, e.g., officials merely appeal to facts about the pedigree of those rules, or do officials also consider the substantive merits or demerits of the rules in evaluating their legality?

Hart's position, then, is a version of "Soft Positivism," since it holds that the *only* constraint on the content of a society's Rule of Recognition comes from the facts about official practice in deciding questions about legality. Soft Positivists honor the positivist doctrine that law and morality are conceptually independent of each other by noting that it is still a conceptual possibility, on the Soft Positivist view, for there to be a Rule of Recognition, hence a legal system, in which morality is *not* a criterion of legal validity. That morality is a criterion of legal validity in some systems is just a contingent fact about the actual official practice in those systems, not a conceptual requirement of positivism's account of law.

Hard Positivists, led by Raz, dispute this.[31] Hard Positivism takes there to be an *additional* constraint on the content of the Rule of Recognition—beyond the fact that it is a social rule—namely, that the criteria of legal validity it sets out must consist in plain facts about the *sources* or *pedigree* of the rules in question. Hard Positivists motivate these arguments by appeal to other features deemed to be central to the concept of law. Thus, most famously, Raz argues that it is part of our concept of law that it makes an intelligible claim to *authority*, even if that claim is often not realized in practice. According to Raz, however, a legal system can only claim authority if it is possible to identify its directives without reference to the underlying ("dependent") reasons for that directive. This is a "prerequisite" for authority because what distinguishes a (practical) authority in the first place is that its directives pre-empt consideration of the underlying reasons (including, e.g., moral reasons) for what we ought to do (and in so doing actually makes it more likely that we will do what we really ought to do). But Soft Positivism makes the identification of law depend on the very reasons that authoritative directives are supposed to pre-empt, and thus makes it impossible in principle for law—more precisely, the Rule of Recognition—to possess authority.

Raz imports into the concept of law not only a claim to authority, but a claim to a very particular concept of authority according to which an authoritative directive performs a *service* for those subject to it, namely, the service of helping them comply more successfully with what "right reason" would require. Raz's claims about authority are controversial in a number of ways,[32] for example, in

---

[31] Dworkin disputes this too, but for different reasons. See the discussion of the "public guidance" argument in Ch. 4, pp. 125–8.

[32] They are *not* controversial, however, in the ways Dworkin discusses in "Thirty Years On" (n. 3 above) pp. 1665–76, since most of the discussion there is predicated on misstatements—sometimes gross misstatements—of Raz's view. So, e.g., Raz plainly does not hold that "no proposition of law is true unless it successfully reports an exercise of legitimate authority" (id., p. 1666) (a proposition can be a proposition of law even if it is not authoritative; more importantly, Raz's Sources Thesis is *not* a doctrine about what makes applied legal statements true); he certainly does not make any "empirical

treating the hallmark of "authority" as its performing a *service*;[33] in arguing that authoritative reasons must be *exclusionary*, i.e., that they pre-empt all consideration of the dependent reasons on which the authoritative directive is based;[34] in supposing that all law *sincerely* claims authority; and in requiring that there be objectively better and worse answers to *practical* questions (without such answers, it would be impossible to assess whether an authority was performing the required "service").

In some cases, Razians have compelling replies to objections to these aspects of the theory of authority,[35] but at least some Hard Positivists have opted for demonstrating that we can get the same constraints on the Rule of Recognition with more modest conceptual claims: so, e.g., Scott Shapiro claims that positivism is committed to the idea that law guides conduct, but that reflection on the concept of being guided by a rule shows that a Rule of Recognition that employed content-based criteria of legal validity could not possibly guide the conduct of officials.[36] If successful, we get a Hard Positivist conclusion from what are supposed to be more minimal (and thus, less contentious) assumptions about what is part of the concept of law.

While I am inclined to the view that Hard Positivism is correct—though not necessarily for the reasons noted above—I will not argue that here. Rather, I want to call attention to two points. First, the Hart/Raz dispute—the dispute about whether there are constraints on the content of the Rule of Recognition as positivists conceive it—is both the most important on-going debate in recent analytical jurisprudence and one that has already moved beyond Dworkin: this debate will be settled on the terms put forth by Raz, Shapiro, W.J. Waluchow, Jules Coleman, and others. Second, if the Hard Positivists are right, then we are still owed some response to Dworkin's challenge that some "principles"—those

assertion" to the effect "that every legal official believes that the laws he enacts create moral obligations" (id., p. 1667) (the theory is conceptual, not empirical); Raz does not hold that "nothing is a law unless it meets all the necessary conditions of having legitimate authority" (id., p. 1668) (law *claims* authority, but often does not actually possess it); Raz does not claim that "it is part of the very concept or essence of authority . . . that nothing can count as an authority if those putatively subject to it must engage in moral reflection to decide whether to obey it" (id., p. 1673) (whether law has a justified claim to authority is different from the question whether we have an obligation to obey the law); Raz manifestly does not believe that "it would be a conceptual mistake to describe ['an exceptionally silly"] statute as law at all" (id., p. 1673) (it would be a conceptual mistake to think that a directive is a *legal* directive if it could not even satisfy, in principle, the non-normative presuppositions of authority, but there are many valid laws that lack authority, and it *would* be a conceptual mistake to deny that); and so on. I am aware of no instance in philosophical debate of recent decades in which one eminent figure has so utterly mischaracterized and misunderstood the views of another eminent figure *in his field*. That Dworkin was also Raz's colleague at Oxford for decades makes the sometimes elementary confusions about Raz's views all the more mystifying.

[33] For doubts, see Thomas Christiano, "Waldron on Law and Disagreement," *Law and Philosophy* 19 (2000), p. 515.

[34] See Stephen R. Perry, "Judicial Obligation, Precedent, and the Common Law," *Oxford Journal of Legal Studies* 7 (1987), esp. p. 223.

[35] See Ch. 4 for a review of some of the debate, a review basically sympathetic to Raz's position.

[36] "On Hart's Way Out" (n. 30 above).

non-conclusive legal standards that Dworkin distinguished from rules—are legally binding. Hard Positivists can, of course, acknowledge, as Hart did, that some principles are legally binding in virtue of pedigree: what are often called "principles of the common law" seem to be a case in point. As to those other non-pedigreed principles that Dworkin would have us treat as legally binding, the Hard Positivist must insist that we not be misled by judicial rhetoric in these cases: non-pedigreed principles are not legally binding, but it is all too obvious why judges should want to write their opinions *as if* they were.

Dworkin's theory was always an odd hybrid—"the third way" John Mackie called it, between positivism and natural law theory[37]—asking neither the factual/descriptive question of classical positivism, nor the explicitly moral question of certain kinds of natural law theory.[38] But if Hart is right, then Dworkin's theory is no third way at all, but merely an exercise in *particular* jurisprudence: Dworkin simply described the Rule of Recognition for those legal systems—perhaps the American—in which there is a conventional practice among judges of deciding questions of legal validity by reference to moral criteria. Rather than disputing Hart's legal positivism, Dworkin is, on this rendering, a case of applied positivism. And if Raz and his followers are right, then Dworkin's theory is no third way because it is simply not an adequate theory of law at all: among other flaws, it renders unintelligible the law's claim to authority, it has no way of discriminating between legally binding and extra-legal references to morality by officials, and it reifies judicial rhetoric about "discovering" the right answer in hard cases, while missing the lawyer's commonplace that judges exercise discretion in hard cases.[39]

What would remain on the table, then, are legal positivism (in whichever form emerges from the Hart/Raz debate) and any natural law theories that present a genuine challenge to positivism. Since Finnis denies, no doubt correctly, that natural lawyers are committed to affirming that morality is necessarily a criterion of legal validity, this familiar way of stating a dispute with positivism is not at issue. (From a dialectical standpoint, Dworkin's greatest advantage was that he did affirm that morality was necessarily a criterion of legal validity.[40]) Indeed, Finnis

[37] See John Mackie, "The Third Theory of Law," in *Ronald Dworkin and Contemporary Jurisprudence*, ed. M. Cohen (London: Duckworth, 1983).

[38] As Larry Alexander put it years ago: "Dworkin asks: what are the most attractive political/moral principles that, if followed, can account for most of the coercive political decisions our society has taken? That is a very odd question." "Striking Back at the Empire" (n. 25 above), p. 419.

[39] Cf. Hart's comment that "it is important to distinguish the ritual language used by judges and lawyers in deciding cases in their courts from their more reflective general statements about the judicial process" in which the "law-making task" is often acknowledged. *The Concept of Law* (n. 2 above), p. 274.

[40] There is now emerging a minor industry of denying that the denial of a "necessary" connection between law and morality is a distinguishing feature of legal positivism. Notable examples include John Gardner, "Legal Positivism: 5½ myths," *American Journal of Jurisprudence* 46 (2000), esp. pp. 222–5 and Leslie J. Green, "Legal Positivism", *The Stanford Encyclopedia of Philosophy* (Spring 2003 Edition), Edward N. Zalta (ed.), <www-philosophy.stanford.edu/fss/ez.html>. Strictly speaking, the claim that "there is no necessary connection between law and morality" is "absurd," as Gardner puts it. Id., p. 223. The fact that Finnis, among others, affirms it (see "On the Incoherence of Legal Positivism" (n. 7 above) p. 1606) might suggest, of course, that there is more to it than that.

admits (as noted earlier) that positivism—understood either in Hart's or Raz's version—gives an adequate account of "what any competent lawyer...would say are (or are not) intra-systemically valid laws, imposing 'legal requirements.'"[41]

Rather than treating this latter concession as an admission that positivism had answered successfully the question it was actually asking, Finnis, instead, lambasts positivism for failing to answer a question it was never asking, to wit, about "the authoritativeness, for an official's or a private citizen's conscience (ultimate rational judgment), of these alleged and imposed [legally valid] requirements" and about "their lack of authority when radically unjust."[42] Positivists can, of course, answer— and have answered such questions[43]—but not in virtue of their particular positivist

Indeed, prior to the recent industry, one would have supposed it obvious that the slogan was a short-hand for at least two different theses that *are* distinctive of legal positivism (much as the absurd-on-its-face slogan "an unjust law is no law at all" is, in fact, a shorthand for theses with some *prima facie* plausibility, as Finnis has shown: see *Natural Law and Natural Rights* (n. 6 above), pp. 363–6.)

One is a proposition Gardner himself endorses, namely, that morality is not necessarily a criterion of legal validity. Gardner, being a Hard Positivist, endorses a stronger doctrine (that entails the weaker), to wit, that morality is necessarily *not* a criterion of legal validity (see his formulation of LP at id., p. 201). Yet Hart appears to endorse the weaker version of the "no necessary connection" thesis in *The Concept of Law* (n. 2 above), pp. 185–6 ("it is in no sense a necessary truth that laws reproduce or satisfy certain demands of morality, though in fact they have often done so"), and does so again in "The Postscript" when he endorses "soft positivism" (id., p. 250–4), citing, among others, Jules Coleman's 1982 article that popularized this "no necessary connection" thesis: "Negative and Positivism Positivism," reprinted in *Ronald Dworkin and Contemporary Jurisprudence* (n. 37 above). Now even if Finnis does not reject this version of the thesis, Dworkin does, and that must surely explain why it has figured prominently in jurisprudential debate.

The second version of the "no necessary connection" thesis is the one suggested, of course, by Hart's 1958 essay on "Positivism and the Separation of Law and Morals," in his *Essays on Jurisprudence and Philosophy* (Oxford: Clarendon Press, 1983), where the slogan is explicated as requiring "the separation of law as it is and law as it ought to be" (id., p. 52). (Note, too, that in further explicating what this positivist doctrine means, Hart offers a version of the first "no necessary connection" thesis: "in the absence of an expressed constitutional or legal provision, it could not follow from the mere fact that a rule violated standards of morality that it was not a rule of law; and, conversely, it could not follow from the mere fact that a rule was morally desirable that it was a rule of law." Id., p. 55.) This version too states an important dispute with positivism's opponents, especially Finnis, whose ch. 1 in *Natural Law and Natural Rights*—about which more below—aims to show that we cannot say what law is without first asking what it ought to be.

41 Finnis, "On the Incoherence of Legal Positivism" (n. 7 above) p. 1611.

42 Id. Thus, when Finnis says, "*Pace* Coleman and Leiter, the laws of South Africa, or some of them, were not binding, albeit widely *regarded and treated and enforced as* binding" (id.), he states no dispute at all with Coleman and Leiter, "Legal Positivism" (n. 24 above), for nothing in Coleman and Leiter claims that the laws of South Africa under apartheid were *morally* binding, only that they were legally valid. And that latter point Finnis does not dispute. Perhaps it is a moral deficiency of Coleman and Leiter, and other positivists, that we do not always ask and answer the questions that interest Finnis, but it hardly shows positivism to be "incoherent"! (Finnis, to be sure, thinks the "incoherence" results from the fact that positivism sets itself an "explanatory task" that it cannot discharge; the difficulty is that the "explanatory task" in question—"whether, when, and why the authority and obligatoriness *claimed* and *enforced* by those who are *acting as* officials of a legal system, and by their directives, are indeed *authoritative reasons* for [officials' or citizens'] own conscientious action" ("On the Incoherence of Legal Positivism" (id.) p. 1611)—is one Finnis sets for positivism, not one legal positivists set for themselves, as noted in the text.)

43 See, e.g., Leslie J. Green, "Law and Obligations," in *The Oxford Handbook of Jurisprudence and Philosophy of Law*, ed. J. Coleman & S. Shapiro (Oxford: Oxford University Press, 2002).

theory of law, but rather their theories of legitimacy and justified authority. Finnis's objections seem to reflect, at bottom, misunderstanding of what John Gardner has aptly called the "comprehensive normative inertness" of legal positivism: "When a philosopher of law asserts a proposition that neither endorses nor criticises what [lawyers] do, but only identifies some necessary feature of what they do, lawyers and law teachers are often frustrated."[44] But as Gardner says, positivism "merely states one feature that all legal guidance necessarily has, viz. that if valid *qua* legal it is valid in virtue of its sources, not its merits."[45]

There remains, however, a more important way of taking the natural law challenge to positivism, also suggested by Finnis's work, namely, as a challenge to the methodology of descriptive jurisprudence. And it is to this issue that we now turn.

II. Jurisprudential Methodology: Is Descriptive Jurisprudence Possible?

These days when philosophers worry about "methodology" they usually worry about the fruitfulness of conceptual analysis and the epistemic status of the intuitions which do so much work in most branches of philosophy.[46] Seen from this perspective, the methodology debate in jurisprudence has been idiosyncratic and narrow: those, like Perry, Postema, and Stavropoulos, who have worried in recent years about the prospects for what Hart called "descriptive jurisprudence" have not taken issue with his commitment to conceptual analysis, or even to the role of intuitions in legal philosophy.[47] Rather, they have taken issue with his assumption that the methodology of jurisprudence can be purely *descriptive* in character. These critics accept that jurisprudence *is* conceptual and intuition-driven, but dispute what Perry usefully calls the "methodological positivism" characteristic of Hart (and, arguably, other legal positivists), namely, his view that "legal theory can . . . offer a normatively neutral description of a particular social phenomenon, namely law."[48] Now it is curious that this kind of methodology debate is found nowhere else in philosophy, not even in the domains of practical philosophy, of

[44] John Gardner, "Legal Positivism: 5½ Myths" (n. 40 above) p. 203.

[45] Id. Gardner, of course, presupposes the truth of Hard Positivism.

[46] See, e.g., Gilbert Harman, "Doubts About Conceptual Analysis," in *Philosophy in Mind*, ed. J. O'Leary-Hawthorne & M. Michael (Dordrecht: Kluwer, 1994); Frank Jackson, *From Metaphysics to Ethics: A Defence of Conceptual Analysis* (Oxford: Clarendon Press, 1998); *Rethinking Intuition: The Psychology of Intuition and Its Role in Philosophical Inquiry*, ed. M. DePaul & W. Ramsey (Lanham, MD: Rowman & Littlefield, 1998); Jaakko Hintikka, "The Emperor's New Intuitions," *Journal of Philosophy* 96 (1999); Jonathan Weinberg, Shaun Nichols, & Stephen Stich, "Normativity and Epistemic Intuitions," *Philosophical Topics* 29 (2001): 429–60.

[47] Stavropoulos has taken issue, to be sure, with Hart's implicit theory of concepts, but not with the project of conceptual analysis *per se*. See Nicos Stavropoulos, "Hart's Semantics," in *Hart's Postscript* (n. 5 above).

[48] "Hart's Methodological Positivism" (n. 5 above) p. 311. In the place marked by the ellipsis in the text, Perry included "and should": but that is irrelevant to the issue here. Our only question is whether legal theory *can* be descriptively neutral.

which Perry insists jurisprudence is properly a branch. It is an interesting question—at least sociologically, perhaps philosophically too—why jurisprudence should have been afflicted with this debate, while moral and political philosophers go about their business only bothered—if bothered at all—by the skeptics about intuitions and concepts. My tentative hypothesis is that, as with much else that is philosophically peculiar in jurisprudential debate, the fault lies with Dworkin.

In *Law's Empire*, Dworkin advanced the idea that law is an "interpretive concept."[49] To say that law is an interpretive concept is to say, among other things, that we cannot understand the concept unless we understand the *value* or *point* of law. And the point of law, according to Dworkin, is to justify the exerice of coercive power by the state.[50] If we accept all this, then we are, indeed, led to the conclusion that jurisprudence cannot be purely *descriptive*: for a jurisprudential account of law must undertake a normative inquiry in to the conditions under which a normative system claiming to be "law" would, in fact, *justify* state coercion. I am going to refer to this, for ease of reference, as "the Normative Concept of Law," that is, the concept of law according to which law discharges a normative task, namely, justifying state coercion. Dworkin's position, then, is that because law is an *interpretive* concept it follows that the pertinent concept of law for jurisprudence is the Normative Concept described above.

If there is an argument here, it must turn on the claim that law is an interpretive concept. It is not clear, however, that the claim about interpretation can bear this weight. As Raz has commented:

An interpretation of something is an explanation of its meaning. Many if not all legal philosophers think of themselves as explaining the essential features of legal practices, and explaining the relations between them and related phenomena such as other forms of social organization, other social practices, and morality....[Hart himself] was seeking to interpret the complex social institution the law is. If Hart and others did not make as extensive use of "interpretation" as Dworkin does, this is in part because fashions dictate the use of terms, and because they may well have wished to avoid being associated with theories that, in their eyes, misconstrued the nature of interpretation.[51]

---

[49] Dworkin, to be sure, also presented the "semantic sting" argument to show that other legal philosophers were engaged in a failed enterprise: finding shared criteria for the application of the word "law." Dworkin's "semantic sting" argument, such as it is, has by now been subjected to so many withering criticisms, that if there is ever to be hope of "progress" in legal philosophy we should be prepared to say that if any argument is no longer worth discussing, it is this one. For a representative critique, see Jules L. Coleman, "Methodology," in *The Oxford Handbook of Jurisprudence and Philosophy of Law*, ed. J. Coleman & S. Shapiro (Oxford: Oxford University Press, 2002), pp. 314–21. As Coleman points out, one natural way to read Dworkin in *Law's Empire* (n. 3 above) is that he is saying that we are driven to Dworkin's understanding of law as an "interpretive concept" by the failure of criterial semantics. This argument, as Coleman notes, is not valid: "It could only be valid were it true that the semantics of concepts must either be criterial or interpretive." Id., p. 316. Even if it were valid, of course, it would still be false, since Dworkin's argument against criterial semantics fails. In the interest of space, I ignore these issues in the text.

[50] See, e.g., *Law's Empire* (n. 3 above), p. 190: "A conception of law must explain how what it takes to be law provides a general justification for the exercise of coercive power by the state..."

[51] Joseph Raz, "Two Views of the Nature of the Theory of Law: A Partial Comparison," in *Hart's Postscript* (n. 5 above), pp. 1–2.

Talk about "intrepretation," in short, is not really doing any work in Dworkin: one can interpret the concept of law without thinking that concept is equivalent to the Normative Concept. The real question is whether Dworkin's explanation of the Normative Concept of Law is an explanation of *our* concept of law: calling his explanation an "interpretation" of the concept goes no distance towards establishing that. I am inclined, alas, to Hart's view[52] that Dworkin has simply changed the topic: the Normative Concept is one concept of law, but it is plainly not *the* concept, since we all recognize (natural law theorists like Finnis included) the existence of law so thoroughly unjust that it could not possibly justify coercion (even if, with Finnis, we want to deny these are "central cases" of law).

That Dworkin has, in fact, no argument for treating the Normative Concept of Law as *the* concept of law may explain why recent critics of Hart's "methodological positivism" like Perry have returned to Finnis: for Finnis, unlike Dworkin, has an *argument*, and in one form or other, it is the argument revived by the recent critics. Showing why Finnis is wrong goes a long way to showing why the recent methodological debate about descriptive jurisprudence should be retired.

"[A] theorist," says Finnis, "cannot give a theoretical description and analysis of social facts [including law] unless he also participates in the work of evaluation, of understanding what is really good for human persons, and what is really required by practical reasonableness,"[53] that is, reasoning about what one ought to do. He cannot do this because "the subject-matter of the theorist's description [namely, law] does not come neatly demarcated from other features of social life and practice."[54] In the case of social phenomena like law, which are constituted by human actions and practices, "the actions, practices, etc., can be fully understood only by understanding their point, that is to say their objective, their value, their significance or importance, as conceived by the people who performed them, engaged in them, etc."[55] The latter observation, however, states no dispute with Hart's descriptive jurisprudence, since Hart too accepts the hermeneutic constraint on accounts of social phenomena: to wit, that an adequate description of a human social practice must attend to how the participants in the practice understand its meaning and purpose. One can, of course, *describe* the *value* a practice has for its participants without engaging in the practice of evaluation. As Hart put it: "Description may still be description, even when what is described is an evaluation."[56]

So if there is a real quarrel with descriptive jurisprudence here it must pertain to the fact that law "does not come neatly demarcated from other features of social life and practice." As Finnis puts it: "there is no escaping the theoretical requirement that a judgment of *significance* and *importance* must be made if theory is to be more than a vast rubbish heap of miscellaneous facts described in a multitude

52 See the discussion, above, circa n. 28 and accompanying text.
53 Finnis, *Natural Law and Natural Rights* (n. 6 above), p. 3.   54 Id., p. 4.
55 Id., p. 3.   56 *The Concept of Law* (n. 2 above), p. 244.

of incommensurable terminologies."[57] Even the proponents of a purely descriptive jurisprudence, like Hart and Raz, believe that the theory is concerned only with the *important* or *significant* features of law. But, asks Finnis, "from what viewpoint, and relative to what concerns, are *importance* and *significance* to be assessed?"[58] The viewpoint from which these matters are assessed, according to Finnis, is a "practical" one, that is, one "with a view to decision and action."[59] Hart and Raz—arbitrarily, Finnis suggests—confine their attention to law as understood from the "internal point of view"—the point of view of the citizen who accepts the law as providing reasons for acting—while "firmly refus[ing] to differentiate further" between "central . . . [and] peripheral cases *of the internal . . . point of view itself.*"[60] Against this arbitrary refusal, Finnis says that:

[T]he evaluations of the theorist himself are an indispensable and decisive component in the selection or formation of any concepts for use in description of such aspects of human affairs as law or legal order. For the theorist cannot identify the central case of that practical viewpoint [the internal point of view] which he uses to identify the central case of his subject-matter, unless he decides what the requirements of practical reasonableness really are, in relation to this whole aspect of human affairs and concerns. In relation to law, the most important things for the theorist to know and describe are the things which, in the judgment of the theorist, make it important from a *practical* viewpoint to have law.[61]

The non-sequitur at the core of this passage, in fact, mirrors the conflations in the work of Perry, Postema, and Stavropoulos.[62] In Finnis's formulation, the non-sequitur occurs in the slide from what I will refer to as the "Banal Truth" that "evaluations . . . are an indispensable and decisive component in the selection or formation of any concepts for use in description of such aspects of human affairs as law or legal order" to the claim that the evaluation in question involves "decid[ing] what the requirements of practical reasonableness really are." I take

[57] *Natural Law and Natural Rights* (n. 6 above), p. 17.   [58] Id., pp. 11–12.
[59] Id., p. 12.   [60] Id., p. 13.
[61] Id., p. 16. Finnis claims to be describing here an insight "reached more rapidly (though on the basis of a much wider social science) by Max Weber." Id., p. 16. Yet the invocation of Weber's notion of an "ideal-type" (id., p. 9) may be misplaced, given Finnis's conclusions. As two commentators on Weber remark: "The term 'ideal' has nothing to do with evaluations of any sort. For analytical purposes, one may construct ideal types of prostitution as well as of religious leaders. The term does not mean that either prophets or harlots are exemplary or should be imitated as representatives of an ideal way of life." H.H. Gerth and C. Wright Mills, "The Man and His Work," in *From Max Weber: Essays in Sociology*, ed. Gerth & Mills (New York: Oxford University Press, 1946), p. 59. The "ideal type" involves, rather, "the construction of certain elements of reality into a logically precise conception" (id.), as a way of "approximat[ing] the multiplicity of specific historical situations" (id. at 60). Thus, "ideal types" are really models, that abstract from certain particulars, and focus on theoretically illuminating features of varied situations; they are, as Weber puts it, "a technical aid which facilitates a more lucid arrangement and terminology" and then allows us "to determine the degree of approximation of the historical phenomenon to the theoretically constructed type." "Religious Rejections of the World and Their Directions," in *From Max Weber* (id.), pp. 323–4.
[62] See, e.g., Stephen R. Perry, "Interpretation and Methodology in Legal Theory," in *Law and Interpretation*, ed. A. Marmor (Oxford: Clarendon Press, 1995); Perry, "Hart's Methodological Positivism," in *Hart's Postscript*, (n. 5 above); Gerald J. Postema, "Jurisprudence as Practical Philosophy," *Legal Theory* 4 (1998): 329–57; Nicos Stavropoulos, "Interpretivism" (unpublished manuscript).

the Banal Truth to be the uncontested legacy of post-Kuhnian and post-Quinean philosophy of science: there is no such thing as a presuppositionless inquiry, of facts that are "theory-free," and so on. But that goes no distance at all to establishing that the presuppositions of the descriptive enterprise require judgments about what Finnis calls "practical reasonableness" or that the viewpoint from which "importance" and "significance" are assessed is the "practical viewpoint."

Let us distinguish between *epistemic* values and *moral* values. Epistemic values specify (what we hope are) the truth-conducive desiderata we aspire to in theory construction and theory choice: evidentiary adequacy ("saving the phenomena"), simplicity, minimum mutilation of well-established theoretical frameworks and methods (methodological conservatism), explanatory consilience, and so forth. Honor those values—even the explicitly pragmatic ones like simplicity—and, we hope, we will acquire knowledge. Moral values are those values that bear on the questions of practical reasonableness, e.g., questions about how one ought to live, what one's obligations are to others, what kind of political institutions one ought to support and obey, and so forth. The question, then, is whether the judgments of "significance" and "importance" that Finnis rightly insists are indispensable in theory-construction must make reference to moral values in addition to epistemic values? Descriptive jurisprudence accepts the Banal Truth in answering this question "no." Descriptive jurisprudence says that epistemic norms, alone, suffice to demarcate legal phenomena for purposes of jurisprudential inquiry.

Consider an analogy. If I want to provide an analysis of the concept of a "city," whatever analysis I proffer had better explain the familiar, shared features of New York and London and Tokyo and Paris. Any analysis of the concept of "city" that does not fit these paradigm instances (what Finnis would call "central cases") is not an analysis of *our* concept of "city." But now we might imagine the following dialogue between the character I will call "the Natural City Theorist" (NCT) and our proponent of descriptive (conceptual) analysis, "the Descriptivist," concerning the concept of a city:

NCT: How do you know that it is the features of *these* places—New York, Paris, London, etc.—that have to figure in an analysis of the concept of city? Why, in other words, are these the "central cases" for purposes of your analysis?
Descriptivist: Well, because they are paradigm instances of *our* concept: someone who didn't think New York or Paris were paradigm instances of cities wouldn't be using the concept of "city" the way we do.
NCT: Yes, but what gives you the right to claim that they are using the concept of "city" wrongly? How, without thinking about what a city really is from a practical viewpoint, can you rule out the non-conforming usages of the concept?
Descriptivist: Actually, I don't have to say the person who denies that New York and Paris are "cities" is using the concept wrongly; I'm not interested in regulating linguistic or conceptual practice, just in understanding what we call "cities" are actually like.[63] If you're right that there are lots of non-conforming usages of the concept of "city," then perhaps I'll

---

[63] I should note that it is not clear that this retort is available to Frank Jackson; see the discussion, below, in Section III.

have to rename my concept "city". But it doesn't matter what you call it: the point is that places like New York and Paris and London have things in common, things that are, in fact, usually picked out with the concept of a "city." I want to understand what those places have in common, and, at the end of the day, I don't care what you call them. In point of fact, of course, they're usually called cities.

NCT: But isn't that then just an appeal to statistically normal usage?

Descriptivist: Yes, and that's fine for settling the quibble about terminology.[64] The main point is that there are real places in the world—what I've been calling "cities"—that have certain important, common features that make it interesting and fruitful to group them together and ask what it is they share.

NCT: Ah-hah! So now you admit that you've made a value judgment about what is "important" and "fruitful," so your project is not really a descriptive one after all.

Descriptivist: It's as descriptive as chemistry or cognitive psychology: none of us can deny the Banal Truth that our subject-matter has to be demarcated for empirical inquiry to be possible. Cognitive psychologists have to individuate the mind, and decide that neural reactions in the brain are pertinent bits of descriptive data to attend to when a subject has received sensory stimuli, while the growth of facial hair is not. We cut the joints of the world with an eye to epistemic values like simplicity, consilience, coherence with other theories, and so forth. To that extent, *no* project is "purely" descriptive.

NCT: But you need more than *epistemic* norms, you need *moral* and *political* norms to delineate your subject-matter. How, after all, can you say what a "city" is—as distinct from a house, or a farm, or a suburb, or a hamlet—without attending to the essentially *practical* question of how one ought to live?

Descriptivist: I just don't see this. To even ask your *practical* question—ought one to be a city-dweller, or a suburbanite, or a farm inhabitant?—we *already* need to understand the difference between city and suburb and farm. *Your* practical questions are, themselves, parasitic on a demarcation made based on purely *epistemic* criteria, criteria like:

(i) statistically normal usage: most people call London and Paris "cities" rather than "suburbs";

(ii) evidentiary adequacy: experience reveals that there are forms of human communal life, across cultures, that differ in striking ways; the "cities," for example, all have high-density populations, elaborate systems of public transport, higher levels of asocial behavior, and so on; and

(iii) explanatory consilience: it would be illuminating if we could have a unified account of the phenomena noted in (ii), rather than simply viewing them as discreet, brute facts about different countries.

These *epistemic* considerations quite naturally lead us to demarcate "cities" from "farms" and "suburbs" (and so on) as a topic for investigation. How humans *ought* to live is simply a different question.

---

[64] Interestingly, Finnis never really considers this response in *Natural Law and Natural Rights* (n. 6 above). The closest he comes is in the context of quoting Raz (id., p. 10) talking about "typical cases" of law. Finnis notes that "the word 'typical' may suggest that the relevant criterion is statistical frequency" but then adds that he prefers to call these the "central cases," where central cases are defined by reference to how well they meet the demands of "practical reasonableness." Alas, "statistical frequency" seems exactly the right way of taking talk about "typicality," and it is unfortunate Finnis bypassed the adequacy of such a criterion so abruptly. (Ultimately, I agree with Finnis that it *may* not be adequate: but more on that in Section III.)

NCT: Yet surely you must admit that the fact that some human beings have organized their communal life in to cities, while others remain on farms and in suburbs, reflects the *practical* interests and *practical* judgments made by these people?

Descriptivist: Of course, there is nothing in my project that requires me to deny that the way the social world is cut up—into cities and suburbs, into schools and hospitals, into legal systems and systems of informal social norms, etc.—reflects the practical concerns of people. I'm not making any claims about the etiology of these features of the social world; whatever the etiology of particular phenomena like "cities" or "legal systems", my goal is to give a satisfactory descriptive account of what we find.

Now does the Descriptivist fare any worse when we switch from the concept of "city" to the concept of "law"? It is not apparent why he should. So, for example, while it is surely worthwhile to ask whether certain cases of legal systems are *just* and *worthy of obedience*—just as it is worthwhile to ask whether life in "cities" is desireable and conducive to human flourishing—that is simply a different question from the descriptive one of what "law" and "legal systems"—or "cities"—are like. And to even ask the practical question it seems we have to have in place a conceptual demarcation of law from other forms of normative control. And so on.

Perry, while often echoing Finnis,[65] takes a slightly different argumentative tack in more recent work. Perry now describes legal philosophy as being centrally concerned with "the problem of the normativity of law."[66] Indeed, he goes so far as to claim that explaining "the (apparent) reason-givingness of law"—i.e., law's normativity—is the "central task" of legal philosophy.[67] But what is the evidence for this strong claim?

Perry says the problem of the normativity of law involves questions like "How is the concept of legal obligation to be analysed?" and "What does it mean to claim authority over someone?"[68] These questions appear to call for purely descriptive answers: an *analysis* of legal obligation, for example, or an explanation of the *claim* to authority. It is trivially true, of course, that the concepts in question are normative ones, but what is called for, in Perry's own formulation, is a *descriptive* explication of those normative concepts.

Now curiously, Perry himself acknowledges that Hart does not even have an analysis of legal obligation—indeed, Hart has nothing to say about the normativity of law in the main text of *The Concept of Law*, beyond a refutation of the Austinian account. As Perry correctly notes, Hart's social rule theory of obligation "is simply a descriptive statement that (a certain proportion of) members of the relevant group regard themselves and all others in the group as obligated to conform to some general practice. This statement uses rather than analyzes the concept of obligation."[69] Hart's descriptive account, to be sure, distinguishes two

---

[65] For example, when he says that "any given social phenomenon can be accurately described in an indefinitely large number of ways" ("Hart's Methodological Positivism" (n. 5 above), p. 327). More generally, the argument in Perry, "Interpretation and Methodology in Legal Theory" (n. 62 above), is strongly inspired by Finnis.   [66] "Hart's Methodological Positivism," Id., p. 330.
[67] Id., pp. 330–1.   [68] Id., p. 330.   [69] Id., pp. 334–5.

kinds of social practices, those where convergent behavior is *merely* habitual and those where it reflects the fact that agents take themselves to have obligations to engage in that behavior. The latter, according to Hart, is a central social phenomenon wherever there is law, but the Scandinavian Realists—Hart's real target in this context—cannot, because of their "external" perspective, demarcate it from mere habitual behavior and so cannot explain the social phenomenon of law.[70] So Hart's "descriptive statement" suffices for his actual theoretical purposes.[71]

The only way for Perry to convert this "descriptive statement" into a theoretical claim that requires positive moral appraisal of law is for Perry to repeatedly *mischaracterize* it. Thus, while Perry's initial characterization of the "problem of the normativity of law" is, as above, quite clearly descriptive (an "analysis" of legal obligation or the "claim" of authority), he soon begins describing the "problem" as follows: "does law in fact obligate us in the way that it purports to do?"[72] As to this question, he says, quite plausibly, that it "arises within the philosophy of practical reason, and it would seem inevitable that its resolution would require normative and probably moral argument."[73] *Yet this is quite plainly a very different question*, and it is equally plainly a question the answer to which is not required to give an analysis of the concept of law according to Hart. So Perry's normativity problem is simply not Hart's problem. Almost all of Perry's argument, alas, appears to trade on a *sotto voce* slippage between descriptive questions about normativity and the truly *normative* questions, as though the two were the same.

Perry fares no better with Raz, the positivist who does indeed have an account of what it is to "claim authority over someone." Here is the crucial passage in Perry:

> Raz's argument for the service conception of authority is moral in nature. If it is right, then the anarchist thesis that the state could never have the moral authority it claims is wrong. The theory sets out moral conditions of legitimacy which Raz holds are implicit in the concept of law and which must be met if the law is to give rise to obligations that people would not otherwise have. Raz's theory of law is thus also a political philosophy that is in direct competition with, among others, Dworkin's integrity theory (itself both a theory of law and a political philosophy).[74]

Every sentence in this paragraph is, as best I can tell, either flatly wrong or dangerously ambiguous. First, Raz does not argue for the service conception of authority

[70] These points are well developed—against an earlier version of Perry's argument against descriptive jurisprudence—by Scott J. Shapiro in his reply to Perry in *The Path of the Law and Its Influence: The Legacy of Oliver Wendell Holmes, Jr.*, ed. S.J. Burton (New York: Cambridge University Press, 2000).

[71] Perry does, to be sure, sometimes try to exploit the unfortunate fact that in the Postscript, Hart appears to view the fact of convergent behavior as a *reason for* (a ground of) an obligation. As Perry says, "it is not . . . entirely clear whether Hart believes that acceptance of a social rule gives rise to an *actual* obligation for the relevant group's members" or whether the theory simply reports what is the case when "people *regard themselves* as obligated to the rule," "Hart's Methodological Positivism," (n. 5 above) pp. 332–3. As argued earlier, however, Hart goes wrong in trying to respond to Dworkin in this way. See the discussion at n. 24 above and accompanying text.

[72] "Hart's Methodological Positivism" (n. 5 above), p. 335.   [73] Id., p. 336.

[74] Id., p. 352.

on the grounds that it is morally attractive or has morally good consequences: he argues that it is *our* concept. That is a descriptive claim. Second, Raz's account of authority is perfectly compatible with "the anarchist thesis that the state [more precisely, the laws of the state] could never have the moral authority it claims," because Raz's thesis is only that all laws (sincerely) *claim* moral authority, not that they actually have it. The anarchist thesis, in Razian terms,[75] is simply the claim that law always fails to satisfy the Normal Justification Thesis. Nothing in Raz's theory of authority or of law precludes it. Third, Raz's theory does hold that law must meet something like "moral conditions of legitimacy" if it is to give rise to obligations, but *qua* theory of law, it holds only that everything that is law *claims* authority, and thus *claims* to give rise to obligations, but not that it actually does so. The latter claims are not part of a "political philosophy," but rather a descriptive analysis of the concept of law and of authority.

It is certainly true that if one holds that descriptive jurisprudence must answer the questions of substantive moral and political philosophy—what *ought* one to do, what laws *ought* one to obey—then it cannot be purely descriptive. But no one ever denied that. The difficulty with Perry's argument is that he wants to treat these latter questions *as if* they were the questions that descriptive jurisprudents were actually asking. But this is just to misread the targets of the criticism.

I want to conclude by considering one final challenge, of sorts, to the claim that descriptive jurisprudence is possible. Recently, Julie Dickson, in the posture of explicating Raz's view, has argued that there is a position intermediate between descriptive jurisprudence and the view of Dworkin and Finnis that jurisprudence requires moral evaluation of law: this is what Dickson calls "indirectly evaluative legal theory." I will argue that, in fact, this kind of legal theory is just an instance of descriptive jurisprudence and its application of what Dickson calls "meta-theoretical" (what I called *epistemic*) values. There is, in short, *no* conceptual space between descriptive jurisprudence (once the Banal Truth is acknowledged) and the normative conception of jurisprudence.

Dickson motivates her presentation of indirectly evaluative legal theory via a quotation from Raz, and so it is worth examining this passage with some care. Raz says:

Legal theory contributes... to an improved understanding of society. But it would be wrong to conclude... that one judges the success of an analysis of the concept of law by its theoretical sociological fruitfulness. To do so is to miss the point that, unlike concepts like "mass" or "electron," "the law" is a concept used by people to understand themselves. We are not free to pick on any fruitful concepts. It is a major task of legal theory to advance our understanding of society by helping us to understand how people understand themselves.[76]

Let us distinguish two claims about concepts that are implicit in this passage. Let us call a "Natural Kind Concept" a concept whose extension is fixed solely by

---

[75] See "Authority, Law and Morality" (n. 29 above).
[76] Id., pp. 321–2. This is quoted in Dickson, *Evaluation and Legal Theory* (n. 5 above), p. 40.

whatever well-confirmed scientific (lawful) generalizations employ the concept. Let us call a "Hermeneutic Concept" any concept which satisfies two conditions: (i) it plays a hermeneutic role, that is, it figures in how humans make themselves and their practices intelligible to themselves, and (ii) its extension is fixed by this hermeneutic role.

Notice, to start, that lots of Natural Kind Concepts do play hermeneutic roles: "gold" in bourgeois societies, for example, or "water" in many religious baptismal rituals, or "wolverine" in Michigan (the "mascot" of the University of Michigan). Yet none of this makes these concepts Hermeneutic Concepts, because we do not take their extension to be fixed by the hermeneutic roles they do or might play: wolverine is a biological category, unaffected by its role in how Michigan residents and football fans make sense of themselves and their social world.

Now Raz's central claim, in the passage quoted above, is that "the law" is a Hermeneutic Concept. This claim is clearly endorsed by every legal philosopher of the last hundred years, with the exception of the Scandinavian Realists. Hart, famously, has an argument (noted above) why we must treat "law" as a Hermeneutic Concept: namely, that we will not be able to distinguish its extension from that of habitual social practices if we fail to treat it as such. Let us suppose that is correct (let us suppose, in other words, that failure to mark that distinction would result in some explanatory failure of a theory of law).[77]

With this terminology in place, we can restate Raz's argument, in the passage quoted earlier, as follows. According to Raz, social-scientific fruitfulness is not a criterion for the adequacy of an analysis of the concept of law because the concept of law is a Hermeneutic Concept, whereas scientifically fruitful theories all concern Natural Kind Concepts.

I realize, of course, that this restatement goes quite a bit beyond what Raz explicitly says in the quoted passage, but it is the only way I can see to make sense of it: for, on the face of things, it is completely mysterious why one should think a fruitful scientific theory whose target is Hermeneutic Concepts should employ criteria of fruitfulness appropriate only to Natural Kind Concepts—i.e., to concepts whose extension is unaffected by their hermeneutic role—unless, of course, one thought that scientific theories *only* had Natural Kind Concepts in their purview. In the heyday of logical positivism, this would seem a reasonable assumption:[78] *of course*, one would say, the only scientifically respectable concepts are those whose extensions *are* essentially the same as (or reducible to) the extensions of concepts in the physical sciences. But logical positivism, in this regard, is

---

[77] I am not sure it is correct, needless to say, and for a simple reason: many concepts play hermeneutic roles, but their extensions are not deemed to be fixed by those roles. Some other kind of theoretical considerations must explain why the hermeneutic role is paramount in the case of "law" but not, e.g., "wolverine." And what those theoretical considerations are, and how they are to be weighed, is a complex question, that is rarely discussed explicitly in legal philosophy.

[78] Of course, most logical positivists would not, strictly speaking, talk in terms of "natural kinds," except perhaps in the deflationary sense later articulated by Quine: see his "Natural Kinds," in *Ontological Relativity and Other Essays* (New York: Columbia University Press, 1969).

happily defunct, and has been for many decades.[79] And thus, insofar as a scientific theory has as its target a Hermeneutic Concept, it is unclear why what Dickson calls meta-theoretic values (what I called epistemic values) will not suffice for a theory of law. Insofar as a descriptive theory of law takes as its target a Hermeneutic Concept, necessarily a comprehensive, simple, and consilient theory—i.e., a descriptively adequate one—must account for how the concept is "used by people to understand themselves."[80]

Dickson's own central example—that of an agnostic's account of Roman Catholic ritual—illustrates clearly that we need nothing more than *epstemic* values to account for Hermeneutic Concepts. Here is what Dickson says:

> Imagine an agnostic observer who wants to understand a Roman Catholic mass which he attends. In order to be successful in his task, this observer will obviously have to engage in evaluative work, for in order to understand the mass, he will have to understand, amongst other things, what it is for mass to be celebrated well. This will require an evaluation of which things it is important for various of the involved parties to do correctly and an understanding of what those actions mean for them. The observer will, therefore, inevitably be making judgments about which are the most important or significant features of the mass, and which ideals a well-celebrated mass should live up to. However, the observer's judgment that a particular feature of the mass is important or significant will not be supported by his own direct evaluations regarding whether that feature or the ideals to which it is alleged to contribute are good or bad, right or wrong—he is agnostic as regards these matters and is not in the business of making any such evaluations. Rather, the observer's indirectly evaluative judgments of the importance of a given feature of the mass will be supported or justified by the role which that feature plays in the self-understandings of those participants in the mass. Those self-understandings will include the attribution of spiritual and moral value in respect of certain aspects of the mass, and those attributions of value indicate the things which matter to participants in the mass and which are thus important to explain. However . . . the agnostic observer need not share those values, nor himself take a stance on whether the participants are correct in their ascriptions of spiritual and moral value, in order to understand which features of the mass are important and significant for those participating in it.[81]

In this example, we treat the Roman Catholic "mass" as a Hermeneutic Concept, whose extension is fixed by how those who participate in the mass understand it. Epistemic values—most obviously "saving the phenomena"—require that our theory of the mass attend to the features of the mass that are "significant" and "important." This requires, in turn, that we attend to how *those who participate in the mass* understand its significance and importance; it does not, by Dickson's own admission, require that we attend to how the theorist (the agnostic) *evaluates* those

---

[79] See, e.g., Richard W. Miller, *Fact and Method: Explanation and Confirmation in the Natural and Social Sciences* (Princeton: Princeton University Press, 1987); Nancy Cartwright, "From Explanation to Causation and Back Again," in *The Future for Philosophy*, ed. B. Leiter (Oxford: Oxford University Press, 2004). For an earlier argument for a similar conclusion, see Dagfinn Føllesdal, "Hermeneutics and the Hypothetico-Deductive Method," *Dialectica* 33 (1979), pp. 319–36.

[80] Raz, "Authority, Law and Morality" (n. 29 above), pp. 323–24.

[81] Dickson, *Evaluation and Legal Theory* (n. 5 above), pp. 68–9.

practices. Thus, the resulting theory is "indirectly evaluative" only in the trivial sense that to account for the extension of a Hermeneutic Concept—one that figures in the *evaluations* of agents who employ the concept—we must attend (descriptively) to *their* evaluative practices.

This is not simply a terminological quibble, with Dickson calling this "indirectly evaluative theory" while I am calling it a descriptive theory of a Hermeneutic Concept. For it is Dickson's central thesis that there is a conceptual space between the view of theorists like Finnis and Dworkin that "in order to understand law adequately, a legal theorist must morally evaluate law" ("the Moral Evaluation Thesis"[82]) and the Hart-style descriptivist who holds that an adequate understanding of law does not require a moral evaluation of law. The difference here is marked by the posture of the theorist—the one who offers the "adequate understanding"—and what role evaluation plays in his undertaking. *Everyone*, on this accounting, acknowledges that the theorist must employ epistemic values in demarcating the object of theoretical inquiry. The *only* question is whether the theorist must also engage in *moral* evaluation in order to have a theory of the object in question. Dickson, like every descriptivist, denies that. So her "indirectly evaluative legal theory" does not stand in any competition with the Moral Evaluation Thesis, since it agrees wholly with the descriptivist that the answer to the last question is negative. The confusion results from the fact that Dickson, like Raz, thinks epistemic values in scientific theory-construction cannot accomodate the distinctive features of Hermeneutic Concepts. But that assumption is motivated by bad philosophy of science—which is to say, it is *unmotivated*—and it is thus insufficient to motivate a kind of legal theory distinct from both descriptive jurisprudence and the Moral Evaluation Thesis.

III. Philosophical Methodology: The Naturalistic Turn

Legal philosophers have, in my view, been having the *wrong* debate about jurisprudential methodology: legal philosophy is, indeed, *descriptive*, and trivially so, in exactly the way most other branches of practical philosophy have an important descriptive component. The real worry about jurisprudence is not that it is descriptive—*of course* it is (or tries to be)—but rather that it relies on two central argumentative devices—analyses of concepts and appeals to intuition—that are epistemologically bankrupt.

Start with concepts. On the dominant view, from Plato through Carnap to Peacocke "every analysis of a concept is inextricably bound to a collection of purported analyticities."[83] But post-Quine, we know (don't we?) that the analytic-synthetic distinction does not mark an epistemic difference but a socio-historical

---

[82] Id., p. 9.
[83] Stephen Laurence & Eric Margolis, "Concepts and Cognitive Science," in *Concepts: Core Readings*, ed. E. Margolis & S. Laurence (Cambridge, Mass.: MIT Press, 1999), p. 18. Even the more

one. Philosophers long thought that some truths were *necessary* while others were *contingent*; in the twentieth century, under the influence of logical positivism, this was taken to be the distinction between those statements that were "true in virtue of meaning" (hence *necessarily* true) and those that were "true in virtue of fact" (hence only *contingently* true). The former "analytic" truths were the proper domain of philosophy; the latter "synthetic" truths the proper domain of empirical science. Quine argued that the distinction could not be sustained: all statements are, in principle, answerable to experience, and, conversely, all statements can be maintained in the face of recalcitrant experience as long as we adjust other parts of our picture of the world. So there is no real distinction between claims that are "true in virtue of meaning" and "true in virtue of facts," or between "necessary" and "contingent" truths; there is simply the socio-historical fact that, at any given point in the history of inquiry, there are some statements we are unlikely to give up in the face of recalcitrant empirical evidence, and others that we are quite willing to give up when empirical evidence conflicts.

Without a domain of analytic truths—truths that are *a priori* and hold in virtue of meaning—it becomes unclear what special domain of expertise for philosophical reflection remains. If all claims are, in principle, revisable in light of empirical evidence, then would not all questions fall to empirical science? Philosophy would be out of business, except perhaps as the abstract, reflective branch of empirical science. And if analytic statements are gone, then so too is conceptual analysis: since any claim of conceptual analysis is vulnerable to the demands of *a posteriori* (i.e., empirical) theory construction, philosophy must proceed in tandem with empirical science, not as the arbiter of its claims, but as a reflective attempt at synoptic clarity about the state of empirical knowledge.

Even the leading contemporary champion of conceptual analysis, Frank Jackson, appears, on closer inspection, to acknowledge the import of the Quinean critique and thus to seriously *deflate* the role of conceptual analysis in philosophy. According to Jackson, conceptual analysis proceeds "by appeal to what seems to us most obvious and central about [the concept in question] . . . as revealed by our intuitions about possible cases."[84] "[T]he general coincidence in intuitive responses," to possible cases, he says, "reveals something about the folk theory of [the concept in question]",[85] where the "folk theory" is just the "ordinary" understanding of the concept, partly explicit, partly implicit in ordinary ways of talking and thinking. But note that Jackson specifically chastises conceptual analysis in its "immodest role," namely when "it gives intuitions . . . too big a place in determining what the world is like":[86] "There is nothing sacrosanct about folk theory," he notes. "It has served us well but not so well that it would be irrational to make changes to it in the light of reflection on exactly what it involves, and in the light

recent "possession-condition" account of concepts developed by Christopher Peacocke still requires that it be *analytic* that certain inferential transitions are privileged by a particular concept.

[84] Jackson, *From Metaphysics to Ethics: A Defence of Conceptual Analysis* (n. 46 above), p. 31.
[85] Id., p. 32.   [86] Id., pp. 43–4.

of one or another empirical discovery about us and our world".[87] The question is, having conceded this much, what remains? Conceptual analysis, as Jackson conceives it, becomes hard to distinguish from banal descriptive sociology of the Gallup-poll variety. Indeed, Jackson says explicitly that he advocates, when necessary, "doing serious opinion polls on people's responses to various cases"![88] But this now seems to blur the line between conceptual analysis and lexicography: for does not lexicography aim to track statistically normal usage of words or concepts,[89] precisely the pattern of usage a well-designed opinion poll would detect?[90]

Jackson would retort, of course, that even opinion polls have a role to play; he says:

[T]he *questions* we ask when we do metaphysics are framed in a language, and thus we need to attend to what the users of the language mean by the words they employ to ask their questions. When bounty hunters go searching, they are searching for a person and not a handbill. But they will not get very far if they fail to attend to the representational property of the handbill on the wanted person. These properties give them their target, or, if you like, define the subject of their search.[91]

But this makes the difference between conceptual analysis and lexicography even more obscure: do not lexicographers attend "to what the users of the language mean by the words they employ" and then write up the results? Is philosophy, on this account, just glorified lexicography?

Glorified lexicography is important, to be sure, but its results are strictly ethnographic and local: one thing such a method cannot deliver are timeless or necessary truths about how things are. But this is exactly what legal philosophers appear to be after (and it is what philosophers *ought* to be after, isn't it?). On the Razian view, for example, as Dickson explains it,

[A]nalytical jurisprudence is concerned with explaining the nature of law by attempting to isolate and explain those features which make law into what it is. A successful theory of law of this type is a theory which consists of propositions about the law which (1) are necessarily true, and (2) adequately explain the nature of law . . . I am using "the nature of law" to refer to those essential properties which a given set of phenomena must exhibit in order to be law.[92]

---

[87] Id., p. 44   [88] Id., p. 36.

[89] Tony Honoré has impressed upon me that this is a caricature of actual lexicography, which has a strong normative element. So take the characterization in the text as describing a new discipline: "pop lexicography," since tracking statistically normal usage does loom large in the popular image of lexicography. Conceptual analysis in Jackson's sense seems to amount to no more than pop lexicography.

[90] Jackson is unusual in admitting, quite directly, that, "Our subject is really the elucidation of the possible situations covered by the *words* we use to ask our questions . . . I use the word 'concept' partly in deference to the traditional terminology . . . and partly to emphasize that though our subject is the elucidation of the various situations covered by bits of language according to one or another language user, or by the folk in general, it is divorced from considerations local to any particular languagae." *From Metaphysics to Ethics* (n. 46 above), p. 33. On this account, then, the only difference from lexicography is that we are not concerned with statistical normalcy internal to a group of users of just one language.

[91] Id., p. 30. Cf. Timothy Williamson's discussion of what remains of the linguistic turn in his contribution to *The Future for Philosophy*, (n. 79 above).

[92] *Evaluation and Legal Theory* (n. 5 above), p. 17.

A jurisprudential theory that employs conceptual analysis to deliver *necessary* truths and illuminate *essential* properties would plainly involve conceptual analysis in its *immodest* form, and thus will find no solace from Jackson.[93] More seriously, such an approach depends on the assumption that Quine is fundamentally wrong about analyticity, an assumption that, at this late date, requires some explicit defense if we are to take the results of jurisprudential inquiry seriously.

Now consider intuitions.[94] On the "modest" form of conceptual analysis recommended by Jackson, we test a purported analysis of a concept against our intuitions about possible cases. Jackson, like many others,[95] takes the Gettier counter-examples to the analysis of knowledge as "justified true belief" to be a central success story for this method.[96] But we now know, thanks to the empirical work of Jonathan Weinberg, Shaun Nichols, and Stephen Stich, that the Gettier counter-examples report merely ethnographic facts about the epistemological intuitions of certain socioeconomic groups and in certain cultures.[97] Gettier sheds no light on the *nature* of knowledge, *per se*, though he shed considerable light on the epistemic intuitions common among people of a certain class in certain societies.[98] But why should *those* intuitions be of any interest? And, in the absence of

[93] Leslie Green has argued that the role of ordinary language philosophy in Hart's project has been overstated. See Green, "The Concept of Law Revisited" (n. 18 above), p. 1688 n. 1. In one sense this is true: there is only one *explicitly* ordinary-language argument in the book, the appeal to the difference in ordinary language between having an "obligation" and being "obliged" to do something as a way of showing that the Austinian analysis of the concept of law mischaracterizes the normativity of law. See *The Concept of Law* (n. 2 above), pp. 82–3. But insofar as Hart also subscribes to the Razian conception of legal theory described by Dickson—and I take it he does—then he shares a philosophically more important affinity with ordinary language philosophy: namely, the assumption (the *confidence*) that there are deep truths about reality, including social reality, to be found via careful consideration of ordinary concepts, whether or not we access those truths via explicit invocation of ordinary language.

[94] The critique of naturalized jurisprudence in Coleman, "Methodology" (n. 49 above), is deficient, among other respects, in treating the attack on traditional philosophical method as exhausted by the Quinean attack on analyticity.

[95] So, e.g., George Bealer has the misfortune of adducing the Gettier examples as evidence of "the on-balance agreement of elementary concrete-case intuitions among human subjects" in "Intuition and the Autonomy of Philosophy," in *Rethinking Intuition* (n. 46 above), pp. 204–05, 214. Bealer was writing prior, of course, to the appearance of the Weinberg, Nichols, & Stich results.

[96] *From Metaphysics to Ethics* (n. 46 above), pp. 31–2.

[97] "Normativity and Epistemic Intuitions" (n. 46 above).

[98] R.M. Hare leveled similar charges years ago against Rawls's method of bringing our general moral principles in to "reflective equilibrium" with our intuitions about particular cases, though the charges have largely gone unanswered. This is unfortunate, since the implications of the Hare challenge, as the Weinberg et al. results show, extend beyond moral philosophy. As Hare wrote:

The appeal to moral intuitions will never do as a basis for a moral system. It is certainly possible, as some thinkers even of our times have done, to collect all the moral opinions of which they and their contemporaries feel most sure, find some relatively simple method or apparatus which can be represented, with a bit of give and take, and making plausible assumptions about the circumstances of life, as generating all these opinions; and then pronounce that that is the moral system which, having reflected, we must acknowledge to be the correct one. But they have absolutely no authority for this claim beyond the original convictions, for which no ground or argument was given. The "equilibrium" they have reached is one between forces which might have been generated by prejudice, and no amount of reflection can make that a solid basis for morality.

R.M. Hare, *Moral Thinking: Its Levels, Method and Point* (Oxford: Clarendon Press, 1981), p. 12.

radical epistemic relativism, how could such intuitions shed any light on the *necessary* conditions for knowledge, the *essential* properties of epistemic justification?

The critique mounted by Weinberg et al. provokes strong reactions, in large part because it represents the "revenge" of the "sophomoric relativist," that familiar philosophical bogeyman. The aggressive college sophomore who says, "Well, that's just *your* view of the concept of law [or knowledge or morality]" all of a sudden has philosophically respectable friends, even some with tenure in good departments! Take Robert Cummins's scathing gloss on the dispute between externalists and internalists about the theory of mental content:

Consider the role of Twin-Earth cases [cases in which the same concept purportedly has different extensions depending on the environment in which someone is thinking that concept] in current theories of content. It is commonplace for researchers in the Theory of Content to proceed as if the relevant intuitions were undisputed... Nor is the reason for this practice far to seek. The Putnamian take on these cases is widely enough shared to allow for a range of thriving intramural sports among believers. Those who do not share the intuitions are simply not invited to the games. This kind of selection allows things to move forward, but it has its price. Since most nonphilosophers do not share the intuition, the resulting theories of content have little weight with them, and this is surely a drawback for a theory that is supposed to form an essential part of the foundations of cognitive psychology. Making a Putnamian conscience an entrance requirement for the theory of content threatens to make it irrelevant. We must take care that such agreement about the intuitions as there is is not merely a selection effect.... If we are honest with ourselves [however] I think we will have to confront the fact that selection effects like this are likely to be pretty widespread in contemporary philosophy.[99]

Is there any reason to think legal philosophy is exempt from the charge? Hardly— and especially not in light of the complete dominance of the field by one school, Oxford University. I am not saying that dominance is unjustified—by the best criteria we can muster, it is obvious that Oxford has deserved to dominate from the 1950s to the present—but rather that that professional and intellectual dominance is likely to have magnified any "selection effect" in Cummins's sense.[100] But it is a question for a different day to show that the Weinberg et al. critique of intuitions in epistemology has a parallel in legal philosophy.

Let us suppose Cummins is correct: what alternative is there? Cummins, a philosophical naturalist, proposes the following alternative to philosophical reliance on intuitions:

We can give up on intuitions about the nature of space and time and ask instead what sort of beasts space and time must be if current physical theory is to be true and explanatory. We can give up on intuitions about our representational content and ask instead what representations must be if current cognitive theory is to be true and explanatory.[101]

---

99 Cummins, "Reflection on Reflective Equilibrium," in *Rethinking Intuition* (n. 46 above), p. 116.
100 American philosophers, especially those who are naturalists—a more common breed on this side of the Atlantic—often joke that Oxford is a place where philosophers take *their* intuitions *very seriously*.
101 "Reflection on Reflective Equilibrium," in *Rethinking Intuition* (n. 46 above), pp. 117–8.

I shall take this as an example of what we may call "the Naturalist Method," which can be understood as comprising two subsidiary theses:

> *Substantive Thesis.* With respect to questions about *what there is* and *what we can know*, we have nothing better to go on than successful scientific theory.

> *Methodological Thesis.* Insofar as philosophy is concerned with what there is and what we can know, it must operate as the abstract branch of successful scientific theory.

The Substantive Thesis of the Naturalistic Method is, to be sure, no *a priori* truth, and nor is it presented as such by naturalists like Quine or his followers. The thesis is also, to be sure, widely denied, and not just by postmodernists and professors of English.[102] Yet, from an historical point of view, it should hardly be controversial. The ontology of our post-Enlightenment world is overwhelmingly the product of the Substantive Thesis. On top of that, the philosophical track record of all forms of *a priori* analysis, conceptual or intuitive, is not especially encouraging. Kant took it to be *a priori* that space necessarily had the structure described by Euclidean geometry; subsequent physics showed his intuitions to be mistaken. As Jaakko Hintikka has recently written:

As far as empirical realities are concerned, the brute fact is that the intimations of intuition do not have any privileged epistemological status. They do not carry any automatic justification with them, no matter how convincing they may be subjectively. Epistemologically, they are on the level of clever guesses or perhaps Aristotle's *endoxa* [common opinions].[103]

The moral naturalists draw from this history is that the only sound reason to prefer one metaphysical or epistemological picture over another is not because it seems intuitively obvious (think of Kant and the Euclidean structure of space) but because it earns its place by facilitating successful *a posteriori* theories of the world. Kant's—and everyone else's—intuitions be damned, it just turned out that physics had a use for non-Euclidean accounts of the structure of space. Philosophy, on this naturalistic story, has no special methods for investigating the world; it is simply the abstract and reflective part of empirical science.

The prospects for naturalism in jurisprudence is now a lively and contested issue, and I do not propose to resolve the issue here. Rather, I want to return to an issue from Section II. For if the Cummins worry is generalizable—if, in fact, we should be skeptical that the intuitions at work in legal philosophy are any better, epistemically, than the intuitions at work in epistemology and the theory of content—then doesn't that lend support precisely to the Finnis critique of decriptive jurisprudence? After all, in Section II, the defense of descriptive jurisprudence turned on a rather uncritical invocation of the claim that we were describing "our"

---

[102] See, e.g., Bealer, "Intuition and the Autonomy of Philosophy," (n. 95 above); many of the essays (esp. Alvin Plantinga's reply to critics) in *Naturalism Defeated? Essays on Plantinga's Evolutionary Argument Against Naturalism*, ed. J. Beilby (Ithaca: Cornell University Press, 2002); *Naturalism: A Critical Appraisal*, ed. S Wagner & R. Warner (South Bend: University of Notre Dame Press, 1993).

[103] "The Emperor's New Intuitions" (n. 46 above), p. 143.

concept, where the first person plural possessive was to be cashed out in terms of statistical frequency. But, of course, that same uncritical invocation underlies three decades' worth of invocations of the Gettier counter-examples, and now we know that this was just rhetoric, *not* an accurate report of any statistical frequency (except within well-defined ethnographic communities). So has not Quine-Stich-Cummins skepticism about the methods of conceptual analysis and appeal to intuition simply led us to Finnis? We can *not* it seems defend what is "important" and "significant" about the Hermeneutic Concept of law by reference *only* to describing "our" concepts and "our" intuitions, since the talk of "our" may prove illusory. We must, it seems, agree with Finnis after all that we have to discriminate among theoretical objects in terms of non-epistemic criteria, criteria like the extent to which the object satisfies the demands of practical reasonableness.

This conclusion would be hasty for two reasons. First, there has, as of yet, been no showing that "our" concept of law is really as illustory as "our" concept of knowledge: perhaps statistical frequency, in conjunction with other epistemic values, will suffice for the traditional project of analysis of the concept of law. Second, and more importantly, the proferred conclusion bypasses, without argument, the Cummins-style solution to the problem, should it be a real one: namely, the Substantive and Methodological Theses of naturalism, as above.

Still, this way of framing the dispute throws in to relief a very different kind of methodology problem in jurisprudence. For now the methodological positivist like Hart has two opponents: the Finnis-style critic who thinks epistemic values are *not* enough to demarcate his subject-matter; and the naturalist critic who thinks epistemic values *conjoined with* Hart's dominant methods—conceptual analysis and appeals to intuition—can deliver no more than ethnographically relative results.

So, too, there would now be two "solutions": the Finnis solution of turning to moral evaluation of law to demarcate the object of jurisprudential inquiry; versus the Naturalistic Method recommended by Cummins, and embodied in the Substantive and Methodological Theses described above. If, with Raz, we take legal theory to be concerned with law's essential[104] properties, then the methodological question is now vivid: in figuring out *what there (essentially) is*, should we turn to morality or to science? I think the answer is clear.[105] But that, alas, is an argument for a different occasion.

---

[104] Understood in Quinean terms, for the naturalist: see n. 77, above.
[105] See Chs. 7 and 8 in this volume.

Postscript to Part II: Science and Methodology in Legal Theory*

The program for a naturalized jurisprudence sketched in Chapters 4–6 might be understood as exploiting two broadly Quinean ideas, one well-expressed by Quine himself, the other by Robert Cummins, a naturalistic philosopher of mind. Quine tells us that naturalism is "the recognition that it is within science itself, and not in some prior philosophy, that reality is to be identified and described."[1] Since empirical science does not employ the two distinctive, interlocking methods of English-speaking philosophy in the twentieth century—namely, analysis of concepts via appeals to intuitions (the two interacting when, per Frank Jackson's formulation,[2] we appeal to intuitions about possible cases to determine the extension of our concepts)—a naturalized philosophy of law, aiming to describe the reality of legal phenomena, should, it seems, eschew such methods as well.[3]

But what then does naturalized jurisprudence put in their place? In the place of conceptual analysis and reliance on intuitions in philosophy of science and mind, Cummins, in a Quinean vein, suggests that,

We can give up on intuitions about the nature of space and time and ask instead what sorts of beasts space and time must be if current physical theory is to be true and explanatory. We can give up on intuitions about our representational content and ask instead what [mental] representations must be if current cognitive theory is to be true and explanatory.[4]

* An earlier version of some of this material benefited from discussion at a conference on philosophical naturalism sponsored by the Rutgers Institute for Law and Philosophy in June 2005. I am grateful to Dennis Patterson for organizing the conference, and to the participants for helpful questions and comments—especially Alvin Goldman, Geert Keil, and Michael Smith. I also was greatly helped by comments by Larry Laudan on an earlier draft of some of this material.

[1] W.V.O. Quine, "Things and Their Place in Theories," in his *Theories and Things* (Cambridge, Mass.: Harvard University Press, 1981), p. 21. Alas, Quine himself never got past the science of the 1930s, and so failed to notice that neither his behaviorism nor his eliminativism were vindicated by actual scientific developments subsequently.

[2] *From Metaphysics to Ethics: A Defence of Conceptual Analysis* (Oxford: Clarendon Press, 1997).

[3] This is not to deny the role that "conceptual analysis," in a more capacious sense, has played in the development of science, as emphasized by Larry Laudan in his seminal *Progress and Its Problems: Toward a Theory of Scientific Growth* (Berkeley: University of California Press, 1977), esp. ch. 2. As Laudan documents, the history of science is replete with examples of debates about *conceptual* problems, either "internal" to a theory (e.g., the theory "exhibits certain internal inconsistencies...or its basic categories of analysis are vague and unclear" [id., p. 49]) or "external" to the theory, but related to how the theory comports with others that are already viewed as rationally vindicated. But in both cases, conceptual problems are not resolved by appeal to intuitions about the extension of the concepts, but rather by reliance on standards of clarity and logical entailment.

[4] Robert Cummins, "Reflection on Reflective Equilibrium," in *Rethinking Intuition: The Psychology of Intuition and Its Role in Philosophical Inquiry*, ed. M. DePaul & W. Ramsey (Lanham, Maryland: Rowman & Littlefield, 1998), pp. 117–18.

We can, to be sure, test our intuitions about possible cases to fix the extension of the concept of "space" or the concept of "representational content," but since such intuitions are hostage to parochial bias, lack of empirical knowledge, and all variety of selection effects,[5] there is no reason to think such intuitions and their deliverances deserve *epistemic weight*. The alternative, favored by Cummins and other Quineans, is to turn to methods that have already *earned* their epistemic *bona fides* many times over, namely, the methods and results of the empirical sciences.[6] Instead of testing "folk" intuitions about the extension of our concepts of space and representational content, why not see what concepts of space and representational content figure in successful empirical science? Philosophers, on this approach, are the abstract and reflective branch of empirical science, clarifying the contours and extensions of concepts that have been vindicated by their role in successful explanation and prediction of empirical phenomena. For a naturalized jurisprudence, this same approach would mean taking seriously the enormous social scientific literature on law and legal institutions to see what concept of law figures in the most powerful explanatory and predictive models of legal phenomena such as judicial behavior.[7]

The implications of the Quinean program of naturalization have given rise in many domains to the charge that naturalizing some subject area of philosophical investigation "changes the subject," that is, misses or abandons what was philosophically distinctive or important about the subject matter, replacing that with questions that are simply *different*. That charge has been put against naturalized jurisprudence by Jules Coleman on various occasions.[8] In his recent book, for

---

[5] As Cummins quips about the debate between externalists and internalists about mental content: "Those who do not share the [relevant] intuitions are simply not invited to the games." Id., p. 116.

[6] Again, we should not be misled by Quine's unQuinean attachment to the science of the 1930s, evident in his loyalty to behaviorism and his eliminativism (though he, finally, abandons the latter in the 1990s). As Jerry Fodor has noted, the distinguishing feature of empirical science in the last half century has not been the reduction of all the others to physics, but rather the proliferation of special sciences. For a pithy account, see Fodor's review of E.O. Wilon's *Consilience* in *London Review of Books* 20 (October 29, 1998).

[7] See, e.g., Glendon Schubert, *The Judicial Mind* (Evantson: Northwestern University Press, 1965); Glendon Schubert, *The Judicial Mind Revisited* (New York: Oxford University Press, 1974); David W. Rhode & Harold J. Spaeth, *Supreme Court Decision Making* (San Francisco: W.H. Freeman, 1976); Harold J. Spaeth, *Supreme Court Policy Making: Explanation and Prediction* (San Francisco: W.H. Freeman, 1979); Jeffrey A. Segal, "Predicting Supreme Court Cases Probabilistically: The Search and Seizure Cases, 1962–1981," *American Political Science Review* 78 (1984), 891–900; Jeffrey A. Segal & Albert D. Cover, "Ideological Values and the Votes of U.S. Supreme Court Justices," *American Political Science Review* 83 (1989), 557–65; Tracey George & Lee Epstein, "On the Nature of Supreme Court Decision-Making," *American Political Science Review* (1992), 323–37; Timothy M. Hagle & Harold J. Spaeth, "The Emergence of a New Ideology: The Business Decisions of the Burger Court," *Journal of Politics* 54 (1992), 120–34; Jeffrey A. Segal & Harold J. Spaeth, *The Supreme Court and the Attitudinal Model* (New York: Cambridge University Press, 1993); Jeffrey A. Segal & Harold J. Spaeth, *The Supreme Court and the Attitudinal Model Revisited* (Cambridge: Cambridge University Press, 2002).

[8] Liam Murphy raises the same kind of challenge in his "Concepts of Law," *Australian Journal of Legal Philosophy* 30 (2005), p. 14.

example, Coleman—commenting on the version of naturalized jurisprudence in Chapters 1 and 2—writes:

There is nothing objectionable about a sociological, psychological, or a psychosocial jurisprudence. No philosopher of law could quarrel with a project of trying to uncover lawlike regularities in judicial decision-making. Such social-scientific laws of judging... might render judgment more predictable, which could have the salutary effect of facilitating coordination and planning; a social science of adjudication would also be valuable on purely theoretical grounds, as a way of making law and legal practice more rationally intelligible. The problem is that there is no reason to think that such a social-scientific project can be a substitute for the philosophical methodology of analytic jurisprudence.[9]

In a subsequent essay on jurisprudential methodology, Coleman continues this line of thought in criticizing my views:

[T]here is absolutely no reason to believe that the facts that interest us as philosophers and social theorists are the facts that social and natural scientific theories are interested in addressing or are designed to address. Is there a social scientific theory that is interested in the difference between validity and legality, between rules that are binding on an official and those that are binding because they are part of the community's law? What social scientific inquiry calls for an explanation of that difference?[10]

This way of framing the objection, however, begs the question against the naturalist, as can be seen easily enough by imagining a theologian taking the same argumentative tack and objecting that,

There is absolutely no reason to believe that the facts that interest us as theologians— namely, facts about sin, the Holy Trinity, and transubstantiation—are the facts that social and natural scientific theories are interested in addressing or are designed to address.

The difficulty, of course, with that kind of rejoinder is that it *takes for granted* the reality of certain "facts" to be explained, when one of the points of methodological naturalism is that the only "real" facts are the ones identified and described in the sciences. That our best current predictive-explanatory theories rule out certain putative facts counts against those facts, not against naturalism, absent some *independent* argument against the Quinean assumption "that it is within science itself, and not in some prior philosophy, that reality is to be identified and described."[11]

Of course, theology is an extreme case, since the "subject" of theology is not just changed, but, in all likelihood, eliminated within a naturalistic framework. But it is, to be sure, possible that some of the distinctions and categories in which jurisprudential theories are presently invested will go the way of transubstantiation. What the conceptual jurisprudents like Coleman need is some argument

---

[9] Jules Coleman, *The Practice of Principle* (Oxford: Clarendon Press, 2001), p. 213.
[10] Jules Coleman, "Methodology," in *The Oxford Handbook of Jurisprudence and Philosophy of Law*, ed. J. Coleman & S. Shapiro (Oxford: Oxford University Press, 2002), p. 350.
[11] To be sure, Quinean fallibilism requires us to allow that today's suspect facts may find a place in tomorrow's science.

against that possibility: such an argument would show that naturalized jurisprudence *unfairly* or *illegitimately* "changes the subject."

But so far we have not even made explicit the "subject" of jurisprudence. What are we talking about or investigating when we do legal philosophy? I shall borrow a crisp, and I believe representative, statement of the "subject" of jurisprudence from Julie Dickson, who is explicating the influential Razian view of the matter. She writes:

[A]nalytical jurisprudence is concerned with explaining the nature of law by attempting to isolate and explain those features which make law into what it is. A successful theory of law of this type is a theory which consists of propositions about the law which (1) are necessarily true, and (2) adequately explain the nature of law.... I am using "the nature of law" to refer to those essential properties which a given set of phenomena must exhibit in order to be law.[12]

One might worry, to be sure, that this kind of task has been successfully discharged in no branch of philosophy, but let us put that worry about the Razian project to the side for now. For naturalists, if you want to know what makes "law into what it is," or what makes any X into what it is, you need to know how Xs are described and explained by the sciences (or how Xs figure in true descriptive and explanatory scientific theories). Thus, assuming we give "necessarily" and "the essential nature of law" suitably Quinean glosses—i.e., assuming we treat them, as we should, as equivalent to "central to the most fruitful explanatory-predictive social science of law we have going"—then a naturalized jurisprudence is concerned with something like the Razian question, the central question in the philosophy of law.

But this is too quick a response, and the non-naturalist can now refine his worry in a way that goes to the heart of his doubts about naturalized jurisprudence. What the non-naturalists in jurisprudence *really* believe is that the concept of law is what I called in Chapter 6 a "Hermeneutic Concept," that is a concept whose extension is fixed by its role "in how humans make themselves and their practices intelligible to themselves."[13] Joseph Raz puts the point this way:

[I]t would be wrong to conclude... that one judges the success of an analysis of law by its theoretical sociological fruitfulness. To do so is to miss the point that, unlike concepts like "mass" or "electron," "the law" is a concept used by people to understand themselves [i.e., it is a Hermeneutic Concept]. We are not free to pick on any fruitful concepts. It is a major task of legal theory to advance our understanding of society by helping us to understand how people understand themselves.[14]

If the concept of law is a Hermeneutic Concept, so the objection to naturalized jurisprudence goes, then the reality it picks it out is not going to be one which the sciences identify and describe.

---

[12] Julie Dickson, *Evaluation and Legal Theory* (Oxford: Hart Publishing, 2001), p. 17.
[13] See p. 173 above.
[14] Joseph Raz, "Authority, Law and Morality," *The Monist* 68 (1995), pp. 321–2.

This objection, however, assumes, falsely, that the sciences must dispense with Hermeneutic Concepts. That assumption, to be sure, would have seemed uncontroversial to philosophers of science fifty years ago, when it was generally accepted that all explanations had to conform to one model—usually drawn from some idealized version of physics—which had no room for explanations that took seriously the *meaningfulness* of certain mental states *qua* causes. But with the defeat of the logical positivist program, such an assumption no longer makes sense: the positivist picture of there being just *one kind* of confirmation, *one kind* of explanation, and so on—each exemplified by that highly idealized version of physics—has been replaced with a new pluralism that recognizes, as one philosopher of science puts it, that "explanatory adequacy is essentially pragmatic and field-specific."[15]

That scientific accounts of social phenomena have room, in principle, for Hermeneutic Concepts does not show, of course, that they make room for the kinds of Hermeneutic Concepts to which conceptual jurisprudents are attached. Consider a leading predictive-explanatory theory of judicial decisions, Segal's and Spaeth's "Attitudinal Model,"[16] bracketing for the moment questions about its adequacy. Developing ideas first broached by the American Legal Realists,[17] Segal and Spaeth argue that the best explanation for judicial decision-making[18] is to be found in the conjunction of the "the facts of the case" and "the ideological attitudes and values of the justices."[19] Segal and Spaeth identify the "ideological attitudes" of judges based on "the judgments in newspaper editorials that characterize nominees prior to confirmation as liberal or conservative" with respect to particular issues (for example, civil rights and liberties).[20] Looking at more than thirty years of search-and-seizure decisions, Segal and Spaeth found that the Attitudinal Model correctly predicted 71% of the votes by justices: that is, the ideological attitudes of the judge towards the underlying factual situations (and their variations) explained the vote of the judge nearly three-quarters of the time.

Of course, to show that their explanation is the best one, Segal and Spaeth must compare the Attitudinal Model with some alternatives—most importantly, for our purposes, with what they call "the Legal Model" of decision.[21] On the Legal Model, it is valid sources of law, in conjunction with valid interpretive methods

[15] Richard W. Miller, *Fact and Method: Explanation, Confirmation and Reality in the Natural and Social Sciences* (Princeton: Princeton University Press, 1987), p. 95. See also, Philip Kitcher, "The Ends of the Sciences," in *The Future for Philosophy*, ed. B. Leiter (Oxford: Clarendon Press, 2004), esp. p. 215, and Nancy Cartwright, "From Explanation to Causation and Back," in *The Future for Philosophy*.   [16] See esp. *The Supreme Court and the Attitudinal Model Revisited* (n. 7 above).
[17] Id., pp. 87–9.
[18] Their focus is on Supreme Court Justices, though other literature ranges more widely.
[19] *The Supreme Court and the Attitudinal Model Revisited* (n. 7 above), p. 86.
[20] Id., p. 321. As Segal & Spaeth remark: "Although this measure is less precise than past votes, it nonetheless avoids the circularity problem, is exogenous to the justices' behavior, and is reliable and replicable." Id.
[21] Id., pp. 48–85. Their treatment of the "Legal Model" is, in several respects, crude; I have cleaned it up considerably for purposes of presentation in the text—precisely the kind of conceptual work, in the capacious sense noted earlier (n. 3), central to progress in empirical science.

applied to those sources, that determine outcomes (call the valid sources and interpretive methods "the class of legal reasons"). The difficulty is that the class of legal reasons is indeterminate: it justifies more than one outcome in appellate disputes.[22] Thus, as Segal and Spaeth write:

> If various aspects of the legal model can support either side of any given dispute that comes before the Court, and the quality of these positions cannot be reliably and validly measured a priori, then the legal model hardly satisfies as an explanation of Supreme Court decisions. By being able to "explain" everything, in the end it explains nothing.[23]

In other words, one can generate no testable predictions from the Legal Model because the class of legal reasons justifies, and thus, predicts, multiple outcomes.[24]

What is important to notice here is that the best causal explanation of decision, the Attitudinal Model, is one that relies centrally on Hermeneutic Concepts: for it is supposed to be the *attitude* of judges towards the *facts* that explains the decision, and "attitudes" are clearly *meaningful* mental states that are assigned a *causal* role in accounting for the outcome (the decision). But a judge's favorable moral attitude towards, e.g., privacy in the home—which might be the attitude explaining some of his votes in search-and-seizure cases—is not the same as the kinds of Hermeneutic Concepts that H.L.A. Hart treats as central to the phenomena of modern legal systems: for example, that officials accept some rules from an internal point of view, that is, as imposing obligations upon them of compliance, and thus also licensing criticism of deviation from the rule and so on. The *normativity of law*, the idea that legally valid norms supply special *reasons for acting* in virtue of their legality, is still missing on this account.

Does the preceding mean that the normativity of law—that central hermeneutic feature of the concept of law to which Hart called our attention—is eliminated within a naturalized jurisprudence whose ontology is populated by the posits required for the Attitudinal Model to work? That conclusion is, in fact, not yet warranted.

Recall, first, Robert Cummins's naturalistic alternative to the analysis of concepts based on appeals to intuitions about possible cases of application—precisely the kind of method that Hart and other conceptual jurisprudents have long employed. Following Cummins, naturalized jurisprudence should ask what must law be if current social-scientific theory of adjudication (namely, the Attitudinal Model) is to be true and explanatory? For the Attitudinal Model to be true and explanatory, there has to be, among other things, a clear demarcation between the ideological attitudes of judges (which are causally effective in determining the

---

[22] Segal & Spaeth clearly recognize the selection effect for Supreme Court cases: "because the Supreme Court does have control over its docket, the justices would refuse to decide . . . a meritless case. Those that the Court does decide tender plausible legal arguments on both sides." Id., p. 93. It is clear from this observation that Segal & Spaeth acknowledge the existence of cases in which the class of legal reasons is rationally determinate, i.e., the legal reasons justify only one outcome.

[23] Id., p. 86.   [24] This is because prediction tracks justification on the Legal Model.

decisions) and the valid sources of law which are central to the Legal Model's competing explanation of judicial decision. Thus, implicit in the Attitudinal Model is quite plainly a concept of law as exhausted by authoritative texts (precedents, statutes, constitutions) which are the raw material of the competing Legal Model, and which exclude the ideological attitudes central to the Attitudinal Model. Since the interpretation of those authoritative texts (i.e., the law) is indeterminate, the Legal Model cannot explain appellate decision-making, according to Segal and Spaeth. As I argued in Chapter 2, the same implicit concept of law was at work in analogous arguments by the American Legal Realists that legal reasoning was indeterminate:

The famous Realist arguments for indeterminacy which focus on the conflicting but equally legitimate ways lawyers have of interpreting statutes and precedents only show that the law is indeterminate on the assumption either that statutes and precedents largely exhaust the authoritative sources of law or that any additional authoritative norms not derived from these sources conflict. It is the former assumption that . . . motivate[s] the Realist arguments.[25]

And now we may add: the same assumption drives Segal and Spaeth's arguments for the inadequacy of the Legal Model and the superiority of the Attitudinal Model. The concept of law, in turn, that vindicates this assumption is none other than the Razian "Hard Positivist" notion of a Rule of Recognition whose criteria of legality are exclusively ones of pedigree: a rule (or canon of interpretation) is part of the law by virtue of having a source in legislative enactments, prior court decisions or judicial practice, or constitutional provisions. That is the view of law required by the Legal Model, and it is the view of law required to vindicate the Attitudinal Model as providing the best explanation of judicial decision. Raz's Hard Positivism, in short, captures what law must be if the Attitudinal Model is true and explanatory.

To be sure, this defense of Hard Positivism is very different from Raz's own:[26] we need no intuitions about whether all authority performs a "service" (as Raz believes), whether authoritative directives are *exclusionary* as opposed to *very weighty* reasons for action, and so on.[27] It suffices, on this approach, that the Hard Positivist concept of law figures in the best explanatory account of legal phenomena.

Now it is also true that there is nothing in this approach that makes "helping us to understand how people understand themselves"—in Raz's formulation—central to how we understand the nature of law. But the Razian approach, I fear, may confuse the central jurisprudential question—what is law?—with a different

---

[25] See p. 72 above.

[26] See Raz, "Authority, Law, and Morality" (n. 14 above) and the discussion in Ch. 4.

[27] For an example of how the game goes when we are reduced to warring intuitions, see the discussion of the Perry-Waluchow objection to Raz (based on one set of intuitions about the nature of *authoritative* reasons) with my rejoinder (based on a different set of intuitions) in Ch. 4, p. 131.

question, namely, what role does the folk concept of "law" play in the self-understanding of agents? But as Dickson put it earlier, in explicating Raz's view, what we are purportedly after in jurisprudence is "the nature of law," that is, "those essential properties which a given set of phenomena must exhibit in order to be law." Armchair sociology about people's self-understandings may or may not be reliable when it comes to finding out what law is essentially like. As Mark Murphy, a defender not of positivism but natural law theory, has aptly remarked:

Ordinary users of the language do not enjoy a final authority on the correctness of analyses of the terms they employ nor on the presuppositions of the practices that they are engaged in.... The starting point for marking out a set of phenomena as law is the practices of human agents, but that does not make those agents infallible about whether they are correct in thinking that any particular instance is a case of law.[28]

Naturalized jurisprudence must insist, needless to say, on that fallibility.

That positivism must be correct if the Attitudinal Model is to be true and explanatory does not yet show, however, that the *normativity of law*—that central hermeneutic feature of law—is part of the positivist picture the Attitudinal Model requires. After all, while the Attitudinal Model needs to demarcate ideological attitudes from law by appeal to the latter's pedigree, the normativity of law is not, itself, a feature of law that is deemed explanatory on the Attitudinal Model: it is a mere rhetorical pose judges adopt in their opinions. Yet according to Hart, and other positivists, a central feature of legal systems is that officials like judges take themselves to have obligations to apply certain criteria of legal validity and to apply the laws so validated. All the Attitudinal Model, like its Legal Realist predecessors, allows is that officials talk *as if* they have obligations under law, when, in fact, their behavior is *really* explained by their ideological attitudes towards the underlying facts of the cases.

Notice, though, that the Attitudinal Model is fundamentally a theory about the behavior of *appellate* officials; it could be that the behavior of lower court officials is, in fact, fruitfully explained by reference to those officials taking legal norms to impose obligations. Indeed, we can go further: there is nothing in the Attitudinal Model, or its critique of the Legal Model, to suggest that the class of legal reasons does not at least *constrain* the possible outcomes even at the appellate level: legal reasons *under*determine the final decision, but they are not irrelevant to it. To the extent that legal reasons circumscribe the range of permissible outcomes, the normativity of law figures in the best explanation of the decision—even if the *final* outcome (chosen from among those that can be rationalized legally) is a product of ideological attitude rather than legal reasoning.[29]

But suppose that no predictive-explanatory theory of legal phenomena emerged in which the normativity of law played a causal role: would this deflation

---

[28] Mark C. Murphy, "Natural Law Jurisprudence," *Legal Theory* 9 (2003), p. 250.
[29] I have made a related point in explicating the views of the American Legal Realists in Ch. 2.

of normativity be fatal to the positivist program? Remember what motivated Hart's introduction of the "internal point of view" in the first place. He was worried that Scandinavian Realists like Alf Ross—who purportedly held that law is just a prediction of what the courts will do[30]—had no way of marking a distinction between two kinds of mass social behavior: namely, the case where everyone "mindlessly" does the same thing, versus the case where everyone does the same thing because they think they *ought* to be doing so. The latter, Hart noted, was distinctive of a legal system: officials are not like herd animals stampeding, *as it happens*, in the same direction; they "go" in the same direction (for example, applying the same criteria of legal validity) because they think that they *must*. For the Scandinavians, so Hart thought, there was no distinction between the two cases: all that counted is *what officials did*, whether it was the consequence of mindless stampede or what was perceived to be obligatory action. This was deemed to be a fatal flaw in the Scandinavian Realist account of law.[31]

Does naturalized jurisprudence commit the same sin? It is crucial to keep in mind that Hart does not suppose that officials *actually* have obligations to do the same thing, just that they *take themselves* to have such obligations. The real objection is to the image of the *stampede*, to the idea that officials act and decide as they do "mindlessly," like the proverbial lemmings heading off the cliff. The Attitudinal Model certainly does not understand judges to be lemmings, but rather, political actors advancing an ideological agenda: they do the same thing, to the extent they do, because they share ideological aims. Moreover, they almost all share one behavior in common: namely, the *concealment* of their ideological aims behind rhetoric which involves purporting to take the normativity of law seriously: judges, of all ideological persuasions, claim that they do what they do *because they have legal obligations to reach these decisions*, not because they feel an obligation to implement their ideology. A complete causal story of judicial behavior would have to explain this striking fact about the practice as well. To date, the Attitudinal Model is largely silent on this familiar rhetorical phenomenon, but there is nothing in that Model that rules out a companion explanation for what I will call this "normativity of law talk" so central to judicial practice in the United States.

To be sure, admitting "normativity of law talk" within our social-scientific theory of adjudication involves a further deflation of the claims of legal obligation beyond the deflation in Hart's original theory: we move from *"judges take themselves to have obligations"* to *"judges talk as if they take themselves to have obligations."* But the crucial fact, from the standpoint of Hart's original, and apparently compelling complaint against the Scandinavians, is that there is nothing in a naturalized jurisprudence that requires us to embrace the "stampede" picture of judicial decision or to ignore, entirely, the *apparent* normativity of law.

---

[30] New research (so far unpublished) by Brian Berry suggests that Hart's characterization of Ross may be unfair, but I put that issue to one side.

[31] Hart, of course, thought the American Legal Realists made the same mistake, but here he was clearly wrong as I argued in Ch. 2.

So the conception of naturalized jurisprudence in Part II does not change the subject of traditional jurisprudence, strictly understood: it simply proposes to address the same and traditional subject by more epistemically credible methods. But that brings us to a far more serious objection, one that is ultimately fatal to this way of conceiving naturalized jurisprudence. For there is no robust, hence epistemically credible, social science of adjudication. It is one thing to turn to space-time physics, whose explanatory and predictive success is extraordinary, to understand the "essential" nature of space or time; it is quite another to think the feeble social scientific models churned out by political scientists are cutting the social world at its causal joints.

The Attitudinal Model, for example, looking only at a limited range of cases, and making some fairly crude assumptions about the competing Legal Model, is able to predict outcomes only 71% of the time. Predictive success of 50% would be achieved by the "flip the coin" model. A 71% success rate is, in short, not the stuff of which scientific credibility is made.

Does the epistemically feeble condition of the predictive-explanatory social sciences of law mean that, as suggested at the end of Chapter 6, our only option is Finnis-style evaluative jurisprudence or, more extremely, what Liam Murphy calls "a practical political method: the best place to locate the boundary of [the concept of] law is where it will have the best effect on our self-understanding as a society, on our political culture"?[32] I will return to Finnis in a moment, but let us pause to consider Murphy. Murphy thinks "there is insufficient agreement in the intuitions that are the data for any philosophical conceptual analysis"[33] of law, adding, "There are just different ways of drawing [the] boundary [between law and morality], preferred by different people."[34] But all of this is as much armchair speculation as its opposite, namely, the confidence of Hartians and Razians that they have limned the deep structure of the "concept" we employ. In both cases, a naturalist has reason to ask for some *empirical* evidence about the "concept" alleged to be current in our practices. This, of course, is one of the tasks that experimental philosophy, the most exciting recent development in naturalistic philosophy, has set itself in fields like epistemology and action theory.[35] Already, we have learned that the armchair intuitions about the extension of the concept of knowledge made famous by Edmund Gettier—and widely taken as a decisive proof that there is more to the concept of "knowledge" than "justified true belief"—are culturally specific, illuminating not the nature of knowledge, but a perhaps still interesting ethnographic fact about the folks whose intuitions are usually thought to count in

---

[32] Liam Murphy, "Concepts of Law," *Australian Journal of Legal Philosophy* 30 (2005), p. 9. This echoes the argument in Murphy's "The Political Question of the Concept of Law," in *Hart's Postscript*, ed. J.L. Coleman (Oxford: Oxford University Press, 2001).   [33] "Concepts of Law," id., p. 7.

[34] Id., p. 9.

[35] See, e.g., Jonathan Weinberg, Shaun Nichols, & Stephen Stich, "Normativity and Epistemic Intuitions," *Philosophical Topics* 29 (2001), 429–60; Joshua Knobe, "Intentional Action in Folk Psychology: An Experimental Investigation," *Philosophical Psychology* 16 (2003), 309–24; Shaun Nichols, "The Folk Psychology of Free Will: Fits and Starts," *Mind & Language* 19 (2004), 473–502.

these games. How will the concept of law fare when subjected to similar empirical scrutiny? As things stand, we simply have no idea, and so no concrete reason to take Murphy's armchair intuitions any more seriously than Raz's.

John Finnis offers a less direct version of the Murphy challenge. He starts by quibbling with my rendering in Chapter 6 of his arguments,[36] though at least some of his grievances seem to depend on his failure to appreciate the resonance between Weberian themes in philosophy of social science (Finnis's point of reference) and the more robust framing of the same points in post-World War II philosophy of science. But Finnis does emphasize a point I had, perhaps imprudently, elided in the earlier essay, and which warrants a response now. Finnis writes:

[G]iven that any general theory of law, however merely descriptive its ambition, necessarily prefers one concept of law over countless others . . . explanations of why this concept is an improved one, to be preferred to other concepts, are designed to show that this concept, this theory, makes better sense of the complex idea that law is something there is reason to have.[37]

This claim, indeed present in the earlier *Natural Law and Natural Rights*, is, as it stands, yet another non-sequitur: for from the fact that a descriptive theory "prefers one concept of law over countless others" it simply does not follow that the criteria for selection pertain to any view about why "law is something there is reason to have." If my cousin Julius thinks "the concept of law" is equivalent to "whatever a bright young thing from Rutgers says it is," I have many grounds for rejecting that analysis quite apart from the fact that that criterion for concept individuation bears no relationship, except accidental, to why "law is something there is reason to have."

Finnis, to be sure, recognizes that so baldly stated, his proposition is a non-sequitur, and so he buttresses it with his well-known claim that there is a "central" or "focal" case of the internal point of view on law which purportedly forces us to his form of concept-individuation:

[T]here must be and is a central case of the so-called internal point of view that plays so structural a role in every contemporary jurisprudence. A reminder or two must suffice. Hart argues, against Kelsen and (in a different way) Bentham and Austin, that rules conferring private power on individuals (e.g., to make a contract) should not be described as mere fragments of obligation-imposing rules. His argument adduces or describes no fact that Bentham, Austin, and Kelsen had failed to describe, other than the truth that there is reason to want and value private powers . . . .[38]

This, alas, is a misstatement of Hart's argument, on a par with Finnis's earlier, and better-known, claim that Hart excludes from consideration the point of view of

---

[36] John Finnis, "Law and What I Truly Should Decide," *American Journal of Jurisprudence* 48 (2003), esp. pp. 115–25. He later repeats some of the misrepresentations of positivism rebutted in Ch. 6, n. 42. I shall not revisit my response to those misleading objections.   [37] Id., p. 119.
[38] Id., p. 120.

the Holmesian "bad man."[39] In fact, Hart expresses no view about how nice (or good or just or desirable) it is to have rules that confer private powers. Hart observes, rather, that the logical structure of power-conferring rules is eviscerated when forced into the Procrustean bed of obligation-imposing rules, since there is a conceptual connection between the standard of conduct a power-conferring rule lays down and the purported "sanction" (namely, nullity) that attaches to failure to live up to the standard—in contrast to obligation-imposing rules, like those in the criminal law, where the standard of behavior is conceptually and logically independent of the sanction.[40] His argument, then, against sanction theorists like Austin and Kelsen is not that it is good or desireable to have power-conferring rules, but rather that paradigmatic instances of legal systems have such rules, and the sanction theorists cannot give an adequate descriptive account of that aspect of the phenomenon of law.[41]

Near the end of his lengthy reply to me, Finnis declares that "there is no necessity to be had save necessity of the kind that good practical reasons pick out for us when we are deliberating about what to want and choose to try to have...."[42] There are, to be sure, no genuine *necessities* to be had anywhere, as all Quinean naturalists would agree, but there are lots of for-all-practical-purposes-here-and-now "necessities" to be had—i.e., the "stuff" we just would not want to give up— but what Finnis and Dworkin (and all other natural law theorists) need is some *argument* why the "necessities" about the concept of law are those related to the demands of practical reason. Murphy's rejoinder, in this regard, is more honest: he admits that he wants us to *choose* our concept of law on the basis of purely practical considerations, while Finnis and Dworkin claim we are *forced* to do so, that any effort at understanding the "concept of law" drives us to asking "what law *ought* to be." Looking back over nearly four decades of writing, it is surprising how little—other than what is now rather familiar dialectical trickery—the natural law theorists have offered in support of this claim.

Julie Dickson, who sides with me on many points against Finnis, has raised a different set of concerns about some of the arguments in Part II.[43] Dickson suggests that I have wrongly construed her position as intermediate between that of "pure" descriptivists like Hart and that of evaluative jurisprudents like Finnis. She remarks:

[W]hen Hart's descriptivism is mischaracterized—in the way that I regard some of Stephen Perry's remarks as mischaracterizing it—then indirectly evaluative legal theory might appear to be an intermediate position between an implausible interpretation of the

---

[39] John Finnis, *Natural Law and Natural Rights* (Oxford: Clarendon Press, 1980), pp. 12–13. Hart denies that the perspective of the "bad man" can *exhaust* the internal point of view on law, not that it is not, itself, one possible perspective on the reason-giving force of legally valid norms.

[40] H.L.A. Hart, *The Concept of Law*, 2nd ed. (Oxford: Clarendon Press, 2004), esp. pp. 33–5.

[41] See, e.g., id., pp. 27, 32.

[42] "Law and What I Should Truly Decide" (n. 36 above), p. 125.

[43] "Methodology in Legal Theory: A Critical Survey," *Legal Theory* 10 (2004), 117–156.

descriptive aspirations of jurisprudence and Finnis's and Dworkin's position. However, in my view, Hart's descriptivism, properly understood, is simply an instance of [what Dickson calls] indirectly evaluate legal theory.[44]

But she then allows that there may be a real dispute over whether or not "epistemic" (as I call them) or "metatheoretic" (as Dickson calls them) values suffice for theory construction in jurisprudence. Helpfully explaining her own view, Dickson writes:

[I]n making indirectly evaluative judgments of importance and significance and in explaining legal phenomena, the legal theorist himself has to be able to discriminate between and make evaluative judgments about participants' self-understandings in order to pick out which are most relevant in understanding law's important and significant features...

[This] does not merely amount to a mirroring or reproductive exercise. Some self-understandings of the participants will be confused, insufficiently focused, or vague. Moreover, some self-understandings will be more important and significant than others in explaining the concept of law...

All this requires the legal theorist not merely to record and reproduce but to *evaluate* the self-understandings of participants in explaining law's important and significance features. Contra Leiter, it seems natural to me to say ... that this is an evaluation—albeit not a moral evaluation—of aspects of legal practices themselves...

Leiter's explicit rejection of this point ("it does not ... require that we attend to how the theorist ... *evaluates* those practices") suggests that a difference of opinion [between Leiter and Dickson] remains ...[45]

The ellipses in the last quotation, however, obscure the fact that the kind of evaluation to which I was referring was an analogue of *moral* rather than *epistemic* evaluation. The context of the sentence Dickson partially quotes was my consideration of Dickson's own very helpful example of the agnostic who tries to make sense of a Roman Catholic mass.[46] My point was that the agnostic's own evaluation of the Catholic mass (for example, that it is a voodoo ritual based on preposterous metaphysical assumptions) need be no part of the enterprise of figuring out what is "significant" and "important" about the mass from the standpoint of understanding it hermeneutically. To be sure, I agree with Dickson that what is called for is not simply "record[ing] and reproduc[ing]" the self-understandings of participants in the Mass. The question elided here is what kinds of normative considerations, *precisely*, are required for a theory of a hermeneutic concept? Dickson and I appear to be agreed that *moral* considerations are not required; but what remains after we exhaust the familiar epistemic (or "metatheoretic") desiderata?

Perhaps what Dickson has in mind is some vaguely Davidsonian/Sellarsian notion[47] to the effect that in interpreting a human social practice, it is a requirement of charity to interpret the actors as more-or-less "making sense" by reference

---

[44] Id., p. 137.   [45] Id., pp. 138–9.
[46] Julie Dickson, *Evaluation and Legal Theory* (Oxford: Hart Publishing, 2001), pp. 68–9.
[47] I owe this suggestion to Brian Berry.

to the interpreter's normative standards of "making sense." Does this involve more, though, than the metatheoretic normative considerations that both Dickson and I think are appropriate to Hermeneutic Concepts? As the debate stands today, I am uncertain what Dickson thinks, but perhaps this last question will focus where the dispute, if there is one, really lies.

In contrast to Dickson, Ian Farrell is worried not about the role of evaluation in jurisprudence, but about the role of *conceptual* analysis itself, and he has raised some doubts about my criticisms which I find persuasive.[48] Others have raised versions of these kinds of concerns,[49] but I will focus on Farrell's formulation as the most cogent to date. Farrell wants to defend the view that "*modest* conceptual analysis [in Frank Jackson's sense] is a legitimate methodology for jurisprudence."[50] As Farrell explains it:

In its modest role, conceptual analysis restricts itself to drawing conclusions about what the *concept* is, illuminating the concept's underlying structure and determining whether particular situations are covered by the concept. . . . [T]his typically involves an exposition of the folk theory of the concept. Modest conceptual analysis goes no further. Specifically, conceptual analysis in its modest form makes no claims about the nature of the universe. It is merely descriptive, and descriptive of the *concept* and not of the *world* (which of course the concept purports to describe, or at least refer to).[51]

Now this appears to be a significant deflation of the analytical ambitions of Hart in writing a book on the "concept" of law. Hart, after all, endorsed the Austinian view that (quoting Austin) we "are looking not merely at words . . . but also at the realities we use words to talk about."[52] But on Farrell's (more plausible) rendering of conceptual analysis, we do not illuminate the reality, i.e., the nature of law, we illuminate, rather, the nature of our "talk" about law. As Farrell puts it:

Conceptual analysis, even in its modest role, attempts to increase our *understanding* of how we use words. The methodology is employed to clarify and to systematize, to make sense of the way we employ certain important terms by making explicit an underlying, inchoate, but nonetheless coherent concept or theory. If we must use an analogy from criminal investigation, modest conceptual analysis would be better compared to image enhancement,

---

[48] Ian P. Farrell, "H.L.A. Hart and the Methodology of Jurisprudence," *Texas Law Review* 84 (2006), 983–1011.

[49] See, e.g., the discussion of Jules Coleman's criticisms earlier in this Postscript. See, more recently, John Oberdiek and Dennis Patterson, "Moral Evaluation and Conceptual Analysis in Jurisprudential Methodology," in *Current Legal Issues: Law and Philosophy*, ed. R. Harrison (Oxford: Oxford University Press, forthcoming), which is otherwise a helpful overview of aspects of the recent debate. Oberdiek and Patterson, like Farrell, want to preserve something of "conceptual analysis" even granting the soundness of Quine's attack on analyticity. They claim, however, that "there are at least four distinct, overlapping methods of conceptual analysis that are not challenged in any serious way by Quinean naturalism." Somewhat bizarrely, two of the "methods" they identify (their first and third) are obviously vulnerable granting the soundness of Quinean naturalism (which Oberdiek and Patterson purport to do), while their second seems to be only stipulatively an example of "conceptual analysis." Their fourth example has some resonance with Farrell's discussion, which I concentrate on in the text.   [50] "H.L.A. Hart and the Methodology of Jurisprudence" (n. 48 above) p. 999.

[51] Id.   [52] Hart, *The Concept of Law* (n. 40 above), p. 14.

whereby an out-of-focus photograph of the perpetrator is enhanced to the extent that the subject's face can be recognized.[53]

The final analogy is suggestive, but we need to be careful to construe it *modestly*: for strictly speaking, what we recognize is not the subject's *actual* face, but rather the contours of the face *as portrayed in the photograph*: it is the photograph, not the person, that comes into focus. *Modest* conceptual analysis illuminates our concepts—our *talk*, as it were—not the referent we might have intended to understand. When the photograph comes into focus, to be sure, we may discover that the person pictured is not the one we have in custody. At the same time, the clearer picture may enable us to pick out the suspect we really want. So, too, then with successful conceptual analysis.

Perhaps this understanding of conceptual analysis is, after all, consonant with Hart's Austinian view, which continues (quoting Austin again): "We are using a sharpened awareness of words to sharpen our perception of phenomena."[54] And perhaps, too, it resonates with Timothy Williamson's recent defense of the continued relevance of "the linguistic turn" in philosophy:

Some contemporary metaphysicians appear to believe that they can safely ignore formal semantics and the philosophy of language because their interest is in a largely extra-mental reality. They resemble an astronomer who thinks that he can safely ignore the physics of telescopes because his interest is in the extra-terrestrial universe. In delicate matters, his attitude makes him all the more likely to project features of his telescope confusedly onto the stars beyond.[55]

Williamson's picture is, I suspect, more modest than Hart's, and thus more amenable to Farrell's deflation of the enterprise of conceptual analysis in law. For on Williamson's picture, if we do not understand our representational medium, we run the risk of projecting the defects of the medium on to its subject-matter. But Hart's Austinian infatuation with language and concepts is less modest: it supposes that if we understand our medium, we understand the nature of the things it represents to us. If Williamson's evocative analogy were really apt for conceptual jurisprudence, the claim would be that an astronomer who understands his telescope understands the nature of the universe! And that is clearly a deeply *immodest* claim, which Farrell's defense of conceptual analysis does not license.

This is not to say that conceptual analysis, even on Farrell's rendering of Hart, is of no interest. Its deliverances are neither simple nor trivial—nor are they merely, as Farrell argues *contra* me, "glorified lexicography". As Farrell points out,[56] one need only look at a typical dictionary definition of "law" and Hart's analysis in *The Concept of Law* to see the difference in results between lexicography and conceptual analysis. These points are well-taken, but do they show that conceptual

---

[53] "H.L.A. Hart and the Methodology of Jurisprudence" (n. 48 above), p. 1001.
[54] *The Concept of Law* (n. 40 above), p. 14.
[55] "Past the Linguistic Turn?" in *The Future for Philosophy* (n. 15 above), p. 128.
[56] "H.L.A. Hart and the Methodology of Jurisprudence" (n. 48 above), p. 1001 and n. 87.

analysis delivers the Razian desideratum of identifying (as Dickson put it) "those essential properties which a given set of phenomena must exhibit in order to be law"?[57] Farrell plainly does not think so:

Hart believes that the folk concept of law is *universal*.... But in developing his theory of the concept of law, Hart makes numerous assertions regarding the intuitions of the educated man. In doing so, he appears to simply assume that all educated persons share his intuitions. And not just well-educated, English men: Hart's assertion of the generality of the concept of law entails that all members of any society with a modern legal system must share Hart's relevant linguistic intuitions. If Hart's views prove not to be representative to this extent, his generality claim would be directly rebutted.[58]

Once again, there is an *empirical* question about how the concept of law is actually employed, and whether or not it exemplifies the coherent structure that Hartians and Razians find, or whether it varies with moral purpose as Murphy claims? Or perhaps (even more radically) the concept of law, at least in certain ethnographic contexts, is like the concept of "morally right," i.e., a concept without any cognitive content, but simply an expressive device for registering a special kind of endorsement?

Finnis declares that empirical inquiry into the perhaps ethnographically relative use of the concept is "scarcely worthy of the name of *philosophy*,"[59] and perhaps he is right. But an argument entailing the demise of *philosophy* of law is a successful *reductio* only on the dubious assumption that its conclusion is, in fact, absurd. Are the methods of philosophy, even supplemented with empirical data about usage, really capable of anything more?

To be sure, there is a more transformative conclusion than Finnis's purported *reductio*. For perhaps the fundamental error in philosophy of law consists in thinking that the concept of "law" is really a worthy subject of analysis at all? Certainly the convoluted directions that analyses of the concept have taken in recent years do not inspire confidence.[60] Consider: philosophers of science no longer spend any time at all analyzing the concept of "science," since the Razian-style enterprise of identifying the "essential properties" of science was a complete failure, indeed, one of the spectacular failures of mid-twentieth-century philosophy of science. Demarcating science from non-science failed, even though everyone still knows physics is science, and astrology is bogus. Perhaps the "problem" of demarcating law from morality will go the same way? There are certainly all kinds of systems of norms in human societies, and some are *clearly* legal (e.g., "don't go faster than 55 miles per hour on this road") and some are *clearly* moral (e.g., "in acting you ought to treat others as ends, not as means"), but perhaps the more fruitful questions for the future will not concern the "essential" features of the distinctively

---

[57] Julie Dickson, *Evaluation and Legal Theory* (Oxford: Hart Publishing, 2001), p. 17.
[58] "H.L.A. Hart and the Methodology of Jurisprudence" (n. 48 above), p. 1008.
[59] "Law and What I Should Truly Decide" (n. 36 above), p. 116.
[60] Consider, e.g., Part Two of Coleman's recent *The Practice of Principle* (n. 9 above).

legal norms. Let the experimental philosophers sort out the facts about people's intuitions about the concept, one might say. Perhaps naturalizing jurisprudence should, in short, *change the subject*, in much the way that the naturalistic revolution in post-positivist philosophy of science has led to a proliferation of philosophies of the special sciences and to the subsumption of scientific practice under more general human activities (e.g., rational belief formation and revision)? These are the kinds of issues that, I hope, will command the attention of naturalistically-minded jurisprudents in the years ahead.

PART III

NATURALISM, MORALITY, AND OBJECTIVITY

7

Moral Facts and Best Explanations*

I. Introduction

Do moral properties[1] figure in the best explanatory account of the world? According to a popular realist argument, if they do then they earn their ontological rights: for only properties that figure in the best explanation of experience are *real* properties.

Although this realist strategy has been widely influential—not just in metaethics, but also in philosophy of mind and science[2]—no one has actually made the case that moral realism requires: namely, that moral facts really will figure in the best explanatory picture of the world. This issue may have been neglected in part because the influential Harman-Sturgeon dialectic on moral explanations[3] has focused the debate on whether moral facts figure in *relevant* explanations.[4] Yet as

* My thanks to Julia Annas and Allan Gibbard for comments on much earlier versions of portions of this material; to Ben Zipursky for comments on a more recent draft; to William Forbath for guidance on historical questions; to Sahotra Sarkar for guidance on evolutionary biology; and to the editors of *Social Philosophy & Policy* and the participants in the "Moral Epistemology" conference in La Jolla in June 2000 for their helpful questions and comments on the penultimate version.

[1] I will use the terms "moral properties" and "moral facts" interchangeably in what follows. So, e.g., one might say that inflicting gratuitous pain on a sentient creature has the property (or feature) of being morally wrong, or one might say that it is a (moral) fact that the infliction of such pain is morally wrong.

[2] See, e.g., Jerry Fodor's defense of the reality of the attitudes in *Psychosemantics* (Cambridge, Mass.: MIT Press, 1987), ch. 1, and Richard Boyd's defense of scientific realism over many years: e.g., his "Scientific Realism and Naturalistic Epistemology," in *PSA 1980, Volume 2*, ed. P. Asquith & R. Giere (East Lansing: Philosophy of Science Association, 1982).

[3] Gilbert Harman, *The Nature of Morality* (New York: Oxford University Press, 1977); Nicholas Sturgeon, "Moral Explanations," reprinted in *Essays on Moral Realism*, ed. G. Sayre-McCord (Ithaca: Cornell University Press, 1988); Gilbert Harman, "Moral Explanations of Natural Facts—Can Moral Claims Be Tested Against Moral Reality?" *Southern Journal of Philosophy* 24 (Supp. 1986): 57–68; Nicholas Sturgeon, "Harman on Moral Explanations of Natural Facts," *Southern Journal of Philosophy* 24 (Supp. 1986): 69–78. In later work, Sturgeon has argued, with some plausibility, that "nonmoral explanations do not always appear to undermine moral ones." "Nonmoral Explanations," *Philosophical Perspectives* 6 (1992): 97–117, at pp. 111–12. But this point, even if correct, has no bearing on the argument here, which supposes that the question is not whether nonmoral explanations undermine moral ones, but which explanations are *best*.

[4] See, e.g., David Brink, *Moral Realism and the Foundations of Ethics* (Cambridge: Cambridge University Press, 1989), pp. 187 ff. which discusses the issue in terms of explanatory "relevance" and "irrelevance."

others have noted, explanatory relevance is *irrelevant* when it comes to realism: it is, after, all, inference to the best explanation that is supposed to confer ontological rights.[5] I propose to ask, then, the relevant question about moral explanations: should we think that moral properties will figure in the best explanatory account of the world?

A preliminary word, however, about the significance of the question is in order. Many moral realists—in particular, the so-called "Cornell" realists[6]—take explanatory potency in the above sense to be *sufficient* for realism. This position, however, no longer seems tenable in light of the powerful criticisms of inference to the best explanation (IBE) as a license for realism.[7] Instead, we should construe explanatory potency only as a necessary—but not sufficient—condition for realism. This would make the debate about explanatory potency a debate about what Geoffrey Sayre-McCord calls the "weak" version of the "Explanatory Criterion": "A hypothesis should not be believed if the hypothesis plays no role in the best explanation we have of our making the observations that we do."[8] "Real" facts—moral or scientific—must still, as Peter Railton puts it, figure "in the explanation of our experience," such that they "cannot be replaced without loss,"[9] but that they do so figure is not by itself sufficient for realism.

II. Best Explanations

Do moral properties, then, figure in the best explanatory account of the world? Of course, we cannot hope to decide here what the "best" explanatory account of the world really is, but we may at least ask whether moral properties will figure in seemingly "better" explanatory accounts. To know whether they will, however, we need to answer two questions that have been sadly neglected in the moral realism literature: first, what makes one explanation better than another; second, *to what* are we comparing moral explanations?

---

[5] See Geoffrey Sayre-McCord, "Moral Theory and Explanatory Impotence," in *Essays on Moral Realism* (n. 3 above), pp. 272–4.

[6] The "Cornell" realists are defenders of moral realism like Richard Boyd and Nicholas Sturgeon (who teach at Cornell), as well as their students, like David Brink.

[7] The IBE arguments for realism claim that we are entitled to infer the real existence of those facts that figure in the best explanation of our experience. Arthur Fine has argued that, as a defense of realism, IBE begs the question, which is precisely about the legitimacy of such an inference (namely, the IBE by which scientists posit unobservable entities). Bas van Fraassen, on the other hand, has asked why we should think what happens to be our best explanation should warrant an inference to truth. See Arthur Fine, "The Natural Ontological Attitude," in *Scientific Realism*, ed. J. Leplin (Berkeley: University of California Press, 1984), pp. 84–91, and Bas van Fraassen, *Laws and Symmetry* (Oxford: Clarendon Press, 1989), pp. 142–9.

[8] "Moral Theory and Explanatory Impotence" (n. 5 above) pp. 267–8.

[9] "Moral Realism," *Philosophical Review* 95 (1986), p. 172. Note that none of this constitutes a bar to realism; Railton's realist program, for example—in both ethics and philosophy of science—eschews IBE. See also his "Explanation and Metaphysical Controversy," in *Scientific Explanation*, ed. P. Kitcher & W. Salmon (Minneapolis: University of Minnesota Press, 1989).

Any account of what makes an explanation "best" or "better" is bound to be contentious, but if the realist is to defend moral facts on explanatory grounds, then he must take some stand on this question. I propose that we start with two intuitively plausible criteria for theory-choice articulated in a well-known paper by Paul Thagard: consilience and simplicity.[10] *Consilience*, according to Thagard, has to do with "*how much* a theory explains." So "one theory is more consilient than another if it explains more classes of facts than the other does".[11] *Simplicity* in a theory is only a virtue when not at the expense of consilience. So "a simple consilient theory not only must explain a range of facts; it must explain those facts without making a host of assumptions with narrow application".[12] Notice that *ontological* or *theoretical* economy is not necessarily a virtue on this view: ontologies and theories can be complex as long as they contribute to consilience.[13] So one explanation will be better than another, on this account, if it explains more and does so with comparable or greater simplicity.

One might, of course, wonder why the moral realist should care about these criteria?[14] One reason is surely that they are intuitively plausible. "Simplicity" is, of course, a mainstay on any checklist of desiderata for theory-choice, while whole theories of explanation have been built around the idea that explanations should advance understanding by unifying disparate phenomena[15]—something which consilient theories (theories that explain different classes of phenomena in terms of some basic explanatory mechanism) would seem to do.

At least for some moral realists, however, a second reason for taking these criteria seriously seems compelling: namely, that they are—as Thagard argues—criteria operative in the history of science. Since for many moral realists—particularly those concerned to vindicate the explanatory power of moral properties—moral inquiry and moral epistemology should be continuous with scientific inquiry and scientific epistemology, it seems fair to expect that moral explanations should satisfy the criteria that inform theory-choice in science.[16]

---

[10] Paul Thagard, "The Best Explanation: Criteria for Theory Choice," *Journal of Philosophy* 75 (1978): 76–92. I ignore a third criterion: "analogy." Analogy is the thought that "other things being equal [i.e. without sacrificing consilience of simplicity], the explanations afforded by a theory are better explanations if the theory is familiar, that is, introduces mechanisms, entities, or concepts that are used in established explanations" (id., p. 91). This criterion is both more contentious and, arguably, more obviously inhospitable to moral explanations.   [11] Id., p. 79.

[12] Id., p. 87.   [13] The simplicity criterion is, then, a relative of Ockham's razor.

[14] This objection, especially with respect to consilience, was urged on me in conversation by Julia Annas.

[15] See Michael Friedman, "Explanation and Scientific Understanding," *Journal of Philosophy* 71 (1974): 5–19.

[16] That Thagard has accurately captured these criteria is nicely illustrated by this passage written by a mathematician reviewing a book by a physicist:

The great ambition of scientists is to grasp the far from obvious nature of the physical world at ever more fundamental levels, and in doing so, to unify our understanding of phenomena that had previously appeared to be disparate. We have been enormously successful in this, demonstrating that complex objects are made from simpler components, and they in turn are made of even simpler ones.... [U]nderlying the immense complexity of life is a simplicity of microscopic composition.

George Ellis, "Good Vibrations," *London Review of Books* (March 30, 2000), p. 14.

In any event, it is clear that to assess the explanatory potency of moral facts we need to have some criteria for assessing moral explanations and Thagard's seem like reasonable candidates. Let the burden fall upon the moral realist to show why these criteria are inappropriate in the case of moral realism—and to suggest appropriate alternatives as well.

Applying Thagard's criteria yields a standard obstacle to putatively real facts, what I will call "the Problem of Explanatory Narrowness" (PEN). A property suffers from PEN if its explanatory role is too peculiar or narrow: if it only explains one class of phenomena to which it seems too neatly tailored.[17] Real explanatory facts, so Thagard's criteria suggest, must have some degree of extra consilience. Properties that "explain," but suffer from PEN, are not "real" properties.

Consider an example. Imagine someone called the Spirit Realist, who holds that various human actions can be explained in terms of the effects of spirits. So, for example, the Spirit Realist holds that Hitler did the evil things he did because possessed by evil spirits.[18] Assume further that the Spirit Realist holds that evil spirits supervene on precisely the evil-making moral properties that supervene on the relevant natural properties. What is wrong, then, with "spirit facts"?

Examples like this are obviously troubling to the moral realist. But one response that is not available here is the one David Brink offers against the defender of the explanatory power of magical facts: "What is objectionable about magical facts ... is that they are incompatible with natural facts. Appeals to magical and natural facts provide competing explanations of the same phenomena."[19] The proposed spirit facts, however, are not magical facts in Brink's sense. The Spirit Realist, like the moral realist, assumes that his preferred facts (spirit facts) supervene on the relevant natural facts, and thus do not compete with them. Only by begging the question against the Spirit Realist could we employ a response like Brink's.

But surely we still have a good response to the Spirit Realist: namely that spirit explanations suffer from PEN, and thus these explanations give us no reason to think spirit properties are real properties. For spirit facts seem to do no explanatory work above and beyond that done by moral facts. The problem for the moral realist will be to show why moral properties should not meet the same fate vis-à-vis the non-moral facts on which they supervene.

III. Naturalistic Explanations

We now know what would make one explanation better than another, but we still lack a precise comparison class for the moral explanations at issue here: we cannot

---

[17]   Cf. Crispin Wright, *Truth and Objectivity* (Cambridge, Mass.: Harvard University Press, 1992).

[18]   Cf. Sturgeon:"I do not believe that Hitler would have done all he did if he had not been morally depraved..." "Moral Explanations" (n. 3 above) p. 245.

[19]   *Moral Realism and the Foundations of Ethics* (n. 5 above), p. 183.

decide whether moral explanations are "best" or "better" unless we know to what kinds of explanations they are to be compared. Rather than positing moral facts to explain our moral observations, Gilbert Harman argued that we "need only make assumptions about the psychology or moral sensibility of the person making the moral observation."[20] In a similar vein, Freud and Nietzsche have appealed to deep facts about human nature and development to explain our moral beliefs and judgments.[21] Freud's account is more detailed, and so I will focus on his here.[22]

There are, it seems at first, two different stories of the development of moral conscience in Freud: in one, conscience arises through the internalization (or "introjection") of the parental super-egos as a way of resolving the Oedipal complex;[23] in the other, conscience arises as a result of the introjection of innate aggressive drives, whose taming is a necessary precondition for the rise of civilization.[24] John Deigh observes that the first (the "standard account") "fits more

---

[20] *The Nature of Morality* (n. 3 above), p. 6.

[21] For Nietzsche's version of these kinds of naturalistic arguments, see the discussion in Leiter, "The Paradox of Fatalism and Self-Creation in Nietzsche," in *Willing and Nothingness: Schopenhauer as Nietzsche's Educator*, ed. C. Janaway (Oxford: Clarendon Press, 1998), esp. pp. 230–5, and in Leiter, "One Health, One Earth, One Sun: Nietzsche's Respect for Natural Science," *Times Literary Supplement* (Oct. 2, 1998), pp. 30–1. For a longer treatment, see Leiter, *Nietzsche on Morality* (London: Routledge, 2002). Nietzsche's and Freud's approaches are compared in the book and in the *TLS* article. For Freud's naturalistic explanation of moral judgment, see especially, "The Dissection of the Psychical Personality," in *New Introductory Lectures in Psychoanalysis*, trans. & ed. J. Strachey (New York: Norton, 1965).

[22] I am assuming—not uncontroversially these days-that Freud's theory is basically true, or at least the part of the theory concerned with explaining the nature of and capacity for moral judgment and conscience. The standard reference point for the contrary view is, of course, Adolf Grünbaum, *The Foundations of Psychoanalysis: A Philosophical Critique* (Berkeley: University of California Press, 1984). (Strictly speaking, of course, Grünbaum argues only that Freud's theory is not warranted by the evidence adduced, not that it is false.) Frederick Crews's shrill polemics notwithstanding, Grünbaum's critique has itself been demolished in a series of papers, of which the most important are: Arthur Fine and Mickey Forbes, "Grünbaum on Freud: Three Grounds for Dissent," *Behavioral and Brain Sciences* 9 (1986): 237–8; Jim Hopkins, "Epistemology and Depth Psychology: Critical Notes on *The Foundations of Psychoanalysis*," in *Mind, Psychoanalysis and Science*, ed. P. Clark & C. Wright (Oxford: Blackwell, 1988); David Sachs, "In Fairness to Freud: A Critical Notice of *The Foundations of Psychoanalysis* by Adolf Grünbaum," *Philosophical Review* 98 (1989): 349–78; Richard Wollheim, "Desire, Belief, and Professor Grünbaum's Freud," in *The Mind and Its Depths* (Cambridge, Mass.: Harvard University Press, 1993). Empirical confirmation of aspects of Freudian theory from non-clinical settings include Henry E. Adams, Lester W. Wright, Jr., & Bethany A. Lohr, "Is Homophobia Associated with Homosexual Arousal?" *Journal of Abnormal Psychology* 105 (1996): 440–5 (reporting experimental evidence of the role of reaction formations in homophobia).

[23] Freud writes: "With his abandonment of the Oedipus complex a child must... renounce the intense object-cathexes which he has deposited with his parents, and it is as a compensation for this loss of objects that there is such a strong intensification of the identifications with his parents which have probably long been present in his ego." "The Dissection of the Psychical Personality" (n. 21 above), p. 57.

[24] Freud writes:

His aggresiveness is introjected, internalized; it is, in point of fact, sent back to where it came from—that is, it is directed towards his own ego. There it is taken over by a portion of the ego as super-ego, and which now, in the form of 'conscience,' is ready to put into action the ego the same harsh aggressiveness that the ego would have liked to satisfy upon other, extraneous individuals....

closely into [Freud's] general theory of how one develops a personality... [while] the other [the "Nietzschean account"] ... gives a more cogent explanation of how one acquires a conscience."[25] Deigh thinks the Nietzschean account marks a *change* in Freud's theory of moral development, especially in explaining the formation of conscience via repression of *aggressive* rather than *sexual* drives. It would take us too far afield into Freud interpretation to resolve the question, but let me at least suggest here that the two accounts can also be understood as complimentary. For the super-ego has a dual function for Freud: the enforcement of moral standards, and the maintenance of an ego ideal to which we may aspire. And as Deigh himself notes elsewhere: "The operations of conscience [for Freud] owe their motivational force to aggressive drives; the operations of the ego ideal owe theirs to sexual drives."[26] Both accounts of the origin of the super-ego, then, would be necessary to explaining the dual functions it performs.

The crucial point, though, for our purposes is that on Freud's account "judgments of morality and value have motivational force that is traceable to these basic [aggressive and sexual] instincts."[27] Moreover, from the standard account we know that the *content* of judgments of morality derives from the identification with the parental super-egos required to resolve the Oedipal complex. So both moral motivation and the content of morality receive a psychoanalytic explanation: there need be no moral facts to explain moral judgments and their force, just innate drives and standard development trajectories through which creatures like us pass.[28]

Some recent moral anti-realists like Simon Blackburn and Allan Gibbard, by contrast, have turned not to Freud, but to evolutionary theory for a naturalistic

---

Civilization, therefore, obtains mastery over the individual's dangerous desire for aggression by weakening and disarming it and by setting up an agency within him to watch over it, like a garrison in a conquered city.

Civilization and Its Discontents, trans. & ed. J. Strachey (New York: Norton, 1961), pp. 78–9. This account, as is well known, mirrors Nietzsche's in the second essay of *On the Genealogy of Morality* (1887).

[25] John Deigh, "Remarks on Some Difficulties in Freud's Theory of Moral Development," reprinted in *The Sources of Moral Agency* (Cambridge: Cambridge University Press, 1996), p. 66.

[26] John Deigh, "Freud, Naturalism, and Modern Moral Philosophy," reprinted in *The Sources of Moral Agency*, id., p. 127.   [27] Id.

[28] Recent years have witnessed an odd marriage of Freudian insights and Kantian strictures in the work of some Anglo-American moral philosophers, including Deigh. See also, Samuel Scheffler, *Human Morality* (New York: Oxford University Press, 1992), ch. 5; J. David Velleman, "A Rational Superego," *Philosophical Review* (forthcoming). These writers believe that Freud's theory can be divested of Freud's explicitly anti-rationalist interpretation. Deigh, for example, complains that "the belief that [moral] judgment has motivational force solely in virtue of its being invested with instinctual force is not philosophically innocent" and that Freud simply begs the question against the rationalist who denies that premise. "Freud, Naturalism, and Modern Moral Philosophy" (n. 26 above) p. 129. The difficulty, of course, is that for Freud this is an *empirical* question, not a philosophical one, and the empirical evidence favors his interpretation—or so Freud believes. (Oddly, Deigh makes the conclusory assertion that Freud did not have "evidence to support it" (id., p. 130), but there is no argument or discussion.)

account of moral judgment.[29] Gibbard's proposal, for example, is to analyze normative judgments as expressing states of norm-acceptance and to explain the latter capacity in terms of its contribution to successful "coordination," where coordination is the "biological function" selected for by evolution.[30] Call this the Evolutionary Explanation (EE). So on this "speculative evolutionary story" supposing that there are "normative facts is gratuitous": we can explain our normative judgments fully without them.[31]

Admittedly, though, Gibbard's account (like Blackburn's) *is* speculative. Research by biologists, fortunately, does provide some help. Many evolutionary biologists have been concerned to explain the existence of altruistic *behavior*, and while *judgments* about the value of altruism are not usually discussed, it seems reasonable to suppose that the existing evolutionary accounts could be extended in that direction: if evolution selects for altruistic behavior, surely it also selects in favor of the normative practices that support such behavior.[32] The central puzzle for evolutionary theory about altruism concerns the level on which natural selection operates. If it operates only on the level of the individual, then it is hard to see why it would favor altruistic behavior by individuals, since all such behavior would seem to detract from the reproductive success of that individual. If the target of selection, however, is in some circumstances the "group" to which the individual

---

[29] Simon Blackburn, "How To Be an Ethical Antirealist," *Midwest Studies in Philosophy* 12 (1988): 361–76; Allan Gibbard, *Wise Choices, Apt Feelings: A Theory of Normative Judgment* (Cambridge, Mass.: Harvard University Press, 1990). See also, Gilbert Harman, "Explaining Value," *Social Philosophy & Policy* 11 (1994): 229–48, esp. at pp. 238–9. For skepticism about such evolutionary accounts, see Nicholas L. Sturgeon's "Critical Study" of Gibbard in *Noûs* 29 (1995): 402–24, esp. at pp. 415–18.

[30] Gibbard, id., pp. 108, 116. Among Sturgeon's more interesting objections to the speculative evolutionary story is the following: "[Gibbard] believes . . . that humans evolved biologically to have a separate motivational faculty, a 'language-infused' norm-acceptance system that emerged as we became language-users . . . [E]valuative language thus emerged to play a special role, that of expressing the norms so accepted." Sturgeon, id., p. 407. But the puzzle, then, is why "we don't now find natural languages better adapted to the function Gibbard identifies." Id. In other words, why did evolution not also select for language with a non-cognitive surface grammar, instead of the cognitive surface grammar that non-cognitivists must work so hard to reinterpret?

In the speculative evolutionary mode which this objection invites, some answers do suggest themselves. For example, it was probably advantageous in terms of facilitating successful co-ordination and co-operation for humans to employ a language with a uniform syntax, rather than to have evolved many specialized syntaxes, especially since evolution has no reason to take sides in the debate between realism and anti-realism (or cognitivism and non-cognitivism). Indeed, cognitive-looking syntax may have enhanced the value of normative talk for co-ordination. Only the fact—on which, to repeat, evolution is utterly neutral—that there are no moral facts creates a dilemma for the philosophical interpretation of normative talk. For recall that a primary motivation for non-cognitivism is the thought that *if* there are no moral facts, *and* we take the syntax of normative discourse at face value, *then* it is mysterious why normative talk persists: why would a putatively fact-stating discourse that states no facts have held on for so long? Non-cognitivism vindicates the point of normative talk even in the absence of normative facts.   [31] Gibbard (n. 29 above), pp. 121, 108.

[32] I will assume, plausibly, that altruism is central to morality, so that we have explained a lot about morality when we have explained why we prize altruism. Altruism is, of course, central to a number of influential moral philosophies—from Schopenhauer's to Thomas Nagel's—and it also enjoys pride of place in common-sense moral thinking as well.

belongs, then an explanation suggests itself. As Darwin, who toyed with but did not develop the idea, puts it in a famous passage:

It must not be forgotten that although a high standard of morality gives but a slight advantage or no advantage to each individual man and his children over the other men of the same tribe...[t]here can be no doubt that a tribe including many members who, from possessing in a high degree the spirit of patriotism, fidelity, obedience, courage, and sympathy, were always ready to aid one another, and to sacrifice themselves for the common good, would be victorious over most other tribes; and this would be natural selection. At all times throughout the world tribes have supplanted other tribes; and as morality is one important element in their success, the standard of morality and the number of well-endowed men will thus everywhere tend to rise and increase.[33]

Group selectionism as an explanation for the rise of altruism (and, following Darwin, we might say "the standard of morality") has recently received a robust defense from Elliott Sober and David Sloan Wilson,[34] but it is still far from having carried the day in biology.[35] Intermediate between individual and group selectionist accounts, and much more widely accepted by biologists, is the "kin selectionism" developed by W.D. Hamilton.[36] Here, the target of selection is held to be larger than the individual, but smaller than the group or the tribe: the constraint is genetic similarity, i.e., kin. Rearing your sibling's kids may sometimes be a better way of passing on (some portion of) your genes than having kids of your own, and thus natural selection could prefer altruistic behavior (and attitudes) towards kin.[37] Of course, the moral value assigned to altruism is not kin-specific (at least *in theory*, as opposed to *in practice*), but we might speculate that kin-specific altruism is more robust when supported by a general moral imperative to care for the welfare of others.

So from psychoanalysis and evolutionary theory we get two different naturalistic accounts of moral behavior and judgment. Let us call all these accounts—which explain moral belief and judgment by appeal to the deterministic forces

---

[33] Charles Darwin, *The Descent of Man and Selection in Relation to Sex* (London: Murray, 1871), p. 166.

[34] *Unto Others: The Evolution and Psychology of Unselfish Behavior* (Cambridge, Mass.: Harvard University Press, 1998).

[35] See, e.g., the review by John Maynard Smith in *Nature* 393 (1998): 639–40, or the polemic in Richard C. Lewontin's review essay in *The New York Review of Books* 45 (October 22, 1998): 59–63.

[36] The theory is first sketched in W.D. Hamilton, "The Evolution of Altruistic Behavior," *American Naturalist* 97 (1963): 354–6, and receives its classic formal expression in: "The Genetical Evolution of Social Behavior I," *Journal of Theoretical Biology* 7 (1964): 1–16, and "The Genetical Evolution of Social Behavior II," *Journal of Theoretical Biology* 7: 17–52. All these papers are reprinted in W.D. Hamilton, *Narrow Roads of Gene Land* (Oxford: W.H. Freeman, 1996). In a 1975 paper, Hamilton himself displays some sympathy for a kind of "group selectionism," though for formal modelling reasons that would take us far afield. See "Innate Social Aptitudes of Man: An Approach from Evolutionary Genetics," reprinted in *Narrow Roads of Gene Land*, esp. p. 337.

[37] Hamilton puts the point as follows in the 1963 paper:

[T]he ultimate criterion which determines whether [gene] *G* will spread is not whether the behavior is to the benefit of the behaver but whether it is to the benefit of the gene *G*; and this will be the case if

operative in one or more of the special sciences (psychology, physiology, biology, etc.)—"Naturalistic Explanations" (NE). I am going to assume in what follows that some NE actually works.[38] We can then pose the comparative question as follows: which are better explanations, moral explanations (MEs) or NEs? If MEs fare worse, then we will have (certainly defeasible) grounds for thinking that moral properties will not make it into the best explanatory account of the world. We may see that, in fact, MEs are inferior by attending again to Thagard's two criteria.

(i) *Consilience*: NEs will always explain more than MEs (they will be more consilient); that is, the mechanisms employed by NEs explain much more than just the class of "moral" phenomena (e.g., moral beliefs and observations), while MEs will only "explain" the "moral" phenomena. This should hardly be surprising: after all, NEs were generally proffered as accounts of other phenomena first, before finding application in the moral cases. Thus, the causal mechanisms underlying Freudian explanations work to explain not only morality, but also various neuroses as well as all the psychopathologies of everyday life. The application of EE to moral phenomena is a relatively recent and sometimes contentious matter; by contrast, evolutionary accounts of physiological characteristics, social phenomena, mental content, etc., abound, and many are now well established.

(ii) *Simplicity*: MEs involve additional "assumptions with narrow application"[38a]—namely assumptions about moral facts—that are not justified by gains in consilience. By contrast, the assumptions of NEs—assumptions, e.g., about unconscious psychic forces, microphysiological processess, natural selection, genetic drift etc.—will involve great gains in consilience, and thus (arguably) justify the increase in theoretical complexity.

Moral properties, in short, suffer from PEN: they are too neatly tailored to only one sort of explanandum—what I am calling the moral phenomena—for us to think that moral properties are real (explanatory) properties. The comparison of MEs with NEs should make this obvious; but even without a comparison, moral facts, like spirit facts, seem to have all the trappings of PEN.

---

the average net result of the behavior is to add to the gene pool a handful of genes containing *G* in a higher concentration than does the gene pool itself. With altruism this will happen only if the affected individual is a relative of the altruist, therefore having an increased chance of carrying the gene, and if the advantage conferred is large enough compared to the personal disadvantage to offet the regression, or 'dilution,' of the altruist's genotype in the relative in question.

Id. at 7.

[38] If no NE works, then moral explanations might seem to win by default. Even that strikes me as doubtful, however. For why should moral explanations be the default position, when they play a role only in parts of folk explanations (and the speculations of various moral realist philosophers) and have been utterly neglected by all serious empirical researchers? Psychoanalytic explanations (more controversially) and evolutionary explanations (uncontroversially) have established their explanatory credentials in many domains, even if details of their account of moral judgment might be disputed.

[38a] Thagard, "The Best Explanation" (n. 10 above), p. 87.

IV. Rejoinder: Opting Out of the Explanatory Debate

How, then, should the moral realist respond to this new argument from explanatory impotence? Two general lines of response have been in evidence in the literature: on the one hand, there are those who simply want to "opt out" of the debate: explanatory potency, they claim, simply does not or should not matter for moral realism. Others, however, want to respond on the (explanatory) merits. Let us deal with each of these approaches in turn.

Why, some philosophers have asked, should moral realists care about explanatory potency? The challenge has come in two main forms: on the one hand, there are those who think explanatory power is *irrelevant* to establishing moral realism; on the other hand, there are those who think explanatory considerations are unfair to moral realism.

Those who make the charge of "irrelevance"[39] claim that the explanatory potency of properties simply does nothing to show whether the properties are moral: for moral properties "justify" or "guide action," rather than "explain." This complaint, however, misunderstands the explanatory argument. Moral realists who invoke explanatory considerations are concerned only with the *reality*, not the *morality* of the properties; thus, the claim is not (*contra* David Copp) that moral theories are "confirmable" on explanatory grounds.[40] Which properties are the "moral" properties—as opposed to the question which properties are real—will have to be answered on other grounds. Railton, for example, suggests that we will need to draw on "our linguistic or moral intuitions" in order to pick out natural properties that "express recognizable notions of goodness and rightness."[41] The "irrelevance" complaint, then, simply misconstrues the point of the debate.

By contrast, the charge of "unfairness" is motivated precisely by an appreciation of the bearing explanatory considerations are usually taken to have upon the question of realism. What motivates the charge is the thought that by making explanatory power a necessary mark of real properties we will have unfairly prejudged the issue against moral facts. This sort of worry is expressed in Thomas Nagel's comment that, "To assume that only what has to be included in the best causal theory of the world is real is to assume that there are no irreducibly normative truths."[42]

---

[39] E.g., Sayre-McCord, "Moral Theory and Explanatory Impotence"; David Copp, "Explanation and Justification in Ethics," *Ethics* 100 (1990): 237–58.

[40] See Peter Railton, "Naturalism and Prescriptivity," in *Foundations of Moral and Political Philosophy*, ed. E.F. Paul et al. (Oxford: Basic Blackwell, 1990).

[41] "Moral Realism" (n. 9 above), p. 205.

[42] *The View From Nowhere* (New York: Oxford University Press, 1986), p. 144. A very interesting and important critique of Nagel's metaethical views in this regard can be found in Sigrún Svavarsdóttir, "Objective Values: Does Metaethics Rest on a Mistake?" in *Objectivity in Law and Morals*, ed. B. Leiter (New York: Cambridge University Press, 2001). Ronald Dworkin has recently objected to the "best explanation" test in terms similar to Nagel's. See "Objectivity and Truth: You'd Better Believe It," *Philosophy & Public Affairs* 25 (1996): 87–139. Dworkin's views are described and criticized in Ch. 8.

This response raises complex epistemological and ontological questions, but a somewhat abbreviated reply will have to suffice here. Much of the interest of recent work on moral realism consists in the fact that it tries to show that such realism is compatible with naturalistic constraints on epistemology and ontology—constraints like causal or explanatory potency. Values, these realists want to claim, can be real in precisely the way everything else in the natural world is. From this perspective, one might make two responses to Nagel. First, we might want to know why we should have to make exceptions for value in our best epistemology of the world? Surely the answer cannot simply be to make room for moral realism! Second, assuming we think the naturalistic constraints are well-motivated, having to make exceptions for particular properties casts doubts on their standing. It is still open to someone to take issue with the metaphysical picture that informs these replies, but the naturalist may be forgiven for thinking it unremarkable that moral (and perhaps many other) facts should make it into our ontology of the world once naturalistic constraints are dropped.[43]

A final, related form of objection does suggest itself at this point: namely, that these "naturalistic constraints" are *too* constraining. As Hilary Putnam puts it: the best-explanation test " 'proves too much'; for if it were right, it *would* apply to cognitive values just as much as to ethical ones!"[44] In other words, the moral realist might charge that the explanatory criterion itself cannot survive the best-explanation test, so the position of the naturalist is self-refuting. This form of argument, however, only works on the assumption that the moral anti-realist must be committed to realism about epistemic norms. But why think that? The moral skeptic should happily be Quinean about epistemic norms, and simply point out that from where we stand in Neurath's boat, the epistemic norms of our best-going science include the best-explanation test, and that is all we have to go on when it comes to the metaphysics and epistemology of anything else. In any case, the naturalistic moral realists at issue here—unlike, say, Putnam—all accept the best-explanation test as a necessary condition for realism.

V. Rejoinder: Arguing the Explanatory Merits

What then of responses on the explanatory merits? Here, again, there appear to be two possible lines of reply. One invokes the possible identity or supervenience of moral properties on the explanatory properties as a way of showing that the

---

[43] John McDowell has built a whole realist program around a sometimes glib contempt for naturalistic constraints, and, not surprisingly, his is a promiscuous ontology, including moral, aesthetic and comical facts, among others. The grounds for this—which, in any event, are not always easy to discern—and their plausibility would require separate examination. For doubts about McDowell's program, see David Sosa, "Pathetic Ethics" in *Objectivity in Law and Morals*, ed. B. Leiter (Cambridge: Cambridge University Press, 2001) and Pt IV of Ch. 8.

[44] Hilary Putnam, "Replies to Brian Leiter and Jules Coleman," *Legal Theory* 1 (1995): 69–80, at p. 81.

explanatory argument for anti-realism is inconclusive. The second reply argues more directly that without moral facts we do, indeed, suffer some explanatory or cognate epistemic loss. I will argue that, in fact, the issue of explanatory loss is the decisive one for the whole debate about moral explanations, even for those who would try to save moral realism through appeal to claims about supervenience or identity. Let us consider, however, each reply in turn.

A. Identity/Supervenience

The explanatory argument, some philosophers argue, simply cannot rule out moral realism: for nothing in the explanatory argument shows that the explanatorily superior facts (e.g., the facts in NEs) are not simply the very facts on which the moral facts supervene or with which they are identical. Think, for example, of the case of color:

> [O]ur best explanations of [why we perceive roses as red] might well make reference to certain characteristics of roses, facts about light, and facts about the psychological and perceptual apparatus of perceivers, but not the *redness* of the roses (and not to any particular feature of the roses that can be reductively identified with redness). Despite this, the availability of such explanations expands our understanding of colors; it does not show that there are not colors.[45]

So in giving the scientific account of color we have simply identified the facts about light and vision that constitute color facts. The suggestion is: so too for morals. For example, in giving the NE, perhaps we have simply identified some of the facts that constitute moral facts. Nothing, it seems, in the explanatory argument for anti-realism rules that out.

Three responses, in ascending order of importance, might be made to the moral realist on this score:

First, the analogy with color may be the wrong place for the moral realist to look. As Paul Boghossian and David Velleman have argued, projectivism about color properties may, indeed, be the right response to the scientific account of color: "The projectivist account of colour experience is...the one that occurs naturally to anyone who learns the rudimentary facts about light and vision. It seemed obvious to Galileo, as it did to Newton and Locke."[46] Now perhaps color

---

[45] Sayre-McCord, "Moral Theory and Explanatory Impotence" (n. 5 above), pp. 274–5; for a similar point, see also Brink, *Moral Realism and the Foundations of Ethics* (n. 4 above), p. 193. Gibbard, it should be noted, agrees on this point; he says: "Even if I am right that normative judgments have coordination as their biological function, that does not by itself show that there is no kind of fact...to which these judgments are adapted to correspond. One might imagine a program of 'normative realism' that proposes a kind of fact to do the job...I, myself, though, have found no kind of fact that works..." *A Theory of Normative Judgment* (n. 29 above), p. 116.

[46] Paul Boghossian & J. David Velleman, "Colour as a Secondary Quality," *Mind* 98 (1989), p. 97. See also their, "Physicalist Theories of Color," *Philosophical Review* 100 (1991): 67–106. Note, of course, that Boghossian and Velleman do not attack color realism on *explanatory* grounds, but rather on the grounds of certain epistemological and phenomenological problems that arise when we

and morality are relevantly different, such that projectivism is not the "obvious" response to learning the naturalistic explanation for moral belief. Much will turn, surely, on the sort of naturalistic explanation in the offing. In any event, the plea I should like to make here is simply for more to be said. For moral realists have been far too glib about invoking the case of color, yet the "scientific" picture may plausibly "explain away" morals *and* colors. As a result, an appeal to the case of color *simpliciter* cannot help the moral realist.[47]

Second, this reply to the explanatory argument changes the terms of the debate about moral realism significantly. The claim under consideration is that the explanatory argument against moral realism is not conclusive because it *might* turn out that the moral facts are simply constituted by the explanatory facts at issue. But note that explanatory considerations will do no work in establishing that claim: we will require some independent argument for taking the moral properties to be identical with or supervenient upon the properties in the apparently better explanation. So to invoke the line of response under consideration here is already to concede that explanatory considerations alone can *not* establish moral realism. This, it seems to me, is an important point often obscured in the recent literature. It suggests that a naturalistic moral realism may still stand or fall upon the traditional obstacle: the plausibility of the posited relation between the "moral" and the "natural."

Third, there still remains a simplicity problem for the moral realist. For the moral realist must now claim that moral facts are explanatory, but only in virtue of their being identical with or supervenient upon explanatory non-moral facts. Yet, plainly, substantive theses about *identity* or *supervenience* add to the complexity of our theory and our ontology in a way that must be justified by some gain in

---

try to construe color properties as identical with or supervenient upon the scientific facts about light and vision that explain them. For a summary see the first article, pp. 82–3; for an extended treatment, see the 1991 paper.

[47] A different route against the color analogy is suggested by Blackburn in "How To Be an Ethical Antirealist" (n. 29 above). Blackburn claims that the naturalistic picture is motivated by two elements: (1) the fundamental identification of the commitment in question as something other than a belief; (2) the existence of a neat natural account of why the state that it is should exist" (p. 363). (1) is what is crucial here: Blackburn's idea is that states of mind that are not beliefs simply lend themselves to naturalistic accounts in a way that belief-states do not: "the fundamental state of mind of one who has an ethical commitment makes natural sense" on the naturalistic story (p. 363)—and this is because this "state of mind starts theoretical life as . . . a stance, or conative state or pressure on choice and action" (p. 363). Now while Blackburn thinks there is an EE for color just as there is for moral value (thus satisfying (2)), he thinks there is a difference as to (1): "[T]here is no way that I can see usefully to contrast color commitments with *beliefs*. Their functional roles do not differ. So, there will be no theory of a parallel kind to develop, explaining why we have propositional attitudes of various kinds toward color talk, or why we speak of knowledge, doubt, proof, and so forth in connection with them" (p. 373). As a result, the naturalistic story about color will not help us make "natural sense" of the "color commitment." For this to be a satisfactory reply, however, much more would have to be said about the first of the two elements in Blackburn's picture: immediately, it is not obvious that naturalism could not consume conative and belief states in its wake (think of the strong programme in the sociology of knowledge).

consilience or some cognate epistemic virtue.[48] When we learn that the observable macroproperty of "being water" is identical to the unobservable microproperty of "being H_2O" we can explain features of the macroproperty (that it freezes, that it evaporates, that it boils away, etc.) and in so doing can effect a certain explanatory unification of the macro-properties of water with other macro-features of the world (e.g. ice, steam, etc.) that would have been obscure without knowledge of the micro-properties and the identity thesis. Thus, there is an epistemic gain (unification of phenomena) from making our theory of the world more complex by accepting the identity of "water" and H_2O that *justifies* that complexity.

Supervenience claims present a related issue. Consider the case of the EE: granted physicalism,[49] evolutionary facts must be identical with, or more likely supervenient upon, physical facts. Yet there are clear gains in consilience by admitting these substantive theses about supervenience into our theory: namely, the now well-known scope of EEs, together with the apparent inability of any other science (e.g., physics) to account for the same phenomena. But if EEs do all the explanatory work that MEs do—plus some—then there seems no reason to add substantive theses about moral property-supervenience into our theory, when we already have the theoretically simpler and more consilient EE. If the supervenience of evolutionary facts will do all the explanatory work, why add the supervenience of moral facts to our best theory of the world?

Claims of identity or supervenience, then, will not—in isolation—save moral realism against the explanatory argument; we must earn our right to such claims by both (a) vindicating the identity/supervenience thesis on non-explanatory grounds; and (b) vindicating the added theoretical complexity involved in these theses by demonstrating that they produce a gain in consilience or some cognate epistemic virtue (e.g., explanatory unification).

B. Explanatory Loss

The moral realist, then, who would defend moral facts on explanatory grounds must claim that *without* moral facts we suffer an explanatory loss:[50] just as physics cannot do the same explanatory work as evolutionary biology, so too evolutionary

---

[48] Perhaps this is not true of *all* identity claims: e.g., the identification of the morning star and the evening star. But reductive identifications—reducing one class of things to a wholly different class of things—plainly require a substantial theoretical edifice to motivate them. It is, to put the matter gently, hardly obvious, for example, that "morally right" just picks out "maximizations of utility." Theoretical complexity, however, requires an epistemic payoff, like consilience, at least when we are comparing explanations.

[49] By physicalism, I will just mean the doctrine that everything that exists is physical, i.e., occupies some discreet points in space and time.

[50] Supervenience claims are the most common in the moral realism literature, so I will focus on that case in what follows.

biology (or psychology or sociology, etc.) cannot do the same explanatory work as moral facts. Can the moral realist sustain this central claim?

Unfortunately, there is no way to approach this question except on a case-by-case basis. No *a priori* considerations can demonstrate that there will never be an explanatory loss from eliminating moral facts from our best account of the world. Two sorts of considerations, however, may make us skeptical of the realist's claim. First, if we go outside the contemporary philosophical debate and look to scholars in other disciplines actually concerned with explanatory questions, I think we will be hard-pressed to find anyone doing serious explanatory work with moral facts. Outside of informal ways of speaking and "folk explanations," moral facts appear to play no role in any developed explanatory theory. The moral realism literature often makes much of these "folk" explanatory theories, but, as the comparison with naturalistic theories suggests, it is doubtful that these folk theories will make it into our best account of the world. Philosophers would perhaps do well not to forget that while, for example, there are Marxist historians using broadly "economic" facts to explain historical events, there is no school of "Moral Historians" using moral facts to do any interesting or complex explanatory work.[51]

A second ground for skepticism about moral explanations is more specific: namely, that the actual candidates preferred in the literature are, by and large, not very promising. Some moral explanations are just patently vacuous,[52] but even the more promising candidates do not, I think, stand up to scrutiny. Let me conclude by considering some examples from the work of Sayre-McCord, Brink, and Joshua Cohen.

Non-reductive moral realists want to defend moral explanations in a way akin to Jerry Fodor's defense of the autonomy of the special sciences:[53] they want to claim that there are distinctive "groupings" and generalizations in moral explanations that cannot be captured by a more "basic" explanatory scheme or science. Just as nothing in physics captures the distinctive categories and generalizations of economics and psychology, so too biology and psychology are supposed to miss the distinctive generalizations of moral theory.

Part of the appeal of Fodor's argument, of course, was that psychology and economics and biology really seemed to be engaged in important explanatory work, so that it would be a real loss if their distinctive facts had to be dropped in a physicalist ontology of the world. If the moral realist is to avail himself of a similar defense, then we must be similarly impressed by moral explanations. Both

---

[51] See, however, the discussion of Railton's program in n. 65, below.

[52] This is true, I think, of almost all of Sturgeon's examples. My own feeling is that if I were seeking an explanation for Hitler's conduct and was offered the account that "He was morally depraved," I would take such an answer to be a bit of a joke: a repetition of the datum rather than an explanation. Contrast Sturgeon's moral "explanation" of Hitler with a sophisticated, and not at all vacuous, account like that in Erik Erikson, *Childhood and Society*, 2nd ed. (New York: Norton, 1963), pp. 326–58. Erikson's account makes no use of putative moral facts to explain Hitler's behavior.

[53] See the "Introduction" to Fodor, *The Language of Thought* (Cambridge, Mass.: Harvard University Press, 1975).

Sayre-McCord and Brink try to suggest as much, but their accounts, I will argue, are not persuasive. Here, for example, is Sayre-McCord pursuing the strategy just described:

[C]ertain regularities—for instance, honesty's engendering trust or justice's commanding allegiance, or kindness' encouraging friendship—are real regularities that are unidentifiable and inexplicable except by appeal to moral properties.[54]

There is, of course, a double claim here, and thus two ways to resist it: first, there must be "real [moral] regularities"; second, it must be the case that we cannot explain or even identify them without moral facts. Sayre-McCord's proposal falters on both. Is "honesty's engendering trust" a "real regularity"? To the contrary, it seems honesty just as often engenders not trust but annoyance or bitterness or alienation: people, as is well known, do not want those around them to be *too* honest.[55] Indeed, someone who is too honest may often be thought untrustworthy, precisely because he or she cannot be expected to guard one's secrets and keep one's counsel. And justice, it seems, provokes opposition as often as it produces allegiance: many people have little interest in just arrangements, and so resist them at every step. And do we necessarily befriend the kindly or simply appreciate them—or perhaps take advantage of them? In sum, it is far from obvious that Sayre-McCord's folksy examples bear much scrutiny; there appears to be little "regular" about these putative regularities.[56]

Sayre-McCord's proposal fails on the second count as well. Do we need moral facts to explain these putative regularities—or just the assumption that people who believe others are honest will trust them?[57] In fact, surely the latter is a *better* explanation: for if there is a regularity here, it requires only the perception of honesty, rather than its actual presence. Perceived honesty should, it seems, engender trust as readily as real honesty; while making real honesty the basis of the regularity will leave out of the explanatory scope those cases where people trust those who only seem honest, but are not really. So, too, what people *believe* or *perceive* to be "just" probably does engender allegiance, whereas the regularity collapses when we talk about *real* justice, which is often a threat to privileged groups. What

[54] "Moral Theory and Explanatory Impotence" (n. 5 above), p. 276.

[55] Trust, of course, also seems engendered by much else besides honesty: in the political realm, it is notorious that people trust their leaders notwithstanding a long and familiar history of deceit (consider Americans during the Persian Gulf War, notwithstanding the experience of Vietnam and Watergate). With respect to government, it seems more likely that it is what the anarchist Randolph Bourne called an attitude of "filial mysticism" toward the state rather than honesty that accounts for the willingness of the citizenry to "trust" the authorities. We might prefer an explanation (if there were one) that would cover all these cases of trust-engendering.

[56] The moral realist might protest that moral explanations, of course, have *ceteris paribus* clauses, and so there will, naturally, be exceptions to the regularities. But the skeptic might ask: what exactly are the parameters of these claimed regularities and their exceptions? Appeal to *ceteris paribus* clauses, without *any* account of what those special conditions are, simply permits the defender of folk moral explanations to discount any counter-example with some handwaving about "*ceteris paribus*."

[57] This, of course, is just a variation on Harman's account of the flaming cat case in *The Nature of Morality* (n. 3 above), ch. 1.

explanatory gain, then, would we get from assuming with Sayre-McCord that there are moral facts (e.g., about honesty or justice)?

Brink, with somewhat greater detail, pursues the same line as Sayre-McCord when he claims that "moral explanans will generalize better than would explanans in terms of the lower-order facts that constitute these moral facts."[58] Brink gives the example of explaining "political instability and social protest in [apartheid] South Africa" in terms of racial oppression (an unjust practice), rather than in terms of the particular social, economic, and political conditions in *which it happens to be realized* in South Africa—since surely "there would still have been racial oppression and instability and protest under somewhat different" conditions.[59] As a result, the "moral explanation . . . "—appealing to the unjust practice of racial oppression—"will occupy a distinct and privileged explanatory role".[60]

But will it? Brink himself notes that "our interest in explanations is typically an interest in understanding past events or predicting future events".[61] During the heyday of the empiricist Covering Law Model of explanation during the 1940s and 1950s, there was supposed to be a strict symmetry between explanation and prediction,[62] but Carl Hempel later relaxed this requirement as follows: "Any rationally acceptable answer to the question 'Why did X occur?' must offer information which shows that X was to be expected—if not definitely, as in the case of . . . explanation [by appeal to a covering law], then at least with reasonable probability."[63] Thus, to think we have understood the past event we must think that if we had known what we now take to explain that event we would have been able to predict its occurrence—at least with reasonable probability.

We still, of course, have to be careful how stringent we make this demand, lest it start to label as pseudo-explanations seemingly sound and familiar explanations, like the sort found in history. Yet Brink's example cannot even satisfy a very weak requirement of predictability. Take the South Africa case: racial oppression existed *for decades* without the significant political unrest and social protest that finally marked the collapse of apartheid. So too with racial oppression in the American South, which existed for nearly a hundred years after the Civil War with only episodic and ineffectual resistance. From the standpoint of the historian, then, what exactly would be the "distinct and privileged explanatory role" of racial oppression? What predictions, if any, follow from knowing that a society is racially oppressive? Does it not seem, instead, that we would have to turn precisely to the particular lower-order social, economic, and political facts to really explain why

---

[58] *Moral Realism and the Foundations of Ethics* (n. 4 above), p. 195.   [59] Id., p.195.
[60] Id.   [61] Id., p. 194.
[62] Hempel and Paul Oppenheim wrote in the classic 1948 paper: "an explanation of a particular event is not fully adequate unless its explanans, if taken account of in time, could have served as a basis for predicting the event in question." "Studies in the Logic of Explanation," reprinted in *Theories of Explanation*, ed. J. Pitt (New York: Oxford University Press, 1988), p. 12.
[63] Carl Hempel, "Aspects of Scientific Explanation," in *Aspects of Scientific Explanation and Other Essays* (New York: Free Press, 1965), p. 369.

social protest arose against racial oppression at the times it actually did? Indeed, we would look in vain for real historians explaining the end of American apartheid by reference to its injustice.[64]

Brink's moral explanation, like Sayre-McCord's, also faces a second difficulty: namely, that it seems sufficient for the explanation (such as it is) that people *believe* racial oppression to be unjust, regardless of whether it really is unjust. That is, it seems sufficient to "explain" the social protest against racial oppression in terms of the protesters' belief that racial oppression is unjust, without assuming that it really is unjust. To be entitled to the additional assumption that it really is unjust, we must know what explanatory gain is to be had by complicating our theory and ontology in this way.

Now we would have such an explanatory gain if

(a) injustice produces certain regular effects (e.g., social instability, revolution, etc.)
   (i) *independent* of what people believe about the justice of some socio-economic arrangement, *or*
   (ii) because of what people believe, where these beliefs themselves are best explained by the reality of injustice; and
(b) the injustice is multiply realized in non-moral states of affairs.

Both conditions are essential. Condition (a) guarantees that it is injustice itself, and not simply people's beliefs, that does the explanatory work. Condition (b) guarantees that the regularity at issue correlates with the moral fact of injustice itself, and not with some non-moral state of affairs to which injustice is (allegedly) reducible. For if injustice is multiply realized in various kinds of non-moral states of affairs, then only the fact of injustice will suffice for identifying the regularity.[65] Of course, as in the case of water, we might argue that even if injustice is not

---

[64] One possible exception is found in Thomas Haskell's account of the demise of slavery in his contribution to *The Antislavery Debate: Capitalism and Abolitionism as a Problem in Historical Interpretation*, ed. T. Bender (Berkeley: University of California Press, 1992), though it is unclear that Haskell's account depends on slavery being *really* wrong or simply on people *believing* it to be wrong (conjoined with the rise of national and international markets, which both altered people's sense of self and responsibility, and made slavery more visible as an institution than ever before). In the case of the demise of segregation, the standard historical accounts emphasize three factors: (1) the migration of Southern blacks to the North (in the wake of the collapse of the Southern agricultural economy) which gave rise in the 1930s and 1940s to Congressional districts in which blacks had real political power; (2) the frustration of World War II black GIs who faced segregationist impediments to seizing GI Bill opportunities, and who, in conjunction with newly empowered black labor unionists, came to constitute much of the leadership of the civil rights movement at the local level; and, most importantly, (3) Cold War imperatives to do something about Jim Crow, which impeded efforts to win the hearts and minds of Africa and Asia.

[65] I am assuming here, with Fodor and others, that multiple realizability blocks reduction. In fact, this seems to me true only on contentious assumptions about reduction, but these issues would take us too far afield. For critical discussion of the multiple realizability argument, see Jaegwon Kim, "Multiple Realization and the Metaphysics of Reduction," reprinted in his *Supervenience and Mind* (Cambridge: Cambridge University Press, 1993); Brian Leiter and Alexander Miller, "Closet Dualism and Mental Causation," *Canadian Journal of Philosophy* 28 (1998): 161–81, esp. at pp. 171–3.

multiply realized, appreciating its micro-reduction base in some non-moral states of affairs permits the unification of what were thought to be disparate macro-phenomena, and thus the added theoretical and ontological complexity of the identity thesis at issue would still earn its place in our best picture of the world. But this is a fragile thesis: for this kind of reduction might be thought to eliminate, rather than vindicate, the macro-property, so everything would turn on the details of the proposed reduction.

Now Joshua Cohen's recent argument that "the injustice of slavery contributed to its demise"[66] seems to offer an account that would satisfy (a) and (b), above. For Cohen explicitly rejects the view that "all that matters [in explaining the demise of slavery] . . . are beliefs about injustice" rather than the injustice of slavery itself.[67] For "the injustice of a social arrangement limits its viability",[68] and thus explains why such arrangements collapse or are overthrown. It is, of course, hardly controversial that slaves, like all people, have interests in "material well-being, autonomy, and dignity"—"fundamental interests" as Cohen calls them[69]—that are violated by the institution of slavery; nor should it be controversial that the fact that "slavery conflicts with the interests of slaves" contributes to "the limited viability of slavery".[70] What is crucial, as Cohen recognizes, is that the "injustice" of violating fundamental interests "conveys information relevant to explaining the demise of slavery that is not conveyed simply by noting that slavery conflicts with the interests of slaves".[71] But why think this is true? Why isn't appeal to the brute conflicts of interests—between slaves and masters—enough?

One possibility is that the moral convictions of some people (e.g., abolitionists) that slavery was unjust contributed causally to the demise of slavery *and* those moral convictions are, themselves, best explained "by the injustice of slavery".[72] As Cohen writes:

[P]art of the explanation for the moral belief [that slavery is unjust] is that slaves have interests in material well-being, autonomy, and dignity, and are recognized as having them; that slavery sharply conflicts with those interests, and is recognized as so conflicting; and that those interests are legitimate, and recognized as such. And why is this sequence of points not naturally captured by saying that people believe slavery to be unjust in part because it is unjust?[73]

The final and putatively rhetorical question, however, simply masks the fact that explanatory considerations are doing no work here. For even Thrasymachus and

---

[66] Joshua Cohen, "The Arc of the Moral Universe," *Philosophy & Public Affairs* 26 (1997): 91–134, at p. 94.
[67] Id., p. 124. Id., p. 95: "I am concerned with the consequences of slavery's injustice . . . and not simply the consequences of the fact that some people think of it as wrong."   [68] Id., p. 93.
[69] Id., p. 116.   [70] Id., p. 94.   [71] Id.
[72] Cohen here fudges, and says only that the moral convictions are "explained in part by the injustice of slavery" (id., p. 123). But this would only suffice if it is shorthand for "the injustice of slavery is part of the *best* explanation for the moral convictions." It is not clear that this is what Cohen claims, or what he is entitled to claim.   [73] Id., pp. 128–9.

Callicles could agree that slaves have the "fundamental interests" Cohen ascribes to them, and that slavery "sharply conflicts with those interests," without agreeing that any of this has anything to do with injustice.[74] That additional theoretical claim depends on the viability of Cohen's substantive account of justice—which, following Rawls and T.M. Scanlon, is "based on an idealized notion of consensus— a free, reasonable, and informed agreement"[75]—that Thrasymachus and Callicles reject. We need, then, an independent argument—one having nothing to do with explanatory considerations—about why *this* is what justice *really* consists in.

What Cohen (and Brink) ultimately need to claim is that "injustice" identifies "features of the system" that "are a source of instability".[76] But they also need the claim that "injustice" is a way of classifying the causally relevant phenomena that identifies regularities we would miss if we only employed the classificatory schema of some underlying domain of facts (e.g., psycho-social facts about interests and their conflict). Sustaining this latter claim would make the argument directly analogous to Fodor's argument that the special sciences give us classificatory schema (and resultant causal regularities) that would be lost if we could avail our-selves only of physics. In the end, though, Cohen never gives us an argument for this claim—essentially, for (b) above. He writes, for example, that one could explain the demise of slavery,

> ... simply [by] stat[ing] the properties of slavery—the conflict between slavery and slave interests—... without taking a position on whether those properties indeed are what makes slavery unjust; in short ... the fact that the properties *are* injustice-making is not itself a part of my argument. Still, they are, and can unobjectionably be presented via the moral classification. Moreover, that mode of presentation is morally important. For the world looks different if we think that injustice-making features limit the viability of systems that have them.[77]

This extraordinary passage, alas, confirms the worry that moral explanations are, as Cohen feared, "simply collages of empirical rumination and reified hope, pasted together with rhetorical flourish".[78] For the only reason Cohen gives for employing the "moral" explanation—a classification, by the way, that is only "unobjectionable" to moral realists of the contractarian variety that Cohen favors[79]—as distinct from the non-moral account of *the same causal features* is that when we talk the language of morality "the world looks different." That is no doubt true, but it hardly counts, on its face, as an epistemic virtue that a classifica-tory scheme makes things "look different." Even our Spirit Realist could claim as

---

[74] It would have to be possible, of course, to define the relevant notion of "interest" without its being a fundamentally *normative* notion. But surely we can equate "interest" with, e.g., what agents would desire under appropriate conditions, without endorsing such desires.

[75] Cohen (n. 66 above), p. 120.   [76] Id., p. 132.   [77] Id., p. 132.   [78] Id., p. 93.

[79] See, e.g., John Rawls, *A Theory of Justice* (Cambridge, Mass.: Harvard University Press, 1971); T.M. Scanlon, *What We Owe to Each Other* (Cambridge, Mass.: Harvard University Press, 1998).

much: a world populated by good and evil spirits does, indeed, look different from a world divested of illusions.

These examples do not, of course, exhaust the possibilities;[80] yet given the absence of moral explanations in the disciplines actually concerned with explanatory questions, the difficulties confronting the actual examples of moral explanations considered above ought to encourage a healthy skepticism about whether the moral realist can carry the explanatory burdens his case requires.

VI. Conclusion

We have seen, then, that the argument from explanatory impotence does not *necessarily* rule out moral realism. The moral realist, however, must bear a double burden. She must either: (a) defend an account of moral facts as supervening on or being identical with explanatory non-moral facts; or (b) argue that dropping moral facts from our ontology results in some explanatory (or cognate) loss. To defend (a), however, the realist must also defend (b): that is, she must defend admitting substantive theses about identity and supervenience into her best theory of the world, presumably on the grounds that without moral facts we suffer

---

[80] In particular, I have said nothing about Railton's theory, the most detailed in the literature. Railton presents us with a slightly different—and also more complex—case, since he is alone among contemporary moral realists in regarding his program as reductionist by way of reforming definitions of moral terms. See his "Moral Realism" (n. 9 above) and "Naturalism and Prescriptivity" (n. 40 above) (all citations are to "Moral Realism"). This still does not, however, relieve Railton of the explanatory burden: if our theory is to include reforming definitions of moral terms in naturalistic terms, there must be some explanatory gain to justify doing so. In rough summary, Railton's approach is this: Railton claims that "what is morally best" is "what is instrumentally rational from a social point of view" (p. 200); but he also claims that we can explain certain historical developments in terms of "a mechanism whereby individuals whose interests are denied are led to form common values and make common cause along lines of shared interests, thereby placing pressure on social practices to approximate more closely to social rationality" (p. 199). So, in short, instrumental social rationality—or deviations therefrom—explains historical change; but instrumental social rationality is just what "morally right" refers to. Railton also seems to argue that we do get a *gain* in consilience from this moral explanation: for on Railton's story, seeing the connection between the explanatory mechanism, social rationality, and morality allows us to appreciate certain general historical tendencies in the evolution of moral norms (pp. 195–6). Note three points about Railton's proposal: (1) for it to work at all Railton's quite specific reforming definition of "morally right" must be independently defended (Kantians and constructivists, among others, will dissent); (2) this reforming definition must really afford us some explanatory gain; and (3) the explanatory theory itself must be a good one if the explanatory considerations are to support moral realism. The refreshing amount of explanatory detail Railton provides also makes his theory a clear target for critics of the explanatory paradigm: see, e.g., Alexander Rosenberg, "Moral Realism and Social Science," *Midwest Studies in Philosophy* 15 (1990): 150–66. Even supposing that Railton's theory could overcome the explanatory objections, it will still falter, I believe, on its proposed reforming definition. Here, however, it will be considerations pertaining to the diversity of recognizably *moral* opinion, rather than explanatory impotence, that will prove fatal to the theory. I plan to address these issues elsewhere.

an explanatory or cognate epistemic loss. Only if these obligations can be discharged will we have some reason for thinking moral facts will figure in the best explanatory picture of the world. If I am right that (b)—which both possible defenses of moral realism require—is probably not sustainable, then moral realism will have been refuted on explanatory grounds. Perhaps then we may, with greater confidence, join Nietzsche in saying that when it comes to ethics, "it is a swindle to talk of 'truth' in this field."[81]

---

[81] *The Will to Power*, Sec. 428.

8

Objectivity, Morality, and Adjudication*

Two familiar features of Ronald Dworkin's theory of adjudication generate a strange predicament. On the one hand, Dworkin maintains that most cases, including most "hard" cases, have "right answers." On the other hand, Dworkin argues that to discover that right answer, judges must avail themselves of moral considerations and moral argument: a party's rights follow from the principle which explains some significant portion of the prior institutional history *and* provides the best justification for that institutional history as a matter of political morality. But if moral considerations figure decisively in determining the answer to a legal dispute, then there can only be a single right answer as a matter of law if there is a single right answer to the question of political morality. Yet if morality is, as many seem to think, "subjective" in some sense, then there may be as many right answers as a matter of morality as there are judges, and thus, consequently, no single right answer as a matter of law. Here is how John Mackie put the worry many years ago:

[W]hat the law is, on Professor Dworkin's view, may crucially depend on what is morally best—what is best, not what is conventionally regarded as best in that society. Now I would argue . . . that moral judgments of this kind have an irreducibly subjective element. If so, then Professor Dworkin's theory automatically injects a corresponding subjectivity into statements about what the law is.[1]

If, in other words, one thinks that adjudication is "objective," in the sense that there are objectively right answers to legal disputes, then it might seem a bad idea to make right answers in law depend on moral considerations as Dworkin does.

Dworkin has not, of course, been insensitive to these concerns; over a period of years now, he has articulated an unusual response to this attack on the "objectivity"

* I am grateful to the students in my Spring 1996 seminar on "Objectivity" at the University of Texas at Austin for help in thinking about these issues and to my colleagues in philosophy—Daniel Bonevac, Cory Juhl, and Robert C. Koons—for useful comments on an earlier draft. I also benefitted from discussion of a later draft by the participants in the 2nd Annual Conference on Analytic Legal Philosophy at Columbia Law School in April 1997; I can recall helpful comments or questions on that occasion from Ruth Chang, William Edmundson, Ken Kress, David Lyons, Andrei Marmor, Thomas Nagel, Joseph Raz, Scott Shapiro and Jeremy Waldron. Finally, thanks to David Sosa and to the students in Jules Coleman's Spring 1999 "Philosophy of Law" seminar at Yale Law School for detailed comments on the penultimate draft.

[1] John Mackie, "The Third Theory of Law," reprinted in Marshall Cohen (ed.), *Ronald Dworkin and Contemporary Jurisprudence* (London: Duckworth, 1983), p. 165.

of morality.[2] According to Dworkin, the root of the problem lies in the understanding of "objectivity" that is implicit in this attack. Once we distinguish, as Dworkin would have us do, between sensible, but defeasible, "internal" attacks on the objectivity of morality from unintelligible, and irrelevant, "external" attacks on the objectivity of morality, we see that Mackie's criticism depends on the latter, and thus reflects a misunderstanding about what is at stake in worrying about the objectivity of morality, and thus in worrying about the objectivity of law. For the only type of objectivity that matters—namely, an "internal" objectivity—Dworkin's theory faces no predicament.[3]

Dworkin's extensive writings on "external" and "internal" skepticism about objectivity have attracted little attention from philosophers or jurisprudents over the years. Indeed, I am not aware of anyone, other than Dworkin, who has found his response on this score satisfactory.[4] In Part I of this paper, I want to review what Dworkin has said about objectivity and why it has seemed to many philosophers to be wrongheaded.

But the purpose of this paper is not simply critical. Although Dworkin may not provide a suitable articulation of the point, I think there is a genuine issue about our understanding of objectivity that is at stake here. This issue, so I will argue in Part II, is best understood as involving two competing paradigms of objectivity. On what I will call the "Naturalistic Conception," objectivity in any domain must be understood on the model of the natural sciences, whose objects of study are objective in the sense of being "mind-independent"[5] and causally efficacious (i.e. in making a causal difference to the course of experience). Such a conception of objectivity informs the work of both philosophers who affirm the objectivity of morality (like Boyd and Railton), as well as those who deny it (like Nietzsche and Mackie). The "Non-Naturalistic Conception," by contrast, denies that the type of objectivity found in the natural sciences is the relevant type of objectivity to aspire

---

[2] Dworkin's main discussions of these issues appear in the following texts: "Can Rights Be Controversial?" in *Taking Rights Seriously* (Cambridge, Mass.: Harvard University Press, 1977) [cited hereafter as TRS]; "Is There Really No Right Answer in Hard Cases?" [cited hereafter as MP1] and "On Interpretation and Objectivity," [MP2] both in *A Matter of Principle* (Cambridge, Mass.: Harvard University Press, 1985); *Law's Empire* (Cambridge, Mass.: Harvard University Press, 1986), 78–86 [cited hereafter as LE]; "Pragmatism, Right Answers, and True Banality," in M. Brint & W. Weaver (eds.), *Pragmatism in Law and Society* (Boulder: Westview, 1991) [cited hereafter as P]; and, most recently, "Objectivity and Truth: You'd Better Believe It," *Philosophy & Public Affairs* 25 (1996): 87–139 [cited hereafter as OT].

[3] I am not going to be concerned with the plausibility of this latter claim here. It bears noting, however, that even if Dworkin were right about the unintelligible "external" perspective, he would still need actually to defeat all "internal" skeptical attacks to support the right-answer thesis.

[4] For a representative critique, see Michael S. Moore, "Metaphysics, Epistemology, and Legal Theory," *Southern California Law Review* 60 (1987): 453–506.

[5] More precisely, these objects are *epistemically* independent of human mind: what we believe, or even what we would be justified in believing, does not fix the nature of these objects. Cf. the discussion of "observer-independence" in Sigrún Svavarsdóttir, "Objective Values: Does Metaethics Rest on a Mistake?" B. Leiter (ed.) *Objectivity in Law and Morals*, (Cambridge: Cambridge University Press, 2001).

to in all domains; some Non-Naturalists claim this because they think Naturalistic Objectivity is unintelligible (or at least, unintelligible as applied to domains like morality). Non-Naturalists typically have positive proposals for how to understand objectivity in domains like ethics or aesthetics. I will concentrate in Part II on only one: John McDowell's notion that objectivity in ethics is a matter of moral views being "susceptible to reasons."[6] We shall see, I think, that the grain of truth in what Dworkin is getting at in his external/internal distinction is really best understood as the difference between a Naturalistic versus a Non-Naturalistic Conception of Objectivity. Dworkin would have us, then, embrace the latter as the only type of objectivity at stake in assessing his theory of adjudication.

In Part III of this paper, however, I will argue that the Non-Naturalistic Conception (at least the McDowell/Dworkin version) is not an adequate account of objectivity: it fails to explain basic intuitions about objectivity (even in ethics), as well as leaving us with a picture of the "objectivity" of ethics that would, in fact, be quite congenial to the non-cognitivism that both McDowell and Dworkin purport to have left behind. If that is right, then the predicament remains a live one for Dworkin's theory. It is my view that the predicament has no solution, and that the law is, in fact, indeterminate.[7] These latter issues are, however, beyond the scope of this paper.

Let us turn first, then, to Dworkin's response to the predicament.

I. Dworkin on Objectivity

A. Introduction

According to Dworkin, when we claim that there is an objective fact about whether one interpretation is better than another, or whether one principle is morally better than another, we are not making a claim *external* to the practice of substantive moral or interpretive argument in which these claims arise. "Slavery is objectively wrong" is simply a *moral* claim internal to the practice of argument in which we offer reasons for the proposition that "Slavery is wrong." Two thousand years of metaphysics notwithstanding, there simply are no *metaphysical* questions about value; there are only *evaluative* questions. To the extent that Protagoras, Plato, Hume, Nietzsche, G. E. Moore, A. J. Ayer, Charles Stevenson, John Mackie,

---

[6] Other adherents to the Non-Naturalist Conception of Objectivity, but not necessarily to McDowell's positive construal of it, would include Thomas Nagel, *The View From Nowhere* (New York: Oxford University Press, 1986) and Hilary Putnam, "Are Moral and Legal Values Made or Discovered?" and "Replies to Brian Leiter and Jules Coleman," *Legal Theory* 1 (1995): 5–19, 69–80. On Nagel's views, see Svavarsdóttir's essay id.

[7] For a more detailed articulation of my views on this subject, see my "Legal Indeterminacy," *Legal Theory* 1 (1995): 481–92, and also my essay on "Legal Realism," in D. M. Patterson (ed.), *A Companion to Philosophy of Law and Legal Theory* (Oxford: Blackwell, 1996). For more on the Realist views, to which I am generally sympathetic, see Ch. 1.

Gilbert Harman, Richard Boyd, Peter Railton, Michael Smith, and Allan Gibbard thought they were answering questions of *meta*-ethics, they are wrong. There is only ethics, only argument about what is right, what is just, what is good, what is evil, and the like. Here is how Dworkin has put the point over the years:

I have no arguments for the objectivity of moral judgments except moral arguments, no arguments for the objectivity of interpretive judgments except interpretive arguments, and so forth. (MP2, 171)

I have yet been given no reason to think that any skeptical argument about morality can be other than a moral argument . . . (MP2, 174)

Any successful—really, any intelligible—argument that evaluative propositions are neither true nor false must be internal to the evaluative domain rather than archimedean about [i.e. external to] it. (OT, 89)

Thomas Nagel, though not quite agreeing with Dworkin, characterizes the view succinctly: "the only way to answer skepticism, relativism, and subjectivism about morality is to meet it with first-order moral arguments. [Dworkin] holds that the skeptical positions must themselves be understood as moral claims—that they are unintelligible as anything else."[8]

If we are not doing metaphysics (or metaethics) when we are worrying about "objectivity," then what are we doing? According to Dworkin, talk about the "objective" wrongness of abortion, for example, is really just disguised *moral* talk, perhaps "a slightly more emphatic form" of abortion is wrong (MP2, 171). All purportedly external statements about the status of the judgment "abortion is wrong" are really "nothing but clarifying or emphatic or metaphorical restatements or elaborations of [the internal moral claim] that abortion is wrong" (OT, 97):

We use the language of objectivity, not to give our ordinary moral or interpretive claims a bizarre metaphysical base, but to *repeat* them, perhaps in a more precise way, to emphasize or qualify their *content*. (LE, 81)

Now at first sight these remarks seem quite obviously wrong. To claim that abortion is *objectively* wrong is, on a natural reading, not simply to "repeat" or "emphasize" that abortion is wrong, but rather to assert a certain metaphysical thesis: to wit, that there exists a property of moral wrongness, which abortion has, and which it has quite independently of what we happen to think about the matter.[9] To talk about "objective" rightness and wrongness is to talk about metaphysical or ontological issues, about what properties the world contains quite apart from what we happen to know about them. Yet this is precisely what Dworkin, in the

---

    [8] Thomas Nagel, *The Last Word* (New York: Oxford University Press, 1997), p. vii.

    [9] Cf. David Brink, *Moral Realism and the Foundations of Ethics* (Cambridge: Cambridge University Press, 1989), p. 20 ("ethics is objective . . . [in the sense that] it concerns facts that hold independently of anyone's beliefs about what is right or wrong"); Peter Railton, "Moral Realism," *Philosophical Review* 95 (1986): 163–207, p. 164 (the issue about objectivity is the issue of "in what ways, if any, does the existence of moral properties depend upon the actual or possible states of mind of intelligent beings").

remarks quoted above, seems to deny. To see how Dworkin motivates this counter-intuitive claim, then, we need to understand a bit more about the distinction Dworkin draws between "internal" and "external" forms of skepticism about morality.

B. The "Internal" and the "External"

Internal skepticism about morality (or any other domain of discourse) is skepticism motivated by first-order moral (aesthetic, interpretive) argument. "The internal skeptic addresses the substance of the claims he challenges" (LE, 78), and in so doing, presupposes the cogency of moral argumentation. The internal skeptic "denies some group of familiar positive claims and justifies that denial by endorsing a different positive moral claim—perhaps a more general or counterfactual or theoretical one" (OT, 89). An internal skeptic, for example, might deny that sexual acts are moral or immoral—he might deny, that is, that they have any *moral value*—by relying on a *moral* view according to which "suffering is the only thing that is inherently bad" (OT, 91). In this sense, he would be *skeptical* about the *moral value* of sexual behavior while at the same time "presuppos[ing] the truth of some positive value judgment" (OT, 89).

It is possible, on Dworkin's view, to be (internally) skeptical not simply about the moral value of some particular behavior, but about moral value as such. Such *global* internal skepticism would itself be motivated by a *moral* view: for example, the view that God is the only plausible basis for morality,[10] conjoined with skepticism about the existence of God (OT, 91). It is crucial, says Dworkin, to recognize that the former conjunct here is itself a view "within" morality, as it were, so that even this global skepticism is generated *internal* to morality.

External skepticism, by contrast, "is a metaphysical theory, not a . . . moral position" (LE, 79); it is "a second-level theory about the philosophical standing or classification of [first-order] claims" (LE, 79–80). External skepticism is both: (1) "austere" in that "it purports to rely [only] on non-moral arguments to defeat" the ordinary or "face-value" view that moral convictions can be objectively true and false (OT, 92); and (2) "neutral" in that "it takes no sides on substantive moral controversies" (OT, 92). John Mackie is the paradigmatic external skeptic for Dworkin.[11] He purports to stand outside the practice of moral argument, appealing instead to "some transcendental metaphysical world" (LE, 78), a world which does not (claims Mackie) contain moral facts of any kind.

---

[10] Dworkin assumes this is a *moral* view, but it is equally plausible understood as a metaphysical view about the aetiology of value, as David Sosa points out to me.

[11] Dworkin is not always clear on this point. In one paper, he describes Mackie as "defend[ing] a kind of internal moral skepticism" (P, 366), but in a more recent paper he says (correctly, in my view) that Mackie "was an external skeptic purporting to rely only on independent, non-moral, philosophical arguments" (OT, 113).

Before going further, we should quickly dispense with two rather facile arguments that Dworkin sometimes invokes against external skepticism in his writings. The first involves the misleading suggestion that the external skeptic is necessarily committed to the existence of a world-in-itself, a "transcendental metaphysical world." In Dworkin's recent work, in particular, the external skeptic is now accused of commitment to "archimedean skepticism" (OT, 92), of "purport[ing] to stand outside a whole body of belief, and to judge it as a whole from premises or attitudes that owe nothing to it" (OT, 88). The force of the charge becomes vivid in his claim that, "We cannot climb outside of morality to judge it from some external archimedean tribunal, any more than we can climb out of reason itself to test it from above" (OT, 127).

This last claim, however, contains a revealing non-sequitur: for the reasons for thinking it incoherent to "climb out of reason itself to test it from above"—reasons familiar from Hegel and Quine, among others—have no bearing on whether we can "climb outside of morality" and assess it from some other standpoint. We cannot step outside "reason"—outside our best current picture of the world—and assess it all at once, because we thereby deprive ourselves of *any* criteria by which to proceed. But we can surely assess various components of that picture—moral, religious, biological, aesthetic—from the standpoint of those other components with which we rest content at the present.

In disclaiming the ability to "climb out of reason itself to test it from above," Dworkin seems to have in mind the famous image of "Neurath's boat." But Neurath's boat is no help to Dworkin in this context. Neurath analogizes our epistemological situation to that of sailors who are trying to rebuild their ship while at sea. Since they cannot rebuild the whole ship at once—they cannot, as it were, "climb out of the ship itself" and rebuild it from scratch—they must choose to stand firm on certain planks in the ship while reconstructing others. They will, of course, choose to stand firm on those planks that work the best—a pragmatic criterion—while rebuilding those that are less dependable or useful or necessary. At a later date, the sailors may choose to rebuild the planks they had stood on previously, and in so doing they will again choose to stand firm on some other planks that serve their practical needs at that time.

Our basic epistemic situation—as Quine, in particular, has argued for many years[12]—is the same: like the sailors at sea, we cannot "climb outside" our best picture of the world, and rebuild it from scratch. We necessarily stand firm on certain "planks" within this picture of the world—various empirical claims, theoretical hypotheses, and epistemic norms—while evaluating other claims. Pragmatic desiderata (at least for Quine) determine which planks we choose to rest critical reflection upon, though nothing precludes the possibility that, at some later date, the claims and criteria we rely on today may themselves be subject to revision. In

---

[12] For a lengthier account of how I understand Quine, see Ch. 5.

the Quinean picture (to which I am basically sympathetic[13]) we are committed to saying that "there is no Archimedean point of cosmic exile from which to leverage our theory of the world."[14] But a theory of *morality* is plainly just one sub-set of a total theory of the world, and there is nothing in the rejection of an "Archimedean point of cosmic exile" that precludes one from assessing the sub-theory from *outside that particular sub-theory*: "Exile" from a "sub-theory" is *not* equivalent to *cosmic* exile. As Quine remarks (in a related context):

Have we . . . so far lowered our sights as to settle for a relativistic doctrine of truth—rating the statements of each theory as true for that theory, and brooking no higher criticism? Not so. The saving consideration is that we continue to take seriously our own particular aggregate science, our own particular world-theory or loose total fabric of quasi-theories, whatever it may be. Unlike Descartes, we own and use our beliefs of the moment, even in the midst of philosophizing, until by what is vaguely called scientific method we change them here and there for the better. Within our total evolving doctrine, we can judge truth as earnestly and absolutely as can be; subject to correction, but that goes without saying.[15]

But which "planks" in our boat should we choose to rest critical reflection and truth upon?

"In my naturalistic stance," says Quine, "I see the question of truth as one to be settled within science, there being no higher tribunal."[16] But science—and the norms of a scientific epistemology, i.e. the implicit norms on which scientific practice relies—are the highest tribunal *not* for any *a priori* reasons, but because— to speak crudely, but not inaccurately—science has, as an *a posteriori* matter, "delivered the goods": it sends the planes into the sky, eradicates certain cancerous growths, makes possible the storage of millions of pages of data on a tiny chip, and the like. Science, for Quine, is simply on a continuum with common sense,[17] since both aim to predict and control the future course of experience—with the difference that science, unlike, say, folk psychology or economics, manages and forecasts experience with greater precision and reliability. "[W]e can never do better than occupy the standpoint of some theory or other, the best we can muster at the time."[18] For Quine, that theory is a scientific one, because that is the theory

---

[13] Minus Quine's austere physicalism, which is detachable from his pragmatism and naturalism. See the useful discussion in Christopher Hookway, *Quine: Language, Experience, and Reality* (Stanford: Stanford University Press, 1988), pp. 63–78, 124.

[14] Roger Gibson, "Willard van Orman Quine," in J. Kim & E. Sosa (eds.), *A Companion to Metaphysics* (Oxford: Blackwell, 1995), p. 427. For related discussion, see Peter Hylton, "Quine's Naturalism," *Midwest Studies in Philosophy* 19 (1994): 261–82.

[15] W. V. O. Quine, *Word and Object* (Cambridge, Mass.: MIT Press, 1960), pp. 24–5.

[16] W. V. O. Quine, "Comments on Lauener," in R. Barrett & R. Gibson (eds.), *Perspectives on Quine* (Oxford: Blackwell, 1990), p. 229.

[17] "Science is self-conscious common sense." *Word and Object* (n. 15 above), p. 3. "The scientist is indistinguishable from the common man in his sense of evidence, except that the scientist is more careful." W. V. O. Quine, "The Scope and Language of Science," in *The Ways of Paradox and Other Essays* (Cambridge, Mass.: Harvard University Press, 1976), p. 233.

[18] *Word and Object* (n. 15 above), p. 22.

that works the best. Yet even Quine concedes that the basic norm of a scientific epistemology (namely, empiricism) "would go by the board" if, say, telepathy delivered on its claims.[19]

Let me now recap: the argument here is that while the external skeptic *might* be committed to a "transcendental metaphysical world," he need not worry still about the objectivity of value. He could well accept the metaphor of Neurath's boat and see the question about the objectivity of value as simply being the question: given the (ontological and epistemological) planks in our best picture of the world on which we currently stand firm, how are we to make sense of putative moral facts? This is a perfectly sensible question for an anti-Archimedean Quinean to ask, and it is the question whose intelligibility Dworkin must defeat if he is to defeat decisively the external skeptic.

There is a second distracting argument Dworkin sometimes makes. Often, he saddles the external skeptic with a commitment to "neutrality," and then accuses the skeptic of failing to be neutral. Unfortunately, this is one of those cases where Dworkin's failure to cite authors who actually hold the views that he implies some real person holds makes it easy for him to set up "straw men" as opponents.[20] Indeed, Dworkin's paradigm external skeptic—Mackie—is, by Dworkin's own admission, *not* "neutral" (OT, 113). While it *is* essential to external skepticism that its arguments against the objectivity of morality be *non-moral* arguments (the "austerity," in Dworkin's terms, of external skepticism), it is not clear why it is essential to the position that "it take . . . no sides on substantive moral controversies" (OT, 93). What marks the skeptic as *external* is that his attack on the objectivity of morality *is not itself a moral attack*. Whether or not this skeptical attack has *implications* for substantive moral controversies—a matter debated among moral realists and skeptics[21]—simply does not impugn the *externality* of the skepticism.

But even if the skeptic were committed to neutrality, would he have to run afoul of this constraint? Dworkin argues that he would. The external skeptic rejects the "face value" view of morality according to which moral rightness and wrongness is an "objective matter" and certain moral "opinions are true . . . and . . . people who disagree are making a bad mistake"(OT, 92). Yet the external skeptic fails to realize that this "face value" view is not some *external* thesis about the status of morality, but is itself "part of substantive morality" (OT, 93). Thus, a skeptic who rejects this view can no longer be *neutral* about morality.

[19] W. V. O. Quine, *Pursuit of Truth* (Cambridge, Mass.: Harvard University Press, 1990), p. 21.
[20] This is a long-standing feature of Dworkin's work, going back to his early articles on H. L. A. Hart's positivism, in which Hart's view is regularly misstated. See, e.g., Hart's postscript to *The Concept of Law*, 2nd ed. (Oxford: Clarendon, 1994); and see also Charles Silver, "Elmer's Case: A Legal Positivist Replies to Dworkin," *Law and Philosophy* 6 (1987): 381–99.
[21] See, e.g., Nicholas L. Sturgeon, "What Difference Does It Make Whether Moral Realism Is True?," in N. Gillespie (ed.), *Moral Realism: Proceedings of the 1985 Spindel Conference, Southern Journal of Philosophy* 24 Supp. (1986): 115–71; Jeremy Waldron, "The Irrelevance of Moral Objectivity," in R. George (ed.), *Natural Law Theory: Contemporary Essays* (Oxford: Clarendon Press, 1992).

The external skeptic can do no better, perhaps, than to concede this trivial point: if in fact claims about the objective status of moral judgments are internal to morality, then the external skeptic does, indeed, reject part of substantive morality. But this makes external skepticism *internal* to the domain of morality only, as it were, by stipulation: by stipulating, that is, that the claim to objectivity is in fact a *moral* claim—which is, presumably, what the Dworkinian external skeptic would want to resist stipulating in the first place. I do not disagree, of course, that ordinary people think that some moral judgments are "objectively true," but to name that a *moral* view and on that basis assail external skepticism for a breach of neutrality seems mere definitional trickery.

With these preliminary points out of the way, we can now ask what the real problem with external skepticism is supposed to be? The volume of Dworkin's rhetoric on this issue is high,[22] but the actual arguments are somewhat elusive. Dworkin's central claim, however, is quite clear: external skepticism is, at bottom, unintelligible, at least as applied to morality. "[T]he external level . . . does not exist" (P, 362) he says. The "issue of objectivity [as conceived by the external skeptic] . . . is a kind of fake" (MP2, 172). The proponent of external skepticism

supposes that we can distinguish between the [language-]game and the real world, that we can distinguish between the claim that slavery is unjust, offered as a move in some collect-ive enterprise in which such judgments are made and debated, and the claim that slavery is really or objectively unjust in the actual world . . . . [But] this is exactly what we cannot do, because the words "objectively" and "really" cannot change the sense of moral . . . judgments. If moral . . . judgments have the sense and force they do because they figure in a collective human enterprise, then such judgments cannot have a "real" sense and a "real" truth value which transcend that enterprise and somehow take hold of the "real" world. (MP2, 174)

In short, the only "intelligible . . . [skeptical] argument that evaluative propos-itions are neither true nor false" must be an *internal* argument (OT, 89).

What are Dworkin's *arguments* for claiming that the "external" skeptic's pos-ition is essentially unintelligible? I can discern two main argumentative strategies in his work: (1) what *look* like external arguments are really *internal* arguments; and (2) the genuinely "external" arguments make either preposterous or question-begging demands on moral discourse. Let me consider the strongest representa-tive of each argument, in order.

C. Internal Arguments All the Way Down

As noted before, a natural way of construing the debate about the objectivity of the judgment "abortion is morally wrong" is as an ontological debate "about the

---

[22] Dworkin objects "to the pointless metaphysical theater, the fierce campaigns against invented fools" (P, 382) and suggests that the challenges of external skeptics are "just bad philosophy" (OT, 139). He expresses the (aptly named) "pious hope" that "the leaden spirits of our age, which nurture [these skeptical challenges], [will] soon lift" (OT, 139). He chastises naturalistic moral realists (like

kinds of properties there are in the world" (OT, 103). The external skeptic says the
world contains no moral properties; the "realist" affirms their existence.[23] We have
already seen one facile argument that Dworkin would make against this way of
understanding the debate: namely, that the external skeptic violates the "neutrality" requirement, since to deny that there are any real moral properties would be
to deny that "some acts really are unjust, or some people really are good, or something of the sort" (OT, 100). But this, as already remarked, is only an interesting
point against the external skeptic if (a) he is committed to neutrality, and (b) the
"really" is part of substantive morality. So let us put this consideration aside.

The most common form the ontological debate has taken in recent years concerns whether "moral" properties are identical with, or supervenient upon,[24] natural properties. According to Dworkin, however, this way of framing the debate
still does not take the skeptic outside substantive morality:

Some philosophers argue that moral properties are identical with natural properties—that
an act's relative rightness, for example, just is its relative power to maximize happiness. On
that view, when we say that the fact that an act promotes happiness causes people to think
it is right, which is often plausible, we might as well say that the fact that it is right causes
people to think it is. But once again this latter claim offers the neutral archimedean no
target, because he cannot reject it without rejecting the identity-of-properties claim, and
that . . . is an abstract moral conviction. (OT, 104)

But is a claim about property-identity a *moral* claim? Moral realists who argue for it
certainly do not do so in *moral* terms; rather it is presented as a certain sort of
semantic or (a posteriori) *metaphysical* thesis. Peter Railton, a self-described "stark-
raving moral realist,"[25] follows Richard Brandt in suggesting that we think of the
identity claim—e.g. the claim that morally right just means instrumentally rational
from a social point of view—as a "reforming definition or an *a posteriori* statement
of property identity" (NP, 157). But to give a reforming, naturalistic definition of
moral rightness (or non-moral goodness) we must, says Railton, draw on "our

Richard Boyd and Peter Railton) for "add[ing] to the confusion by accepting the [external skeptic's]
challenge as sensible and trying to meet it" and dismisses them for falling prey to "the fallacy of the
[external skeptics], which is to suppose that some sense can be assigned to supposedly metaphysical
claims that is not itself a normative sense" (OT, 127).

[23] More precisely, the full-blooded realist holds that: (a) the statements in some domain of discourse are cognitive, i.e. apt for evaluation in terms of their truth and falsity; (b) the truth-value of
these statements is an objective matter (e.g. the truth-conditions of these statements are, in principle,
evidence-transcendent); and (c) at least some statements in the domain are true. For a related, but
slightly different, characterization, see Philip Pettit, "Embracing Objectivity in Ethics" in *Objectivity
in Law and Morals* (n. 5 above).

[24] I am convinced by Jaegwon Kim's arguments that there is no intelligible doctrine of "supervenience" intermediate between dualism and reduction. See especially Chapters 4, 5, 14, and 16 in
Kim's *Supervenience and Mind* (Cambridge: Cambridge University Press, 1993). One advantage of
Railton's realist program is that it deals squarely with the issue of formulating reductive identity
claims between the "moral" and the "natural," rather than hiding behind the fig-leaf of "mere" supervenience. See especially, Peter Railton, "Naturalism and Prescriptivity," in E. F. Paul et al. (eds.),
Foundations of Moral and Political Philosophy (Oxford: Blackwell, 1990) [cited hereafter as "NP" in
the body of the text].   [25] Railton, "Moral Realism" (n. 9 above) p. 165.

linguistic or moral intuitions" so as to "express recognizable notions of goodness and rightness."[26] The appeal here is to our intuitions about the use of language, not to moral argument.

Consider an analogue in the doctrine of "moon realism,"[27] that is, realism regarding talk about the moon. The moon realist holds that propositions like, "The moon has a circumference of 14,000 miles" are *objectively* true or false. But to have any idea what would count as the truth-condition for this statement, we have to have some notion what we are referring to when we talk about the "moon." We have to know, in other words, that when we make claims about the "moon" we are talking about that celestial body that stands in a certain spatial relation to the earth, and not, say, the Empire State Building: it is facts about this celestial body, and not facts about the Empire State Building, that determine the truth or falsity of statements about the "moon." To give a definition (reforming or otherwise) of some putatively cognitive predicate—whether it be "the moon" or "morally right"—is just to specify the domain of facts which constitute the locus for the truth-conditions for sentences in that domain. In specifying that domain, we can do no better than appeal to our intuitions about how the concept ("moon" or "morally right") is used. But appealing to linguistic intuitions about the use of "moon" is not an activity internal to arguments in astronomy, just as appealing to linguistic intuitions about the use of "morally right" is not an activity internal to the practice of moral argument. Thus, the external skeptic about these claims would not make a *moral* argument against the proposed definition, but a *semantic* one to the effect that the proposed identity does not, in fact, capture "recognizable notions" of moral rightness, that it omits, for example, the element of *endorsement* characteristic of moral language.[28]

Naturalistic moral realists like Railton recognize that while the reductionist tries to "capture most of the central intuitions in [the] area," he cannot do justice to all of them, and thus "must do something to lessen the force of those which he cannot capture" (NP, 169). The reduction aims for "tolerable revisionism" (NP, 159) that "permits one to account for the correlations and truisms associated" with the moral predicate at issue (NP, 162). But ultimately, the proposed claim of property-identity "must earn its place by facilitating the construction of worthwhile theories" (NP, 157), that is theories that "locate value properties among features of the world that are accessible to us through ordinary experience and that play a role in empirical explanation" (NP, 154).[29] The claim of property-identity,

[26] Id., p. 205.
[27] I have used the example before. See Brian Leiter, "Tort Theory and the Objectivity of Corrective Justice," *Arizona Law Review* 37 (1995): 45–51, p. 48.
[28] See, e.g., Allan Gibbard, *Wise Choices, Apt Feelings: A Theory of Normative Judgment* (Cambridge, Mass.: Harvard University Press, 1990), pp. 10 ff.
[29] For more on these issues, see also Peter Railton, "What the Noncognitivist Helps Us to See, the Naturalist Must Help Us to Explain," in J. Haldane & C. Wright (eds.), *Reality, Representation and Projection* (New York: Oxford University Press, 1993).

then, is ultimately predicated on appeals to semantic intuitions and the desiderata of theory-construction; the external skeptic, conversely, can contest the reduction on either ground. Nowhere in this dispute does there seem to be any need for distinctively *moral* argumentation.

D. External Skepticism: Unintelligible or Question-Begging

Having ruled out the leading naturalistic attempt to make ontological sense of moral facts proves crucial for Dworkin's second main argumentative strategy against external skepticism. For Dworkin concedes that it *is* a legitimately *external* argument to deny the objectivity of morality on the grounds that it does not meet the constraints imposed by what we might call a "scientific epistemology" which says—in part, and quite roughly—that: (a) only that which makes a causal difference to experience can be known; and (b) only that which makes a causal difference to experience is real.[30] Dworkin's response is that such a demand, made about morality, is either preposterous (i.e. unintelligible) or question-begging.

It is preposterous because it would commit us to what Dworkin calls "the absurd moral-field thesis" (OT, 117), the thesis that,

the universe houses, among its numerous particles of energy and matter, some special particles—morons—whose energy and momentum establish fields that at once constitute the morality or immorality, or virtue or vice, of particular human acts and institutions and also interact in some way with human nervous systems so as to make people aware of the morality or immorality or of the virtue or vice. (OT, 104)[31]

Now both the naturalistic realist and his skeptical opponent could agree that *this* thesis is, indeed, quite absurd, that it is "barely intelligible" (OT, 127). *But it is precisely for this reason that the realist wanted to identify moral properties with natural properties in the first place!* The motivation for the naturalistic reduction, in short, is to find a place for the "moral" within a scientific epistemology. Yet we have just seen that Dworkin rules out this move on the grounds that any argument for a property-identification is an essentially *moral* argument, and so not sufficiently "austere" for the externalist's debate.[32] I have already contested this characterization of the debate about reduction, but since Dworkin thinks property reductions violate austerity, he is prepared to dismiss the externalist demand for

---

[30] A scientific epistemology must, of course, encompass more than a commitment to inference to the best explanation. We need, for example, a basic empiricist doctrine—the senses can be a source of knowledge—as well as certain epistemic norms which satisfy neither the empircist nor the abductive criteria. These epistemic norms admit of only a *pragmatic* defense, as discussed earlier.

[31] I take it this is what Dworkin is getting at also when he derides the external skeptic for complaining that moral claims "are not descriptions that can be proved or tested like physics" and that they are not "part of what he calls (in one of the maddening metaphors that seem crucial to any statement of his view) the 'fabric' of the universe" (LE, 79–80).

[32] I take it this is the flip-side of Dworkin's claim that the skeptical rejection of a naturalistic reduction of a moral predicate violates neutrality.

conformity with a scientific epistemology on the grounds that it supposes the preposterous moral-field thesis.

But is Dworkin entitled to do this, even granting his internalist construal of the property-reduction debate? In fact, it seems he is not. If the demand that moral properties find a place within a scientific epistemology leads to the "absurd" moral-field thesis, the skeptic might well conclude that this just shows that there can be no moral facts: the "absurdity" of "morons" shows *not* that the external skeptic is misguided, but that he is right, that there is no intelligible sense in which the world could contain moral facts. What Dworkin really needs is an argument against the skeptical demand that moral facts be made to fit the requirements of a scientific epistemology. This, in a nutshell, is the *crucial* issue for Dworkin's whole position.

Now Dworkin, in fact, considers this question explicitly. He describes an "epistemological hierarchy" argument the skeptic might make according to which,

it makes no sense to suppose that acts or events or institutions have moral properties unless we have some plausible account of how human beings could be "in touch with" or aware of such properties, and if we reject the explanation offered by the moral-field thesis we must appeal to some other account of a moral faculty that would be equally occult. (OT, 117)

What Dworkin describes here is just the demand that moral facts satisfy the demands of a scientific epistemology—something they cannot do, he concedes, in a way that is not "occult."

How does Dworkin resist, then, the epistemological argument? One argument he offers involves a familiar appeal to moral phenomenology, to the "evidence in my own experience . . . of a capacity to make moral judgments that bring conviction, that are mainly durable, that agree with the judgments of a great many others, and that are amenable to the normal logical combinations and operations" (OT, 118). Yet this is, quite transparently, a non-starter: no one—neither realist nor skeptic—contests the *phenomenology* of moral experience and judgment. The question has always been how this experience is to be explained, whether it can be accepted at face value, or whether it must be explained in quite different terms in order to locate this experience within our best picture of how the world works. Phenomenology is simply a datum, not an argument.

This brings us to the crucial move in Dworkin's argument: the repudiation of the demand that moral experience be made to fit within a scientific epistemology. Dworkin objects that the external skeptic's

hierarchical epistemology . . . tries to establish standards for reliable belief *a priori*, ignoring the differences in content between different domains of belief, and taking no account of the range of beliefs we already hold to be reliable. (OT, 118–19)

If a scientific epistemology "does seem appropriate to beliefs about the physical world" (OT, 119), it makes no sense for moral beliefs "[s]ince morality and the other evaluative domains make no causal claims" (OT, 120). If we accept the demand that moral facts must figure in the "best explanation" of experience, it will follow that,

> no moral (or aesthetic or mathematical or philosophical) belief is reliable. But we can reverse that judgment: if any moral belief is reliable, the "best explanation" test is not universally sound. Either direction of argument... begs the question in the same way. (OT, 119)

But the question is begged only if we grant Dworkin's false assumption that the demand for conformity to a scientific epistemology is really an arbitrary, *a priori* demand.[33] This assumption, however, reveals a complete misunderstanding of what drives the debate between external realist and skeptic about morals.

Recall Quine's posture, which assigns priority to the scientific epistemology. Quine takes science as "the highest tribunal" not for any *a priori* reasons, but because, as an *a posteriori* matter, science has "delivered the goods." Science has earned its claim to be a guide to the real and the unreal by depopulating our world of gods and witches and ethers, and substituting a picture of the world and how it works of immense practical value. A scientific epistemology—predicated on such seemingly simple notions as "evidence matters" (theories must answer to experience, not simply authority)—is one of the most precious legacies of the Enlightenment, a legacy under attack from those corners of the academy where bad philosophy reigns supreme. Oddly, with his off-the-cuff slur of a scientific epistemology as "*a priori*," Dworkin sounds more like the postmodernists he otherwise denounces with great moral earnestness.[34]

The demand to find a place for moral facts within a scientific epistemology is neither arbitrary nor *a priori*, but simply the natural question to ask given the *a posteriori* success of science. It is not that moral claims are simply exempt from a scientific epistemology because they do not involve causal claims; it is, rather, that (crudely speaking) causal power has shown itself over the past few centuries to be the best-going indicia of the knowable and the real, and therefore it is natural to subject any putative fact to this test. Naturalistic moral realists like Boyd and Railton are not "bad metaphysicians" (OT, 127); rather, they recognize (as Dworkin apparently does not) the epistemological pressure generated by the success of empirical inquiry that honors a scientific epistemology. Given that we have a useful guide to the true and the real already in hand—namely, science and its epistemic norms—why not see, these moral realists essentially ask, whether or not

---

[33] As an aside, let me point out that whether *beliefs* in general and *mathematics* in particular (as distinct from beliefs *about* mathematics) would figure in the best explanation of our experience is an open question—the latter depending, for example, on whether or not mathematics is indispensable to science.

[34] E.g.: Dworkin complains about the post-modernist "*auto-da-fe* of truth [which] has compromised public and political as well as academic discussion" (OT, 89). This strikes me as unduly melodramatic on the former count: surely "public and political" discussion was utterly compromised long before Derrida came on the scene. I would agree, though, that the fact that public discourse should have reached new lows of Orwellian double-speak just at the time when deconstruction became all the rage in the academy (the 1980s) surely does cry out for socio-economic explanation—though both phenomena are, I suspect, epiphenomenal.

"moral facts" can meet these demands (rather than suffer the same fate as witches and the ether).

Now no one should be surprised that if we repudiate the demands of a scientific epistemology we get a promiscuous ontology, replete with moral facts, aesthetic facts, theological facts and the like. But unless we are given a good reason for repudiating this epistemology—other than the patently question-begging reason of making room for our favorite (heretofore) suspect facts—the real question about any putative facts is whether they can answer to our best-going criteria of the knowable and the real.[35] This is what motivates the debate between external realist and external skeptic. Rather than showing their debate to be unintelligible, Dworkin has simply betrayed his misunderstanding of both *what* they are arguing about and *why* they are doing so. What we have yet to find in Dworkin is any *argument* for insulating the domain of morality from the demands of the scientific epistemology which has otherwise served us well.

But perhaps there are the beginnings of such an argument in the writings under consideration. Consider, for example, one of the ways Dworkin frames his repudiation of the "best explanation" test of a scientific epistemology:

Since morality and the other evaluative domains make no causal claims...such tests can play no role in any plausible test for them. We do need tests for reliability of our moral opinions, but these must be appropriate to the content of these opinions. That is why an epistemological challenge that comes to nothing more than insisting that moral properties are not physical properties must fail. (OT, 120)[36]

We may get a better idea what Dworkin is, perhaps, getting at in remarks like these by first taking a detour through a debate about the nature of objectivity suggested by the work of John McDowell.

II. Two Kinds of Objectivity

A. McDowell on Objectivity

In a series of influential papers,[37] McDowell has advanced what he calls a "realist" view about the objectivity of semantic, ethical, and other evaluative facts, but one

---

[35] Anyone who would repudiate a scientific epistemology must also provide some new, principled account of the distinction between the real and the unreal, demonstrating that while it makes room for, e.g., moral facts, it still excludes from our best picture of the world various pseudo-facts.

[36] For discussion of Gerald Postema's development of this argument, and its limitations, see Ch. 9, pp. 274–5.

[37] See John McDowell, "Anti-Realism and the Epistemology of Understanding," in H. Parret & J. Bouveresse (eds.), *Meaning and Understanding* (Berlin: de Gruyter, 1981) [cited as AREU]; "Non-Cognivitism and Rule-Following," in S. Holtzman & C. Leich (eds.), *Wittgenstein: To Follow a Rule* (London: Routledge, 1981) [cited as NCRF]; "Wittgenstein on Following a Rule," *Synthese* 58 (1984): 325–63; Critical Notice of Bernard Williams, *Ethics and the Limits of Philosophy*, *Mind* 95 (1986): 377–86 [cited as CN]; "In Defence of Modesty," in B. Taylor (ed.), *Michael Dummett: Contributions to Philosophy* (Dordrecht: M. Nijhoff, 1987); "Projection and Truth in Ethics," Lindley

that is predicated on an explicit repudiation of a certain "scientistic" view of what such objectivity must consist in.[38] We may think of McDowell's work as a sustained attack on the idea that the conception of objectivity we inherit from the natural sciences—what I called the "Naturalistic Conception"—is the *only* viable conception and, in particular, that it must apply to the domain of value. According to the Naturalistic Conception, it will be recalled, a fact is "objective" if it: (a) is "mind-independent" (in some appropriate sense); and (b) makes a causal difference to the course of our experience.

McDowell's attack on this conception is, unfortunately, disproportionately directed at the requirement of mind-independence. Like Dworkin, he repeatedly charges the skeptic about morality with holding a certain (untenable) conception of objective reality: "how things really are is how things are in themselves—that is, independently of how they strike the occupants of this or that particular point of view" (NCRF, 141). The thrust of McDowell's critique, then, is to show that such a conception of reality is unintelligible: "We cannot occupy the independent perspective that platonism envisages; and it is only because we confusedly think we can that we think we can make any sense of it" (NCRF, 150). Famously, he thinks that the correct understanding of Wittgenstein's remarks on rule-following will reveal the problems with this conception of objective reality. Roughly, the argument proceeds as follows.

Any satisfactory philosophical account of rule-following must explain two features of the phenomenon: it must show rules to be "objective" in some sense (i.e. it cannot be the case that whatever anyone thinks the rule means just determines what the rule means); and it must account for the "normativity" of rules (i.e. the fact that rules constrain conduct, that they set criteria of rightness and wrongness for those trying to follow them). The two features are connected: if rules are *not* objective, then they cannot be normative. If whatever I take the rule to mean fixes the content of the rule, then there is no meaningful sense in which the rule can constrain (or serve as a yardstick) for my subsequent conduct.

Wittgenstein's remarks on rule-following are then construed as undermining one conception of the "objectivity" of rules, which McDowell calls "platonistic." Platonism involves a certain interpretation of the "mind-independence" requirement—what we might call "Strong Objectivity." A fact is strongly objective if its existence and character does not depend (epistemically) on what we do know or *could* know about it (even at the ideal limit).[39] The Strong Objectivist about rules thinks of them as "the inexorable workings of a machine . . . [which are]

Lecture, Department of Philosophy, University of Kansas (1988) [cited as PTE]. McDowell's recent *Mind and World* (Cambridge, Mass.: Harvard University Press, 1994) is only indirectly concerned with these issues, and could not, in any event, be thought to mark an advance in philosophical clarity over the earlier papers.

[38] Cf. the attack on "scientism" in PTE, 12.

[39] I borrow here from some of the discussion in my "Objectivity and the Problems of Jurisprudence," *Texas Law Review* 72 (1993): 187–209, esp. pp. 190–6.

independent of the activities and responses that make up our... practice [of following the rule]" (NCRF, 151).

Such a conception of rules, according to McDowell's reading of Wittgenstein, fails for two reasons: it cannot account for the *normativity* of rules and it "always transcends any grounds there may be for postulating it" (NCRF, 147). It fails to account for normativity because it is unclear how a rule whose content is in-principle unknowable by us could discharge its *normative* function.[40] ("How could something unknown obligate us?" as Nietzsche puts it.[41]) And the Platonist's version of the rule is never warranted by the available evidence, since the available evidence (past behavior, physical and mental) underdetermines the content of the rule.[42] The moral, for McDowell, is always the same: facts about what a rule means, just like moral facts and semantic facts, are all real and knowable, but only from *within* the relevant practices (of rule-following, or moral argument, or language-use); the idea that we could stand outside these practices and identify any facts is nonsensical. Here is how McDowell has put the point over the years:

(1) [I]t is only because of our own involvement in our "whirl of organism" [i.e. "the activities and responses that make up our... practice"] that we can understand a form of words as conferring, on the judgment that some move is the correct one at a given point, the special compellingness [i.e. normativity] possessed by [a rule]. (NCRF, 151)

(2) [I]f we are simply and normally immersed in our practices, we do not wonder how their relation to the world would look from outside them, and feel the need for a solid foundation discernible from an external point of view. (NCRF, 153)

(3) [M]oral values are there in the world, and make demands on our reason. This is not a platonism about value...; the world in which moral values are said to be is not the externally characterizable world that a moral platonism would envisage. (NCRF, 156–57)

(4) [T]here is no standpoint from which we can give a sense-making characterization of linguistic practice [or moral practice] other than that of immersion in the practice. (AREU, 248).

(5) We have no point of vantage on the question what can be the case, that is, what can be a fact, external to the modes of thought and speech we know our way around in, with whatever understanding of what counts as better and worse execution of them our mastery of them can give us. (PTE, 11)

---

[40] For a more explicit verson of this "normativity" argument, see Crispin Wright, "Introduction," in *Realism, Meaning and Truth* (Oxford: Blackwell, 1987), pp. 24–5.

[41] "How the True World Finally Became a Fable," in *Twilight of the Idols*, in W. Kaufmann (ed.), *The Portable Nietzsche* (New York: Viking, 1954).

[42] This point is related to the famous skeptical argument developed in Saul Kripke, *Wittgenstein on Rules and Private Language* (Cambridge, Mass.: Harvard University Press, 1982). Kripkenstein, however, supposes that even all the evidence available to an *ideal* knower would still underdetermine the content of the rule. McDowell's objection to Kripke, in turn, is that he construes the argument as issuing in a *skeptical* conclusion, rather than showing only that we must conceive of the objectivity of rule-following in non-platonistic terms (in addition to purging from our account the assumption that all understanding requires *interpretation*). (I also grant, for purposes of the argument in the text, that if the content of the rule is underdetermined then belief in any particular version of the rule is not warranted; but this could be contested.)

Now the hardcore realist—as opposed to the non-Archimedean Quinean realist—would want to contest this Wittgensteinian attack on the intelligibility of the "external" vantage point, on the notion of a world-as-it-is-in-itself. But I want to grant McDowell the general metaphysical point, because it is actually quite irrelevant to the debate between skeptic and realist. As we saw before in rebutting Dworkin's similar charge of "Archimedeanism," there is nothing in the skeptical position that requires the intelligibility of an "external" vantage point in the objectionable sense. One could very well think that from where we stand in Neurath's boat, it is a live question of the post-Enlightenment world how moral facts are to be squared with everything else we take ourselves to understand about the world and its processes. Or, to put this in terms of McDowell's favored metaphors: the question of how to place morality is one that arises *within* our practices, not external to them. Indeed, even within our moral practices, the issue of the objectivity of morality remains a *live* issue precisely because we find within our practices the sorts of intractable moral disagreements that invite skepticism in the first place.[43]

So the skeptic can agree with McDowell in resisting the "philosophical temptation to connect objectivity with a suitable relation to how things would look from outside" (CN, 385), and still think there is a serious issue from *within* our best-going theory of the world about what room, if any, there remains for moral facts.

McDowell, however, has another argument against the "external" skeptic, one that can be viewed as a complement to Dworkin's failed appeal to moral phenomenology. I argued earlier that moral experience is simply a datum, and that the key question (accordingly) is whether our moral experience is best explained in realist or skeptical terms. McDowell has argued that, in fact, the skeptic cannot give a *coherent* account of moral phenomenology, that he must presuppose the existence of moral facts in the very process of explaining them. The dilemma is most acute for the "projectivist," the external skeptic who holds that moral properties are simply a *projection* of our subjective responses to various features of the world onto the world. McDowell's objection to the projectivist is essentially this: the projectivist cannot identify the subjective state that is being projected without already presupposing the concept to be explained. Here is the crucial passage:

> [I]t undermines a projective account of a concept if we cannot home in on the subjective state whose projection is supposed to result in the seeming feature of reality in question without the aid of the concept of that feature, the concept that was to be projectively explained. (PTE, 6)

Try, in other words, to pick out the subjective response that is projected on the world when something seems "funny" without appealing to some concept of

---

[43] This argument, it is worth noting, does not involve a commitment to verificationism, as Dworkin has misleadingly maintained at various places in his work (e.g. TRS, 281–2; MP1, 137). One need not believe that any fact must be demonstrable to be real. All one need accept is the principle of "inference to the best explanation." The skeptical argument, then, is that the best explanation for intractable moral disagreement is that there are no objective moral facts.

the "funny" or "comic," and you will be at a loss. The natural subjective states to identify—"a disposition to laugh" or "to find something funny"—already presuppose the explanandum at issue.

This argument only works, however, on the assumption that one is committed to the reality of any property (e.g. "the funny" or "the morally right") simply in virtue of knowing how to apply the associated concept. But why should the skeptic agree to that assumption? The skeptical claim is an *ontological* claim about what exists. The projectivist skeptic says moral facts are not part of the world's basic furniture, that they are simply projections of various subjective states onto the world. That the projectivist must, in turn, appeal to moral *concepts* in order to characterize these responses simply does not show that he is committed to the existence of moral *facts*.

So it seems that McDowell, like Dworkin, has no good argument against the Naturalistic Conception of objectivity. McDowell's more ambitious argument from phenomenology fails to show the skeptic's position to be incoherent. And McDowell's Wittgensteinian argument attacks a metaphysical position that the skeptic need not presuppose. Moreover, in both cases the attack is only on the Naturalistic demand of "mind-independence," rather than causal efficacy. We could even grant to McDowell that moral facts are response-dependent facts in some sense[44]—that they are not robustly mind-independent—and still think that they: (a) are sufficiently independent of actual human response for objectivity (in virtue of the idealization of response-conditions built in to all the current accounts of response-dependent facts); yet (b) fail to be objective because they do not figure in the causal explanation of experience. Against this latter demand, I do not see that McDowell has any direct response. Putting this problem aside, however, we can at least ask what McDowell's Non-Naturalist alternative for objectivity in ethics amounts to.[45]

McDowell speaks about "truth," not objectivity, in ethics, though the difference will not matter for purposes here. The crucial skeptical challenge to truth in

[44] A popular proposal as of late. For versions, see Philip Pettit, "Realism and Response-Dependence," *Mind* 100 (1991): 587–626; Pettit, "Embracing Objectivity in Ethics" (n. 23 above); Michael Smith, *The Moral Problem* (Oxford: Blackwell, 1994); and Mark Johnston, "Dispositional Theories of Value," *Proceedings of the Aristotelian Society*, supp. vol. 62 (1989): 139–74. For a critique of the notion that moral facts are response-dependent facts, see Crispin Wright, *Truth and Objectivity* (Cambridge, Mass.: Harvard University Press, 1992).

[45] McDowell would presumably contest the label "Non-Naturalist," since much of his recent work has tried to recapture a different meaning for "naturalism," one which would include his own view. Roughly, his idea seems to be that it is "natural" in some (loosely Aristotelian) sense for human beings to develop certain responsive capacities (e.g. to right and wrong, etc.), and thus there is no special problem (from the standpoint of a naturalistic world view) about the epistemic or ontological status of the facts whose existence depends on these responsive capacities. See esp. *Mind and World*, (Cambridge, Mass.: Harvard University Press, 1994) pp. 77–86; John McDowell, "Two Sorts of Naturalism," in R. Hursthouse et al. (eds.), *Virtues and Reasons: Philippa Foot and Moral Theory* (Oxford: Clarendon Press, 1995). (For penetrating criticism of this account, see Crispin Wright's review, "Human Nature?" *European Journal of Philosophy* 5 (1996): 235–54.) McDowell, though, is certainly a Non-Naturalist in my sense, i.e. someone who rejects the Naturalistic Conception of objectivity.

ethics comes, McDowell claims, from philosophers like Alasdair MacIntyre and Charles Stevenson who think "we lack . . . a conception of better and worse ways to think about ethical questions" (PTE, 4). But, objects McDowell,

we do after all have at our disposal a conception of reasons for ethical thinking which is sufficiently rich and substantial to mark off rationally induced improvements in ethical stances from alterations induced by merely manipulative persuasion. (PTE, 5)[46]

What we need, then, for truth or objectivity in ethics is not that moral facts be severed from human responses, but only that ethical thought "allow . . . for a sufficiently substantial conception of reasons" (PTE, 8). "Susceptibility to reasons" is the hallmark of objectivity in ethics, and, "The threat to truth is from the thought that there is not enough substance to our conception of reasons for ethical stances" (PTE, 9). Notice, in particular, that McDowell is *not* saying that convergence in ethical responses is enough for truth in ethics, for such convergence might simply be "a mere coincidence of subjectivities rather than agreement on a range of truths— the sort of view that would be natural if everyone came to prefer one flavor of ice cream to any other" (PTE, 8). It is the possibility of convergence *backed by substantial reasons* that demarcates genuinely objective domains from those marked by "a mere coincidence of subjectivities."

   Now against the Naturalist who complains that the question about objectivity in ethics is necessarily the ontological question, McDowell simply falls back upon something like Dworkin's (mistaken) charge of arbitrary, *a priori*-ness. "[H]ow good are the credentials," McDowell asks, "of a 'metaphysical understanding' [of the kinds of facts the world contains] that blankly excludes values and instances of the comic from the world in advance of any philosophical enquiry into truth"? (PTE, 12) "What is missing," he adds, "is a reason to suppose that natural science has a foundational status in philosophical reflection about truth—that there can be no facts other than those that would figure in a scientific understanding of the world" (PTE, 12). Yet, once again, to the Quinean this all looks very strange. For it is not some inexplicable or accidental prejudice that privileges a scientific epistemology over all others. Rather, such a posture is the natural one to adopt (at least initially) given the tremendous success such an epistemology has enjoyed to date. To simply push the scientific epistemology aside opens the ontological floodgates to a whole pre-Enlightenment conception of the world that we seem to do better without.

B. McDowell and Dworkin

Whatever its drawbacks, I hope it is now apparent how McDowell's discussion— and the distinction between Naturalistic and Non-Naturalistic Conceptions of

---

[46] This point echoes a familiar complaint about emotivism, first broached by Richard Brandt in "The Emotive Theory of Ethics," *Philosophical Review* 59 (1950): 305–18.

objectivity—resonates with some of what we saw Dworkin trying to get at in the prior section. Indeed, there are even places in the Dworkinian corpus where he comes very close to naming the distinction at issue. For example, in a 1978 essay, he says that we should "suppose that there is something else in the world beside hard facts" (MP1, p. 138), where "hard facts" are just "physical facts and facts about behavior (including the thoughts and attitudes) of people" (MP1, p. 137) or "the sort of fact that is...in principle demonstrable by ordinary scientific methods" (MP1, p. 139). Moral facts and, for example, facts about the best interpretation of a story would be cases of non-hard facts, in Dworkin's view. More recently, he writes that, "Morality is a distinct, independent dimension of our experience, and it exercises its own sovereignty" (OT, 127) and endorses as a general epistemic "principle of tolerance" (my phrase, not Dworkin's) the following:

[T]he epistemology of any domain must be sufficiently internal to its content to provide reasons, viewed from the perspective of those who begin holding convictions within it, for testing, modifying or abandoning those convictions. (OT, 120)

As a blanket principle, of course, this could not be right. Think of the adherents of the Church of Scientology, who embrace the bizarre Hubbardian cosmology. It is natural to say that theirs is *not* an objective account of the universe, even though: (a) there are probably no reasons "internal" to the domain that would lead its adherents to abandon it; and (b) the reasons "external" to the domain—e.g. the reasons provided by physics, astronomy and evolutionary biology—would not shake the "convictions" of the devout Scientologists.

Dworkin, however, does not mean his principle of tolerance to apply to those domains that make claims at odds with the claims of science. He explicitly says that since astrology and orthodox religion "purport to offer causal explanations" they can be subjected to the best-explanation test. But, he adds,

Since morality and the other evaluative domains make no causal claims...such tests can play no role in any plausible test for them. We do need tests for reliability of our moral opinions, but these must be appropriate to the content of these opinions. That is why an epistemological challenge that comes to nothing more than insisting that moral properties are not physical properties must fail. (OT, 120)

So the principle of tolerance covers those domains which do not make causal claims; for these domains we need a non-Naturalistic criterion of objectivity.

But why suppose these domains are objective in the first place? Dworkin's central intuition—the one that undergirds, I think, the often confused attack on external skepticism discussed above—might be put as follows:

So you, Mr. Skeptic, have shown that moral properties do not figure in our best explanatory picture of the world, that they do not deserve a place in a suitably scientific ontology—that is all well and good, but it is hardly of much concern to me. For even though "moral wrongness" is not a property that slavery possesses objectively (in your Naturalistic sense of that term), it is still the case that my arguments for the wrongness of slavery are strong and persuasive ones, and that you have given me no argument to cease believing that slavery is wrong. Who cares (as it were) about the ontological status of moral facts: what I want to know is whether you have a good (i.e. internal) argument that slavery is not wrong?

If this is what Dworkin's view comes to, then it is important to recognize that his real position is not that external skepticism is unintelligible, but that it is irrelevant.[47] Debate about the ontology of moral facts as much as you want, Dworkin might say; none of this affects one bit one's ability to argue for and against different moral propositions. The only objectivity that "counts," as it were, resides in the potentialities of this moral argument.

That this is the crux of Dworkin's view is suggested in various papers. He says, for example, that, "We do have reasons for thinking that slavery is wrong and that the Greeks were therefore in error: we have all the moral reasons we would cite in a moral debate about the matter" (OT, 122). Elsewhere, he says:

> *We* do not say (nor can we understand anyone who does say) that . . . moral values are "out there" or can be proved. We can only say, with different emphases, that . . . slavery is wrong. The practice . . . of morality give[s] [this] claim all the meaning [it] need[s] or could have. (LE, 83)

Similarly, in the context of discussing a dispute about an "interpretive fact"—say, the best way to make sense of certain events in the novel *David Copperfield*— Dworkin says that participants in such a discussion,

> are trained to subject their responses to the disciplines of reflection and consistency, and then to make certain assertions that their training authorizes them to make on the authority of these responses so disciplined. The exercise, conducted by participants so trained, serves some purpose—perhaps recreational or cultural—other than to increase our collective knowledge of the external world . . . [The participants] certainly do not think that narrative consistency is the same sort of thing as the weight of iron, or that it is part of the external world in anything like the way the weight of iron is . . . . Whatever sense [i.e. objectivity] statements about narrative consistency may have, they are given that sense by the enterprise that trains participants to make and respond to such statements. (MP1, 140, 141).

I take Dworkin to be making essentially McDowell's point in passages like these: that objectivity in ethics is a matter of "susceptibility to reasons"; that to attack the objectivity of an ethical position is to give ethical reasons against holding it (not epistemological or ontological arguments); that the capacity for such reasoning is nurtured within certain practices of moral argumentation, and that we simply have nothing else to go on in assessing moral arguments than the sensibilities and capacities so nurtured. Dworkin, in short, should endorse McDowell's slogan that

---

[47] I confess that this would be a somewhat strange complaint for Dworkin to make, since for external skepticism to be "relevant" would be for it to be non-neutral, which, as we have seen, Dworkin claims it must not be.

"truth in ethics [is] earned from within ethical thinking" (PTE, 10), and could equally well agree (with certain obvious additions) that,

The threat to truth [in ethics] is from the [internally skeptical] thought that there is not enough substance to our conception of reasons for ethical stances. When we try to meet this [internally skeptical] threat, there is no reason not to appeal to all the resources at our disposal, including all the ethical concepts that we can lay our hands on, so long as they survive critical scrutiny; and there need be no basis for critical scrutiny of one ethical concept except others, so the necessary scrutiny does not involve stepping outside the point of view constituted by an ethical sensibility. (PTE, 9)

If Dworkin and McDowell are both Non-Naturalists about objectivity of roughly the same sort, it still remains the case that they have no substantial argument against the Naturalistic Conception except, perhaps, the irrelevance argument sketched above. We must consider, then, whether this argument suffices to defeat the external skeptic.

III. Against Non-Naturalism

In this section, I argue that Non-Naturalism is not a suitable conception of objectivity, even for ethics, for two reasons. First, in many cases (including ethics), we can get no purchase on the notion of a discourse being "objective" (even in the sense of being "susceptible to reasons") without implicit reliance on the Naturalistic sense of objectivity: unless there are Naturalistically objective facts to which the discourse must answer we will often be unable to make sense of better and worse ways of reasoning.[48] Second, even the skeptic does not deny that people's moral views are "susceptible to reasons;" what he denies is that what is distinctively *moral* in their view is open to reasoned consideration. Dworkin and McDowell have done nothing to show that moral views are susceptible to reasons in this stronger sense, the sense necessary to distinguish their view from that of, say, the non-cognitivist.[49]

[48] I hedge here because of the case of mathematics, a paradigmatic objective domain. At least parts of mathematics—those parts which are indispensable to scientific practice—can, in theory, have their objectivity vindicated in conventionally naturalistic terms; but other parts of mathematics present a more difficult case. There are several possible lines of response: (1) we might suppose that the objectivity of math (and, say, logic) is simply conventional, so that math is not, appearances to the contrary, robustly objective in the way the objects studied by the natural sciences are; (2) we might think there is some Humean story to be told about why creatures like us experience the compulsion of the mathematical and logical "must" or "ought" ("$2+2$ *must* elicit the response 4")—indeed, such a story might be conjoined with a version of the conventionalism suggested under (1); (3) finally, we might concede that math and logic are objective, even though this objectivity cannot be explained naturalistically, but question whether the features which warrant our confidence in their objectivity (the cross-cultural, and often timeless, quality of mathematical and logical truths) really give us reason to think that morality will also turn out to be objective in some non-naturalistic way. (I am grateful to Ed Stein and Jules Coleman for help in thinking about this question.)

[49] By "non-cognitivism," I mean a view about the *semantics* of moral discourse to the effect that the meaning of moral language is its role in *expressing* certain non-cognitive attitudes. Universal

A. Is Naturalistic Objectivity Irrelevant?

On the interpretation proposed above, Dworkin's key challenge to Naturalistic Objectivity is that it is irrelevant to moral argument in the double sense that the (naturalistically) objective status of a moral position: (a) has no bearing on the objectivity of ethics, which is a matter of there being better and worse reasons for ethical stances; and (b) would not change anyone's first-order moral views. I propose to show that Dworkin is wrong on both counts.

Imagine there arose a practice of making arguments about the merits of different flavors of ice cream, say chocolate and vanilla. Parties to this discourse might argue for the superiority of chocolate in the following way:

> What distinguishes chocolate is the richness and seriousness of the flavor, in comparison to the fleetingness of the sensation of vanilla. Chocolate grips the palate, it takes over the mouth, it washes away all the prior flavors. It is a total and encompassing taste experience, unlike vanilla. The creaminess of chocolate—that quintessential trait of great ice cream—is so unlike the creaminess of vanilla, which is hard to distinguish from mere milkiness. Chocolate ice cream is just *substantial*, in a way that vanilla could never be.

Suppose, too, that a consensus (backed by canonical forms of reasoning like the preceding) arises according to which chocolate really is the better flavor: we have, in other words, a *hegemonic* convention of reasons (call it "the Chocolate Convention") which always supports the conclusion that chocolate is to be preferred. The convention is "hegemonic" not in the sense that no other reasons can be heard or appreciated—the parties are, by hypothesis, *susceptible* to reasons—but only in the sense that everyone comes to find the reasons favoring chocolate persuasive.

According to Non-Naturalism, we should have to say that it is an *objective* fact that chocolate is better than vanilla. Ice cream flavors are, after all, susceptible to reasons in this scenario. But since there has arisen a hegemonic convention of finding the arguments for chocolate to be the strongest, there is no indefeasible *internal* skeptical attack on objectivity to be mounted. So on the Non-Naturalist picture, chocolate is objectively better than vanilla.

Now this conclusion strikes me as quite bizarre. My intuition is that the "taste" of ice cream flavors is the paradigm of a subjective property (what seems right to the judger just is right). So regardless of how compelling people find the "reasons"

prescriptivists (Hare), norm-expressivists (Gibbard), crude emotivists (Ayer), and sophisticated emotivists (Stevenson) all differ about the attitudes expressed, but agree about the basic semantic thesis. They also agree with the skeptical ontological thesis that there are no moral facts. Mackie accepts this latter thesis, but rejects the semantic one: he construes moral language as *cognitive*—i.e. as apt for evaluation in terms of its truth and falsity—but, given his ontology, thinks all moral statements are false. Mackie's error theory has the drawback of making it puzzling why anyone should engage in moral discourse: what could be the point of a putatively fact-stating discourse that states no facts? Non-cognitivists are moved by the same ontological considerations to try to find a way to preserve the point of moral discourse by proposing a revisionary semantics.

favoring chocolate, and regardless of how vigorously they argue, one wants to say that the parties to the Chocolate Convention are talking nonsense: there are no *objective* facts about the "tastiness" of ice cream flavors; the "tastiness" of chocolate or vanilla is merely *subjective*. But we can only articulate this intuition by appeal to an *external* conception of objectivity, by appeal to the notion that any particular discourse—no matter how robust it looks—must ultimately answer to the facts, naturalistically conceived. The Chocolate Convention simply cannot do that, since there are no objective facts about the "tastiness" of ice cream flavors to answer to.

We can generalize the point: Naturalistic Objectivity is relevant to assessing the objectivity of most domains of discourse precisely because it is always *possible* for hegemonic conventions of argumentation (like the Chocolate Convention) to grow up around non-factual matters. The Non-Naturalist, however, has no resources for responding to this possibility, no way to say that a hegemonic convention of reasons is, in fact, not objective. Non-Naturalism, in short, renders it a conceptual impossibility for there to be a hegemonic convention of reasons about a non-objective domain. But such conventions seem not only to be *conceptual* possibilities, but *actualities* (think of scholastic debates about the number of angels that might fit on the head of a pin). Surely it is implausible that objectivity should accrue to judgments solely in virtue of the fact that they are not *successfully* challenged, that they are parts of hegemonic conventions for which no *persuasive* internal skeptic can be found. The Naturalistic Conception of objectivity, then, does make a difference to how we would assess the objectivity of such domains of discourse.

McDowell, it seems, has two possible responses. First, he might deny that the Chocolate Convention is really a case of people being *susceptible* to reasons; that it is, rather, merely the façade of the kind of susceptibility to reasons that we find in evaluative discourse.[50] Unfortunately, I see no non-question-begging way for McDowell to articulate this thought. How do we know that our "moral reasoning" is, itself, not a hegemonic convention like the Chocolate Convention? Is that not that precisely what is at issue here? At least with discourses concerning matters that are objective in the Naturalistic sense, we have some way of weeding out cases of *mere* hegemony of one type of reasoning. But McDowell cannot avail himself of that consideration. What McDowell would need, but does not offer, is a robust account of "susceptibility" to reasons, one that does not beg the question against the skeptic about our moral discourse. I do not see such an account in the offing.

McDowell might, then, take a different line, and simply "bite the bullet" and reject the intuition that the "tastiness" of ice cream is a subjective property. If, in fact, a practice of reasoning like the Chocolate Convention really were sustainable, then, the McDowellian might claim, we *should* view "tastiness" as objective.

---

50 Thanks to C. J. Summers for pressing this line of response.

There are two difficulties, however, with such a response. First, as already noted, we must be prepared to generalize beyond this one case and claim something much stronger: namely, that it is a conceptual impossibility for a hegemonic convention of reasons to arise concerning matters that are subjective; susceptibility to reasons simply *suffices* for objectivity, even within hegemonic conventions. Yet this general claim seems too strong: surely it makes conceptual sense to think of a domain being susceptible to reasons even though it is not objective. The difficulty for the McDowellian is to account for this possibility without recourse to the "external" perspective. Second, biting the bullet seems too radical a response, compared with simply admitting the relevance of the "external" perspective. Why—except for a dogmatic commitment to Non-Naturalism—should we "bite the bullet" if an "external" perspective on objectivity suffices to account for the natural intuition that objectivity requires that reasons answer to facts about the world?

But now consider a rather different gustatory claim: namely, that chocolate ice cream is tastier than excrement.[51] Surely our *intuitions* about this case are the opposite of the prior case: we are tempted to say precisely that *this* is an objective fact about relative tastiness. Does this intuition help vindicate the McDowellian view?

The answer depends on how we go about explaining the sense in which it is an objective fact that chocolate ice cream is tastier than excrement. It does not appear that the explanation for this fact resides in the choice between chocolate and excrement being "susceptible to reasons." (To the contrary, we are inclined to think that if someone could give *reasons* for preferring excrement, that this would go no distance to changing the fact-of-the-matter.) Chocolate is surely better than excrement *intersubjectively*, i.e. there is a near-universal consensus on this point. Perhaps this is all "objectivity" comes to in this context, but if so, that will not be enough to save McDowell's view. Yet chocolate might even turn out to be *objectively* better than excrement if it turns out that, in these extreme cases, the property of tastiness just supervenes upon or is identical with some cluster of chemical-physical facts about the micro- and macro-constitutions of the substances at issue and their chemical-physical interaction with the human sensory apparatus. In other words, if it is an objective (as opposed to just intersubjective) fact that chocolate tastes better than excrement, this would be objectivity in the familiar Naturalistic sense.[52]

Does external skepticism also affect one's first-order moral beliefs? I think it does, for much the same reasons that it makes a difference to one's assessment of the

---

[51] I owe this challenge to Rob Koons, who put it in slightly more colorful terms.

[52] The same should be said about, e.g., the taste of wines. To the extent that there actually are objective reasons concerning the quality of wines, this too is surely because there is an underlying naturalistic story to be told about the microconstitution of wines, and their physico-chemical interaction with the human sensory apparatus. Of course, this would have to be argued on a case-by-case basis. Often it may turn out that questions of taste which purport to be part of domains in which reasons prevail are really better explicable in debunking sociological terms. See, e.g., Pierre Bourdieu, *Distinction: A Social Critique of the Judgment of Taste*, trans. R. Nice (Cambridge, Mass.: Harvard University Press, 1984).

objectivity of hegemonic conventions of discourse. It is surely a (defeasible) norm for belief that we should believe in objective facts. According to Non-Naturalism, in the case of the Chocolate Convention there is a (non-naturalistically) objective fact about the superiority of chocolate to vanilla. Therefore, by our defeasible epistemic norm, we should believe that chocolate is superior to vanilla.

Now along comes the external skeptic who casts doubt on the deliverances of our hegemonic convention, for the reasons already given. But once we become skeptical about whether it really is an *objective* fact that chocolate is better than vanilla, should that not affect our first-order view that chocolate *is* better than vanilla? We might, at that point, revert to an internally agnostic position or, if we were secret partisans of vanilla all along (merely swept up by the seeming force of the Chocolate Convention), we might now openly proclaim our preference for vanilla, without embarrassment.

We might sum up the general problem here in a slogan: "Talk is cheap." That we can talk about something *as though it were real*, that we can nurture a practice of giving reasons, does not suffice to underwrite the objectivity of any domain. Objective domains must generally answer to the world at some point: only then can we distinguish mere hegemonic conventions from practices of argument about genuinely objective domains. What the example of the Chocolate Convention brings out is our deeply held intuition that there is a difference between what is real and what we merely talk about as though it were real. Only the "external" perspective permits us to do any justice to that intuition.

Now it is true that naturalistically objective domains *are* susceptible to reasons (e.g. physics). But what demarcates genuine "susceptibility to reasons," of a sort sufficient to underwrite realism, from pseudo-susceptiblity is precisely the possibility of the external perspective (even, to repeat, if it is still a perspective taken from within Neurath's boat).

B. Susceptibility to Reasons

We have already seen that susceptibility to reasons, by itself, is not sufficient to undergird our intuitions about objectivity; we also require the "external" perspective, some picture of what facts there are in the world to which genuinely objective discourses must answer. But now I want to argue that even the notion of "susceptibility to reasons" does not suffice to distance the Dworkin/McDowell view from the view of skeptics like the ethical non-cognitivist. For even non-cognitivists think that moral positions are susceptible to reasons, since moral views typically depend—causally and/or logically—on various *empirical* and *factual* assumptions. Since these assumptions are "susceptible to reasons" (even for the Naturalist), it follows that people with differing moral positions have a space of reasons within which to argue.[53]

---

[53] At one point, Dworkin does make the following rather striking (Nietzschean!) claim: "No matter what we learn about the physical or mental world, it must remain an open question, and one

What Dworkin and McDowell want to claim, of course, is that the "ethical stance" *itself* is susceptible to reasons, quite apart from any factual assumptions. The evidence for the objectivity of ethics is supposed to reside, on this Non-Naturalist view, in what is distinctively *moral* in a moral debate being open to reasoned and critical reflection. Yet Dworkin and McDowell, quite strikingly, never make a case for this claim. Dworkin, for example, says things like: "We do have reasons for thinking that slavery is wrong and that the Greeks were therefore in error: we have all the moral reasons we would cite in a moral debate about the matter" (OT, 122). No skeptic need disagree with this, except to point out that the "error" of the Greeks lay in a set of false empirical assumptions about human beings and human potentialities. It just turns out to be false, as a matter of empirical psychology and biology, that (as Aristotle thought), "Some humans are...natural slaves, who altogether lack the capacity for deliberation."[54] What Dworkin needs to show is that the "error" of the Greeks lay *not* in their faulty factual assumptions, but in their distinctively *ethical* stance on this issue.

To illustrate why I think this demonstration will not be forthcoming, let me propose a pseudo-Nietzschean argument for the morality of slavery.[55] The argument is suggested by an actual passage from Nietzsche:

Every enhancement of the type "man" has so far been the work of an aristocratic society...a society that believes in the long ladder of an order of rank and differences in value between man and man, and that needs slavery in some sense or other. Without that *pathos of distance* which grows out of the ingrained difference between strata—when the ruling caste constantly looks afar and looks down upon subjects and instruments and just as constantly practices obedience and command, keeping down and keeping at a distance—that other, more mysterious pathos could not have grown up either—the craving for an ever new widening of distances within the soul itself, the development of ever higher, rarer, more

that calls for a moral rather than any other kind of judgment, how we ought to respond" (OT, 127). This way of putting the point, however, simply conflates *moral* value with all other kinds of value (including, especially, *epistemic* value). No one need disagree that *norms* figure in all judgments, including judgments about uncontroversially *factual* matters. But I take Dworkin's potentially interesting thesis—to which most of his work on this question is devoted—to be that *moral* norms are always implicated in moral skepticism. This is the claim Dworkin argues for, and which I have been arguing against.

54   C. C. W. Taylor, "Politics," in J. Barnes (ed.), *The Cambridge Companion to Aristotle* (Cambridge: Cambridge University Press, 1995), p. 255. It is true, of course, that some people—e.g. those suffering certain forms of mental retardation—lack the ability to deliberate, and it is also true that we know some normal adults who tend to act on impulse and instinct, and so seem to be poor deliberators. But these are *not* the special situations Aristotle has in mind. Moreover, the empirical claims are embedded in a larger claim: to wit, that the "natural slaves" are better off being slaves, under the direction of masters. Yet this is far from being obvious, to put the matter gently.

55   Although Nietzsche makes ambiguous remarks about slavery, I do not actually think there is any support for thinking he had a political program that required the institution of slavery. Nietzsche, in my view, is an "esoteric" moralist, addressing his remarks to select individuals who suffer from the "false consciousness" of thinking that the dominant morality is really *good for them*. For more on these issues, see my "Morality in the Pejorative Sense: On the Logic of Nietzsche's Critique of Morality," *British Journal for the History of Philosophy* 3 (1995): 113–45, and Leiter, "Nietzsche and the Morality Critics," *Ethics* 107 (1997): 250–85.

remote, further-stretching, more comprehensive states—in brief, simply the enhancement of the type "man," the continual "self-overcoming of man," to use a moral formula in a supra-moral sense.[56]

The logic of this argument, in the hands of the pseudo-Nietzsche ("P-Nietzsche") becomes the following:

(1) Any form of socio-economic organization that maximizes the good is itself morally valuable.
(2) The highest good is the enhancement of the "type" man, i.e. the breeding or production of truly great human beings like Beethoven and Goethe.
(3) Slavery is a form of socio-economic organization that maximizes the highest good.

Therefore, slavery is morally valuable.

Most of the quoted passage is devoted to giving empirical support to (3). Here the argument depends on a certain sort of speculative empirical psychology to the effect that nurturing greatness in a human being requires that the person be driven to want to "overcome" himself, to view his current self as unsatisfactory, to always want to become something "higher." Persons, however, only learn to be so driven by seeing mirrored in the social world a similar hierarchy between "higher" and "lower"—"greater" and "lesser"—persons. When society teaches that there are "higher" and "lower" people, this plants in the mind of the potentially great human being the idea that he, himself, may be at present a contemptible "lower" person, thus giving him the impetus to "overcome" himself and realize his greatness.

Now we can well imagine arguing with P-Nietzsche about the empirical assumptions that undergird (3). This, of course, is a debate that even the external skeptic thinks is both possible and relevant to one's ultimate moral view. But for the Non-Naturalist view to be plausible, it has to be the case that premises (1) and (2) are also susceptible to reasoned discussion. What reasoned debate might they have?

Dworkin presumably might differ with P-Nietzsche over two issues: first, that the moral value of an act is to be assessed in terms of its maximizing some value; and second, even granting the consequentialist form of reasoning, that the "highest" value is really the production of human greatness (such that this consideration trumps all competing values).

As to the first question, it is true that there has been substantial literature arguing, e.g., that deontology is irrational (an argument that will not help Dworkin),[57] or that consequentialism would lead to counter-intuitive violations of individual rights. Now this latter objection, at least, will not be any help here, because it simply presupposes an answer to the basic question about value. But even the former argument—the one against deontology—is not a *moral* argument, but an

[56] Friedrich Nietzsche, *Beyond Good and Evil*, ed. & trans. W. Kaufmann (New York: Vintage, 1966), Section 257.
[57] See, e.g., Samuel Scheffler, "Agent-Centered Restrictions, Rationality, and the Virtues," *Mind* 94 (1985), 409–19.

argument that appeals to a certain *epistemic value*, i.e. that one ought not to hold irrational beliefs.[58]

But what about someone who wants to contest that the value of producing great human beings trumps all other considerations? Is the basic ethical stance here—"the highest good is the existence of great human beings"—susceptible to reasons? What distinctively *moral* argument is there that P-Nietzsche's posture is mistaken? Is it that P-Nietzsche does not give enough weight to the basic happiness or well-being of the great mass of humanity? But that is no argument: it is no different than saying to the partisan of vanilla that he has failed to give sufficient weight to the creaminess of chocolate. The partisan of vanilla is neither impressed by nor interested in the "creaminess" of chocolate; so too, P-Nietzsche is neither impressed by nor interested in the happiness of most people. Is it that P-Nietzsche is just not being sensitive to the moral claim that the welfare of others has upon us? Yet this sounds more like a repetition of the disagreement, than an *argument*. (Has the partisan of vanilla just not been sensitive to the "tastiness" claim that the richness of chocolate makes upon us?) We could go on in this fashion for some time, but I do not think we would arrive at anything that looks like a *moral* reason for adopting one ethical stance over the other.

Dworkin, at least, admits as much, though perhaps without realizing how it vitiates the whole position. For sometimes, he concedes, when confronted with a moral disagreement we may simply have to say of our opponents that,

> they did not "see" or show sufficient "sensitivity" to what we "see" or "sense," and these metaphors may have nothing behind them but the bare and unsubstantiated conviction that our capacity for moral judgment functions better than theirs did. (OT, 121–22)

Once we countenance this bit of posturing as a genuine response, however, we have surely conceded that being susceptible to reasons is just a fig-leaf for unrepentant intuitionism,[59] of the sort that Strawson demolished fifty years ago[60] and which even McDowell explicitly renounces as a serious option (cf. PTE, 5–7). Any domain can now be objective if we are permitted to fall back on our superior "sensitivity" and "sense" as vindicating the factuality of our judgments. The ontological floodgates are now thrown so wide that even a Pre-Enlightenment ontology would look unduly austere.

In order to avoid this unseemly consequence, we must, I think, concede the correctness of the conventional non-cognitivist view: yes, moral positions are susceptible to reasons in the familiar sense that people are typically responsive to the

---

[58] Skepticism about *moral* value need not go hand-in-hand with skepticism about all kinds of value: it depends on the sorts of arguments being advanced for skepticism. In the case of the moral skepticism at issue here, it is motivated precisely by accepting first certain *epistemic* values for essentially pragmatic reasons, as discussed earlier.

[59] Do all forms of intuitionism require repentance? Perhaps not. The type one finds in Aristotle and Sidgwick, for example, does not seem to depend on the now discredited perceptual metaphors, that Dworkin invokes here. I do not venture an opinion on this large and difficult question.

[60] See P. F. Strawson, "Ethical Intuitionism," *Philosophy* 24 (1949): 23–33.

demands of logical consistency and factual accuracy; but once *these* are exhausted, there is nothing left but brute and opposed evaluative attitudes or "tastes." At that point, we have left the space of reasons behind.

IV. Conclusion

Dworkin's defense to the charge that his Right-Answer thesis (the claim that all, or most cases have right answers as a matter of law) is incompatible with his view that moral considerations play a decisive role in fixing the rights of litigants has turned on his insistence that his critics misunderstand the sense in which moral considerations need to be objective. At its core, Dworkin's view seems to be McDowell's: that the Naturalistic Conception of objectivity appropriate, say, for natural science, is irrelevant in the evaluative domain. What suffices for objectivity in evaluative matters is that we be able to subject our evaluative stances to reasoned discussion. I have argued that this Non-Naturalistic Conception of objectivity does not give an adequate account of objectivity, even in ethics. If I am right, and if no naturalistic moral realist response to the skeptic succeeds, then Mackie's charge some twenty years ago stands: Dworkin's theory of adjudication "injects a corresponding subjectivity into statements about what the law is" with the result that there is no "single right answer" to questions of law.

9

Law and Objectivity*

We can only discuss issues about the objectivity of law if we first have at our disposal some appropriate philosophical tools.

There are two main kinds of philosophical questions about objectivity: metaphysical and epistemological. *Metaphysical* objectivity concerns the extent to which the existence and character of some class of entities depends on the states of mind of persons (i.e., their knowledge, judgment, belief, perception, or response). *Epistemological* objectivity concerns the extent to which we are capable of achieving *knowledge* about those things that are metaphysically objective. Many philosophers working in the Anglo-American traditions also worry about *semantic* objectivity, that is, about whether or not the propositions in some realm of discourse (physics, psychology, ethics, law, etc.) can be evaluated in terms of their truth or falsity. For a discourse to be semantically objective, and for the statements in the discourse to be true, then the things referred to by the terms of that discourse (i.e., quarks, desires, justice, legal facts) must be metaphysically objective.

I. Metaphysical Objectivity

An entity (or a class of entities) is metaphysically objective if its existence and character is *independent* of the human mind. This "independence requirement" is central to metaphysical objectivity,[1] though its proper interpretation raises two important questions: first, *in what way* must a metaphysically objective thing be "independent" of the human mind; and second, *how much* independence of the relevant kind is required?

A. What Kind of Independence?

The existence and character of some entity might be *independent* of the human mind in three senses: causally, constitutionally, and cognitively. Only the last two will matter for metaphysical objectivity.

* I am grateful to Professor Yasuji Nosaka for his probing questions and our fruitful discussions of many of these issues during his year as a Visiting Scholar at the University of Texas, 1999–2000. Thanks also to Philip Pettit and Scott Shapiro for comments on earlier versions of portions of this material.
  1 B. Brower, "Dispositional Ethical Realism," *Ethics* 103 (1993) 221–49; E. Sober, "Realism and Independence," *Noûs* 16 (1982) 369–85.

An entity is *causally* independent of the human mind as long as the causal trajectory producing it did not involve the human mind. Shoes, for example, are causally *dependent* on the human mind because the existence and character of any particular pair of shoes depends causally on a cobbler having had certain beliefs and desires (e.g., a desire to make a particular kind of shoe, and true beliefs about what needed to be done to produce such shoes). By contrast, the existence and character of the earth is causally *independent* of the human mind: no human intentions played a causal role in bringing about the existence of the earth or its specific character. Metaphysical objectivity, however, *does not require causal independence*. Even entities that are *causally dependent* on the human mind can be mind-independent in one of the other two senses (below), and thus still be metaphysically objective.

An entity is *constitutionally* independent of the human mind if its existence and character is not constituted by or identical with the mind. Certain historical forms of philosophical "idealism" (such as those of Bishop Berkeley and Hegel) held that the world was constitutionally *dependent* on the mind (the human mind, or perhaps the mind of God). Conversely, the claim that some entity is metaphysically objective almost always involves denying its constitutional dependence on the mind. The exception is for psychological entities (e.g., beliefs, desires, emotions): such things cannot be constitutionally independent of the mind since they just are facets of the mind. Yet surely psychological facts may also be metaphysically objective. If so, they must be "independent" of the mind in the final sense.

An entity is *cognitively* independent of the human mind if its existence and character does not depend on any *cognizing* state of persons: for example, belief, sensory perception, judgment, response, etc. (A "cognizing" state is one which is receptive to features of the world and thus is a potential source of knowledge of the world.) A metaphysically objective thing is, accordingly, what it is independent of what anyone *believes* or would be *justified* in believing about it (or what anyone perceives it to be or would perceive it to be under certain conditions, etc.). On this account, psychological facts about a person are metaphysically objective in virtue of not depending on what an observer of that person believes or would be justified in believing about that person's psychological state. (This assumes that mental content is "narrow," not "wide," a technical debate in the philosophy of psychology that must be set aside here.)

Any kind of metaphysically objective fact (except for psychological facts) must necessarily be *constitutionally* independent of the mind. All metaphysically objective facts must also be *cognitively* independent. The common sense picture of the natural world presumes that its contents are metaphysically objective in this sense: ordinary people think that atoms and zebras and sulfur are not simply identical with the mind and that they are what they are independent of what people may believe or be justified in believing about them. Science, then, aspires to epistemological objectivity by trying to accurately depict the way things (objectively) are.

B. How Much Independence?

There can be degrees of cognitive *independence*, and thus degrees of objectivity that may be distinguished; not everything that is objective may prove to be objective in the sense in which common sense understands the constituent elements of the natural world to be objective. (This point is important for understanding the objectivity of law, as we will discuss shortly.) The crucial notion for cognitive independence is independence from the *cognizing* states of persons: beliefs, sensory perceptions, judgments, responses, and the like. Thus, this notion of objectivity supposes that there is always a difference between what "seems right" about some state of affairs and what actually "is right." For example, it may seem right to John (based on a sensory perception) that there is a table in front of him, but it may not be right that there is a table there: it could be an optical illusion. The table, then, is objective *in some sense* since its existence is *independent* of what "seems right" to John.

It is possible, then, to distinguish four kinds of claims about objectivity:[2]

According to *subjectivism*, what seems right to the cognizer determines what is right.

According to *minimal objectivism*, what seems right to the *community of cognizers* determines what is right.

According to *modest objectivism*, what seems right to cognizers *under appropriate or ideal conditions* determines what is right.

According to *strong objectivism*, what seems right to cognizers *never* determines what is right.

Subjectivism and strong objectivism represent the two classical and opposed philosophical positions of antiquity: Protagoras held that "man is the measure of all things" (subjectivism) (Plato, *Theaetetus* *152a, *166a–*168b), while Plato embraced a kind of strong objectivism (Plato, *Phaedo* *741–*75b, *Republic* *475–*480, *508d–e). The Protagorean position denies the objectivity of the world and everything in it: whatever each individual takes to be the case *is* the case (for that individual), and thus the existence and character of any particular thing depends (epistemically) on the (individual) human mind. By contrast, the Platonist affirms the complete and absolute objectivity of the world: What really is the case about the world is never fixed by what any person or all persons believe, has (or have) reasons to believe, or could have reasons to believe. Mistake, on a global scale, even under ideal epistemic conditions, is a possibility for the Platonist. This latter position is often described as "realism" (or "metaphysical realism").

Minimal objectivism and modest objectivism occupy conceptual space between these two familiar, historical positions. Minimal objectivism holds that whatever the community of cognizers takes to be the case is the case. This view, like its pure Protagorean cousin, issues in a kind of relativism (what is the case is

---

² B. Leiter, "Objectivity and the Problems of Jurisprudence," *Texas Law Review*, (1993) 187–209.

relative to a particular community of cognizers), but by abstracting away from the subjectivity of the individual cognizer, it introduces a *minimum* amount of objectivity. It is also a kind of objectivity with some useful domains of application. What is and is not fashionable, for example, is probably minimally objective. What seems right to John about what is fashionable can be objectively wrong: John may be out of sync with the styles of his community, and thus it would be correct to say, "John is mistaken in thinking that a plaid shirt and striped pants go well together." But it does not seem that the entire community can be wrong about what is fashionable: in that sense, what seems right to the community determines what really is fashionable.

In most domains, however, minimal objectivity would be viewed as too close to subjectivism for comfort. Modest objectivity thus abstracts even further away from dependence on *actual* cognizers, individual or communal. Something is modestly objective if its existence and character depends only on what cognizers would believe under certain *idealized* conditions for cognition, conditions like full information and evidence, perfect rationality, and the like. (By hypothesis, under *ideal* conditions, all cognizers would come to the same belief about things.) Everyone on the planet can be wrong in his or her beliefs about a modestly objective entity; beliefs formed under ideal epistemic conditions, however, can never be wrong. This latter point is what differentiates modest from strong objectivity.

Some philosophers have defended the idea that truth is at best modestly objective (e.g., the doctrine Hilary Putnam calls "Internal Realism"[3]): what is true in any domain is simply whatever inquirers would agree upon under epistemically ideal conditions. Versions of this idea have since been subjected to withering criticisms,[4] and it has few adherents. Still, modest objectivity, like the other conceptions, may be particularly apt in certain domains. Consider, for example, facts about color. It seems natural to say that there are (modestly) objective facts about color even though the color of an object is not fully independent of the human mind. For example, we might say that something is red if and only if normal perceivers under normal viewing conditions would be disposed to see it as red. Color, on this account, depends on the human mind—on human response or perception—but only on human response under *appropriate* conditions. One important recent idea is that evaluative facts might be modestly objective in a similar way:[5] evaluative facts would depend on human responses to morally significant situations under appropriate conditions. In both cases, however, it is important to specify the conditions under which human response fixes the reference of a concept in a non-question begging way. It obviously will not do, for example, to define "normalcy" of perceivers and of viewing conditions by reference to their getting the right result (i.e., seeing all and only the red things as red). Some philosophers

[3] H. Putnam, *Reason, Truth and History* (Cambridge: Cambridge University Press, 1981).
[4] M. Johnston, "Objectivity refigured: Pragmatism without verificationism," in J. Haldane and C. Wright (eds.), *Reality, Representation and Projection* (Oxford: Oxford University Press, 1993).
[5] E.g., P. Pettit, "Realism and Response-Dependence," *Mind* 100 (1991) 587–626.

doubt whether the conditions can be specified in a non-question-begging way.[6] We shall consider the prospects for modest objectivity about law, below.

II. Epistemological Objectivity

The demand for epistemological objectivity is the demand to be free of *bias* and other factors that *distort* cognition, that prevent the things being cognized from presenting themselves as they really (metaphysically) are. More precisely, epistemological objectivity requires that the cognitive processes and mechanisms by which beliefs about the world are formed be constituted in such a way that they at least *tend* toward the production of accurate representations of how things are. Notice that epistemological objectivity does not require that cognitive processes always yield true representations: that would demand more than is attainable and more than is even expected. Epistemological objectivity obtains when either of the following is true: (1) the cognitive processes at issue *reliably* arrive at accurate representations, or (2) the cognitive processes are free of factors that are known to produce inaccurate representations.

The obstacles to epistemological objectivity will vary with the domain under consideration. In law, bias for or against one party, or ignorance of pertinent rules or facts, will be obvious hindrances to epistemological objectivity. In the sciences, and the social sciences in particular, "values" are often thought to present a special obstacle to epistemological objectivity insofar as they influence the choice of research topics and, most seriously, the selection and evaluation of evidence. As one contemporary author explains: "Values are thought to damage inquiry epistemically because they are held to be subjective—they come from us, not the world. Therefore to allow values to influence inquiry into the nature of the world is to allow such inquiry to be subject to a control other than the world itself".[7] Epistemic values or norms—for example, norms about when evidence warrants belief—must of course play a role in all scientific inquiry; the worry is about non-epistemic values or norms, like the political ideology of the inquirer or the political climate in which inquiry takes place.

Yet one "need not require freedom from all value and bias in order to have objective inquiry" since "there may yet exist mechanisms of belief-formation that incorporate feedback from the object to the inquiring subject".[8] The mechanism at issue is *causal*: metaphysically objective things make themselves felt *causally*, whatever our theoretical preconceptions and values. No matter what bias leads me to deny that there is a closed door in front of me, my attempt to walk through it will be thwarted (causally) by reality: the door will stop me.

---

[6] E.g., C. Wright, *Truth and Objectivity* (Cambridge, Mass.: Harvard University Press, 1992).

[7] P. Railton, "Marx and the Objectivity of Science," in F. Suppe and P. Asquith (eds.), *PSA* 1984 vol 2 (Lansing, MI: Philosophy of Science Association, 1985) p. 818. Also reprinted in R. Boyd et al (eds.), *The Philosophy of Science* (Cambridge, Mass.: MIT Press, 1991).   [8] Id., p. 818.

The causal impact of reality, however, gives us merely an *external* criterion for objectivity, and does not yet show how inquirers could determine whether or not their inquiry is epistemologically objective. Here, however, inquirers might look for certain familiar markers of epistemological objectivity, like the existence of intersubjective agreement in judgment, the publicity of evidence and standards of proof, and the reproducibility of the evidence for a judgment by different inquirers: "when these conditions are met, subjective contributions and biases will be excluded as far as possible".[9] That physics constitutes a cross-cultural, global community of inquirers strongly suggests that it is epistemologically objective: if it were not, then one would expect local differences (in interests, ideology, and the like) to lead to markedly different discourses of physics. Of course, the absence of intersubjective agreement does not *by itself* demonstrate lack of epistemological objectivity; the question is always what the best explanation for lack of such agreement is supposed to be.[10] In the case of the social sciences, where objective truths may conflict with entrenched interests, it should hardly be surprising that there should be no agreement about certain social scientific questions. In other cases, though, the suspicion will be strong that it is entrenched interests and values that distort cognition of the social world and warp scientific inquiry accordingly.

III. Semantic Objectivity

Semantic objectivity is a property of statements, rather than things or cognitive mechanisms. Philosophers in the Anglo-American traditions of the twentieth century, who approach most philosophical problems by framing them first as problems about language and its relationship to the world, have been most concerned with questions of semantic objectivity. Typically, philosophers are concerned with a class of statements characteristic of a particular branch of discourse: say, physics or psychology or ethics or aesthetics. Some branch of discourse enjoys semantic objectivity when its statements are generally apt for evaluation in terms of their truth and falsity. (Not every statement in the discourse need be determinately true or false—the property of "bivalence"—since few discourses outside pure mathematics are bivalent.) *Cognitivism* is the doctrine that some branch of discourse is semantically objective.[11]

---

⁹ Id.

¹⁰ Dworkin has often attributed to skeptics about his right-answer thesis a bad verificationist argument to the effect that "a proposition cannot be true unless there is some agreed test through which its truth might be demonstrated". *Taking Rights Seriously* (Cambridge, Mass.: Harvard University Press, 1977) p. 282. But the right way to interpret skepticism about the existence of right answers in hard cases is as a "best explanation" challenge: where there is deep and intractable disagreement about the right answer, what is the best explanation for that fact? The skeptic says the best explanation in the legal case is that there is no right answer.

¹¹ Wright (n. 6 above) disputes whether truth-aptness is the relevant criterion for demarcating semantically objective discourses; most discourses satisfy the minimum syntactic requirements to

Thus, for example, the discourse of natural science is presumed to be a cognitive discourse: scientific statements about the natural world are generally either true or false. But what of statements in ethics like, "That distribution of resources is unjust," or "Harming a defenseless animal is morally wrong"? Many philosophers have thought that there are, *as a metaphysical matter*, no facts in the world corresponding to the "injustice" of a distribution or the "moral wrongness" of an action.[12] Most philosophers who deny the metaphysical objectivity of morality claim that its semantics is non-cognitive: rather than stating facts (that either obtain or do not obtain), ethical statements, according to *non-cognitivism*, express attitudes or feelings of various kinds.[13] Non-cognitivists bear the burden, then, of explaining away the surface grammar and logical structure of ethical discourse which make it indistinguishable from ordinary empirical discourse (compare: "This distribution is unjust," with "That chair is red").

A minority of philosophers, however, agree that morality is *not* metaphysically objective, but nonetheless maintain that the surface grammar of ethical discourse should be taken at face value: ethical discourse purports to state facts, and is thus a cognitive discourse. It is, unfortunately, a cognitive discourse almost all of whose statements are false (since there are no metaphysically objective moral facts in the world). (The only true ethical statements, on this view, will be *negations* of ethical judgments: "No, slavery is not really morally wrong.") This doctrine is known as "error theory".[14] Error theories about any discourse make it puzzling, however, why the discourse should persist, let alone occupy the central role that ethical discourse does in human lives: why would people continue to engage in a putatively fact-stating discourse that never succeeds in stating any facts? Non-cognitivism, as a semantic doctrine, at least identifies an important role for ethical discourse: namely, the expression of feelings and attitudes about matters of real moment to human beings and their social existence.

Most philosophers who accept that ethical discourse is cognitive do so because they also believe that morality is metaphysically objective (in some sense):[15] if there are metaphysically objective moral facts, then moral statements will not be systematically false as error theory has it. How could there be such facts? One important strand of argument (that has also been influential in legal philosophy) presupposes the truth of Kripke-Putnam semantics, according to which there can

---

make use of the truth-predicate appropriate. The issue about the objectivity of the discourse must be located elsewhere according to Wright.

[12] A. Gibbard, *Wise Choices, Apt Feelings: A Theory of Normative Judgment* (Cambridge, Mass.: Harvard University Press, 1990); J. Mackie, *Ethics: Inventing Right and Wrong* (London: Penguin, 1977); C. Stevenson, *Ethics and Language* (New Haven: Yale University Press, 1944).

[13] C. Stevenson and A. Gibbard (id.) are the most sophisticated versions of this view.

[14] Mackie (n. 12 above).

[15] D. Brink, *Moral Realism and the Foundations of Ethics* (New York: Cambridge University Press, 1989); Brower (n. 1 above); Pettit (n. 5 above); P. Railton, "Moral Realism," *Philosophical Review* 95 (1986) 163–207.

be necessary truths (e.g., "water is H_2O") that are discoverable only *a posteriori*.[16] For those who think moral facts are *strongly* objective,[17] the central idea is that moral facts are simply identical with (or supervenient upon) natural facts: just as there are necessary, *a posteriori* statements of property identity about water, so too there are such statements about moral facts.[18] For example, perhaps the property of being "morally right" is just identical with the property of "maximizing human well-being," where the latter may be understood in purely psychological and physiological terms. In that case, whether an action X is morally right is a strongly objective matter, since it is simply a scientific question whether action X will in fact maximize the relevant kinds of psychological and physiological states in the world.[19] The crucial claim, plainly, is that moral facts are to be identified with (or treated as supervenient upon) certain kinds of natural facts. Again, many philosophers are skeptical that this claim can be made out.[20]

IV. Law and Objectivity

In law, issues about objectivity arise along a variety of dimensions.[21] For example: (1) We expect the content of our laws to be objective in the sense of treating

---

[16] Kripke, *Naming and Necessity* (Cambridge, Mass.: Harvard University Press, 1980); Putnam, "The Meaning of 'Meaning'," *Mind, Language and Reality: Philosophical Papers, Volume 2* (Cambridge: Cambridge University Press, 1975). Brink provides an accessible introduction to the main themes of the "new" or "causal" theory of reference associated with Kripke and Putnam. (Brink, "Legal Theory, Legal Interpretation and Judicial Review," *Philosophy and Public Affairs* 17 (1988) 105–48 and Brink, "Legal Interpretation, Objectivity, and Morality," in Leiter (ed.), *Objectivity in Law and Morals* (New York: Cambridge University Press, 2001)). A more detailed treatment of the issues in philosophical semantics, again with an eye to issues of legal philosophy, may be found in Stavropoulos, *Objectivity in Law* (Oxford: Clarendon Press, 1996) pp. 17–34, 53–76.

[17] Brink (n. 16 above), P. Railton, "Moral Realism," *Philosophical Review* 95 (1986) 163–207.

[18] This allows moral realists to deflect G.E. Moore's famous "open question" argument. That it was an "open question" in 1400 whether "water was H_2O" has no bearing on the necessity of the identity relation, since the necessary identity here was an *a posteriori* discovery. So too, the fact that it might be an "open question" whether "what is pleasurable is good" shows nothing about the real nature of goodness, since what constitutes goodness may also be discoverable only *a posteriori*.

The Moorean argument can be given a new twist by reframing it in the language of internalism: the doctrine that there is a necessary connection between judging that "X is good," and feeling some motivational pull to do or have X. Even if there are necessary *a posteriori* relations between moral facts and natural facts, there does not seem to be any guarantee that discovering *a posteriori* that "what is good is pleasure" will necessarily exert any motivational force for the judging agent. "So pleasure is what is good. So what? Why should I care about pleasure?" seems a completely intelligible question for the judger to ask. Most moral realists (e.g., Railton, id.) respond to this dilemma by simply denying that internalism is true.

[19] Most naturalistic moral realisms are based on versions of utilitarianism, precisely because it is easy to see what the naturalistic base of moral properties would be in a utilitarian schema. One peculiar feature of the moral realism of Moore (M. Moore, "Moral Reality Revisited," *Michigan Law Review* 90 (1992) 2424–533) is that it is conjoined with a deontological moral theory, yet within a purportedly naturalistic moral realist framework. [20] E.g., A. Gibbard (n. 12 above).

[21] See, e.g., K. Greenawalt, *Law and Objectivity* (New York: Oxford University Press, 1992) for a wide-ranging survey, though one that is a bit thin in its treatment of the philosophical issues.

people the same unless they are "relevantly" different. (2) We expect judges to be objective in the sense of not being biased against one party or the other. (3) We expect legal decisions to be objective in the sense of reaching the result that the law *really* requires without letting bias or prejudice intervene. (4) In some areas of law, we expect the law to employ "objective" standards of conduct (like "reasonable person" standards) that do not permit actors to excuse their conduct based on their subjective perceptions at the time.

Recently, a substantial literature has emerged on the objectivity of law primarily with respect to the issues posed in (3). Indeed, it is here, in particular, that questions about the objectivity of ethics intersect with those about law. We may think of the central problematic in the following way.

Judges must decide cases. They must consult and interpret the relevant legal sources (statutes, precedent, custom, etc.) in order to determine the governing legal principles and rules, and then decide how these are to apply to the facts of the case. Let us call the "class of legal reasons" the class of reasons that judges may legitimately consider in deciding a legal question.[22] If the law is "rationally determinate" on some point that means the class of legal reasons justifies a unique answer on that point: there is, as is commonly said, a single right answer as a matter of law.

We may now speak of the law as objective along two possible dimensions:

(1) The law is metaphysically objective insofar as there exist right answers as a matter of law.
(2) The law is epistemically objective insofar as the mechanisms for discovering right answers (e.g., adjudication, legal reasoning) are free of distorting factors that would obscure right answers.

Where the law is metaphysically objective, we may say there exists a "legal fact": if it is rationally determinate, as a matter of law, that "Leiter is liable for his negligence in these circumstances," then it is a legal fact that Leiter is negligent.

The scope of these claims about the objectivity of law may vary. We may think the law is metaphysically objective only with respect to a narrow range of cases (as the American Legal Realists do), or with respect to nearly all cases (as Dworkin does). We may think the law is epistemically objective some of the time or almost none of the time. The claims to objectivity can diverge as well. The law may be metaphysically objective, but fail to be epistemically objective. On the other hand, the above characterization of epistemic objectivity presupposes for its intelligibility that the law be metaphysically objective: we can get no purchase on the notion of a "distorting factor" without reference to the "things" we are trying to know.[23]

---

[22] See B. Leiter, "Legal Indeterminacy," *Legal Theory* 1 (1995) 481–92 for this way of conceptualizing indeterminacy.

[23] Not all writers accept this link (e.g., G. Postema, "Objectivity Fit for Law," in *Objectivity in Law and Morals* (n. 16 above). See the further discussion in Section VI.

Often, the objectivity of ethics is implicated in the objectivity of law. The metaphysical objectivity of law, as we have seen, is a matter of its rational determinacy, i.e., it is a matter of the class of legal reasons justifying a unique outcome. If the class of legal reasons, however, includes *moral* reasons, then the law can be objective only if morality (and moral reasoning) is objective. The class of legal reasons can come to include moral reasons in two ways.

First, and most obviously, the familiar sources of law—like statutes and constitutional provisions—may include moral concepts or considerations. The United States Constitution provides the most familiar examples, since it speaks of "equal protection," "liberty," and other inherently moral notions. For courts to apply these provisions is for them necessarily to apply the incorporated moral concepts. For the law to be metaphysically objective in these cases requires that these moral concepts have objective content. Of course, this objective content need not be fixed in virtue of morality being objective: an interpretive principle like "Interpret each provision as the framers of the provision would have intended" may suffice to make the application of the Equal Protection Clause of the Fourteenth Amendment determinate, without presupposing anything about the "objective" meaning of "equality." Yet in some cases, and under some theories of interpretation, what will be required is precisely to understand what equality *really* requires.[24]

Second, moral reasons might be part of the class of legal reasons because they are part of the very criteria of legal validity. Natural lawyers hold that for a norm to be a legal norm it must satisfy moral criteria:[25] thus, a judge wondering whether a particular norm (relevant to a particular case) is a valid legal norm must necessarily engage in moral reasoning. Some Legal Positivists ("Soft" or "Inclusive" Positivists) accept a similar view: they hold that, as a contingent matter, morality can be a criterion of legal validity if it is the practice of legal officials in some society to employ moral considerations as criteria of legal validity. For these Positivists—who include the century's leading defender of the doctrine, H.L.A. Hart—legal reasoning in such societies will include moral reasoning.

Of course, even those Positivists ("Hard" or "Exclusive" Positivists) who deny that morality is ever a criterion of legality may still hold that it is a judge's duty in exercising discretion in hard cases to reach the morally correct result. Thus, while the objectivity of morality will not, for these Positivists, affect the objectivity of law, it will still matter in thinking about what judges ought to do in hard cases.

In all these ways, then, the objectivity of morality may be implicated in how we think about the objectivity of law (or the objectivity of the adjudicative process).

[24] Examples of this kind of approach include D. Brink (1988, 2001) (n. 16 above), M. Moore, "A Natural Law Theory of Interpretation," *Southern California Law Review* 58 (1985) 277–398, and N. Stavropoulos (n. 16 above).

[25] Satisfying the moral criteria might be *necessary* for a norm to be a legal norm, or it might be both necessary and sufficient. The strongest forms of natural law theory hold the latter.

V. How Objective Is Law?

Most writers who have considered this question have done so largely within the kind of philosophical framework sketched in the prior sections.[26] Writers like Brink and Moore, for example, have developed an account of law as Strongly Objective, applying the realist semantics (the "new" or "causal" theory of reference) of Kripke and Putnam to issues of legal interpretation. As Stavropoulos explains it:

Both Kripke and Putnam attack what they call the traditional theory of reference. That theory holds that an expression refers to whatever fits the description with which speakers associate the expression. The relevant description . . . captures necessary properties of the referent which are knowable *a priori*, as in the case of knowing that a bachelor is an unmarried man. This cannot be true, Kripke and Putnam argue, since expressions refer to the same object in the lips of speakers who can only associate the expression with vague or mistaken descriptions. Indeed, not only individual speakers but the community as a whole can be in error about the true properties of the relevant object . . . The important suggestion being made by Kripke and Putnam is that reference is *object-dependent*. *Which* object 'Aristotle' or 'water' refers to is not determined by the associated description, but turns instead on a matter of fact, namely which object the name-using or term-using practice is directed at.[27]

Thus, if on the old view the "meaning" of an expression (the descriptions speakers associated with it) fixed the reference of the expression, on the new theory, the referent fixes the meaning. "Water" picks out whatever stuff we happened to baptize with the name "water" at the beginning of the "term-using practice." As it happens, that stuff has a distinctive micro-constitution: it is H_2O. Thus, "water" refers to stuff that is H_2O, and that is what the term means: the stuff that is H_2O. If we can apply the new theory of reference to the expressions that figure in legal rules, then we can vindicate an account of law as Strongly Objective: the meaning of the rule determines its application, and the meaning is Strongly Objective, i.e., the *real* referents of the terms in the legal rule determine the rule's meaning, and the entire community can be mistaken about what that referent is.

    Problems arise at several different levels with this account of the law's objectivity, though all are traceable to the reliance on the new theory of reference. To begin, there are reasons to be skeptical about whether the new theory of reference

---

[26] D. Brink (1988, 2001) (n. 16 above); J.L. Coleman, "Truth and Objectivity in Law," *Legal Theory 1* (1995) 33–68; J.L. Coleman and B. Leiter, "Determinancy, Objectivity and Authority," *University of Pennsylvania Law Review* 142 (1993) 549–637. Also reprinted in A. Marmor (ed.), *Law and Interpretation* (Oxford: Clarendon Press, 1995); M. Moore (1985) (n. 24 above); M. Moore, "Law as a Functional Kind," in R. George (ed.), *Natural Law Theory: Contemporary Essays* (Oxford: Clarendon Press, 1992); N. Stavropoulos (n. 16 above).

[27] Stavropoulos (n. 17 above), p. 8. There are also more general doubts about semantic realism, associated with the work of Michael Dummett, Crispin Wright, and Saul Kripke's reading of Wittgenstein. These problems are reviewed in Coleman and Leiter (n. 26 above) pp. 568–72, 605–07.

is correct.[28] This debate in philosophical semantics would, however, take us far afield, though the reader should at least be aware that the confidence in the correctness of the theory expressed by Brink, Moore, and others is perhaps not warranted.

Even granting, however, the correctness of the new theory, it is not obvious how it helps in the case of law. After all, the new theory always seemed most plausible for a limited class of expressions: proper names and natural kind terms (i.e., terms that pick out the natural features of the world about which science states lawful generalizations). The reason has to do with the implicit essentialism required for the new theory: unless referents have *essential* characteristics—just as "water" has a distinctive and essential molecular constitution—they cannot fix meanings. But what is the essence of "due process" or "equal protection"? We would first need to accept some version of moral realism before the new theory of reference would help.[29]

Finally, even if the new theory of reference gives the correct account of the meaning of some terms (like natural kind terms), that still does not show that it gives us the right account of meaning for purposes of legal interpretation.[30] Suppose the legislature prohibits the killing of "fish" within 100 miles of the coast, intending quite clearly (as the legislative history reveals) to protect whales, but not realizing that "fish" is a natural kind term that does not include whales within its extension. The new theory of reference tells us that the statute protects sea bass but not whales, yet surely a court that interpreted the statute as also protecting whales would not be making a mistake. Indeed, one might think the reverse is true: for a court *not* to protect whales would be to contravene the will of the legislature, and thus, indirectly, the will of the people. What the example suggests is that the correct theory of legal interpretation is *not* a mere matter of philosophical semantics: issues about *political legitimacy*—about the conditions under which the exercise of coercive power by courts can be justified—must inform theories of legal interpretation, and such considerations may even trump considerations of semantics.[31]

---

[28] E.g., G. Evans, "The Causal Theory of Names," (1973) reprinted in *The Varieties of Reference* (Oxford: Clarendon Press, 1982); T. Blackburn, "The Elusiveness of Reference," *Midwest Studies in Philosophy* 12 (1988) 179–94.

[29] Both D. Brink (n. 16 above) and M. Moore (n. 19 above) do accept moral realism. Perhaps for non-moral terms in law, their essential characteristics are *functional* ones, rather than *constitutional*: e.g., since cars can be made out of all kinds of materials, what is essential to "carhood" is not its molecular constitution but its distinctive *functions*. Cf. Moore (n. 26 above), pp. 207–08.

[30] A version of this point was first made by S. Munzer, "Realistic Limits on Realist Interpretation," *Southern California Law Review* 58 (1985) 459–75, in criticizing M. Moore (n. 24 above).

[31] I take the point in the text to be compatible with Stavropoulos's observation that the real problem is that "there can be no principled exclusion of whales" from the protection of the statute, and *not* simply a semantic dispute about "what it is to be a fish" (n. 16 above, p. 192). He continues: "Mistaken theory of fish-hood prevalent when the statute was drafted *explains* why the word 'fish' was mistakenly used to pick out marine life... [but] what makes the legislators' view that whales should not be excluded count is the principle justifying the provision" (id.). But the justifying principle is, of course, not a deliverance of any philosophical theory of meaning or reference.

Strong Objectivity about legal facts raises another set of problems, apart from the problems in philosophical semantics.[32] If the existence and nature of legal facts are independent of what lawyers and judges (even under ideal conditions) believe about them, then how do judges gain access to such facts? In other words, what reason is there, on the Strong Objectivist view, for thinking that ordinary adjudicative practices are epistemologically objective, i.e., involve reliable mechanisms for discovering Strongly Objective legal facts?[33] The "externalism" about epistemological objectivity discussed earlier (Section II) seems an unhappy answer in the legal context. Recall that on the externalist view, one's beliefs are justified *externally*, i.e., independent of one's own experience or awareness of their being justified. *Even if* we had reason to think adjudication was a *reliable* mechanism for generating true beliefs about legal facts—and we have, as yet, no reason for thinking that—it seems bizarre to say that,

(1) A legal decision can be justified *even though no lawyers or judges know it to be justified, or may ever know it to be justified*; or
(2) A legal decision is not justified *even though all lawyers and judges take it to be justified.*

Yet (1) and (2) follow from the conjunction of Strong Objectivity about legal facts with externalism about justification. Indeed, Strong Objectivity about legal facts alone entails the counter-intuitive claims that,

(A) It is a legal fact that "Leiter is liable for his negligence" *even though no lawyer or judge believes it, or will ever believe it*; and
(B) It is not a legal fact that "Leiter is liable for his negligence" *even though all lawyers and judges believe Leiter is liable, indeed even though all lawyers and judges under ideal conditions would believe Leiter is liable.*

If these appeals to intuition are correct, this might suggest that law is only *Modestly* or perhaps *Minimally* Objective. Recall that law is Modestly Objective if,

X is a legal fact if *under ideal conditions* lawyers and judges take it to be a legal fact.

Recall that law is Minimally Objective if,

X is a legal fact if the community of lawyers and judges takes it to be a legal fact.

On both accounts, what the law is is *epistemically* constrained. Which view of the objectivity of law—Minimal or Modest—is correct depends, in turn, on whether we think our concept of law is one that allows that all legal practitioners at a given time can be mistaken about what the law "really" is: if we think that idea is nonsensical, then we are committed to the Minimal Objectivity of law; if we think it makes good sense, then we are committed to the Modest Objectivity of law.[34]

---

[32] Cf. J.L. Coleman and B. Leiter (n. 26 above), pp. 612–16.

[33] M. Moore (n. 29 above) embraces a coherentist epistemology, though that sits uneasily with his commitment to Strong Objectivity. Why should the fact that a set of beliefs cohere for a judge be a reason for thinking that those beliefs track the way the world really is?

[34] Prospects and problems for minimal and modest objectivity are explored in Coleman and Leiter (n. 26 above), pp. 616–32 and in Coleman (n. 26 above). Dworkin's view might be interpreted

Of course, any account of the law as Modestly Objective must specify the ideal conditions for judgment in a non-question begging way. What are the conditions such that judgment rendered under them would fix what the legal facts are? Coleman and Leiter describe the ideal judge (i.e., one whose judgments are rendered under ideal epistemic conditions) as:

(1) fully informed both about (a) all relevant factual information, and (b) all authoritative legal sources (statutes, prior court decisions);
(2) fully rational, e.g., observant of the rules of logic;
(3) free of personal bias for or against either party;
(4) maximally empathetic and imaginative, where cases require, for example, the weighing of affected interests; and
(5) conversant with and sensitive to informal cultural and social knowledge of the sort essential to analogical reasoning, in which differences and distinctions must be marked as "relevant" or "irrelevant."[35]

One might worry though that the notions of "relevant" facts (in 1), "maximal" empathy and imagination (in 3), and "informal" knowledge necessary for judgments of "relevance" (in 5) can not themselves be fleshed out in a non question-begging way, i.e., without presupposing what the right answer is as a matter of law.

In addition, we still confront the question of *epistemic* access to legal facts conceived as Modestly Objective. Let us distinguish "*de jure* inaccessibility" from "*de facto* inaccessibility".[36] A fact is *de jure* inaccessible if our very concept of the fact means there is no conceptual connection between its existence and our knowledge of it. A fact is *de facto* inaccessible if there is a conceptual connection between the fact and our knowledge of it, but it happens, as a contingent matter in some case, that we do not know what the fact is. According to Strong Objectivity, legal facts are *de jure* inaccessible because what we can epistemically access *never* determines what is the case. (Legal facts may, of course, turn out to be *de facto* accessible.) By contrast, Modestly Objective legal facts will only be *de jure* inaccessible if the ideal conditions specified by the theory are themselves *de jure* (that is, in principle or by the terms of the theory) unattainable by humans. The Modest Objectivist must claim, then, that the ideal epistemic conditions for legal judgment (assuming they can be specified in a non-question-begging way) are realizable by creatures like us. If they are not, of course, then it will follow that legal facts are *de facto* inaccessible as well.

---

as a version of Modest Objectivity, insofar as what Hercules takes the right answer to be seems to fix what the right answer is, and Hercules is just an ideal judge, i.e., one with unlimited time, knowledge, and powers of rational and philosophical reflection (Dworkin 1977 (n. 10 above), p. 105). For this kind of reading of Dworkin, see Coleman and Leiter (id.), pp. 633–4. As we will see in the next section, however, Dworkin contests the entire way of conceptualizing objectivity involved in this characterization of his views.

[35] J.L. Coleman and B. Leiter (n. 26 above), p. 630.   [36] Id., p. 631.

But this suggests a further worry about Strong and Modest Objectivity.[37] Part of the concept of law is that it is *normative*, or *reason-giving*. Law cannot be normative, however, if *unknown*. This is why we need an answer to the question of epistemic access, for undetectable legal facts cannot *give* reasons, i.e., cannot be normative. Any conception of the law as Strongly or Modestly Objective raises the specter of the law being unable to fulfill its normative function, insofar as the specter of *de facto* inaccessibility seems a live one. Only a conception of the law as Minimally Objective is, it seems, guaranteed to be compatible with the normativity of law, precisely because (1) communal consensus is constitutive of legal facts, and (2) such consensus is necessarily accessible to that community.

VI. Other Approaches to the Objectivity of Law

Some philosophers recently have disputed whether the traditional ways of conceptualizing objectivity are adequate.[38] In particular, these philosophers have raised two kinds of doubts about the earlier characterizations of objectivity. First, these philosophers (especially Dworkin and McDowell) question whether the conception of metaphysical objectivity (especially *strong* metaphysical objectivity) does not presuppose a vantage point on the way things "really" are to which we can have no access. It is not clear, however, that doubts about, say, the objectivity of morality require such a vantage point: even from "within" our practices questions can arise about the objectivity of morality because, for example, of the apparent diversity of moral views, or because moral facts do not appear to play a role in causal explanations of experience.[39]

Second, some of these philosophers wonder whether the conception of metaphysical objectivity as mind-independence is not a paradigm too closely tied to a picture of the objectivity of the natural world, and thus either does not make sense or should not be applied with respect to the objectivity of domains like ethics or aesthetics. In these evaluative domains, it makes no sense to ask about whether there are evaluative facts "out there" in the world. The objectivity of evaluative discourse is simply a matter of its susceptibility to reasons, of our ability to subject ethical positions to rational scrutiny and discussion.

---

[37] Cf. B. Leiter (n. 2 above), pp. 207–08.

[38] These revisionary views of objectivity have been extensively criticized (see Ch. 8, as well as Svavarsdóttir, "Objective Values: Does Metaethics Rest on a Mistake?" in B. Leiter (n. 17 above); C. Wright (n. 8 above); R. Dworkin, "Objectivity and Truth: You'd Better Believe it," *Philosophy & Public Affairs* 25 (1996): 87–139; J. McDowell, "Projection and Truth in Ethics," in S. Darwall et al (eds.) *Moral Discourse and Practice: Some Philosophical Approaches* (New York: Oxford University Press, 1996); T. Nagel, *The Last Word* (New York: Oxford University Press, 1997); G. Postema (n. 23 above); H. Putnam, "Replies to Brian Leiter and Jules Coleman," *Legal Theory* 1 (1995) 69–80.

[39] Some philosophers who share with Dworkin and McDowell skepticism about the conceptualization of objectivity nonetheless concede this last point (e.g., Postema (n. 23 above)).

According to Dworkin, for example, when we claim that there is an objective fact about whether one interpretation is better than another, or whether one principle is morally better than another, we are not making a claim *external* to the practice of substantive moral or interpretive argument in which these claims arise. "Slavery is objectively wrong" is simply a *moral* claim internal to the practice of argument in which we offer reasons for the proposition that "Slavery is wrong." Two thousand years of metaphysics notwithstanding, there simply are no "external," *metaphysical* questions about value; there is only ethics, only argument about what is right, what is just, what is good, what is evil, and the like. As Dworkin puts it: "Any successful—really, any intelligible—argument that evaluative propositions are neither true nor false must be internal to the evaluative domain rather than archimedean about [i.e. external to] it".[40] Nagel, though not quite agreeing with Dworkin, characterizes the view succinctly: "the only way to answer skepticism, relativism, and subjectivism about morality is to meet it with first-order moral arguments. [Dworkin] holds that the skeptical positions must themselves be understood as moral claims—that they are unintelligible as anything else".[41]

If we are not doing metaphysics (or metaethics) when we are worrying about "objectivity," then what are we doing? According to Dworkin, talk about the "objective" wrongness of abortion, for example, is really just disguised *moral* talk, "nothing but clarifying or emphatic or metaphorical restatements or elaborations of [the internal moral claim] that abortion is wrong".[42]

At first sight these remarks seem quite obviously wrong. To claim that abortion is *objectively* wrong is, on a natural reading, not simply to "repeat" or "emphasize" that abortion is wrong, but rather to assert a certain metaphysical thesis: to wit, that there exists a property of moral wrongness, which abortion has, and which it has quite independently of what we happen to think about the matter.[43] To talk about "objective" rightness and wrongness is to talk about metaphysical or ontological issues, about what properties the world contains quite apart from what we happen to know about them. Yet this is precisely what Dworkin seems to deny. Dworkin's arguments have been extensively criticized elsewhere;[44] let us focus here on the *crux* of his position.

Dworkin concedes that it *is* a legitimately *external* argument to deny the objectivity of morality on the grounds that it does not meet the constraints imposed by what we might call a "scientific epistemology" which says—in part, and quite roughly—that: (a) only that which makes a causal difference to experience can be known; and (b) only that which makes a causal difference to experience is real.[45]

---

[40] R. Dworkin (n. 38 above), p. 89.   [41] T. Nagel (n. 38 above), p. vii.

[42] R. Dworkin (n. 38 above), p. 97.

[43] Cf. Brink (n. 16 above), p. 20 ("ethics is objective... [in the sense that] it concerns facts that hold independently of anyone's beliefs about what is right or wrong"); Railton (n. 18 above), p. 164 (the issue about objectivity is the issue of "in what ways, if any, does the existence of moral properties depend upon the actual or possible states of mind of intelligent beings?").   [44] See Ch. 8.

[45] A scientific epistemology must, of course, encompass more than a commitment to inference to the best explanation. We need, for example, a basic empiricist doctrine—the senses can be a source of

Dworkin's response is that such a demand, made about morality, is question-begging. Dworkin objects that the external skeptic's "hierarchical epistemology . . . tries to establish standards for reliable belief *a priori*, ignoring the differences in content between different domains of belief, and taking no account of the range of beliefs we already hold to be reliable".[46] If a scientific epistemology "does seem appropriate to beliefs about the physical world",[47] it makes no sense for moral beliefs "[s]ince morality and the other evaluative domains make no causal claims".[48] If we accept the demand that moral facts must figure in the "best explanation" of experience, it will follow that "no moral (or aesthetic or mathematical or philosophical) belief is reliable. But we can reverse that judgment: if any moral belief is reliable, the 'best explanation' test is not universally sound. Either direction of argument . . . begs the question in the same way".[49]

But the question is begged only if we grant Dworkin's false assumption that the demand for conformity to a scientific epistemology is really an arbitrary, *a priori* demand.[50] This assumption, however, reveals a complete misunderstanding of what drives the debate between external realist and skeptic about morals. What motivates both "external" realism and skepticism is precisely the thought that in the post-Enlightenment world, the *only* tenable guide to the real and the unreal is science, and the epistemological standards we have inherited from successful scientific practice. Science (and its associated epistemology) has earned this place of honor by *delivering the goods*: by sending planes in to the sky, transplanting hearts, refrigerating food, and so on. A scientific epistemology—predicated on such seemingly simple notions as "evidence matters" (theories must answer to experience, not simply authority)—is one of the most precious legacies of the Enlightenment, a legacy under attack from those corners of the academy where bad philosophy reigns supreme.

The demand to find a place for moral facts within a scientific epistemology is neither arbitrary nor *a priori*, but simply the natural question to ask given the *a posteriori* success of science. It is not that moral claims are simply exempt from a scientific epistemology because they do not involve causal claims; it is, rather, that (crudely speaking) causal power has shown itself over the past few centuries to be the best-going indicia of the knowable and the real, and therefore it is natural to subject any putative fact to this test. Naturalistic moral realists like Brink and Railton are not "bad metaphysicians";[51] rather, they recognize (as Dworkin apparently does not) the epistemological pressure generated by the success of empirical

---

knowledge—as well as certain epistemic norms which satisfy neither the empircist nor the abductive criteria. These epistemic norms admit of only a *pragmatic* defense, as discussed in the text.

[46] R. Dworkin (n. 38 above), pp. 118–19.   [47] Id., p. 119.

[48] Id., p. 120.   [49] Id., p. 119.

[50] As an aside, let me point out that whether *beliefs* in general and *mathematics* in particular (as distinct from beliefs *about* mathematics) would figure in the best explanation of our experience is an open question—the latter, depending, for example, on whether or not mathematics is indispensable to science.   [51] R. Dworkin (n. 38 above), p. 127.

inquiry that honors a scientific epistemology. Given that we have a useful guide to the true and the real already in hand—namely, science and its epistemic norms—why not see, these moral realists essentially ask, whether or not "moral facts" can meet these demands (rather than suffer the same fate as witches and the ether).

Now no one should be surprised that if we repudiate the demands of a scientific epistemology we get a promiscuous ontology, replete with moral facts, aesthetic facts, theological facts and the like. But unless we are given a good reason for repudiating this epistemology—other than the patently question-begging reason of making room for our favorite (heretofore) suspect facts—the real question about any putative facts is whether they can answer to our best-going criteria of the knowable and the real.[52] This is what motivates the debate between external realist and external skeptic. Rather than showing their debate to be unintelligible, Dworkin has simply betrayed his misunderstanding of both *what* they are arguing about and *why* they are doing so. What we have yet to find in Dworkin is any *argument* for insulating the domain of morality from the demands of the scientific epistemology which has otherwise served us well.

Recently, Postema has come to Dworkin's defense on this score.[53] Even if a scientific epistemology has been successful in its domains, this gives us no reason to expect it to apply in all contexts. He writes:

[T]he "success" of natural science depends at least in part on the fact that it self-consciously brackets, and thus remains silent about, large portions of human experience (notably the normative dimensions of that experience). Moreover, normative discourse does not deal in the base currency of natural science—causal explanations; why, then, should we accept that success in charting the world organized under the category of causation gives license to determine the tools for reasoning our way around the practical world?[54]

Unfortunately, both claims are, at best, misleading, and at worst, false. What has been distinctive of the growth of science in the twentieth-century has *not* been its tendency to "bracket" domains of human experience, but rather to expand its coverage to subsume them. In the normative domain, one need only think of psychoanalytic accounts of morality and moral motivation at the dawn of the twentieth century or the evolutionary accounts that now dominate scientific study of normative experience at the dawn of the twenty-first. This expansion of science and a scientific epistemology is, indeed, the predictable consequence of its practical success in its original domains of application.

---

[52] Anyone who would repudiate a scientific epistemology must also provide some new, principled account of the distinction between the real and the unreal, demonstrating that while it makes room for, e.g., moral facts, it still excludes from our best picture of the world various pseudo-facts.

[53] Postema (n. 23 above) defends a conception of objectivity that is *specific* to law—what he calls "objectivity as publicity"—and which deems legal judgments objective if they issue from a process of public practical reasoning. Cf. the notion of "procedural objectivity" discussed in Coleman and Leiter (n. 26 above, pp. 595–7) and the "democratic" notion in Putnam, "Are Moral and Legal Values Made or Discovered?" *Legal Theory 1* (1995): 5–19.   [54] G. Postema (n. 24 above), p. 134.

Now if in some sense it is true that the "base currency" of science is "causal explanations," it is wrong to suggest that "normative discourse" does not deal in such currency at all. The moral explanations literature[55] is replete with examples of the role of causal claims in ordinary normative discourse (e.g., "Of course he betrayed them, he's an evil person"). It is perfectly reasonable then, even on the terms established by normative discourse itself, to inquire whether these explanations are *good* ones, let alone *best* explanations for the phenomena in question.[56] But whether or not any branch of discourse makes *causal* claims is irrelevant to the applicability of a scientific epistemology: the point is precisely that, so far, *causal power is all we have to go on in ontology.*

This brings us to what Postema calls the "Pandora's Box argument," which "puts a challenge to any methodological [i.e., non-metaphysical] account [of objectivity]" to propose an alternative to causal power adequate for distinguishing the objective from the non-objective.[57] Surprisingly, Postema concedes, "I have no specific test to offer".[58] Instead, he suggests a self-referential paradox afflicts a commitment to a scientific epistemology: such an epistemology is not objective by its own criteria.[59] The real argument for embracing a scientific epistemology, however, is not itself epistemic but pragmatic: such an epistemology, as noted earlier, has *delivered the goods.* We have already seen that Postema's attempt to dispute that pragmatic claim failed. Thus, without an alternative criterion of objectivity in hand, Pandora's box is, indeed, opened. In the end, then, Postema is in as vulnerable a position as Dworkin: neither has succeeded in showing how, when thinking about objectivity, we can do *without* metaphysics, nor how we can avoid relying on a scientific epistemology to flesh out this metaphysics.[60]

---

[55] E.g., N. Sturgeon, "Moral Explanations," (1985) reprinted in G. Sayre-McCord (ed.) *Essays on Moral Realism*, (Ithaca: Cornell University Press, 1988).

[56] For a negative answer to the question, see Ch. 7.   [57] G. Postema (n. 24 above), p. 135.

[58] Id., p. 136.

[59] Id., p. 135. Cf. Putnam (n. 39 above), p. 71 for a related objection to the argument in Brian Leiter, "The Middle Way," *Legal Theory 1* (1995): 21–31.

[60] Suppose our metaphysics of legal facts is Modest or Minimal Objectivity: how would that square with a scientific epistmology? Such facts are, of course, mind-independent, *just not to the same degree as Strongly Objective facts.* And they will be causally efficacious to the extent that they (or the psychological facts with which they are identical or on which they supervene) figure in the explanations of, e.g., judicial decisions. We have, admittedly, no showing that that will turn out to be the case, but nor has there been any showing of the opposite. The question demands further consideration.

Index